Praise *for* The Overlooked Americans

"*The Overlooked Americans* is a much-needed reassessment of small-town life in rural America. Based on detailed research, the book reveals life in rural America to be complex and varied—and in many cases better off than conventional wisdom would have us believe. This timely book belies the narrative of a nation sharply polarized across an urban-rural divide. Instead, Elizabeth Currid-Halkett shows that Americans aren't nearly as divided by geography as the punditry and media would have us believe. Urban, suburban, and rural Americans have more in common than we think. A modern-day version of Michael Harrington's classic, *The Other America*, this moving book is essential reading for all who care about the future of our country and its people."

—Richard Florida, author of *The New Urban Crisis*

"What is America really? Currid-Halkett pierces through the noise and challenges mainstream narratives with this timely, rigorous, and heartfelt analysis. *The Overlooked Americans* tears down entrenched definitions and stereotypes and builds a new image of rural America that is not hopelessly divided from urban America. Nuanced, cogent, and empathetic, this book deserves attention from politicians, pundits, and the public."

—Jane Harman, University of Southern California, former member of Congress (CA, 36)

"Currid-Halkett has long been a formidable observer of cultural trends, but with *The Overlooked Americans*, she deftly combines qualitative and quantitative research to create a riveting, clear-eyed, and often-surprising portrait of small-town America."

—Sloane Crosley, author of *Cult Classic*

THE
OVERLOOKED
AMERICANS

THE OVERLOOKED AMERICANS

THE RESILIENCE OF OUR RURAL TOWNS AND WHAT IT MEANS FOR OUR COUNTRY

ELIZABETH CURRID-HALKETT

BASIC BOOKS

New York

Basic Books
Hachette Book Group
1290 Avenue of the Americas, New York, NY 10104
www.basicbooks.com

Printed in the United States of America
First Edition: June 2023

Published by Basic Books, an imprint of Perseus Books, LLC, a subsidiary of Hachette Book Group, Inc. The Basic Books name and logo is a trademark of the Hachette Book Group.

The Hachette Speakers Bureau provides a wide range of authors for speaking events. To find out more, go to hachettespeakersbureau.com or email HachetteSpeakers@hbgusa.com.

Basic books may be purchased in bulk for business, educational, or promotional use. For information, please contact your local bookseller or Hachette Book Group Special Markets Department at special.markets@hbgusa.com.

The publisher is not responsible for websites (or their content) that are not owned by the publisher.

Print book interior design by Linda Mark.

Library of Congress Cataloging-in-Publication Data
Names: Currid-Halkett, Elizabeth, 1978- author.
Title: The overlooked Americans : the resilience of our rural towns and
    what it means for our country / Elizabeth Currid-Halkett.
Description: First edition. | New York, NY : Basic Books, [2023] |
    Includes bibliographical references and index.
Identifiers: LCCN 2022057988 | ISBN 9781541646728 (hardcover) |
    ISBN 9781541646711 (epub)
Subjects: LCSH: Cities and towns—United States. |
    Rural-urban relations—United States.
Classification: LCC HT123 .C84 2023 | DDC 307.760973—dc23/eng/20230111
LC record available at https://lccn.loc.gov/2022057988

ISBNs: 9781541646728 (hardcover), 9781541646711 (ebook)

LSC-C

Printing 1, 2023

Oliver, Ezra, and Eliot

To my beautiful, wild, and magnificent children.

If we all looked at the world through your eyes,
judgment would not exist—only love.

In the end, it is the only way.

Everybody's somebody's beloved, or should be. . . . So in other words, if somebody is beloved to anybody then anything that happens to that person is a story.

—George Saunders, *Paris Review*, 2019

Contents

INTRODUCTION

Getting into the Room

What do you value most?
"Love is the first thing that came to mind."

Do you believe this is what most Americans value?
*"I do. I think it's really hard to look at our country and
not see that."*
—Clay, Oneida, Kentucky

I WAS BORN IN PARKERSBURG, WEST VIRGINIA, WHERE MY PARENTS
chose to land when they emigrated from Ireland. As my parents
went through graduate school and my mother did her medical residency, we hopped from Parkersburg to Pittsburgh, Pennsylvania,
where my siblings were born. When she finished her residency, my
mother was offered a position in Cambridge, Massachusetts, and
another job at a rural hospital in northeast Pennsylvania. With
three kids spaced less than two years apart and massive debt from
their first years in America, my parents couldn't afford to live in an
expensive city, so in 1984 my mom took the job in rural Pennsylvania, where she would work for almost forty years.

And so I grew up in Danville, Pennsylvania, a rural town of five
thousand off Interstate 80.

Danville is not poor, it is not rich, and it is neither uneducated nor flooded with elite college degrees. The median household income is approximately $36,000, and the poverty rate is 13 percent.[1] Unemployment hovers at just under 5 percent.[2] Over 23 percent of the population has a bachelor's degree. Statistically, Danville is representative of much of small-town America.[3]

Danville is also a picture of America's once affordable good life—the life everyone is supposed to have an opportunity to pass through as a member of the middle class. Everyone has a yard and a TV and air conditioning. Parents drive minivans and trucks. Families attend Memorial Day barbecues, and kids swim at the local pool in the summertime and sled down the town's snowy hills after the first winter storm. Some residents work at the local hospital, Geisinger Medical Center, others at a branch of the Merck pharmaceutical company. Some work at coffee shops and ice cream parlors, and several own their own toy shops and restaurants and hardware stores. There are plenty of nurses, lawyers, mechanics, barbers, handymen, and small business owners. There are farmers who sell strawberries and factory workers too. Danville, like many other northeast towns, is rooted in the industrial era of iron and coal and steel. You could, as Philip Roth put it, "touch your toes where America began."[4]

My parents believed in the American dream and worked hard to move up the socioeconomic ladder. Yet even as they assimilated, the subtleties of American culture managed to elude them: how to cut the orange slices for American Youth Soccer Organization games, the importance of the minivan (finally, in 1995 they bought a silver Plymouth Voyager), that multiple pairs of Umbro shorts were a staple of a middle school child's wardrobe, that our babysitter Mrs. Pritchard's very old, baby-blue Chevy Impala was anomalous and a source of embarrassment to impressionable children at school pickup. Having a full-time babysitter (we didn't call them nannies in rural Pennsylvania) because my mom worked was also unusual and not a marker of elite status, as it might be today.

I lived in Danville for thirteen years before I left for college in Pittsburgh, then went to graduate school in New York City, and finally moved to Los Angeles for my job as a professor. I still visit Danville every few years to see my friends and family. One thing I hear over and over again—on campus, in the news, at dinner parties—is how angry small-town America is. But here's what strikes me every time I return to Danville: People are content, even happy. In this highly divisive moment in our history, the people of Danville don't seem particularly angry at the world, as the media has characterized rural folks. Here's the second thing I notice: Those who talk about rural America know little about the people who live there, their hopes, dreams, and cares. Academics, journalists, and pundits know far more about those who dwell in cities, where major media outlets and universities tend to be based, than about small-town Americans.

When we choose to disparage or dismiss those not like us, when we do not attempt to understand other human beings, we ultimately fail to appreciate that our differences can coexist, rather than divide us as they do today. Different forms and expressions of cultural capital, social organization, and economic development shape the specificity of people and places. Our current characterization of rural and urban America, Republicans and Democrats, coastal elites and the flyover states hides a more complicated and nuanced reality of this country, one that I reveal in the course of this book. I have found that we are not as different from one another as we may think. Our sense of division is driven by extremes, not by the views of ordinary Americans.

WHEN DONALD TRUMP won the White House in 2016, many people saw his victory as a threat to democratic values and a reckoning for educated liberals. Elites of all stripes swiftly blamed rural America for his explosive rise and upset win. Stunned by the success of Trump's campaign, academics, publishing houses, and the media spun a narrative that members of the white working class had a whole lot of anger toward coastal liberals and even more toward the DC "deep state," big banks, and institutions in general.

These Americans were represented in the bleakest of terms: poorly educated, without job opportunities, and beset by opioid addiction. They were said to have rebelled against their declining status by electing to the presidency a man whom liberals and progressives considered an existential threat to the nation. Understanding these rural people, the leitmotif went, would allow us to understand how America went wrong and why it is so divided.

As Trump rose to power, dozens of articles and books were published on small-town America's rage toward the country's elite. Books like *Hillbilly Elegy*, *White Trash*, and *White Working Class* and essays in the *New Yorker* and *Guardian* painted a portrait of an irate and disillusioned America, where poor, conservative small towns were at war with wealthy, progressive cities. Much was made of how rural America felt "left behind," as Princeton sociologist Robert Wuthnow put it.[5] Then there were articles—so many articles, in seemingly every newspaper and magazine and website. At dinner parties, many of my friends and colleagues discussed how America's coastal elites didn't get it. We were aghast at our own oversight, having ignored the rage of rural America.

But I often sat at these dinner parties scratching my head. Even if I was surprised that Hillary Clinton hadn't won—I voted for her, and I cried when she lost—I didn't think she lost because small towns were angry. This narrative didn't fit with my experience of rural America. One might say that Montour County, Pennsylvania, where Danville resides, is an exception, but it's actually an exemplar—a once Democratic bastion that flipped Republican for John McCain in 2008.

These conversations about the urban-rural divide continue at fever pitch. Today when we talk about "American culture" or "the

American people," the conversation often revolves around two almost diametrically opposed populations. UCLA geographer Michael Storper calls this phenomenon "separate worlds," whereby economic development and political preferences align to create a chasm between the more and less fortunate. George Packer, a staff writer at the *Atlantic*, divides the country into "four Americas": Free America (libertarians), Real America (small, rural towns), Smart America (old-school liberal meritocrats), and Just America (progressives and social justice movements). In all of these frameworks, the country's socioeconomic, demographic, political, and geographic factions are ultimately at odds with one another. But what is America really? I wanted to escape the binary. I wanted to uncover what sociologist Arlie Hochschild calls "the deep story" of the nation.

Despite the ink spilled, the podcast minutes aired, and the pixels devoted; despite the time spent debating Republicans versus Democrats, populists versus progressives, the coasts versus the middle, cities versus rural areas; despite the Democratic Party's great debate over engaging those who are different versus characterizing them as "deplorables," to use Hillary Clinton's term, or as those who hold on to their "guns and religion," as President Obama said—despite all this, there has been a lack of rigorous qualitative and quantitative research on this topic. I hope to answer that urgent need with this book.

WHEN YOU LOOK closely at the data, the 2016 presidential election no longer seems like an anomaly. Let's step back in time. The depiction of rural America as a cultural backwater, rife with pathologies and problems, existed way before Trump won the White House. Even prior to the 2016 election, rural America was conceptualized in soundbites and static images filled with negativity, hopelessness, condescension, and pity. In the 1960s and 1970s, *The Beverly Hillbillies*, a sitcom about a poor family from the Ozarks striking it rich and moving to California, portrayed these rural Americans as uncouth and gauche.

In 2007, Thomas Frank's *What's the Matter with Kansas?* mocked rural American support of the Republican Party as a form of "derangement," dismissing and illegitimizing the fact that, for many conservative voters, cultural issues were more important to them than economic ones (as they are for many of us). In 2008, years before Trump entered the arena in a meaningful way, Jon Stewart's "Understanding Real America in Wasilla" segment on *The Daily Show* revealed what elites really thought of rural Americans. While the segment was ostensibly humorous and poking fun at vice presidential candidate Sarah Palin, it was also full of snide condescension and disdain for the people who lived in Wasilla, Alaska.

Even if rural America isn't being made fun of, it is rarely cast in a positive light. In a 2012 *Atlantic* piece, journalist Josh Kron writes of the "urban-rural divide splitting America." "Virtually every major city...in the United States of America has a different outlook from the less populous areas that are closest to it. The difference is no longer about where people live, it's about how people live."[6] Other articles focus on the negative impact of globalization, on population decline and brain drain, or on poverty and health disparities.[7]

As the narrative goes, in the 2016 election, the rural people—castigated and pathologized for decades—mobilized into a political force. Over 60 percent of them supported Trump.[8] In response, the mainstream media and Democratic politicians tapped into long-standing, stereotyped depictions of rural Americans to make sense of why they had overwhelmingly supported a candidate whom liberals viewed as reprehensible.

Ultimately, the liberal establishment concluded that small towns supported the antiestablishment Trump because rural Americans everywhere faced severely limited opportunities and resented the success of America's multicultural cities. Rural Americans were enraged, the logic went, and so they wanted a political outsider to tear down the system. Trump reinforced this narrative in his speeches, positioning himself as a spokesperson for "the forgotten men and women of our country."

But rural America's mobilization did not necessarily emerge solely from anger at being left behind. In fact, rural Americans have been increasingly voting for the conservative candidate for almost a generation.[9] And importantly, data shows that many Trump supporters were wealthy and that most of his voters come from urban America. Case in point: Los Angeles gave Trump 1.1 million votes—as many votes as in the six hundred most rural counties put together.[10] This observation isn't to minimize the impact of the rural vote. Many rural Americans may have found, for better and for worse, someone who appeared to advocate for and understand them as people, not just as a group to be pitied.

After all, Donald Trump was ridiculed and ostracized by the very same progressive elite that had discounted rural Americans. He understood where they came from and why they felt perplexed by the current moment in society, connecting with rural America's deep story. Trump was, to use Max Weber's term, rural America's charismatic authority. He told small-town Americans he hadn't forgotten them. Trump oriented his 2016 campaign around their concerns and values, and he won their votes.

YET, DESPITE HOW the region is represented in the popular imagination, rural America is in fact a varied and diverse place that's not hopelessly divided from other parts of the country. Many rural Americans supported Trump for complex reasons other than economic distress or grievance, and middle America is not defined by its supposed anger toward the coasts. Even as small towns offer a different way of living than cities, rural Americans share many core values and opinions with their urban counterparts.[11] And, contrary to one popular narrative, most of rural America is not rapidly deteriorating; in reality,

the region has experienced fairly little population decline over the last
several decades.[12] More recently, many rural towns have experienced
a pandemic boom, as previously urban workers who are now able to
work from home seek out outdoor amenities and lower costs of living.[13]
This more nuanced picture of rural America isn't as compelling as the
typical story precisely because it isn't sensational, attention-grabbing,
and divisive. Yet, to ignore it is to overlook a key part of our country.
Ninety-seven percent of the United States' land mass is rural, and 20
percent of Americans live there.[14] If you look closely, there is a complicated story that doesn't involve red versus blue states, progressives
versus conservatives, or rural Americans versus coastal elites.

Most rural Americans do not neatly fit into stereotypes, and
close research has revealed that most have justifiable reasons for their
perspectives. In 2016, Theda Skocpol and Vanessa Williamson published the results of a study of grassroots Republican conservatism.
They found that many seeming contradictions observed in Republican voters' political preferences—for example, being anti–big government while depending on social services—make sense within
their communities. Arlie Hochschild's *Strangers in Their Own Land*
echoes this finding, offering a sympathetic portrayal of Tea Party
activists in Louisiana, who, despite living in one of the most polluted
states in the country, support the very politicians who would like to
dismantle the Environmental Protection Agency. Why? Because,
for these conservatives, their cultural values matter more to them
than their economic interests and even their future health. This, for
Hochschild, is the deep story: how people understand themselves
and their value systems. As she observes, the story doesn't have to
be accurate, but it has to feel authentic.[15] People in Louisiana may
seem like they are voting against their political interests, but the
politicians who speak to their values—to their wariness of a liberal,
secular world gone wild—are the ones who get their support.

But one only finds answers to these contradictions by talking
to people and truly engaging with them. When Hochschild found

what she calls "the Great Paradox" in Louisianans' political leanings and economic interests, she did not judge. Instead, she sought to understand the deep story.

THIS BOOK DIVES deeply into "overlooked America" and the people who choose to live and work there. For my entire scholarly career, I have found great strength in blending qualitative and quantitative research methods. Through talking to people and studying data, I have tried to create what I believe is a more complex but accurate portrayal of rural Americans, particularly how they are and are not so different from urban folks. I have collected and analyzed a wide variety of statistical data, drawn from four major data sets: the Census (general demographics), the Bureau of Labor Statistics (industry and employment data), University of Chicago's General Social Survey (belief systems, values, levels of happiness), and the Nielsen Retail Scanner (consumer behavior and purchases). I've also teamed up with my colleagues at the University of Southern California Schaeffer Center for Health Policy to analyze health data from the University of Michigan Health and Retirement Study (health habits and disease). I analyzed the most spatially granular data available, and have looked specifically at the interplay of geography and a number of variables, including education, household income, social and religious beliefs, race, local industry, and the consumption of particular goods.

What did I find? Geography has become too much of a convenient container. The notion of a stark rural-urban geographic divide fails to offer an accurate picture of America's social, cultural, and economic landscape. Rural is not synonymous with decline. The spatial manifestation of these forces is far more complicated. You cannot compare, for example, the relationship between New York City and its hinterlands to that of Akron, Ohio, and its rural enclaves forty miles out. Yes, the perception of rural America tends to be that it is less educated and more conservative, but even this observation is not a determinant but rather the result of many interrelated and intricate variables.

What does this all mean? Our current characterization of both urban and rural communities hides a more complicated reality. Here, in the data, in conversations, without preconceived assumptions, I examine the real shape of overlooked America and take the time to understand the people and places that have been out of the spotlight but that offer a more candid account of our country.

There are poor rural places. This is a fact. But it is not the only story—not by a long shot. Case in point: even without controlling for cost of living, parts of small-town West Virginia adjacent to Pittsburgh have higher income levels than the city. Yes, parts of small-town America are suffering due to economic abandonment, but this is a story of regional divergence. Northeastern small towns' prosperity reflects the vitality of the region's cities, just as lackluster economic prospects in the South blanket the entire region, not just rural towns.

When we look at America through the lens of consumerism, we see that the cultural capital embedded in what we buy—whether that's craft beer or Coca-Cola—is not simply a reflection of coastal elites versus rural populists but rather the difference between levels of wealth and education, irrespective of geography. This data tells us that broad notions of rural and urban do not advance the discussion. Places, like people, are multitudes. To understand Appalachian Kentucky is not to understand the farmers of Iowa or the unemployed factory workers of Ohio or the thriving retirees of bucolic Massachusetts. To unpack America, to truly understand it, we have to understand the specificity of people and places while striving to find our commonalities.

The data we use to understand places may provide information, but people give us their truths. As a social scientist, I believe we get to the deep story when we talk to people and really listen to what they have to say. For the research for this book, I had planned to take my family of five (three boisterous boys included) on a road trip across America. We would travel up the Central Valley of California. We would travel into Florida and through the woods of Kentucky. We would spend a few weeks in Pennsylvania, in my hometown, getting a sense of the place and how it has changed. We would visit my birthplace, Parkersburg, West Virginia. It would be amazing and novel, a proper road trip to understand this country and meet its people.

Then the pandemic hit, and the world shut down. No one could go anywhere, let alone into unknown communities, spending hours at a time talking face-to-face. Like many parents of young children, I spent over a year with my life almost completely oriented around their care and education. My littlest one, Eliot, was just eight months old when Covid-19 reached America. Like everyone else, we were scared and locked down. With no travel across the country, no visits to small-town America, how on earth would I write my book? How would I even find people to talk to? There was no walking into a diner or meeting people at a local town-hall meeting. There was no time anyway, between breastfeeding Eliot, making lunches and snacks, and keeping my older two children—one of whom was a reluctant Zoom kindergartener—on track with their education. All of my hopes for how to write a book about America were dashed. And then I talked to my mom.

"Maybe I can find you a few people," she said, when I called her for the fifth time that day in tears about my now completely nonexistent work-life balance. A few hours later, an email from my mom's Hotmail account came through with a list of five women she knew in Danville who agreed to speak with me, complete with telephone numbers and email addresses. Mom's idea inspired me to send text messages to a few high school friends. Did they know anyone who might talk to me? My sister dug up a few names from her former workplace, tracking down former colleagues who might have relatives in various parts of rural America. Here in Los Angeles, a friend up the street who grew up in Wisconsin sent over a few names of people from high school, warily and with hesitation, remarking, "Some of these people are really conservative…Trump supporters. Do you want that?" "Yes, yes I do! Very much so!" I said with appreciation.

Over the next several weeks, a list of contacts came together. A pastor in rural Wisconsin, a former businessman in Minnesota, a retired nurse and handyman in Pennsylvania, an artist in Tennessee, another pastor from Missouri. The list got bigger and bigger. Over the coming months, I spent hundreds of hours interviewing dozens of Americans in places with populations from a few hundred to a few thousand.

To compare perspectives across geographic lines, I interviewed some city dwellers too. And to gain a deeper understanding of the sociology and economics of rural America, I interviewed experts on religion, small towns, health economics, education, and social mobility. I also spoke to experts who could provide a deeper knowledge of the macro issues in society. My interviews with ordinary Americans lasted one to two hours, spanning a wide range of questions from "What is your favorite food?" to "Do you believe equality exists in America?" to "What do you value most?" I asked the same set of questions to rural and urban Americans, seeking out not their political allegiances but rather who they were, what they valued, and how they understood themselves, their communities, and their country. I wasn't interested in their divisions; I was interested in their humanity.

With a number of the Americans I chose to profile in this book, I followed up with additional email and text correspondences and interviews. Almost every person I spoke to offered names of other potential interviewees, and those people offered names, and within a few months I had veritably covered the entire country entirely through the kindness of the good people I had spoken to and bonded with over the phone. These people owed me nothing. They were under no obligation to return the calls or emails some complete stranger had sent.

But, boy, did I learn something about America in the very process of trying to reach Americans. People are really kind. Interviewees took hours out of their day to talk to me and then more time to follow up. They sent me photos of their high school days and their grandkids; they sent their own poetry and book recommendations. One man invited me to visit his farm. A pastor and his wife offered me almost ten potential interviewees. Many of these people thanked me for writing a book devoted to understanding the America they live in, the one that is so often overlooked. "I have hope because of people like you," said a woman from Kentucky, regarding the future of America.

By and large, I let people speak for themselves. I did not always agree, and sometimes very much disagreed, with their opinions. But it was not my place to cast judgment. My job was to empathize with them and present them as they are, in all of their contradictions. I respected them as I would want my own viewpoints and idiosyncrasies to be respected. I simply want their voices to be heard, these voices and perspectives that do not dominate the headlines or appear in best-selling memoirs. To understand them is to get a deep sense of what America is to many who live here. Through both the questions on quotidian matters and those on larger issues, I found that if I just listened—if I didn't judge or criticize—that people wanted to talk.

You might think that there is bias built into snowballing, the interview technique I used, which relies on interviewees offering other potential contacts to the researcher. I am sure there is. Equally, however, I found that the diversity of the people I spoke to—by class, race, education, geography, profession, political leanings, and age—would suggest that this group really captured the range of experience in small-town America. I interviewed conspiracy theorists, avid Trump supporters, and socialists in the heart of Kentucky; progressives in Milwaukee; Republicans who I thought were Democrats until halfway through the interview; and a young Black woman who remarked, "I'm going to say it. I'm going to be the Black woman who says America offers a chance for everyone. Because we know what equality is. We will attain it."

We make a lot of mistakes about people when we know what they look like and how they choose to present themselves. We judge who we think they are, and we don't bother to listen. We see a man in a MAGA hat, and we assume we know exactly what he stands for. We see a woman in a faded UC Berkeley sweatshirt, and we assume her politics. When all we have is a voice, we are forced to simply listen. For me, hearing dozens of voices through the line and having no preconceived notions about what these people look like and who they might be was an extraordinary strength of my accidental research approach. When I picked up the phone to dial, I did not know the person's race, age, religion, or political affiliation. These facts emerged as we spoke, as they wanted to tell them to me. And, in listening nonjudgmentally to all of these wonderful people, I heard their voices and their truths.

WHAT DID I find? Our descriptions of Americans are woefully inadequate. This observation is especially true for the quiet rural Americans who do not necessarily fit the stereotype of feeling left behind or angry. When I studied the numbers, I found that on most measures—cultural, social, economic—rural America is doing just fine. Of course, not all rural Americans are thriving. But neither are all urban Americans—far from it. Extreme poverty, chronic unemployment, intolerance, and economic and social resentment exist in rural America (and always have), but these problems exist in our cities too. Exceptional places like Appalachia and the Deep South are indeed in trouble, a topic I will go into in more detail in this book.

But by basic measures such as median income, homeownership, inequality, and unemployment, rural America is doing well, despite not being as educated as urban America. Even in that respect, rural America is not completely without college degrees. And while rural America is often thought of as less racially open, the greatest proponents of government support for the Black community are the least educated (both urban and rural), not college-educated city dwellers, as one might presume. Even on measures of culture and values, I found that rural and urban Americans care about the same things, even if they use different language to describe their beliefs.

For example, rural folks may not use the word "environmentalism," but they care about the land and the earth in real and effective ways. They have their own vegetable gardens and compost piles, and they recycle and buy less stuff. There is just no cultural capital imbued in their environmental behaviors in the same way that such actions might be lauded in our coastal cities. And, according to the data, rural Americans are not necessarily more religious than urban Americans, but religion plays a more important function in their social and cultural lives.

Notably, most rural Americans are not avidly political. They may have voted for Donald Trump, they may have voted for Joe Biden, but rarely did they express extreme political views. And that is true of all of us. As political scientists have observed, only 15 to 20 percent of people are truly politically active, but these active voters' views dominate headlines and create our sense of a "divided America."[16] Most Americans are not politically strident, and most Americans aren't interested in a political debate with their in-laws. I found in my interviews that most rural Americans, like most urban Americans, are not highly engaged in politics. They care about their families, they worry about their kids, they vote with their wallets and their core values, and they are not deeply resentful of the coasts. As a whole, my data and my interviews point toward a rural America that is far more content, moderate, and similar in its views on democracy, equality, and family to urban America than so many journalists, politicians, and public intellectuals have claimed. Americans are not so different from one another, after all.

Knowing that America isn't so polarized along geographic lines challenges us to think differently. I have come to believe that overlooked Americans often represent the best of America. Some are Republican, some are Democrat, it really doesn't matter—I rarely found much difference in their values, hopes, and views. A die-hard Trump supporter often answered almost identically to a lifelong Democrat on the topics of equality and democracy. While many of the people I interviewed have so much less economically and educationally than many coastal elites, the truth is that plenty of people in this country do not wish to possess what the global meritocratic economy tells them they should. Do not mistake their eschewing of these aspirations for resentment; they are simply living their lives.

Sensational and impassioned rhetoric about a "divided America" and the "culture wars" in fact sows division and exacerbates what differences we do have. Even discussions of the "left behind" among rural Americans obfuscate the complexities within this population. Some may feel left behind, true, but others are standing still. What I came to realize is the "politics of resentment," to quote the political scientist Cathy Kramer, that has so defined the political dialogue in the post-Obama era, may actually be a politics of contentment. I found that most people are focused on things other than politics: their families, upcoming holidays, paying their bills, their church and faith.

A sense of resentment did not dominate any of my conversations, regardless of the interviewees' location, occupation, age, or political affiliation. But I knew that many people on the coasts think that rural Americans—and those who voted for Trump—are intolerant, angry "deplorables."

When I began research for this project, only once—in high school many years ago—had I come across someone who might fit that description. Still, I felt that part of my book should address this issue. I looked everywhere. I interviewed people in the backwoods of Appalachia, in ultraconservative Pennsylvania, and in midwestern towns with populations of less than a thousand. While people held very conservative views and expressed ambivalence toward liberal issues I take for granted, not one person was disrespectful or hateful, even if their views were not mine.

All across America, I met the loveliest, kindest people in the places most vilified by mainstream media and liberal elites. One hundred percent of the Americans I spoke to were decent and thoughtful; they held beliefs that, even when they differed from my own, were almost always understandable. I'm not saying intolerant, deplorable people don't exist in America. I'm saying I didn't come across them. And even though hate-filled, racist, homophobic people do exist, and that is an awful thing, these people simply cannot be the dominant group in rural America. We must not have such a low opinion of Americans who live in places that are not home to us, or who hold views different from our own.

The Overlooked Americans will, I hope, help us rethink our views about rural Americans and their relationship to the rest of the nation through data, interviews, and analysis. In other words, I am not trying to convince you of my perspective, but rather I want to share with you what the people in rural America are experiencing and what they are saying about the important issues of our time.

First, I look at how the economic metrics of rural America suggest a place that is far more vibrant and resilient than we think. Compared to many cities, unemployment in rural America is lower, homeownership is higher, and median income is on par.

I also find that rural Americans are less prejudiced, more diverse, and more apolitical than is commonly thought. Through interviewees' responses to some of the key social, cultural, and political issues of our time—religion, democracy, race-based government aid, same-sex marriage—I will show how rural and urban Americans are far more alike than different. The same can be said about many of their socioeconomic attributes, from homeownership to employment to median income.

Even as rural America is doing well by many measures, the dominant view is that it's in decline. I will argue that, particularly over the past couple decades, the plight of Appalachia has commanded our attention and distorted our views. Encouraged by sensational books and media, as well as the heartbreaking findings of respectable researchers, we have collectively fixated on a particular place and conflated it with all of rural America. This perspective prevents us from targeting intervention and help toward the people who need it most. The coverage of the opioid epidemic has evolved into poverty porn, creating a caricature of rural America as pathological, instead of encouraging deep engagement with the few states that are suffering. Similarly, rural America is often cast in pop culture and the liberal media as backward and alien from the rest of the nation.

Why does the media, with the encouragement of progressive elites, perpetuate this sense of division? Much of it has to do with three key areas: education, religion, and cultural capital. In these realms, rural America conspicuously deviates from the values of progressive elites, earning their ire. Many already recognize that urban and rural America differ sharply on these points, but our current understanding is still too simplistic. For instance, rural Americans are less educated and less fixated on the meritocratic pipeline for their children. The extent to which this will negatively impact their children is debatable. And while rural Americans are often portrayed as distinctly religious, the fundamental beliefs in family, religion, and community are not so different across the rural-urban divide. Many urban Americans believe in God. Similarly, plenty of rural Americans care about racial equality and environmentalism. However, how these values manifest in our day-to-day lives—our cultural capital—can look very different, which creates an appearance of deep division. Ultimately, the conclusion I've reached is that the United States is a far less divided place than our media and politicians would like us to believe.

In recent years, it is true that political battles have raged between conservatives and progressives. Increasingly, extremists on both sides of the aisle dominate political discourse, and in particular, far-right state legislatures and the Supreme Court have decisively reshaped the nation's laws. Their actions do not necessarily reflect the desires of most Americans. Most Americans are not even politically active, and most are moderates. Across geography and the political spectrum, the majority of Americans are aligned on key issues, even hot-button ones: over half of Americans support a woman's right to choose and want stronger gun control. Our current Supreme Court, then, is reflective not of a wide swath of our country but rather of a small conservative subset. In order to fully erase the simulacrum of insurmountable fault lines, we must listen to one another, regardless of whether this causes cognitive dissonance or flies in the face of our own beliefs. So long as people are coming from a place of love, not hate, they deserve to be heard.

I've learned a lot about our country's overlooked Americans. But I've also learned a lot from them. When you sit down with someone, when you hear them talk about their granddaughter's death, or the school they are proud to run, or the conflict they feel between progressive worldviews and their deep adherence to scripture, you understand that we are all fundamentally just human beings navigating life. Or, as Barack Obama put it, "Most folks actually are persuadable. . . . They kind of want the same things. They want a good job. They want to be able to support a family. They want safe neighborhoods." Even with regard to our country's biggest issues—such as race and marriage equality—most people are not interested in hurting others. "What they [Americans] are concerned about is not being taken advantage of, or is their way of life and traditions slipping away from them?" President Obama explains. "Is their status being undermined by changes in society? And if you have a conversation with folks, you can usually assuage those fears. But they have to be able to hear you. You have to be able to get into the room."[17]

In an interview with journalist Ezra Klein, the writer George Saunders remarked on the current state of division in America. "It was really made dramatically clear to me," Saunders observed regarding anti-immigration sentiment, "that agitation...was largely a projection that flourishes in the absence of experience."[18] Saunders's brilliant remark could be applied to many aspects of the current state of America. I, a highly educated liberal living on the West Coast, had much in common with many deeply religious Republicans living in small towns across America. We discovered our similarities once we had the experience of connecting. We laughed together, and they shared their stories, sometimes their pride, sometimes their tears, sometimes deeply personal tragedy. Without the opportunity to speak to people so different from me, I would have assumed a division that perhaps doesn't exist. Getting into the room with anyone immediately lessens animosity and allows us to see those who are different as human beings. It allows us to find the origin of where they are coming from, to appreciate their perspective. We may not agree with them, but we can understand them.

I got into the metaphorical room with Americans. I had conversations with people, even ones very different from me, without angst. Removed from the divisive rhetoric of today's politics and media, we didn't talk about the culture wars; we talked about our lives, our beliefs, our values, and the meaning of America. Very different people, I found, can coexist in our country. Our diversity of opinions and beliefs can be a strength. People who have different views from us need not be vilified. They should be understood. Fundamentally, and most importantly, most people come from a place of love, not hate. For this book, I wanted to get to the truth of America, the deep story. What if there's another version of America? A story we haven't told? I needed to find out. So I talked to Americans.

This is their story.

1

WE ARE NOT SO DIFFERENT, YOU AND ME

Maybe stories are just data with a soul.
—BRENÉ BROWN[1]

CLAY SPENCER IS A POET AND FORMER SOCIALIST WHO LIVES in rock-ribbed, conservative Clay County, Kentucky, which has voted Republican since the Civil War. In the last presidential election, the county voted almost 90 percent for Trump. Clay is now a registered Democrat who considers himself "leftist," but, as he puts it, "I don't much care about the implied binary of that term." Clay grew up in the small town of Oneida—population 427, in the heart of Appalachia—the son of a pastor who worked at a small Southern Baptist boarding school.

As a young adult, Clay moved away for some years to go to college and explore living in a new place. By the time we first speak in the spring of 2021, he is thirty-two years old and has moved back to Oneida, renting a room at the boarding school. When Clay was twenty-one years old, his father died, and being home allows him a chance to be near his mother, who still works at the school. Clay gets his water from the local spring and rarely turns on the heat, even when it gets cold. While some of these choices are environmental, as a poet working service jobs and more recently as a farmhand to make ends meet, Clay is also financially strapped. When I ask him how he feels about the economy, he is quiet at first. "I don't think the economy tends to work for most people," he remarks plainly. "I have a lot of distress and a lot of confusion around questions of economics. The etymology of the word 'economy' and the word 'ecology' come from the same Greek word 'eco,' which is life, and I think we are failing on both counts." Despite his own clear financial hardship, there is not an ounce of anger or resentment in his remarks, just observation.

Clay goes on, "The way the country is set up is to keep the wealthy at the top and keep the poor poor—that rhetoric of the hardworking American that overlooks things that are tied to it. We don't have a country that accumulated wealth without slave labor. We have this compounded wealth that is from the sweat of other people, an economy that produces for a few, and there are illusions of movement, promotions, but I don't think it's very likely [that someone moves from one class to another]." Clay would know. Five of the nation's poorest twenty counties are in Kentucky. Clay County is fifteenth, with a median household income of $30,000. To put this figure in context, the US average median household income is almost $70,000. San Francisco's closes in on $100,000.

Clay and I move from topic to topic, and at times I am so moved by his turn of phrase that I don't know how to respond. When I ask Clay if he relates to fellow Americans, he simply says, "I certainly do, yes. I can't imagine not relating to someone who was also a person." Clay admits his views are "hippieish," but to me they are more substantiated versions of what my progressive friends in Los Angeles might say. What is remarkable is Clay's complete lack of resentment to where he is financially and socially. When we spoke, he discussed various books he'd read on economics, his own poetry, and this country's most pressing political issues. I can't help but ask him about his views on J. D. Vance's best-selling memoir *Hillbilly Elegy*, the story of a small Kentucky town, not too far from Oneida, that describes an angry and dysfunctional community unable to achieve social and economic mobility. Vance, a conservative public intellectual and a newly minted Republican senator from Ohio, narrates the town's decline and his own coming-of-age story as the son of a drug-addicted mother.

While Vance grew up in a small town in Ohio, his family heralded from a part of Kentucky rife with addiction and poverty and steeped in what Vance describes as a contradictory brew of Appalachian culture: loyalty and belief in America, but also what he characterizes as a pathological resistance to hard work and an endless stream of blame toward others for their impoverished situation. Vance observes that his relatives brought this worldview with them to Butler County, Ohio, a Rust Belt region experiencing very similar problems to those in Appalachia. When his mother checked into rehab, Vance's grandparents became his caregivers. Ultimately, through his own wits and hard work and his Mamaw's unrelenting support, he landed at Ohio State University and then Yale Law School, where he felt the deep conflict between his roots and the infinite doors to his future that were suddenly opened.

I ask Clay whether he thought Vance's book was a fair account of his region. Clay, like my graduate students, was troubled by the book, as were many of his friends. Vance blames individuals' moral failings and the region's culture as much as, if not more than, systemic forces for the decline of Appalachia. When it was first published in 2016, the book attained great acclaim for capturing a part of America seemingly misunderstood and forgotten. Vance has since been criticized by many for writing about a place that for most of his later adolescence was not his home but rather somewhere he visited. While *Hillbilly Elegy* offers some insights into the world of rural southern poverty, Vance arguably lacks true empathy for the people he describes, and he seems unappreciative of the larger social forces that make it difficult for most Appalachians to triumph over intergenerational dysfunction, addiction, and poverty as he did.

I find this missing empathy in Clay. "Appalachians should be telling their own story. Somebody who's not from the region should not be grabbing the narrative and putting it into the popular narrative of Americans. It's caused nothing but damage. In this region, there's a lot more nuance than people give it credit. And the more people tell their stories, [the more] we tend to discover, don't we? No need to eulogize us. We're still here."

L ET ME BACK up. For this book, I have spent hours and hours talking to people from Appalachia to San Francisco about their lives. Through this process, I had a list of questions that I went through with everyone to see how people of different ages, locations, income levels, education, and races might answer. While the interviewees and I chatted about all sorts of things—favorite holidays, favorite foods, where they grew up—within these questions was a deep story of their life, belief system, and identity that I was trying to uncover. I wanted to understand how Americans really feel about their fundamental values, each other, and the nation. In particular, I wanted to understand rural Americans. I wanted a peek into the quotidian parts of their lives along with hearing their answers to the big philosophical questions. My sense was that there is a real disconnect between how we Americans view each other and who we really are, and this is perhaps most true in how we see rural Americans.

Clay helps me get closer to the deep story I'm seeking. He is one of many interviewees who disrupt the mainstream ideas about what rural America is and who rural Americans are. Clay County, like much of rural America, is very Republican and predominately non-Hispanic white. Clay County is also far poorer and less educated than most of rural America. Socioeconomically, the town where Clay grew up aligns well with how the media represents rural America. Contrary to our stereotypes, however, Clay is anything but angry, disenfranchised, and reactionary. He speaks sensitively and empathetically about his hometown's past and future, and he lives an idiosyncratic life. He attests to the diversity and complexity to be found among rural Americans, suggesting that our current scripts about this population are wrong. Thing is, he was but one of many people I interviewed from this part of the world, and none of them fit the caricature. There's also strong quantitative evidence that suggests rural Americans are far more nuanced than we give them credit.

I have often thought that Americans, regardless of where we live or whom we vote for, get distracted by sensational media headlines and superficial lifestyle differences. Culture is important, but what I am most interested in is our humanity and how we relate to each other when we strip away our agitation and the cultural signifiers. If we can establish a deeper connection, we can get past our differences and find some form of reconciliation and compromise.

A few months after my conversation with Clay, my research took me over five hundred miles north. On an early December day in 2020, I had interviews with two men from Milwaukee, just hours apart. One of the men was a public defender in the city, and the other a radiologist. Both had graduate degrees and were married with children in college. Both were almost fifty years old at the time of the interviews. The person who made these introductions for me "warned" that one of them was a die-hard Republican who had twice voted for President Trump, and that the other was a far-left progressive. Given the politics of my contact, I was fairly certain the warning had to do with the Trump supporter, and I was quite curious as to what he meant. By this time, I had interviewed many Trump supporters and had found them—like almost all of the people I had interviewed—pleasant, respectful, and reasonable.

I asked these two interviewees, Nathan and Mike, the same questions as I did of almost all of my interviewees: their feelings on democracy, equality (and its existence in America), and the role of government, as well as their perspective on a variety of more personal issues such as education, food, and health. *Do you feel anyone has a right to marry anyone?* I asked. "Yes," replied Nathan. "Yes," replied Mike when I asked him several hours later. Mike continued, "I don't think there's a lot of people who say, 'These people shouldn't be allowed to do this thing.'"

What is your definition of equality? Does it exist in America? "What's my definition of it?" asked Nathan. "Hmm. Equal opportunities come to my mind. People have similar opportunities presented to them despite their race, gender, orientation, but I certainly don't think it exists right now, and it's why I do the work I do, why we live where we live. Striving for equality is a big part of why I live the way I live." I asked the same question of Mike. "The culture and the country should strive for it," Mike responded. "In every way that there could be equality there won't be [complete] equality.... Try to eliminate [inequality], but you will unearth more."

What is the role of government? Is our government too involved or not involved enough? "I believe in what our Constitution says about the limits that need to be on our government," explained Nathan. "Allowing us our personal freedoms, that generally the government should stay out of our business.... However, I think it's important that the government can ensure civil rights, to ensure equality, to strive for that. I want the police out of my business, but I want the government to make it so that people can't hire in a racist fashion or discriminate in a racist or sexist fashion." Mike responded, "You know, the government's role should be making efforts toward equality but staying out of day-to-day life other than to provide the basic necessities: roads, police officers, and schools and social nets. Beyond the basics they should be concentrating on equality and equal opportunity." Can you guess from these interview responses who is the twice-Trump-supporting Republican and who is the progressive Democrat? I wouldn't blame you if you can't, even though we're conditioned to believe the two men's responses should be antithetical.

It's not just people like Clay living in rural America that we get wrong. There is a story in this country that Americans do not see eye to eye on the big stuff. You can divide us by race or religion or geography or income; you can divide us into Republicans and Democrats, conservatives and progressives, the coasts and the middle of America. Supposedly, the country is beset by cultural, social, and political fault lines, and it's all but impossible to find common ground. This very morning as I sit down to drink a cup of coffee and look at the news, I am barraged by frightening headlines—"We're Edging Closer to Civil War," "America's Anti-Democratic Movement," "The Upcoming Elections That Could Shake Both Parties"—and this outcry is only the homepage of the *New York Times*, my favorite newspaper. On Fox News, Newt Gingrich is reporting that Democrats are "paying off" their allies before the midterm "catastrophe." CNN reports that American democracy may hinge on the 2022 election. The same article goes on to quote Governor Jay Inslee of Washington State, who observes of the 2020 election that "we were one vice president away from a coup."[2] Coup. Catastrophe. Civil war. Democracy, the very essence of our country, is in an acute emergency state, as told by our journalists, public intellectuals, and leaders. Is this Haiti? Sudan? Syria? No, it's the United States of America, and to use the same terms for our country that are used to describe war-torn nations with tyrannical governments is an offense to the latter.

Americans are still free to protest nonviolently, and for all the political turmoil of recent years, this is still their preferred tactic. Whether demonstrating against the Supreme Court's recent ruling on abortion or in support of Black Lives Matter, whether lobbying for gun rights or nonviolently protesting the Biden administration, people are free to express their dissatisfaction in the streets, to pen essays and opinion pieces, and to organize political groups. Americans mobilize. They get excited about winning the midterms. There may be schadenfreude when an opposing politician is mired in scandal or an incumbent loses to an upstart from the other party, but it's not civil war.

And yet sensational stories about the end of democracy or an imminent civil war appear daily. These stories often rely on misleading tactics. The polling approach often used by mainstream outlets has its own bias in the methodology. These surveys often use either "binary choice" (yes/no) or "forced choice" (scales of agreeing or disagreeing) questions, which may create ostensibly unambiguous findings but not uncover the variation in how people actually feel.[3] Responding that you perceive "no threat at all" to the future of democracy—a political system known to be messy, difficult, and volatile—would be a naive answer in the best of times. The newspapers and institutions who do the polling may also have a vested interest in producing clear majority and minority responses to hotbutton issues.[4]

The media—motivated by clickbait and profits—popularizes the story of a besieged country under threat. Peddling the sensational idea that America is on the brink of social collapse attracts readers and, in turn, revenue, a far more lucrative approach than acknowledging that America is both rife with difference and tied together by long-standing norms and values. The media is not maliciously motivated or bent on deepening social division, but is rather highly responsive to a changing landscape. Traditional media outlets must now compete with social media, blogs, and YouTube, where disinformation and misinformation often spread.[5] In order to attract eyeballs in this crowded marketplace, larger media institutions adopt sensationalism. Indeed, both traditional and social media contribute to a sense of crisis and division in America and shape information through their own bias.

These tactics do our democracy a deep disservice. Americans are increasingly fatigued by the media putting us on high alert.[6] Day after day, week after week, the average Monday morning brings the distressing headlines I mentioned. We should not be surprised that Americans are tired and skeptical, or that they have lost faith that the government and the media will tell them a fair and balanced story.[7] As the psychologist Steven Pinker points out, if Americans do read the news—which is almost always reporting a crisis—they feel negative and a sense of doom.[8] Many Americans have become desensitized to alarming headlines, even as the media they consume pushes them to be more pessimistic about our government.[9] And yet, these feelings do not translate toward their fellow countrymen.

In a 2015 *New York Review of Books* conversation between then president Barack Obama and the Pulitzer Prize–winning writer Marilynne Robinson, the two great thinkers lament the impact of our politics and media on the nature of democracy. But they equally ask us to recognize that our system of government is worthy of respect and praise. As Obama remarks, "When I was growing up, if the President had spoken to the country, there were three stations, and you know, every city had its own newspaper and they were going to cover that story and that would last for a couple of weeks." Obama observes that the twenty-four-hour news cycle and emphasis on sensationalism creates a sense of despair because this is the type of news that sells. "I believe it creates a pessimism about the country because all those quiet, sturdy voices…they're not heard. It's not interesting to hear a story about some good people in some quiet place that did something sensible and figured out how to get along."

Robinson notes that when the United States was founded, democracy was not taken for granted. It was thought to be a great achievement. "You know, it wasn't simply the most efficient modern system," she observes. "It was something that people collectively made, and that they understood they held it together by valuing it…the human respect…it sort of compounds itself in a respect for the personified achievement of a democratic culture, which is a hard thing." Robinson then goes on to explain that so many other countries have failed to achieve a democratic political system. "I think one of the things we have to realize and talk about is that we cannot take it for granted," she concludes. "It is a main thing that we remake continuously."

Robinson's words are wise, and they reveal how important it is to be conscious citizens of our country. I believe many people share her view of the United States. Not a single person I spoke to was truly scared that democracy might be lost, and nor did they want it to be. No one spoke poorly of others who had different viewpoints than theirs. They valued our political system and their fellow citizens.

This revelation starts with a single question. I asked my interviewees—rural and urban alike: *What does democracy mean to you?* Time and time again, they shared a similar vision. "I guess just empowering people to have a decision in choices, and things that happen in their life and an ability to effect change," said one college-educated woman from Pennsylvania. "I would say living with your freedoms…being able to vote, and [choosing] who you want to represent you," said a high-school-educated man from the same state. "Living in a nation where we can make our own choices. The government is of the people and for the people," responded a pastor from Missouri. "The right to speak your values and beliefs and vote for who you want as your leader," explained a PhD-educated woman from San Francisco. "Multiple opinions coming to a majority consensus," summed up a young woman from Houston. "I think of it as everybody has a choice, everybody has a vote, everyone mattering," said a single mom in Appalachia. "Where everyone gets a fair say with decision-making, to some extent.…People should help make decisions for the country and to have the freedom to have free speech and practice any religion, without being persecuted," explained a neurologist from Memphis. "I am trying to get all of the media influences out of my head. What democracy is? Could it be as simple as one person, one vote?" observed a tech executive from Berkeley. What struck me was, despite how different these people are from one another, their answers are similar. People believe in the same basic functions of government and importance of equality and democracy, irrespective of where they live, their education, or occupation.

The same held true when I asked my interviewees about a "divided America." I asked several questions to get at people's perceptions of national cohesion: *Do you believe Americans have a shared sense of values?, Do you feel left behind?, Do you feel you relate to fellow Americans, particularly those who live in totally different places?,* and finally, *The media has said our country has "two Americas." Is that a statement you believe?* While I listened to folks answer these questions in various ways, one thing was clear: whatever division they perceived in America, they did not feel divided from other Americans. Yes, some people believed that America was divided—almost all the urban, educated interviewees and about half of the rural ones—but they didn't blame their fellow Americans. Many instead pointed to the media for fostering and amplifying a sense of division. Others blamed increasing class inequality, Washington dysfunction, and self-interested politicians. Rarely was an unkind word spoken of other citizens. Even as my new friends worried that the country was fracturing, they felt they could relate to one another as human beings. As Clay Spencer in Kentucky put it, "Being American is enough of a specificity that we had something in common that we could relate to." The media and politicians insist the country is acutely divided, but most of my interviewees still felt they could empathize with other Americans and find common ground.

For the most part, the people I interviewed also didn't feel particularly left behind. As a man from Missouri who asked to remain anonymous remarked, "The truth is, Elizabeth, we don't feel left behind. We want to be left alone." He meant by the government and the media, which he felt encroached on his way of life. People weren't angry with other ordinary Americans. If they did feel alienated, it was because they resented the giant political machine of Washington, which felt beyond their control and yet dictated their lives. Even those I spoke with who were largely comfortable with their situation saw Washington and politics as far removed from their daily experience.

In fact, both the educated coastal elites and those in the smallest of rural towns shared a belief that they could relate to one another. Barring the rare indecisive response, almost everyone shared this sentiment. One Harvard-educated schoolteacher from Berkeley put it like this: "We spent two weeks in Tennessee, and we were at this trampoline park every day, and while we were there talking to a lot of parents [who were very different from parents back in Berkeley]. It's so interesting because [despite this], I feel like there were a lot of points of connection. I felt there were a bunch of moms I met [and] we could have been friends had I actually lived in that area." This woman's observations were not unique. The sense I got from all of my interviewees was that, irrespective of differences, when they talked with others, they could easily find connections.

These interviews aligned with what large-scale studies of American society, such as the University of Chicago's General Social Survey (GSS), reveal.[10] Established in 1972, the GSS collects data on American attitudes, opinions, and beliefs on topics from race to mobility to morality. Year after year, the GSS allows researchers to study what Americans of different ages, races, income levels, and residences think of a variety of topics. Using the most recent data available (2018) and incorporating earlier years as necessary (some questions are not asked every year), I was able to get a wide and deep sense of Americans' views on many important topics.[11] Taking a look at the GSS responses, I found that rural America differs dramatically from our perception of it, and that rural and urban

Americans share a lot of common ground with regard to our most pressing social and political issues.

Consider the responses to questions regarding democracy and the US government. Americans are not disillusioned with democracy. However, they are disillusioned with our government, and this sentiment is not specific to rural or urban folks. Approximately 47 percent of urban and 44 percent of rural respondents to the GSS had "hardly any" confidence in the executive branch. Forty-two percent of those surveyed, across geographies, had "only some" confidence in the executive branch. Similar responses can be found in questions directed toward the legislative branch: 48 percent of urban and 44 percent of rural respondents had "hardly any" confidence in it, while 43 percent and 47 percent of urban and rural respondents, respectively, had "only some" confidence. Put another way, of the urban- and rural-dwelling Americans surveyed in the GSS, only roughly 12 percent and 9 percent, respectively, had "a great deal of confidence" in the executive and legislative branches. Incidentally, while half of rural and urban Americans had "only some" confidence in the Supreme Court, the second-most popular response for both groups was "a great deal" of confidence in the Supreme Court, with 30 percent of urban and 23 percent of rural respondents supportive of the judicial branch.

Despite their misgivings about the government itself, reflected in both my interviews and the GSS, most Americans are proud of their democracy and feel that it more or less works. Almost 50 percent of respondents overall are "somewhat proud" of American democracy. About a quarter of both urban and rural respondents are "very proud" of American democracy. Only 2 percent of urban and 1 percent of rural respondents feel democracy works "very poorly" in America (5 percent and 3 percent of urban and rural respondents, respectively, think it works "very well"). On a scale of zero to ten, with zero being "very poorly" and ten being "very well," most people answered the question of how well democracy works in America with a five, six, seven, or eight.

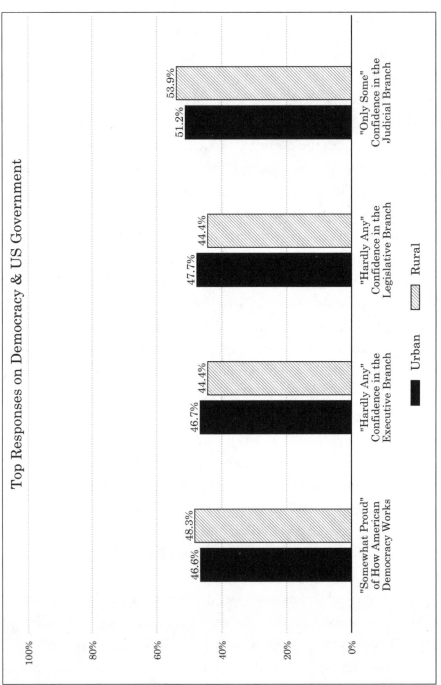

Top Responses on Democracy & US Government

"Only Some" Confidence in the Judicial Branch — 51.2% / 53.9%

"Hardly Any" Confidence in the Legislative Branch — 47.7% / 44.4%

"Hardly Any" Confidence in the Executive Branch — 46.7% / 44.4%

"Somewhat Proud" of How American Democracy Works — 46.6% / 48.3%

Urban / Rural

Source: University of Chicago General Social Survey, 2014 and 2018

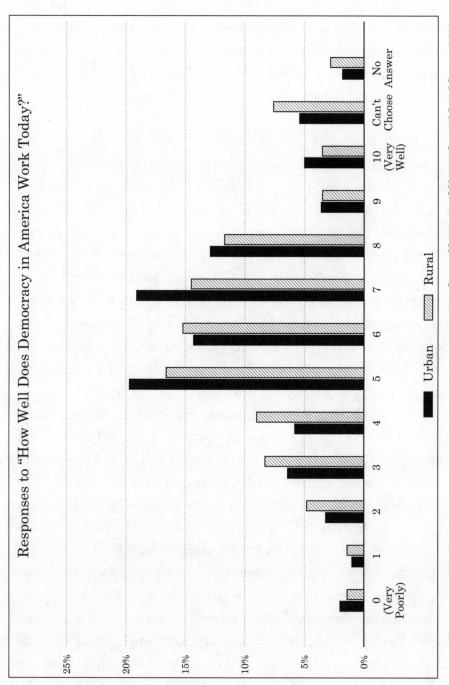

Responses to "How Well Does Democracy in America Work Today?"

Source: University of Chicago General Social Survey, 2014

In total, these results indicate that three-quarters of our country feels pretty good about our system of government and well over half feel that democracy is more or less working, even as most Americans do not feel positively toward the institutions that run the government itself. The same was true of many of my interviewees' remarks around democracy. They still believe in it.

R EGARDLESS OF WHERE they are from, the people I interviewed also believe in equality and do not believe it exists in America. Racial discrimination was the most frequently mentioned example of how the United States remains unequal for some. When I ask, *What is your definition of equality? Does it exist in America?*, the majority of people respond similarly to Craig from Iowa and Denise from Kentucky: people should be treated equally, but often are not, especially on matters of race. "I guess I go back to all men are created equal and should be able to succeed. Hope and pray they do, but unfortunately some people don't. No, [it] doesn't exist. Some is what we inherit. I inherited a great deal, and there's all kinds of discrimination," says Craig, with resignation in his voice. "Well, I would think of it as everybody being treated the same, judged by the same standards," Denise explains. "I think there's still a lot of people who do not get treated equally, maybe because of their skin color."

Other interviewees are acutely aware of the racism and inequality they've witnessed in their own lives, and they discuss their efforts to combat it, hearkening back even to childhood. "When I was in high school, my dad hired a Black boy," says a Republican businessman from Missouri who asked to remain anonymous. "A cross was burned in our front yard," he explains. "I grew an Afro to relate to my Black brothers, and by the time I graduated a Black boy was elected to class president....I've seen [racism] firsthand. I see the tremendous progress we've made, but I still see the darkness." For most people, the issues of racial discrimination are straightforward.

Their worldview rejects racism, and they find it to be an ongoing scourge in our country. For others, race relations are more complicated and introduce uncomfortable viewpoints with no clear solution.

"For all people to be treated equally, period," Shannon responds when I ask her for her definition of equality. "I believe that there's a lot of people who want [equality] to exist. I do believe the media is doing everything in its power to destroy it." Shannon is from Manchester, Kentucky, where she lives with her husband and two of their three kids in a mobile home. While still a small community, the town has grown almost 75 percent since 2010, and today it boasts a population of 2,195. The average house value is $83,704 (compared to almost $300,000 for the United States), and household income is about $35,000, 45 percent less than the national average.[12] Shannon was born and raised in Manchester along with her seven brothers. Twice divorced, she lives with her third husband, his child from a previous marriage (whom she recently adopted), and her son from a previous marriage—all part of her big, blended, cohesive family.

I met Shannon through a sinuous route that started in New York City and then traveled through Missouri and finally to Kentucky, where I met Denise, from Oneida. She suggested Shannon, a woman from her church who lived a town over, as a good person to interview. Denise expressed quite liberal views despite the conservative nature of where she lived, and she noted that Shannon might offer a different perspective than her own.

In our first conversation of many, Shannon and I discuss some hot-button issues. Like many rural folks, she has a thoughtful and layered answer to the question of equality, which almost always coincides in my interviews with a discussion of race. She believes the media has made race relations worse. Perhaps more importantly, she personally has never viewed people through the lens of race, and, by extension, has not judged people for the color of their skin. "I have a very specific answer," Shannon elaborates on her initial response. "Here in Manchester, there were no differences ever made between

Black and white. My best friend when I was growing up was Black. I didn't even know he was Black. We are all the same."

Shannon then goes on to describe a recent personal incident as evidence of her resentment toward the media. "[Louisville, Kentucky] is where Breonna Taylor was killed. What happened was that media is blowing it up. My friend, Black friend from Louisville, deleted me on Facebook because of my political views." Shannon is angry. She sees the media as wrongly framing race relations as political and, in particular, as fostering a negative view of Donald Trump, for whom she voted. "She looked at my Twitter page and it has my little girl singing happy birthday to President Trump and that's why she deleted me. I supported Trump, and media has made him look bad. And that is why she deleted me." Shannon explains that she feels the media had so negatively portrayed Trump that, as racial tensions heated up in the summer of 2020, anyone associated with him was unfairly seen as contributing to racial injustice and unrest. In her view, until the media began to frame Trump supporters as racist, she had got along well with people of all races, and she felt she had never really considered how race distinctions had shaped her own life. From Shannon's perspective, the media was responsible for political polarization and tense race relations.

Jason, a white Mormon man, shared a similar view. Jason grew up very poor in the South but as an adult became a successful and well-off nurse anesthetist. At the time I interviewed him, he was living and working in small-town Pennsylvania, married with three boys. He subsequently moved to the Midwest to a community with a bigger Mormon presence, where he felt he could better raise his kids. "I lived in California for a couple of years, in Orange County. I was out there for two years and we lived with members of the congregation. I saw some of the richest people in my life," Jason says. "I grew up in Memphis, Tennessee.... I actually grew up on the wrong side of the tracks. Poor, school was 90 percent Black. Biggest shock moving to PA was going to a place where everyone was white. I didn't understand how Black people were a minority. Most common statement [I hear from people], 'There is still a lot of racism in the South.'" At this point Jason pauses, almost incredulous. "And here I'm talking to someone in a place where there are three Black people and I'm like, 'How many Black people have you even spoken to in your life?' So that was a big wake-up for me. It was kind of offensive for me."

Jason carries on, and I listen intently. I see how his experience could make him feel confused and angry. "A big thing [with the 2008 election] was if you didn't vote for Obama you were racist. But in Memphis, it was [also accepted that] I could just not want to vote for Obama but that doesn't make me racist. In California, this dawned on me. Y'all have no clue what racism really is.... A couple, who are college professors who are pretty liberal, we were talking and [I tell them that] my best friend growing up is a Black guy, and [the professor's] comment was, 'Wow, your best friend was Black? Wow, that must have been really neat!'" Jason pauses. I can imagine him shaking his head. "Neat? It was normal."

Jason goes on to describe the rest of that conversation. The professor laments the lack of diversity in her hometown, which houses the university where she teaches. Jason, laughing, tells me what he was thinking as he spoke to her: "You have no idea what you are talking about.... You don't even have a friend that is Black." I feel embarrassment for my fellow academic. I can see the *Saturday Night Live* skit of the naive progressive, well-meaning but also painfully out of touch. I know people like her. They are plentiful in my liberal Los Angeles neighborhood, which is also almost 100 percent white and smattered with "In This House, We Believe" signs, even though so many people who display them rarely, if ever, face the grievances these signs purportedly stand against: racism, xenophobia, Islamophobia, classism, transphobia. I support equality for all too. Yet, I realize these signs are fundamentally performative, meant to signal the virtue of their owner. Almost none of us white, well-to-do, overly educated liberals have ever faced any of these forms of discrimination, and few of us actively challenge them in our own lives. We don't know what it feels like to be Jason, and we don't know what it feels like to be Black.

Jason continues, "I do believe racism is alive and well, but I'll be honest, racism is a double-edged sword." I brace myself for what he might say, feeling my own liberal hackles coming up. "I have been on the other end of this. I had a girlfriend who broke up with me because I was white. I've been jumped. I had a friend who, when I went to his house and when they saw I was white, I was never allowed back. I experienced [this] too. I grew up and became a rich white man and lost my ability to have an opinion. I was raised in Memphis in a low-income place, and I could have opinions. I'm the first college-educated person in my family, and yet now because I'm a rich, educated white man I can't speak. I don't have a right to my opinion."

I struggle with these conversations. I am gaining an understanding of where Shannon's and Jason's perspectives come from, but I feel really ambivalent. I can hear Jason's frustration with what he thinks is a complicated—and at times hypocritical—dynamic. Shannon does not appear overtly racist and resents that she's been caught up in what she sees as a politically charged tidal wave. I understand they feel they have experienced unfair judgment and lost friends as a result of tense race relations. It's hard, however, writing in the era of Black Lives Matter with increased awareness of police brutality against minorities, to truly believe that anyone who is not Black can identify with the extent of discrimination and prejudice directed toward this population.

As I am trying to make sense of these responses, I share my results and thoughts with my doctoral student Greg. A few days later, he sends me a recent article in the *Atlantic* by the novelist and essayist Danzy Senna, who also happens to be a colleague of mine at the University of Southern California. In her article "Robin DiAngelo and the Problem with Anti-racist Self-Help," Senna is frustrated with how many well-meaning, educated, liberal white people are preoccupied with race in ways that do not help anyone, except perhaps themselves. "How we have wished that white people would leave us out of their self-preoccupied, ham-fisted, kindergarten-level discussions of race," writes Senna, who is Black, part Irish, and part Afro-Mexican. In particular, she takes aim at Robin DiAngelo, the white woke evangelist and author of *White Fragility* and *Nice Racism*, and Courtney Martin, who had just published *Learning in Public*, her memoir of being a white, privileged liberal who sends her child to an academically failing, predominantly Black public school in Oakland, California, in a guilt-ridden attempt to create social change. For Senna, these writers appear unable to see nuance or any positivity in current race relations. "Interracial worlds, friendships, marriages—Black and white lives inextricably linked, for good and for bad, with racism and with hope—are all but erased," Senna writes.[13] Smoothing over the complexities of race relations, she explains, including being blind to or suppressing the positive, was not bettering society.

This is a point that April Simpson, a Black writer for the Pew Charitable Trust, makes in her report "Why Rural America Is Joining the Movement for Black Lives." "Those who study or live in rural America know that residents' lives are intertwined across races," Simpson writes. "Families may have lived among each other for generations." There is something quite profound in what Senna and Simpson describe, and it captures what I believe Jason and Shannon are expressing.

For me, what is heartening about these conversations is that, to the best of their ability, Shannon and Jason are trying to find ways to understand the experience of others. They acknowledge the existence of racism and inequality, expressing that they do not want racial divides in their own lives. They appear, philosophically and emotionally, on the right side of things. Many people are in fact coming from the same position of a desire for racial equality, for open and caring relationships across racial lines. Yet, the solutions favored by different parts of society are almost antithetical to one another.

Research on contemporary rural views on racial issues highlights the complexity of race in the region. A 2022 *Social Science Quarterly* article by Justin Curtis finds that the protests following the death of George Floyd did very little to change rural respondents' views of the police and their attitudes toward reparations, while having only a muted effect on racial prejudice, even as the country as a whole became less supportive of police, more attuned to discrimination toward Black people, and more in favor of reparations. This is somewhat surprising given that social justice protests in the wake of Floyd's murder could be found across the country, including in rural towns. Curtis speculates that part of this unchanged view is due to the fact that rural folks perceived the protests as urban and progressive, so their attitudes may not have been a rejection of the cause so much as a rejection of its origin.[14] "On the one hand, rural respondents may have been likely to have lower favorability of the police after the death of George Floyd because this example of police brutality would resonate with rural communities that may be more resistant to a powerful state," writes Curtis. "On the other hand, rural respondents may have viewed the social and political movement that emerged in response to Floyd's death as an urban movement to be resisted, and so they may express higher levels of support for the police."

In April Simpson's report on rural America, she offers another explanation. She observes that small-town social justice protests occurred everywhere. Nationwide, people in rural America showed their support for Black people and demonstrated that they are concerned about discrimination. But, Simpson explains, many of them had personal relationships with law enforcement and did not necessarily know how to square their support for racial justice with their friendships with police. "Unlike their urban counterparts, members of the local police force are often neighbors. People may know where the sheriff likes to grab lunch. Some have his cellphone number in

their phones. Locals know which officers they can build a relationship with and which to avoid," writes Simpson. "Close relationships
among local law enforcement, public officials and one another make
the rural response to Floyd's killing uniquely personal." And yet,
many rural folks showed up to protests in their hometowns (despite
threats from residents who attempted to stop them). Importantly,
these events did not draw outsiders from cities or elsewhere. People within rural towns protested out of their own desire to do so.
One interviewee in Simpson's article called this "a civic engagement
awakening."[15] This may very well have been true for many rural
communities. Still, it cannot be ignored that, even if rural Americans
are more supportive of Black Lives Matter than progressives might
have thought, there is far less support than one would find in cities.[16]

The GSS findings mostly concur with this research and with
my interviews, but they offered some surprises as well. On issues of
race and gender, urban and rural respondents do not offer wildly different views, despite the preconception that rural areas are far more
discriminatory than cities. In fact, on some issues, rural Americans,
particularly the least educated, are the most supportive of policies
addressing inequality based on race and gender.

When it comes to Americans' feelings about government support for the Black community, education, not geography, is most
associated with the responses. Surprisingly, the greatest proponents of government support for the Black community are the least
educated—that is, those without a high school education—both
urban and rural, not the educated and urban, as the current cultural climate might suggest. Of educated Americans, more rural
folks than city dwellers support aid for the Black community. The
biggest difference within an educational group is that of high school
graduates, where urban respondents are more likely than rural ones
to support such aid. More generally, those with only a high school
degree are the least supportive of government aid for the Black community and are the least supportive of any race-based intervention.

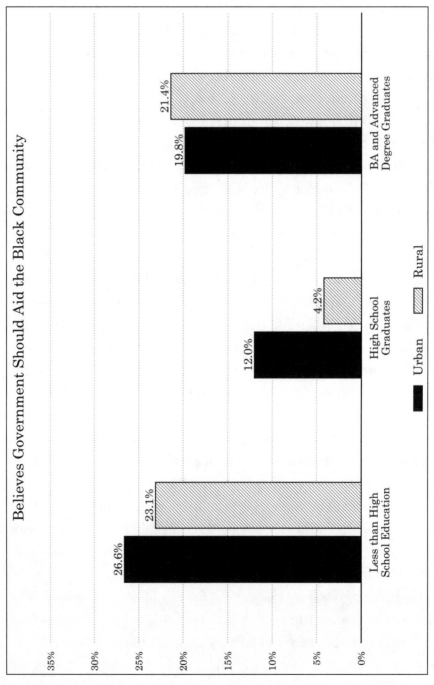

Believes Government Should Aid the Black Community

Source: University of Chicago General Social Survey, 2018

More generally, the majority of those surveyed by the GSS felt something needed to be done to improve equality. Both urban and rural respondents believe "too little" is being done to "improve conditions for Blacks." A quarter of both urban and rural Americans feel "close to Blacks" and 20 percent of rural Americans (versus 16 percent of urban Americans) "strongly support" "preference in hiring Blacks." While only 10 percent of rural Americans answer the question "Should government aid Blacks?" with "Government should help Blacks," the results for urban Americans are surprisingly low, too, at just 17 percent. A quarter of both urban and rural Americans "strongly favor" a relative marrying a Black person. These questions were asked of all survey respondents, irrespective of their own race.

Similarly, when looking at policies directed toward racial equity, responses are largely similar across geographies, with rural folks and the least educated being the most supportive. Overall, 40 percent of urban and rural folks without a high school degree, urban inhabitants with just a high school degree, and rural inhabitants with a bachelor's or above do not believe affirmative action hurts white people. While educated urban residents are the least concerned about the impact of affirmative action on them, their socioeconomic position is far more secure than those who are largely uneducated, for whom any perceived preferential treatment may appear as a threat.

Notably, the majority of Americans, regardless of education or geography, are not supportive of preferential hiring for Black people. For example, 63 percent of educated urban residents and 72 percent of educated rural respondents oppose or strongly oppose preferential hiring for Black people. But even though this idea is unpopular overall, at almost 40 percent, the most likely group to support or strongly support such a policy is rural residents without a high school degree.

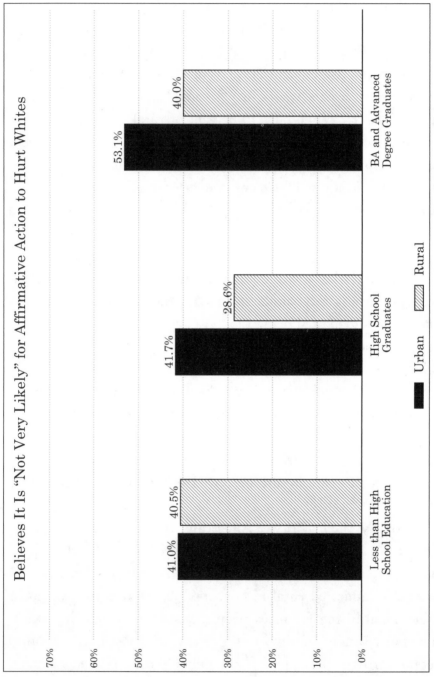

Believes It Is "Not Very Likely" for Affirmative Action to Hurt Whites

Source: University of Chicago General Social Survey, 2018

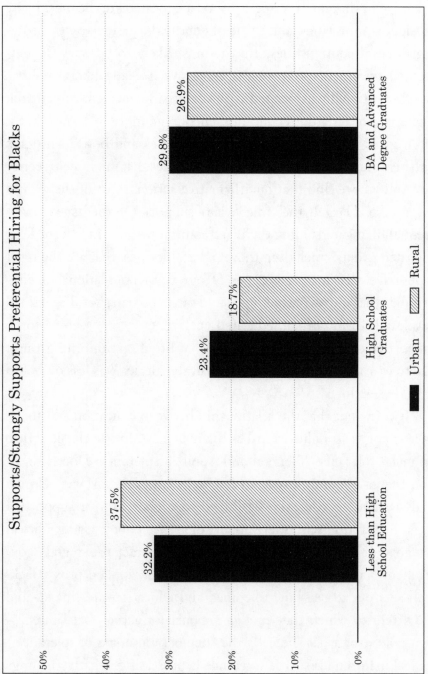

Supports/Strongly Supports Preferential Hiring for Blacks

Less than High School Education
- Urban: 32.2%
- Rural: 37.5%

High School Graduates
- Urban: 23.4%
- Rural: 18.7%

BA and Advanced Degree Graduates
- Urban: 29.8%
- Rural: 26.9%

■ Urban   ▨ Rural

Source: University of Chicago General Social Survey, 2018

I found these results bewildering. As the political and cultural narrative in this country goes, the most educated are the most likely to support minorities, and the least educated, particularly those living in rural communities, are the most likely to be wary of preferential treatment of anyone. Progressive, socially liberal politics are conventionally associated with the urban educated. As research suggests, not only does education encourage more tolerance, but it often gives people—through college courses and books—insights into historical discrimination and the policies that might help rectify it.[17] And yet we find that on affirmative action, most of the groups surveyed feel largely the same level of support. On the issue of preferential hiring and aiding the Black community, it is in fact the least educated groups, including those in rural locales, that are the most supportive, defying stereotypes of our rural population but confirming what my own experience told me to be true. Yet, I remained perplexed. In my urban, educated enclave, everyone seemed to be supportive of practices and policies that lifted up minority groups. There was a widespread belief that rural America was less on board with these efforts.

It turns out that the relationship between education and tolerance is not as straightforward as many believe. In her classic article on racial tolerance "General and Applied Tolerance: Does Education Increase Commitment to Racial Integration?" Mary Jackman finds that more education is linked to higher *abstract* support of racial integration but lower support of *applied* policy. Using a broad category of "support integration" as the abstract proxy and "government action" (for example, busing) as the applied proxy, Jackman sets out to see how tolerance and education are linked, and the extent to which they predict support for actual racial integration policy, or what she calls the "democratic norm of tolerance." As Jackman remarks, true tolerance is possessing negative feelings for a group—immigrants, Black people, women—and yet still supporting a positive policy toward them. To that end, Jackman finds that "the relationship between education and policy orientation is considerably weaker rather than stronger as one moves from general principles to more specific policies." Put another way, once an abstract notion of integration becomes a policy that may affect the educated person's life, a type of NIMBYism emerges.

But Jackman doesn't stop with the educated. She finds a curious link between lack of education and tolerance, which may explain the seemingly contradictory results I found in my analysis of the GSS. Unlike the educated subjects, those with the least education do not have a preference for abstract or applied policy on racial integration. If anything, the least educated lean toward more support for applied policy. Over the three time periods Jackman studied between 1964 and 1973, there was no difference in support for applied policy between the educated and uneducated. In fact, Jackman found in 1964 that those with only a grade school education who had "cold feelings" toward Black people were still more supportive than those with a high school or college education of government action to support African Americans. After considering and dismissing various possible flaws in questions and the reliability of respondents, Jackman concludes, "Increasing years of education lead to a greater familiarity with the appropriate democratic position on racial integration but not a stronger commitment on racial integration." Jackman suggests that "the well-educated are more likely to have genuinely 'learned' abstract democratic principle, but that learning is relatively superficial.... Formal education can produce citizens who have more knowledge, skills and worldly sophistication but it does not seem to instill a deeper commitment to the democratic norm of tolerance."[18]

Jackman's research is backed up by more recent studies. A 2003 Pew study found not dissimilar contradictions between support of the abstract notion of equity versus its application. While well over half of people surveyed supported affirmative action and efforts to increase the numbers of Black people and minorities in college, support dropped to just 24 percent when asked if they should be given preferential treatment. A 2019 Pew survey found that while 75 percent of people supported taking racial and ethnic diversity into account, 72 percent oppose giving preference to Black Americans in hiring and promotion practices.[19] In both of these more recent studies, the results corroborate Jackman's finding that society values helping minorities in theory, but people are less supportive when that aid becomes more concrete and may directly impact them.[20]

In his 2018 book *Whiteshift*, University of London professor Eric Kaufmann finds that the biggest differences are not around the policies themselves but rather the extent to which a particular group finds a policy to be either racist or helpful. Part of what he observes is the shrinking of the once-dominant ethnic white majorities in the West, what he calls "whiteshift." In the United States (and the United Kingdom), this decline of the white majority can explain some of the rise of populist movements and the polarization we see in the electorate. But Kaufmann argues that the animosity arising from these demographic shifts is not only about race but also about what these changes mean for the historically dominant group. In an interview with the *New Yorker*, Kaufmann remarks that "it's about attachment to one's own group rather than hatred of other groups. This is an important distinction."[21] As such, policies that involve race and ethnicity are received differently depending on where one's identity is found. "The country is not divided by racial conflict, but by conflict over racial ideology," writes Kaufmann. He notes that white liberals tend to be the most self-loathing, embracing what he calls the "anti-white ideology of the cultural left." For this group, being white is not a part of their identity but rather symbolic of the structural and historical oppression directed toward minorities, and they wish to correct for their whiteness.

By extension, Kaufmann argues that educated, white respondents are acutely sensitive to racial dynamics, sometimes even more so than the very minority groups who would be most affected. Case in point, Kaufmann finds that white liberals are the most likely to view the proposed wall between the United States and Mexico as racist.

Ninety-one percent of white Hillary Clinton voters with a graduate degree saw the wall as racist, while less than half of minority voters agreed. Fifty-five percent of minorities felt that the wall was in their racial self-interest. Similarly, a full 83 percent of white Clinton supporters believed that diversity makes America better, while just 54 percent of Black people and 46 percent of Hispanics agreed.[22] This data suggests what both Jackman and, many decades later, Danzy Senna have observed through different lenses. White, educated people are very good at knowing what they should care about and how they should feel about certain issues, even if research suggests that they resist the application of policies addressing social injustice. Many have gone so far as to argue that liberal cultural capital rests on being perceived as progressive, woke, and anti-racist—a very different set of identity attributes than those valued by other Americans.

IF EDUCATION AND city dwelling didn't drive positive support for racially tolerant policies, I wondered if some of the responses on the GSS were dependent on the race of the person being asked. Curious, I went back to the GSS and studied responses by race. It turns out that urban support for many racial policies was driven by Black and minority responses. In fact, any increased urban support for such policies compared to rural responses was not due to the white urban population. Consider the case of preferential hiring for Black people. When we look at urban support or opposition as a whole, we see that 26.6 percent of all urban respondents are supportive, while 66.3 percent are opposed. Rural numbers are 19.3 percent and 70.6 percent, respectively. When these responses are studied by race, white support is less than the aggregate support, and minority support is markedly higher. The same general trend can be seen with regard to the question on whether the government should aid the Black community.

Two findings stuck out to me in this analysis: First, was the extent to which race drives people's responses to these questions. At first blush, it appears that urban America is more open-minded and supportive of equity initiatives, but these surveys uncover that Black and minority responses are particularly influential in determining the urban statistics. In other words, minority respondents reside in urban areas at higher rates than they do in rural ones, and they tend to be more supportive of racially tolerant policies than average (which is unsurprising given their lived experience). Second, and perhaps more important for the topic at hand, was that when white Americans are looked at in isolation, rural white Americans do not provide significantly different responses to these questions than white Americans who live in cities. In some instances, rural whites and rural minorities share almost identical responses. Case in point: exactly 34 percent of rural whites and rural minorities believe affirmative action is "not very likely" to hurt whites (white and minority people in cities have a much greater difference between their responses). It may indeed be true that everyone should be more invested in equity policies, but singling out rural America as the root of racism in the country is unhelpful and inaccurate.

In spite of these findings, I still couldn't square the various contradictions in the research. My interviews and the GSS point to a more open rural America when it comes to issues of race, particularly race-based policy. As I researched for this book, however, I also came across articles that suggested rural America was not as on board with Black Lives Matter as urban America. And despite good people like Jason, Denise, and Shannon, some research suggests that minorities experience more racial and ethnic intolerance in rural America than in urban America.[23]

During this time, I came across the article "Historical Roots of Implicit Bias in Slavery," from the *Proceedings of the National Academy of Sciences*, written by three psychologists. To study the extent to which historical structural racism influences current people's implicit biases, the psychologists looked at places with large enslaved populations in

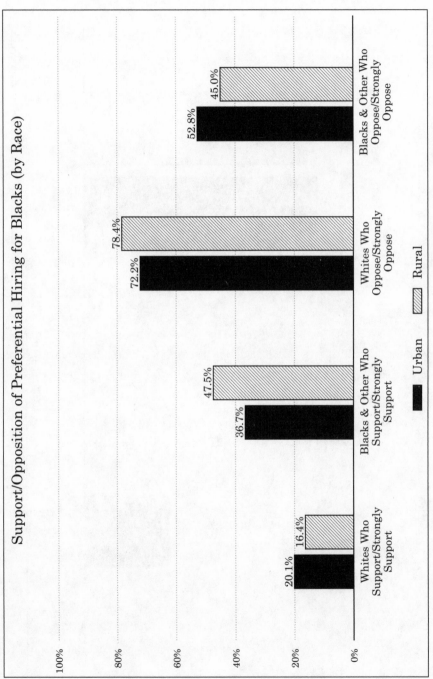

Support/Opposition of Preferential Hiring for Blacks (by Race)

Source: University of Chicago General Social Survey, 2018

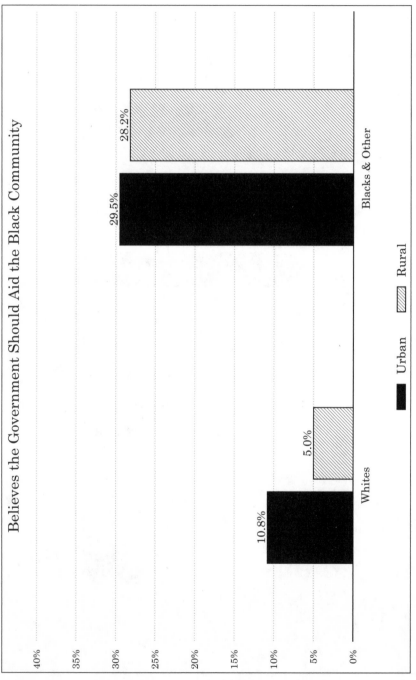

Believes the Government Should Aid the Black Community

28.2%

29.5%

Blacks & Other

5.0%

10.8%

Whites

Urban

Rural

Source: University of Chicago General Social Survey, 2018

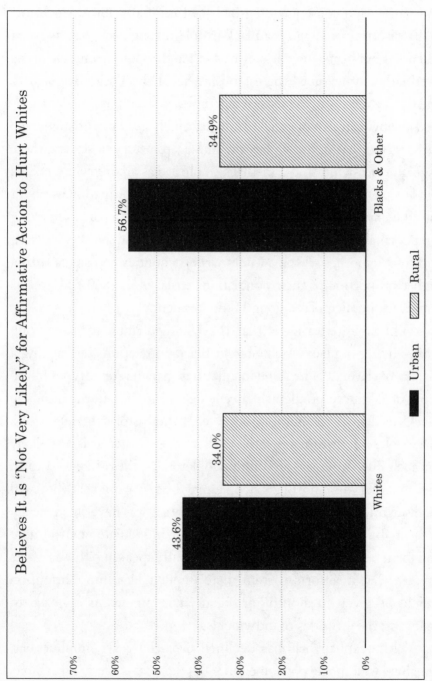

Believes It Is "Not Very Likely" for Affirmative Action to Hurt Whites

Source: University of Chicago General Social Survey, 2018

1860. These areas in the South were more resistant to mandates to end slavery and consequently established Jim Crow laws, which formally discriminated against Black people through schools, housing, and other public means, a legacy that lasted through the middle of the twentieth century until the establishment of the Voting Rights Act and Civil Rights Act. Structural outcomes as a result of Jim Crow created an environment of racial inequality and bias. Unsurprisingly, the authors find that in these places with a deep history of slavery, there is greater pro-white and anti-Black implicit bias among white people and less pro-white bias among Black people. Discrimination was built into the environment of these places and remained a part of life long after formal discrimination mechanisms were banned. "Consistent with our hypothesis," the authors write, "counties and states with a higher proportion of their populations enslaved in 1860 had greater anti-Black implicit bias among White residents."

What is interesting is that they find no implicit bias among whites living in places with current Black populations but lacking a history of slavery. "The same inequalities that cue stereotypes in the mind of White respondents may cue discrimination in the minds of Black residents," the authors observe. If the historical context of a place is less discriminatory, the authors argue, then it is less likely for such cues to emerge. White people may be less likely to form racist stereotypes and Black people may be less wary that they will be discriminated against because that context was never historically present. In short, people respond to their immediate environment and form perceptions as a result. "Practically speaking, these results suggest that in efforts to remediate implicit bias, more attention should be given to modifying social environments as opposed to changing the attitudes of individuals."

While explicit bias has declined over the years, implicit bias remains a widespread phenomenon.[24] Explicit bias is overt and exhibits prejudice or favoritism. Implicit bias is far more subtle and involves the forming of opinions or judgments toward someone due to their skin color, sexuality, or gender without even being conscious of it. Implicit bias is a perpetual problem even for those who actively reject prejudice. Implicit bias is not always obvious in day-to-day life, but it is easy to uncover through cognition tests of "mental associations triggered automatically on thinking about social groups," rather than, say, vocalizing one's opinion.

But, the authors argue, people are often implicitly biased as a result of social environments, and their feelings may be fleeting. "For any individual, activated biases may be idiosyncratic and ephemeral," they write. "However, implicit bias operates like the 'wisdom of crowds' phenomenon, in which independently assessed knowledge, when aggregated, tends to be more accurate than the partial knowledge of any individual." The authors call this "bias of crowds." Some of this bias can be cultural—ways of behaving, what constitutes accepted social capital—and some can be structural, representing historical legacies of discrimination.[25] But these streams of implicit bias overlap. Your social capital may be a function of your socioeconomic position or the color of your skin. Thus, what appear to be cultural differences have generational impacts on those who are excluded from the larger cultural and social hegemony.

While this article was not written about rural America, I came to think of it as a lens through which to understand the conflicting data on rural racial views. My interviewees and the GSS data suggested that rural Americans have more open and less racially biased views than is generally thought, but perhaps implicit bias exists in the rural environment in a way that is not fully clear to its residents. This is likely a reasonable observation about much of humanity. As I conducted my interviews and research for this book, I kept in mind that, while my interviewees were not explicitly racially biased, they may have been implicitly biased. The goal of my research was not to tease out implicit bias, and it was hard for me to truly gauge its presence in the people to whom I spoke.

Even with this limitation in mind, it is clear to me that rural people are sensitively aware and concerned with matters of race. From my hours of conversation with this population, I have come to intimately understand that many rural Americans are much more open-minded than those on the coasts perceive them to be. Rural Americans are not the hard-nosed, ignorant, and intolerant caricatures portrayed by countless books and movies. Awful, bigoted people exist in all sorts of places, I am sure, but sensational journalism makes us think that more of those people exist than actually do and that they typically reside in our small towns. Support for racially tolerant policies is not strongly tied to geography but rather to race and education. What's more, when you speak to them, most Americans express support and hope for racial equality. The difference is not the goal but rather the path to get there. What I've found talking to my fellow Americans, rural and urban, is that there is an enormous amount of empathy out there among all of us. We shouldn't forget that.

This is even more true for religious tolerance. While I did not interview people specifically on their views about other religions, the GSS captures these opinions. On the whole, most people do not exhibit religious intolerance or discrimination: 82 percent of urban and 67 percent of rural respondents have a neutral to very positive attitude toward Muslims. While there are some negative views toward Muslims, Hindus, and atheists, this negativity is in the minority. Negative attitudes toward these faiths may be due to ethnic associations with the 9/11 attacks (a source of Islamophobia) and, in rural America, the smaller populations of these religious groups in predominantly Christian towns.[26] These possibilities are not excuses but rather possible explanations for what the data revealed. Overall, there was little bias for any religion other than in favor of Christianity, which I suspect is due to the overwhelming Christian affiliation of most Americans. Despite these caveats, the predominant trend is that most people do not care what religion others choose to practice, or if they choose to be religious at all. To me, that neutrality is a good sign. We don't need to feel strongly about our fellow Americans' faith decisions; we just need to not judge others negatively on account of how they choose to worship.

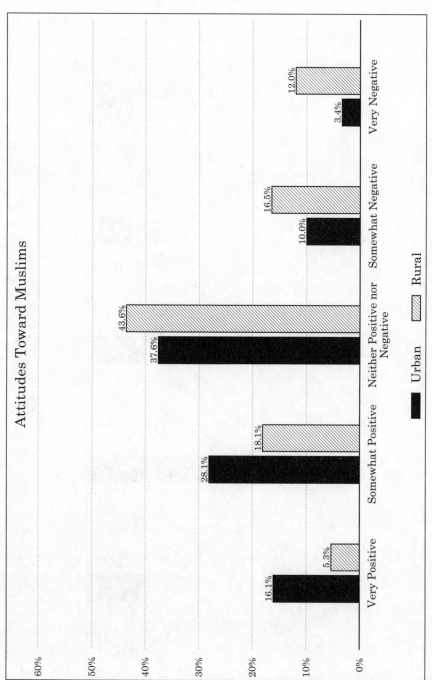

Attitudes Toward Muslims

Source: University of Chicago General Social Survey, 2018

Urban ■ Rural ▨

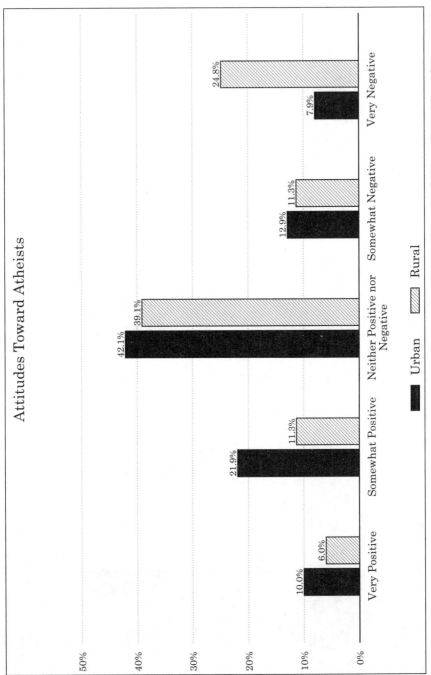

Attitudes Toward Atheists

Very Positive — Rural 6.0%, Urban 10.0%

Somewhat Positive — Rural 11.3%, Urban 21.9%

Neither Positive nor Negative — Rural 39.1%, Urban 42.1%

Somewhat Negative — Rural 11.3%, Urban 12.9%

Very Negative — Rural 24.8%, Urban 7.9%

Urban ■   Rural ▨

Source: University of Chicago General Social Survey, 2018

On the issue of marriage equality, most rural people are fairly supportive. When I asked each interviewee, *Do you think anyone has a right to marry anyone?*, almost everyone said yes. "Love is love" was mentioned more than once by my interview subjects. "I think if two people love each other, they should get married," commented one man from Wisconsin. "As long as they are going to be committed. People are going to do what they want to be happy. We don't really need rules on that, do we?"

Most rural people, regardless of education, did not have a lot to say about the topic of gay marriage compared to subjects such as race, but they did generally support it. These responses were no different from those of the educated urban people I interviewed, with the exception that rural respondents were less likely to be passionate about the topic. Their relative indifference aligns with research showing that people become decreasingly antigay as governments pass legislation supporting marriage equality.[27] Regardless of their own sexual orientation, many of the urban people I interviewed were enthusiastically pro–marriage equality and saw it as an important issue to champion. Among rural folks who were very religious, a few of them mentioned their ambivalence—that they found it hard to reconcile the Bible with the fact that they fundamentally didn't really mind what people did with their personal lives. As one very religious Republican woman from Reno explained, "I'm not that [type of] Christian...so hung up that it has to be between a man and a woman. I've seen some very happy gay couples, with kids." There were a number of religious people I spoke to who said they supported civil unions but not marriage with regard to the church and a union under God. A pastor I spoke with put it like this: "Same-sex marriage is a foreign object to me." He went on, "I believe there should be a mechanism on the secular side to solidify a marriage of some kind, a partnership, mainly because the government should make this necessary. So [gay couples] can get the same benefits....As a priest in a church I have trouble with it because of the sacrament of holy matrimony. I have no trouble with a gay couple; I have a problem with creating a marriage, so that's where I am."

The pastor captured the sentiment of most of the religious people who were not supportive of gay marriage but were supportive of civil unions: a belief that an option for a legal union is important but that marriage has a specific role within the church, and that it is between a man and a woman for procreation. For those who weren't unequivocally supportive of marriage equality, this position seemed to be a struggle. These were good people who weren't sure how to square their religious beliefs with modern society. Rarely did anyone express overt discrimination or homophobia. For those who interpret the Bible literally, there was a cognitive dissonance that they were trying to settle.

Only twice did I encounter people who were intolerant on the topic of marriage equality. A seventy-three-year-old woman from Wisconsin explained to me, "I come from a Christian worldview: from time immemorial, one man, one woman is marriage, and it's for the purpose for the protection and nurturing of children. I think homosexuality is sin and it is fighting God." She defined homosexuality as "I want what I want, and I want it right now." "I worry about gay people because I think they're doomed," she said. "I think they're going to be hurt, and I don't want them to be hurt, but I see it as a way to die early, to not live to your full potential." This was a very hard conversation, and the most extreme response I heard through the course of my many interviews. The only other person who adamantly disagreed with marriage equality did so in a very succinct way; there was no overt judgment, nor did they express any bigoted opinions. This woman, however, decried homosexuality in such a judgmental and misinformed way that it was very hard to keep talking to her after that. I was really angry. But this is where it gets tough. As a researcher, it was not my place to challenge her views. I was there to listen. How could she be honest with me if she felt my judgment? This is not a part of my experience as an interviewer that I have been able to resolve.

The GSS offers a different lens into opinions on marriage equality and reveals much more anti–marriage equality sentiment than my interviews suggest. I pondered as to whether this meant my interviewees had been wary of expressing their true sentiments, but I did not find the same mismatch problem with regard to race. In the GSS, while rural sentiment against gay marriage and sex was higher than urban opposition, the chart reveals that both groups are bifurcated, tending to answer with great support or great opposition rather than more neutral responses. Same-sex sexual relations are also more disapproved of than marriage by people in general, but more so by rural respondents, where over 40 percent of those surveyed believe that same-sex sexual relations are "always wrong" (a quarter of urban respondents gave the same answer). Almost 60 percent of rural respondents support gay marriage, yet over 40 percent of these same respondents say that homosexual sex is always wrong? This didn't add up to me.

While these numbers suggested intolerance among both rural and urban respondents, I saw something slightly different. I was going for a walk with my mother in the autumn of 2021, discussing these seemingly contradictory responses, and she said, "Well, I don't want to think about anyone, gay or straight, having sex, to be honest!" This made me wonder if it's more the directness of the question—asking about something most people avoid talking about—that garners such a contradictory response. People don't always tell the truth in surveys about sex, out of a desire to fit in or to not appear deviant. It takes a particular way of asking someone a question about sex for them to answer honestly.[28] Was it, I speculated, the explicitness of asking about gay sex that put people off, given that most people seem supportive of gay marriage?

When I thought of these seemingly contradictory responses, I thought of Craig Parker from Iowa. Craig didn't seem to mind what people did with their time, and he didn't feel he needed to have a strong opinion on others' intimate affairs. During our initial call,

64

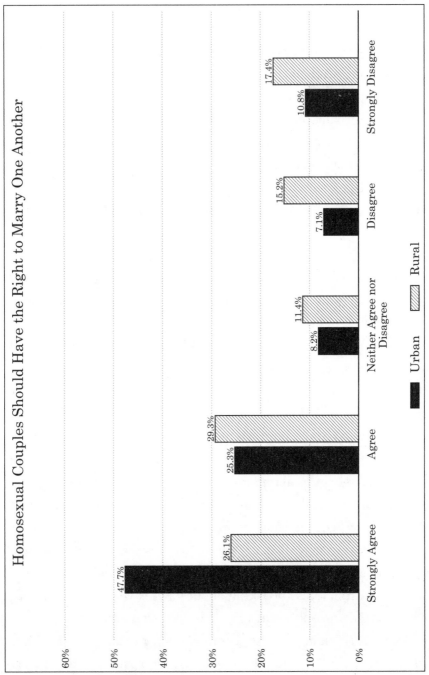

Homosexual Couples Should Have the Right to Marry One Another

Strongly Agree
Urban 47.7%
Rural 26.1%

Agree
Urban 25.3%
Rural 29.3%

Neither Agree nor Disagree
Urban 8.2%
Rural 11.4%

Disagree
Urban 7.1%
Rural 15.2%

Strongly Disagree
Urban 10.8%
Rural 17.4%

■ Urban ▨ Rural

Source: University of Chicago General Social Survey, 2018

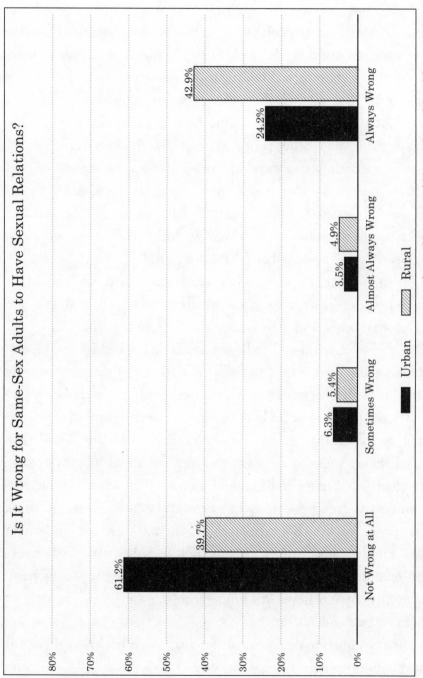

Is It Wrong for Same-Sex Adults to Have Sexual Relations?

Source: University of Chicago General Social Survey, 2018

he certainly never expressed racist or homophobic beliefs. When I called Craig a few months after our first conversation, I asked him again about his feelings on gay marriage to clarify his response. He was more open and explicit in his opinion this second time around. "I think everyone should be free to be who they are and who they want to be. But some of these things get so stigmatized. How do I say it?" Craig paused. "You should be free to be who you are, but don't stuff it down other people's throat. Be who you are.

"Some of these cases where somebody sues someone who doesn't want to make a wedding cake?" he rhetorically questioned. "Come on, guys! If someone doesn't want to make my wedding cake, then I don't want them to make my wedding cake. Forcing people to do things they don't want to do, that's not right."

What struck me about Craig's response and those from other interviewees was that, for the most part, these people didn't care about what others did. Just as importantly, however, they don't want to be told what to do—or to be condescended to by highly educated liberals telling them how to live. I don't know if Craig personally has a problem with homosexuality; he certainly never explicitly said so. It's possible that he and others, due to the strictures of their religion, feel cognitive dissonance around homosexuality. Their faith may instruct them to view gay marriage or sex as morally wrong, but their belief that people should do what they want without government intervention holds stronger sway. I may, for example, think adultery or smoking pot excessively is not good behavior, but I might also think the government has no right to police infidelity or recreational drug use. The two views are not inherently inconsistent, especially if one believes in a limited role of government, as many of my rural respondents do.

In the efforts to demarcate differences, we often lose sight of our quiet commonalities. I found this when I first spoke with Craig, who has lived in Jesup, Iowa, population 2,806, his entire life. At the time we spoke, he was sixty-nine years old. "My great-great-grandfather came to Iowa in 1857," Craig says to me with pride. "At the time, they were building a railroad from Chicago to Littleton. He sold his gold pocket watch and opened a business of a blacksmith. Then they found gold in Jesup, and so they redirected and moved his business from Littleton to Jesup." After our first conversation, Craig sends me a photo of his son, his grandchildren, and himself riding a green Oliver tractor with vast fields and a melancholy sky in the backdrop. "Three generations of Parker men at the tree farm," Craig writes. A tall man who looks years younger than his age, Craig has something that, for me, encapsulates the notion of a decent man. When we talk, his tone is even and level. He's an easy person to interview because he speaks slowly and deliberately, with rich detail. His remarks come across as deep and thoughtful, his values solid and clear in his mind.

Craig inherited his great-grandfather's farm and grows vegetables and trees on his land. He is mainly self-sufficient. "I go outside and play with my chain saws each day the weather is fit," Craig says. While chain saws don't come across as a natural hobby to me, I get what he means about doing something he loves just for its own sake. Craig is a very happy man. Part of his happiness is due to the fact that, as he puts it, "I can come and go as I please. I don't have to worry. We don't live a high standard here. I get up and do what I want to do. I go down and fish, work hard. I can eat what I want to eat."

Craig is the first to admit he's lived a very privileged life, but his definition of privilege isn't in terms of material wealth. Craig has "inherited" the chance to be treated equally, and he is very conscious of the fact that many people are not given such a chance. As he puts it, he has never been discriminated against because of the color of his skin and has always had the freedom to achieve. "We had a guest pastor and he talked about white privilege. I'd never thought about it that way—a pretty sheltered life. Everyone should have the opportunity to do things for themselves. Nobody should have to sleep in the streets or go home hungry." As Craig is a lifelong Republican, I am curious about his views on immigration and former president Trump's border wall. Craig surprises me: "Well, there should be a way for people to come to this country and follow their dreams and build up." When I push him on the wall, he pauses, then, "I would back up and say we need a program where people don't die in the desert."

In retrospect, I realize Craig's responses are consistent. He is conservative, deeply religious, and believes in working hard and making something of oneself. Within that belief is the assumption that everyone else should have that chance too. Even his view on gay marriage is complex. "I still struggle with it," Craig admits. "How do I say this... Yes, in a civil sense, but in a religious sense—how do I say it—still struggling with that." Then, without any judgment or moral overtones, he remarks, "My wife said the other night, 'It's like being born right-handed or left-handed.' When we were in Des Moines, we went to a church where many of the people were gay folks, and I think it's about who the community is that you're serving. There's room for all of us in our beliefs."

Craig believes in equality. He feels empathy for immigrants and wants a better and safer path for them to arrive in our country. Due to his religious beliefs, he may not understand gay marriage fully—and he's the first to admit it—but he is not against civil marriages or gay people. But to get to that understanding, I had to listen, truly listen, to his words. When I stripped away Craig's obvious discomfort, when I took away the liberal script used to discuss hot-button issues, when I listened closely and got to the very heart of what he was trying to express, I found that his sentiments were pure and good, and the distance between rural Iowa and urban Los Angeles was not so wide. Craig doesn't celebrate marriage equality the way I do (near the time of the Supreme Court ruling, my kids all wore T-shirts with the word "Love" written in rainbow). Craig can "struggle" and yet still support gay people and their rights. Craig can be wary of Democratic immigration views and still be deeply concerned for those trying to cross the border. Craig can be skeptical of certain social policies, even as he feels empathy for those with less. Craig can recognize the advantages he's had in life because of his whiteness, even if he doesn't use the term "white privilege" to frame his experiences. Craig doesn't have to think exactly like me or you or share the same language to connect with his more liberal countrymen.

A MONG MY INTERVIEWEES, rural people like Craig felt particularly strongly about people doing things for themselves and being left alone. There was a strong ethos of making one's own opportunities, and many of the people I interviewed had done that for themselves. They were not rich or wildly successful, but they were self-made.

Our small towns' culture of individualism may drive the divergence, depicted by the GSS, between rural and urban responses to the idea of race-based preferential treatment. Rural respondents expressed a philosophy of life that eschewed government help. These were people who didn't believe in handouts or special treatment for anyone and who believed in making something of themselves, an achievement that had nothing to do with accolades or a luxurious lifestyle. Being the first to attend college, holding down a job, owning a house, taking care of one's family, and having a good relationship with God were the hallmarks of success. So, when I looked at the results on how rural whites viewed social programs, it appeared that this broad philosophical stance drove their responses.

Going through the weeds of the GSS, it became increasingly clear that most rural folks expressed no deep-seated racist responses.[29] They were less likely than urban respondents to think Black people were poor or unintelligent and less likely to allow racists to speak.

However, there was a trend in the data that suggested that rural people were more likely to believe that racial differences were due to lack of will or hard work. Over 70 percent of rural respondents believe Black people should overcome prejudice "without favors," contrasted with just 52 percent of urban respondents agreeing with this statement. To be clear, the situation for Black people in America is far more complicated than such a simple question, and systemic racism has been and remains profoundly destructive.[30] The trend of individualism in the GSS responses, however, resonated with what I found in my interviews with rural America.

Irrespective of background and circumstances, rural Americans believe you make your own destiny. The people I spoke with talked about how it was important to live within your means, to save, and to work hard. "I was the first in my family to go to college. My dad worked in a printing press. He worked ungodly hours; he worked six days a week. My dad worked hard, my mom saved, they built a house outside of York," remarked Wayne, a man from Neenah, Wisconsin. "I helped pay with my paper route. I got a scholarship to go to Lehigh [University]. I went to graduate school; it was free. Kimberly-Clark sent me to the University of Chicago to get my MBA. [To this day] I work hard. I don't spend all I make." Wayne concluded, "I don't have a lot of sympathy for those who piss everything away and expect the government to take care of them."

I wondered about the context in which respondents formed these views of government and self-sufficiency. Was it anti-government, or was it that they did not see the benefits of social welfare policies in their own towns? Indeed, research on rural social welfare points to significantly constrained resources compared to metropolitan areas, resulting in less effective programs.[31] As the United States became an increasingly industrialized and professionalized economy, social welfare moved from the community to the state level, and consequently rural areas were left out.[32] I was curious whether the culture of individualism and self-reliance not only shaped rural people's responses to questions about government interventions but also was a result of their own experience with ineffective social policy.

Interestingly enough, in a 2018 Pew survey with urban, rural, and suburban dwellers, the majority of all respondents felt rural America got "less than their fair share" of federal dollars. Rural Americans did not perceive getting help from the government, or perhaps were unconvinced of the role government intervention could play in solving their problems. In fact, most people surveyed felt rural America did not get much aid from the government. Rural Americans also felt their values were different from others, more so than the other groups surveyed.

These two streams of responses overlap, as Katherine J. Cramer found in her book *The Politics of Resentment*, an analysis of Wisconsin's allegiance to Governor Scott Walker despite his policies being against many residents' self-interest. For rural Americans, the conflict has to do with both their values being in opposition to liberal elites and the feeling that they are not getting their fair share. They worry that liberal platforms run against who they are and what they believe in—in other words, their deep story. In my interviews, I wondered if what seemed like contradictions in who rural residents voted for and what was best for them actually indicated that they considered their culture and values—strong adherence to the Bible and the right to live one's life without government interference—as much more important than any individual policy or economic platform, even if the latter would benefit them.

IF I WERE to point to one dividing line between rural and urban America, it would be how each region approaches the topic of privilege. Rural Americans' resentment toward "handouts" is linked to the fact that they personally believe they didn't receive any. "The notion of white privilege," said an exasperated man from Missouri. "It's a little hard to talk to my [white] friends who grew up on a dirt floor about racism, for us to be called racists. My wife [had] no parents, [siblings] raised each other, went off to college. Then, the next generation did better," he explained of his wife, who ultimately became a judge. "Where in that chain do you say, 'My wife is a judge because she has white privilege'?"

There was also a sense that it was okay that not everyone had the same opportunities; the point was to do what you could with what you had. "I would say it was important that [my children] get an education," Craig remarked during one of our conversations. "Big fancy school—I am not into Harvard, Yale, Stanford, and all that. Get education to better themselves and be all they can be." These responses were emblematic of the larger sentiment among interviewees in rural America. They didn't feel it was everyone's right to have a chance at everything, that everyone was entitled to the best, but rather that you made do and did your best with what you were given. "Equity" and "equality" were not terms used with regard to their own life, even those who experienced a tough and impoverished upbringing.

The responses from those I interviewed in urban America rang closer to home and reminded me of Rachel Sherman's book *Uneasy Street: The Anxieties of Affluence*.[33] Sherman, a sociology professor at the New School, interviewed fifty wealthy parents in New York City about everything from their nannies to their child-rearing styles to the brand of bread they buy (the cost of which they hide from their nannies). What Sherman found was that rich people need to morally justify the elite space in which they exist. They make extravagant consumption choices that are ostensibly normal or practical—similar to David Brooks's "bobos," or bohemian bourgeois, who are uncomfortable that their bohemian sensibilities run against their six-figure salaries. Because they are so aware of their privilege, the rich attempt to justify their purchases, whether $10 loaves of bread or performative constraint around what they buy for their children.[34] They want to believe they live, as Sherman puts it, "a very expensive ordinary life."[35]

Like Sherman's interviewees, my urban respondents were self-conscious of their privilege. They wrestled with guilt about their class position, a feeling that was completely absent in those I interviewed in rural America. The sense that these urban respondents had so much—too much, more than they deserved—echoed in the interviews I did with those in Los Angeles, New York, and San Francisco. "For me personally, America is great for me," observed a well-to-do woman who worked in development for a major art museum. "Because I have extraordinary class privilege, I haven't struggled a day in my life. I think America sucks for people who are not like me. When I look at America today, it is inhumane." A media executive remarked that she found the homeless encampments that she drove by unbearable. A few beats later, she said, "I think I am privileged, so I should be happy. But I'm never happy. I'm always working to find out what is next." When I asked a woman from San Francisco about whether she was happy, she responded, "Part of this is being privileged and having the time to read the news and stay informed. There's a bit of, 'Am I doing everything I can, given my privilege and knowledge?' For some people, I think that may be where some of the hesitation [to say I'm happy] comes in," she explained. "And I don't have a God to turn to."

In my interviews with both rural and urban respondents, I found that getting closer to them—"leaning in to the vulnerability," to use Brené Brown's term—allowed me to see that the very attributes that might be a source of division were actually a point of connection. Coastal elites may be privileged. However, they are all too aware of it, and their privilege does not guarantee them happiness. They are incredibly self-conscious and guilt-ridden and show deep humanity when discussing the opportunities given to them. They constantly question themselves, what they are doing with their lives, and what they can do to give back. The rural Americans to whom I spoke might seem ignorant to notions of racial equity and social justice, but they are not coming from a place of racism or hatred. Rather, their resistance to particular social policies is deeply rooted in their belief that people need to achieve things on their own, without the aid of the government.[36] These rural Americans come from a complicated place of depending on only themselves, and many of them hail from disadvantaged backgrounds. What seem like vast differences in opinion or values may actually be differences in levels of privilege and differences in how we grew up. My sense is that if we can appreciate where each of us comes from, we might gain a greater understanding of how we can meet halfway.

This is where the nuance is so important. People are not either-or. They are layers of emotions, characteristics, and often contradictory belief systems. There is nothing wrong with that; it is part of being human. Rural Americans can be both "not racist" and totally oblivious to having a leg up because of the color of their skin. Religious Americans can be both "not homophobic" and antiquated in their views of marriage. Urban, educated Americans can be elite and condescending but also deeply self-aware of their privilege and active in their desire to correct the imbalance.

In the aforementioned 2018 Pew survey, the researchers found that most people, irrespective of where they live, felt that those who did not live in the same locale did not share their values. Almost 60 percent of rural respondents felt that those living in cities didn't share their values, and just over half of urban respondents felt rural folks didn't share theirs. These results are different from my own interviews, where I encountered rural Americans who did not feel disconnected from urban Americans. However, they did often feel pulled into a woke, progressive battlefield, even though they never possessed the views of which they were being accused. The truth is that both the GSS and the rural Americans I spoke to reveal a population who, for the most part, is open and tolerant of all walks of life and does not possess the anger that is so stereotypically associated with them. They share values that I have come to see as strongly associated with many Americans: family, holidays, democracy, and a sense of faith and wonder, whether in the universe, science, or God.

Interviewing Americans about their lives has been an extraordinary thing. I will not use the usual boilerplate words of privilege, honor, blessing, and so forth. Let me just tell you that to sit on the phone for an hour or so with each of these people—Americans I've never met in person, many of whom I'll never get to go for a walk or share a coffee with—was one of the most heartening experiences of my life. What they told me was not all good. Some of it was terrible and heartbreaking. Jane, a rural Pennsylvania grandmother, lost her granddaughter to cystic fibrosis. Because the mother was unable to take care of the child, Jane nursed and cared for her granddaughter until she died in 2018. I admired Jane's strength and ability to persevere. She had grown up as one of six children. "We were poor," she says and then laughs. "We had no idea." She worked her way up from cashier at the local hospital to a vice president, taking night classes along the way. When her granddaughter got too sick, she took a step back from work to care for her. As she tells me the story, I cannot help myself. I start crying. Jane says softly, "That's okay. That's my response too." There was another beautiful woman, Elizabeth, who lived in Kentucky, whose girlfriend was dying of stage four metastatic cancer. I asked, so naively, so stupidly, "Is she going to be okay?" Elizabeth responded, "No. People with her type of cancer have a 0 to 8 percent chance of survival after five years." This woman had already lost her sister to pneumonia ("She had borderline [personality disorder], so hard to be around, but I still loved her"), her father to suicide, and her boyfriend to suicide. When we spoke, I was almost breathless. I couldn't understand how this woman faced each day. And yet she did.

At the time of these interviews, I was grieving my own personal tragedy related to the health of someone whom I deeply love. It was not easy in the midst of a pandemic, homeschooling, worry for my older parents, and fear of illness to also try to make sense of my private catastrophe. But my new friends helped. For I saw their strength in heartbreak, and I valued their ability to somehow find joy and happiness nevertheless. To know there were people out there grappling with loss and stress and finding a way through gave me comfort. I will always be grateful to them, although it is impossible to share my appreciation explicitly with them on this matter.

At this point, it seems a strange time to show you a chart. Rather than see it as another bar chart, please see it as a visualization of hope. Most people are happy. They are happy with their lives, their jobs, their marriages. This is true regardless of whether they are rural or urban, rich or poor. Working-class folks feel as happy and as satisfied as the middle class and the upper class.

I found the soul of Americans through their storytelling, and I can tell you that happiness comes to people *despite* the fact that life gives them what appear to be unsurmountable challenges: A child dying. A scary diagnosis. Suicide. Drug addiction. Poverty. And yet. And yet. According to the GSS, over 80 percent of people would call themselves pretty or very happy. In my own conversations with them, Americans had many reasons for why they felt happy and found a deep sense of meaning in their lives. Some pointed toward the role of religion. Indeed, many people discussed their happiness with regard to their relationship to God and their faith. Many also mentioned their family and friends. As Jane said, "I can honestly say I'm happy because I live comfortably. I have people who love me, people who I love. I have good friends. I have the ability to do what I like. I get to read. I get to walk. I have a partner, someone who cares about me very much. I have grandkids. I am very happy." Even Elizabeth, whose life seems so incredibly, unbearably sad and difficult, said, "With my girlfriend's cancer, it is very stressful. I am not happy, but I am hopeful."

When I say that I feel I have a good sense of Americans—rich or poor, from Kentucky or California—I really mean it. The consistency of their manner, their responses, and their engagement with

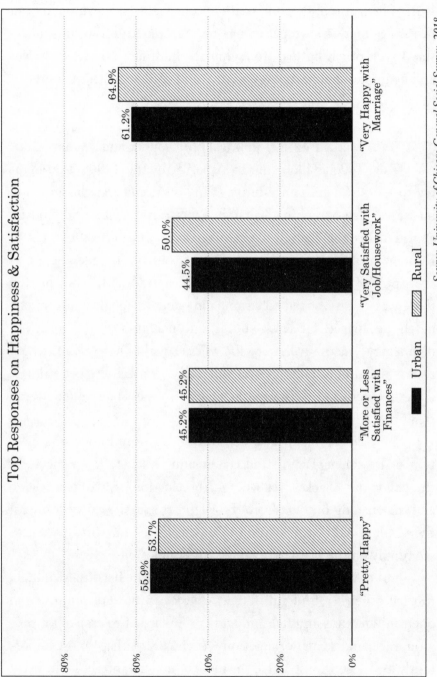

Top Responses on Happiness & Satisfaction

"Pretty Happy"
55.9%
53.7%

"More or Less Satisfied with Finances"
45.2%
45.2%

"Very Satisfied with Job/Housework"
44.5%
50.0%

"Very Happy with Marriage"
61.2%
64.9%

Urban
Rural

Source: University of Chicago General Social Survey, 2018

me showed me an America that we have lost sight of. The good stuff. The fact that most of us are reasonable, well-meaning, decent people. Sometimes we get things wrong, sometimes we misunderstand each other, but we are trying all the time to better ourselves and be intentional in the way we live and connect with each other.

WHEN THE FRENCH political philosopher and scholar Alexis de Tocqueville came to America in the 1800s, the country was a bustle and hurly-burly of industry, cultural changes, and increased demographic diversity. American society and politics appeared, as the Cambridge University political scientist David Runciman observed, completely out of control. Tocqueville, however, persisted. He saw more of America, and as he did, he saw there was civility, social cohesion, and belief in equality just underneath the surface. He saw, to put it in Runciman's words, "a faith in democracy... actually living a life where equality was real." Democracy was almost a religion. And still today, there is the "central paradox of American life": a superficial explosiveness but an underlying steadiness.[37]

The past six years have certainly been tumultuous: the election of President Trump and the ensuing outrage from the Left, the pandemic, Black Lives Matter, the election of President Biden and the ensuing outrage from the Right, the January 6 storming of the Capitol. All of this, yes all of it, speaks to volatility, a country seemingly on the brink of madness and implosion.

But I don't think so. If we stay away from the headlines and talk to each other, we find a different America: a place of promise and open-mindedness and live and let live. A place of tolerance for religion, race, and sexual orientation—even, and perhaps most importantly, by those who struggle the most to understand those different from themselves. "Whether they saw Jan. 6 as 'just another day' or like 'the Civil War,' there was one abiding through line of unity between the groups," writes a *New York Times* editor of the paper's late 2021 focus groups with Republicans and Democrats. "[They shared] care and concern about the future of America."[38]

Tocqueville's America still exists. The things he worried about are also still present: we are volatile, and there is a darkness always on the fringes threatening our great experiment. But we are not passively awaiting our fate, and we still believe in a place where equality is prized, even if we haven't gotten there yet. Tocqueville's initial understanding of America rings true today. We are chaotic superficially but cohesive underneath, and we must not lose sight of that connectivity. The fabric underpinning America is still there, and it will save us.

2

YOU'D BE SURPRISED HOW WELL
WE ARE DOING

*Cities and country have a common history, so their stories
are best told together.*
—William Cronon, *Nature's Metropolis*[1]

THERE ARE 60 MILLION PEOPLE, ALMOST ONE IN FIVE AMERI-cans, living in hamlets, on farms, and in small towns across the landscape," writes Eduardo Porter in a 2018 *New York Times* essay. "For the last quarter century, the story of these places has been one of relentless decline." In "The Hard Truths of Trying to 'Save' the Rural Economy," Porter goes on to point out that the people in small towns are older, there are fewer of them, and they make less money than people living in big cities. He cites even more dire statistics on the future of employment in rural America: most of the region is witnessing declines in manufacturing, while urban America is seeing an increase in technology jobs. "Factory jobs can no longer keep small-town America afloat," writes Porter. "Robots and workers in China put together most of the manufactured goods that Americans buy, and the high-tech industries powering the economy today don't have much need for the cheap labor that rural communities contributed to

America's industrial past. They mostly need highly educated workers. They find those most easily in big cities, not in small towns." He proceeds to cite a small town in Lake County, Tennessee, which lost 250 of its 500 manufacturing jobs between the years 2013 and 2017.

Porter's despair is echoed by many economists and geographers. There is a dominant and, I believe, corrosive narrative that America is deeply divided, both economically and geographically, between affluent cities and impoverished rural communities. Not so dissimilar from the tale of the country mouse and the city mouse, the story goes that (primarily white) poor and working-class people live in rural America, intimidated and forgotten by wealthy elites who reside in the nation's cities. In high-profile books, many scholars and journalists—such as Joan C. Williams in *White Working Class*, Sarah Smarsh in *Heartland*, Nicholas Kristof and Sheryl WuDunn in *Tightrope*, and Amy Goldstein in *Janesville*—have written about small-town America being economically abandoned. Economists Katharine Abraham and Melissa Kearney argue that globalization and technology, which favor cities, explain the problem.

I've known this well-trodden story since my days in graduate school. Many within and outside of academia have explained America's present economic geography through the rise of the knowledge economy in urban America and the vast decline of industry in rural America over the latter half of the twentieth century. My graduate school adviser, Richard Florida, who wrote the groundbreaking 2002 book *The Rise of the Creative Class*, has argued that creativity and innovation drive the world economy and that the people who possess these qualities, whom he calls the "creative class," are drawn to particular cities, catalyzing a talent drain everywhere else. As Jane Jacobs, Saskia Sassen, and, later, Harvard economist Edward Glaeser have documented, much of the West experienced deindustrialization, but only cities—and only some cities at that—were able to find a new road to prosperity through highly educated people, finance, professional services, and the tech industry.

I did not think this story was disputable until I looked closely at the data. While it is not wrong, it is not wholly right either. Glaeser is correct that cities like New York City did rebound from manufacturing's decline better than places like Cleveland and Buffalo, and, as Florida rightly argues, talented people drive the economy, not widget making. But if we look closely at the data for rural and small-town America—at places not associated with the creative class or the knowledge economy—they are doing far better than our dominant story line suggests, and not entirely through different means. What the data shows is that the region where you live—for example, the South, Midwest, Northeast, or Coastal West—is what determines your fortunes, not whether you live in the city versus a small rural town. Poor people live in rural America, but they are also struggling to get by in Los Angeles, New York, and Chicago. Rich people reside in San Francisco penthouses, but they also own expensive ranches and cabins in the Midwest. There are struggling white people in rural America, and there are struggling Black people in urban America, and vice versa.

When we lump huge parts of rural America together and compare it to an aggregate urban America, we hide what is really going on. I studied decades of data on rural and urban America, and I have found that rural America's fortunes have improved. On the whole, most people living outside of cities own their own homes, are employed, and make comparable money, among other positive outcomes. In addition, rural towns are far less unequal than our cities, and their poverty rate is not significantly worse. Parts of rural America are struggling, but that is true of urban America as well. However, by most economic metrics, rural Americans are doing surprisingly well.

L ET'S RETURN TO 2016. When Trump won the presidency, the media was shocked by his meteoric rise to power and frantically searched for an explanation. Because of his special connection with rural Americans, who made up an important part of his base, journalists began to paint a portrait of an irate and disillusioned America, where impoverished, resentful small towns were jealous of and at war with affluent, progressive, coastal cities. As the story goes, rural Americans, feeling economically behind and socially excluded, voted for Trump in protest. The underlying argument is that a populist movement sought to blow up an elite political process that had long since abandoned and ignored them. I knew something wasn't right. Sure, there were (and are) rural voters who are angry with a progressive coastal elite. But equally, there were plenty of conservative wealthy elites who cast their vote for Trump, and there were plenty of people in the heartland who voted for Trump not out of anger but because they preferred him to Hillary Clinton. I knew this because I grew up with these people. I spent almost two years talking to them, and they weren't angry and desirous of dismantling the status quo. Many people who voted for President Trump in 2016 were Republicans and thus voted Republican.

I wasn't the only one skeptical of the overarching Trump narrative. In their academic article "The White Working Class and the 2016 Election," the political scientists Nicholas Carnes and Noam Lupu challenge the notion that Trump "uniquely appealed to the white working class," many members of which reside in rural and small-town America. What they find is that this same bloc of voters had been voting for the Republican candidate for decades. Mitt Romney, both Bushes, and Ronald Reagan were all beneficiaries of the same demographic. The white working class's changing allegiance from Democrat to Republican has been a long, slow, generational shift, not a wild reckoning in the wake of Trump's cult of personality. Not to mention, Carnes and Lupu show that 40 percent of the white working class voted for Hillary Clinton in 2016.[2] From this analysis, the majority of these voters were always going to vote Republican. So why, then, did the narrative of the angry, rural, working-class Trump voter persist?

Perplexed by this misunderstanding, I started looking more closely at urban and rural socioeconomics and its interplay with election outcomes. My doctoral student Andy Eisenlohr and I pored over rows and rows of the most granular data from 2012 and 2016 (presidential election years) and 2018 (midterm elections). We studied government socioeconomic and demographic data for every Census-designated place in America: thousands of communities, from major cities like San Francisco to rural towns like Danville, Pennsylvania. We divided these places into cities (population greater than one hundred thousand), small towns significantly outside of cities (five thousand to fifteen thousand inhabitants), and rural America (under five thousand inhabitants). We tracked homeownership, unemployment, white unemployment, mortgage payment, and household income, along with demographic measures such as education and ethnic diversity. What we discovered defied conventional stereotypes. By most measures other than education, median households in small-town America tend to be doing at least as well as their counterparts in urban America.

The myth of the poor, rural Trump voter also didn't stack up with the data. Congressional districts that voted Republican in both 2016 and 2018 tended to have higher median incomes than those that went Democratic in both years. Of the forty-five states Andy and I studied in detail, twenty-eight have a lower share of significant poverty (defined as family income of under $10,000 a year) in small towns than in urban centers. Fifteen of these states have a higher median household income in small towns than in cities. That share would undoubtedly be higher if adjusted for cost of living, which is lower in small towns. Forty of the forty-five states we analyzed had lower unemployment rates in small towns than in cities.

These results hold true for rural America, the places with the fewest residents. Take the Mid-Atlantic, where 90 percent of all communities with fewer than five thousand people voted Republican for president in 2016. The median homeownership rate for these places is around 73 percent, compared with 32 percent in New York City and 52 percent in Philadelphia. Fifty-eight percent of rural communities have a higher median household income than that of the largest city within their state. Between 2012 and 2016, these rural places had a median unemployment rate of 6 percent, which is lower than in New York City (9 percent), Philadelphia (13 percent), and Washington, DC (9 percent). Midwestern rural communities, 96 percent of which voted Republican in 2016, show similar trends, with a median unemployment rate of 5 percent, both overall and for the non-Hispanic white population. Forty-two percent of these rural places have higher median household incomes than cities such as Saint Louis, Chicago, and Milwaukee. In New England, these results are even starker. Sixty percent of rural communities have a higher median household income than the nearby cities. Rural New England has a 66 percent homeownership rate, in contrast with Boston (34.7 percent); Providence, Rhode Island (34 percent); and Manchester, New Hampshire (47 percent). Homeownership, which is strongly associated with intergenerational mobility, is almost always lower in cities.

At least in the current moment, the reality of rural and small-town America doesn't fit the preconceived notion that it is poor, without jobs, and angry as a result. The racial demographics of the nation, too, are more complicated than the media's narrative would suggest. On measures of diversity, the least diverse places are the Midwest, the Interior Northwest, and New England, where the majority of residents are non-Hispanic white. New England's urban population is 75 percent white. The urban Coastal West—unsurprisingly, due to the dramatic increase in the Latino population from 1990 to the early 2000s—is the most diverse region of the country, with minorities comprising almost half of its population. The South is the most diverse rural region in the country and second-most diverse urban region (with the typical county's white population share at 64 percent and 61 percent, respectively). These statistics reveal a surprising degree of diversity in the South, despite its reputation for being more culturally and racially intolerant. New England, a progressive stronghold, is extremely racially homogenous. Both of these empirical findings differ from the mainstream narrative. I wondered how the ethnic and racial realities of these different geographies have shaped their residents' views, and if perhaps we have been ignoring the experiences of those who live there.

As I continued to develop the ideas for this book, I realized I needed more than a snapshot of sample counties' current statistics. Perhaps today's economic divides were actually connected to historical socioeconomic differences. I needed to look at all of the United States, across regions, over the course of a few decades. With Andy (who at this point had finished his PhD and was living in Washington, DC) and my doctoral student Marley Randazzo, I set out to understand the complexities of urban and rural America over the last thirty years. During this time period, manufacturing expanded, contracted, and expanded again; college degrees became more prized; and cities witnessed a resurgence. When I expanded my analysis across many decades and to a broader section of the United States, many of the numbers actually improved for rural America.

By the time we started this analysis, another presidential election cycle had occurred. While Joe Biden had won squarely, the results indicated deep strongholds of support for former president Donald Trump. Revisiting the analysis that Andy and I did for the 2016 and 2018 election cycles, we expanded to look at the entire United States in 2020, studying the profile of urban and rural regions where there were greater shares of Republican or Democratic voters to see if there were salient qualities that set them apart from one another. In particular, I wanted to see if there was any merit in the ongoing narrative of the poor, angry Trump voter. Our previous work had suggested that the story is more complicated, but the political world now seemed more divided than even a few years ago.

When Andy and I looked at the parts of the country that were more Democratic or more Republican, we found again that the dominant narrative didn't fully add up. Case in point: in 2020, of all the regions in the United States, the Interior Northwest—Idaho, Montana, and Wyoming—demonstrated the greatest support for Donald Trump, with over 60 percent of urban and almost 75 percent of rural votes going to him. By our common perceptions of the rural Trump voter, these should be places with unemployed and downwardly mobile or poor voters, people resentful of cultural elites, and die-hard supporters of Donald Trump.[3]

These folks are Trump supporters, but not for the reasons we might think. If you look at the socioeconomic data for this region, it has the lowest unemployment rate (median levels of 4 percent and 3.7 percent for urban and rural counties, respectively) and one of the highest rural median incomes. The typical county's homeownership rate is at almost 75 percent. The Interior Northwest is second only to New England for share of the rural population with a bachelor's degree; over 20 percent of those in the typical rural Interior Northwest county have a bachelor's, which results in almost a quarter more educated residents than the median for all of the rural United States.

Of course, by political measures, the Interior Northwest and New England (Connecticut, Maine, Massachusetts, New Hampshire, Rhode Island, and Vermont) could not be more different. While the Interior Northwest is a Republican stronghold, much of New England is Democratic (although its rural areas are slightly more Republican than its cities). More to the point, of all regions in the United States, urban New England showed the greatest support for President Biden in the 2020 election. And yet, the unemployment rate for the typical urban county in New England is 4.8 percent, higher than that of the typical urban county in the Interior Northwest. New England also happens to be the most unequal region,

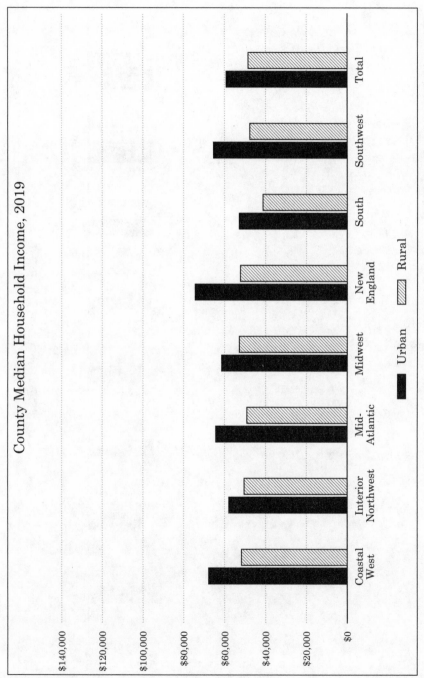

County Median Household Income, 2019

Urban ■   Rural ▨

Source: American Community Survey, 2019

90

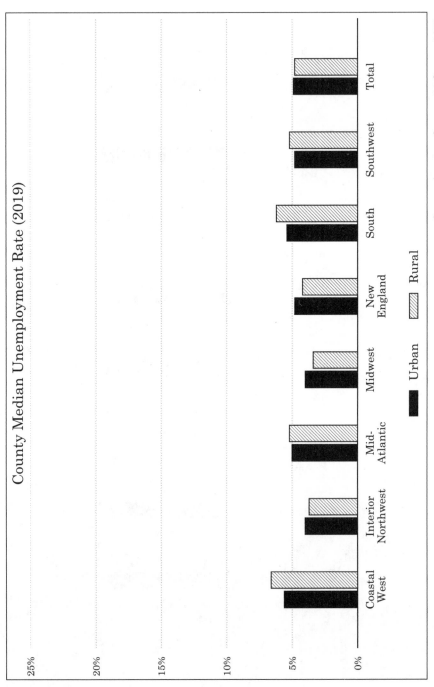

County Median Unemployment Rate (2019)

Urban ■   Rural ▨

Source: *American Community Survey, 2019*

with the greatest share of incomes at the tails (less than $10,000 or greater than $150,000) and the greatest share of households making over $150,000, at over 20 percent. In the Midwest, Trump received almost three-quarters of the rural vote, yet this region possesses the highest rural median income, lowest unemployment, and almost 80 percent homeownership. When we look at inequality more broadly, it does not seem to have the relationship to political affiliation that has been conventionally thought. Take the typical urban and rural counties in New England, the South, and the Coastal West. All of these regions have broadly similar shares of households at the lower end of the income range and yet express vastly different voting patterns.

What stands out to me in looking at this data is that Trump voters are in regions with high homeownership and low unemployment, while urban New England and the urban Coastal West, which lean Democratic, are associated with extreme wealth and income inequality. In short, we would be hard-pressed to come up with an accurate explanation for why rural voters vote the way they do based solely on economics. In fact, while Democratic strongholds align with our view of educated, well-to-do, urban coastal elites, our perception of rural Republicans is inaccurate. While rural folks do vote for Republicans many times over Democratic candidates, it is not because they are economically distressed, jobless, or particularly vulnerable to feeling left behind. Overall, the data suggests the opposite. Many of these people own homes, are gainfully employed, and make decent money. In fact, the median income for the typical rural Interior Northwest county is higher than the national rural median and just $8,700 less than the median for the urban United States. (Keep in mind that the lower cost of living in rural areas essentially erases this difference.)

Were Trump's supporters all angry and economically disenfranchised? Looking at the states most supportive of Trump, the answer is clearly no. Many Democrats, academics, and those in the liberal

Share of Households Earning Less Than $10k (2019)
Rural–Urban Gap

Coastal West	0.7%
Interior Northwest	1.1%
Mid-Atlantic	1.2%
Midwest	1.3%
New England	1.5%
South	1.8%
Southwest	2.1%
Total	2.4%

Source: American Community Survey, 2019

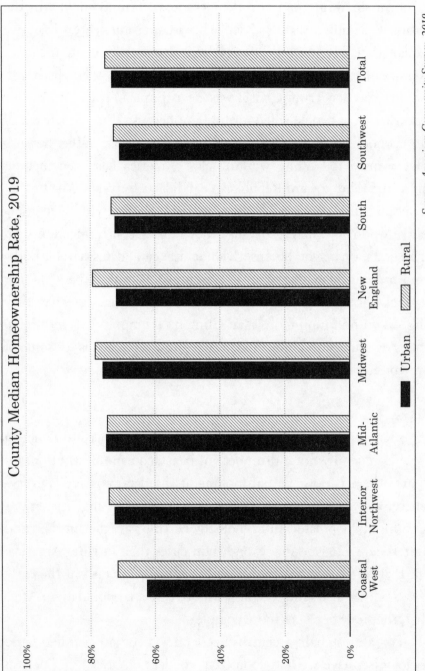

County Median Homeownership Rate, 2019

Urban Rural

Source: American Community Survey, 2019

media found it unfathomable that someone who was—in their view—as norm-shattering and anti-democratic as Trump could win the national election in 2016, particularly without some acute, disruptive explanation. The headline of rural Americans sticking it to the elites is more intriguing than their ambient inclination toward the Right. I didn't vote for Trump, but it was clear to me after looking at this data that most people voted for him not because they felt left out of the economic system or desired a deep reckoning, but rather because they wanted to. White working-class America has been inching more and more toward Republican candidates for years. Maybe that is because rural Americans' values are more aligned with the conservative worldview, maybe because they don't feel a connection with the coasts, or maybe because Democratic candidates haven't bothered to connect with them. These rural folks may have felt—not strongly or angrily but rather quite matter-of-factly—that they aligned with Trump more than Clinton. Trump understood them, and they understood him. And, as uncomfortable as it is for some of our country to accept, maybe that's that.

ONE THING IS clear from my research: life in rural America is generally not a drumbeat of heartache and destitution. Of course there is poverty, but looking at the data, poverty is everywhere, as is wealth. Some things were not surprising: In regions with highly populated cities, homeownership is higher in the rural hinterlands. House value is higher in cities than in rural America, but that difference was muted with the housing crash in the early 2000s. Cities also tend to house a more educated population. After that, the story becomes more complex.

For almost half a century, economists, urban planners, and sociologists have written about the wonders of cities. As a person with a doctorate in urban planning, I am one of those who sees cities as magical, important places for creativity, innovation, and diversity. As early as the 1920s, urban scholars in the Chicago School of sociology argued that cities offer a diversity of experience and existence in a way that small towns are unable to. After the publication of Jane Jacobs's 1961 book *The Death and Life of Great American Cities* and her 1969 book *The Economy of Cities*, we understood that a concentration of people and diverse businesses, industry, and amenities enables resilient economic growth and development. Jacobs points to the importance of mixed-aged buildings—to allow a variety of businesses and people who can afford different rents and require different uses from buildings—and short blocks that create opportunities for the unexpected run-ins of city life that produce new ideas. Fundamentally, Jacobs's view of urban development revolves around the ability of diverse people and businesses to interact and innovate fluidly, spurring economic growth known as "Jacobs externalities" (the Nobel Prize winner Robert Lucas Jr. thought Jacobs should win a Nobel Prize herself).

Fast-forward almost half a century, and social scientists call this concentration of people "human capital," and it is thought to be the key to economic growth everywhere. Edward Glaeser has found that cities with skilled human capital grow faster than those without.[4] In the 1990s, Saskia Sassen came up with the term "the global city." Her argument is that cities were transforming into important sites of intellectual production and centers of "command and control," where the professional-managerial class reigned. The people mattered because the industries that mattered required skilled workers.[5] Richard Florida has argued that cities draw creative people who seek out open and tolerant environments. In short, cities have increasingly become the centers of the educated, and that gap is growing wider.

The numbers reflect this transformation. While in 1990 there was a 3.8 percentage-point difference in the typical urban and rural

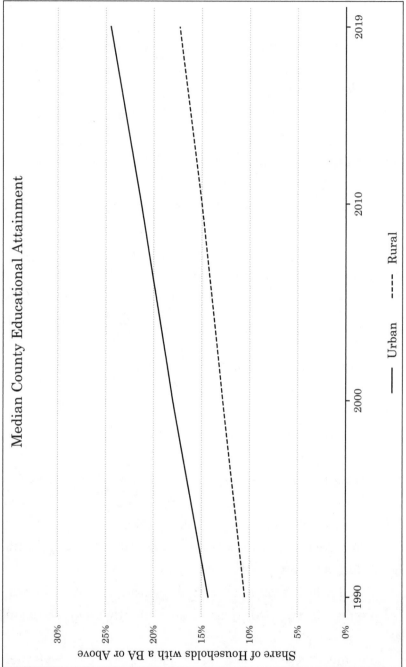

Median County Educational Attainment

Share of Households with a BA or Above

—— Urban   ---- Rural

Source: American Community Survey, 1990, 2000, 2010, 2019

areas' educated classes, by 2019 that number jumped to 7.2. In 2019, 24.5 percent of the typical urban county's dwellers had a bachelor's degree or above, while just 17.3 percent of the typical rural county's did. Keep in mind that this is the median number for all urban areas, not the average. Unless otherwise noted, all statistics reflect median numbers. Places like San Francisco and Boston have much higher numbers of college graduates, and some cities in the South have much lower.

If we look at the rate of change across years, we see that the difference in educational attainment between urban and rural populations has generally widened. In other words, from 1990 to 2010, the number of college-educated urbanites grew much faster than the number of their rural counterparts. By 2019, the rate of change was ever so slightly greater for rural folks, but the earlier faster education growth rate for the urban population meant that the gap between urban and rural had grown by almost four percentage points between 1990 and 2019. In 1990, the urban population had 36 percent more college graduates than small-town America. By 2000, this number had increased to 41 percent. To be more specific, using 2018 data, almost half of Austin, Texas, residents have a bachelor's degree, versus just 12 percent of all southern rural dwellers. The same contrast exists for Minneapolis and Boston compared with the rural Midwest and New England. While the general trend of an urban-rural education divide holds true, it's worth noting that the United States exhibits gaps in education across its cities too. For example, while 60 percent of people living in Seattle have a college degree, only 12 percent of people in Santa Ana, California, do.

Education patterns are geographically and regionally diverging as well. While rural populations are, in general, less likely to be educated, parts of the country are increasingly isolated from the growing rates of college degrees. For example, in 2019 in New England, 38 percent of urban residents and 30 percent of rural residents possessed a bachelor's degree. New England has always been home to the most educated population in America. This tradition stems back to the Enlightenment and New England's role as the center of American intellectual life. One of the biggest gaps between urban and rural education is in the Coastal West, where almost 30 percent of urban inhabitants have a bachelor's degree compared to 19.8 percent of the rural population. From 2010 to 2019, the gap grew by almost 80 percent, likely due to the expanding technology and gaming industries in Silicon Valley, San Francisco, and Los Angeles. In the South, on the other hand, the gap in education between urban and rural areas is not as extreme, because both have depressed education levels. In the South, only 14 percent of the typical rural county's population and 21 percent of the typical urban county's population have college degrees. To put that into perspective, approximately 35 percent of all Americans have a bachelor's degree. The southern share of the population with a college degree is less than that of New England's some thirty years ago.

When I first saw these numbers, I was deeply worried for the potential implications for our country. In a world where a college degree is seemingly the bare minimum for upward mobility, the depressed levels of education among rural Americans is cause for concern. I began to look more closely at income levels, assuming that the lack of education will be reflected in how much people make and levels of inequality. But I didn't see that at all. In fact, I noticed something quite strange. Median income levels in rural America are almost the same as urban America. And despite urban Americans becoming more educated from 1990 to 2019, the gap between urban and rural median income has been closing over the same time period.

In 2019, the difference in median income levels between urban and rural populations was just $10,642 per year (this figure is in 2020 dollars). While certain regions show bigger disparities—New England's urban population makes $22,000 more than those living in its rural towns—the cost of living in cities has become more and more expensive. Even $22,000 is not a lot compared to the expense of living in Cambridge versus Gosnold, Massachusetts. Controlling for cost of living, that $10,642 advantage dwindles down to nothing, and one might even say that the relative median income for rural America is actually more than for urban areas with regard to purchasing power. From that perspective, economically, the median rural American is doing better than in previous years, and median income is more or less the same as that in a city.

This data does not take into account the tails—that is, the extremely poor and the extremely rich. The highest income groups especially saw their earnings take off stratospherically over this time period. But these numbers also challenge our assumption that the highest earners are in cities and the lowest earners live in rural America. In 1990, a similar share of urban and rural households made $150,000 or more, just around 1 percent. By 2019, the number had increased significantly for all households, but much more for those in cities. While in 1990, the difference in the urban and rural share of households earning $150,000 was less than half a percentage point, by 2019, that number increased to four points, with more wealthy households in urban areas, a trend clearly in line with the mega wealth created by the finance and technology firms that predominantly reside in our global cities.[6]

At the same time, rural America decreased the number of households in poverty, bringing this number down to almost the same share as in urban areas. In 1990, almost a quarter of median rural households earned less than $10,000 a year. By 2019, that number had diminished to 6.8 percent. At the same time, the urban share of households making less than $10,000 a year dropped too—from 16.3 percent to 5.6 percent—but the rate of decline wasn't as fast as in rural America. By 2019, despite the increased cost of living in urban areas, the overall share of households making less than $10,000 was virtually the same in both urban and rural America.

100

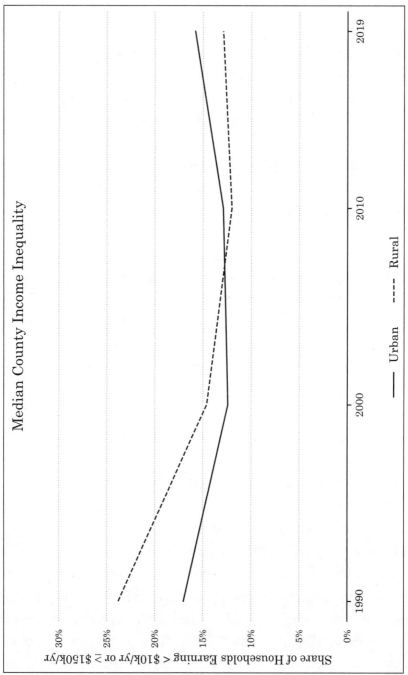

Median County Income Inequality

Share of Households Earning < $10k/yr or ≥ $150k/yr

30% 25% 20% 15% 10% 5% 0%

1990   2000   2010   2019

—— Urban   - - - Rural

Source: American Community Survey, 1990, 2000, 2010, 2019

When we look at inequality—the number of those making less than $10,000 and more than $150,000—we find a greater proportion of people at the extremes in cities. While for some this may seem obvious, this urban inequality was not always the case. In 1990, rural America was a more unequal place: 23.8 percent of rural Americans fell into one of the extremes, almost predominantly driven by poverty. By 2019, 15.8 percent of urban America fell into one of the income tails, while 12.9 percent of rural America followed this pattern, a decline of almost half over the course of thirty years.[7]

Take the cases of Pittsburgh and Philadelphia. Both of these cities have a much higher educated population than rural Pennsylvania and West Virginia (just over the border from Pittsburgh), but the economics do not align. There is a higher share of those making less than $10,000 in Philadelphia (13 percent) and Pittsburgh (7 percent) than in rural Pennsylvania (6 percent). Unemployment numbers reinforce this trend: Philadelphia has a higher unemployment rate than the hinterlands. There are more wealthy people in the cities but, controlling for cost of living, the gap is not as great as one might expect. In Philadelphia, for example, 9 percent of the population makes more than $150,000, compared to 6 percent in rural Pennsylvania. If we focus on small towns, with slightly bigger populations than rural areas, the gap between the number of wealthy people grows smaller. While 3 percent of Philadelphia residents make over $200,000, so do 2.1 percent of those living in small-town Pennsylvania. A greater share of small-town Pennsylvanians make $100,000 to $150,000 than do Philadelphians, and the proportions making $150,000 to $200,000 are similar (2.9 percent in small towns versus 3.4 percent in the city). The same trend holds in Pittsburgh compared with the small towns of West Virginia. While 17.7 percent of Pittsburghers make $100,000 or more, 18.5 percent of small-town West Virginians fall within this income bracket.[8]

Of course, in real numbers, there are more households making more than $150,000 in cities than in rural areas, but the point here is that an upper-middle-class life is accessible in rural and small-town America. While there are unlikely to be as many multimillionaires in rural Pennsylvania as there are in New York City, rural America has other things going for it that cities do not: a higher home-ownership rate, lower unemployment, less income inequality, and a comparable median income. These may not be the tickets to a pent-house apartment, but they do offer a chance at a good and decent life. I began to wonder, as the old statistical adage goes, if this data shows that the differences within urban and rural America might be greater than those between them. The problem with the conventional narrative is that it lumps all of urban America together (whether San Francisco or Cleveland) and compares it to all of rural America (whether Appalachia or Cape Cod), concluding that the latter is, across the board, in deep economic despair.[9] Zoom out, and the generalizations only provide hopelessness. Zoom in, and we can find the dismal town emblematic of the point we are trying to make. Zoom out, our cities are beacons of the global knowledge economy. Zoom in, and New York, San Francisco, and Los Angeles are self-selected, glowing examples of this phenomenon. But these optics distort reality at both ends of the spectrum.

To be honest, this was the sentiment I felt growing up in one of those rural towns in Pennsylvania. Having lived in rural America and then in major global cities, I've seen the economic idiosyncrasies of both ways of life firsthand. Many people I went to high school with were far from rich. Their parents did not attend an elite college, and many hadn't attended university at all. I remember when the TRW Automotive plant closed in my hometown and the gray, rainy day sitting in my best friend's minivan, in tears, as our other best friend (we were a trio) told us she had to move to Ohio so her father could relocate with the company. In my hometown, some people were less well-off and some were children of doctors; some parents were schoolteachers while others worked at the Merck factory. Nevertheless, we coexisted, and we were not homogenously

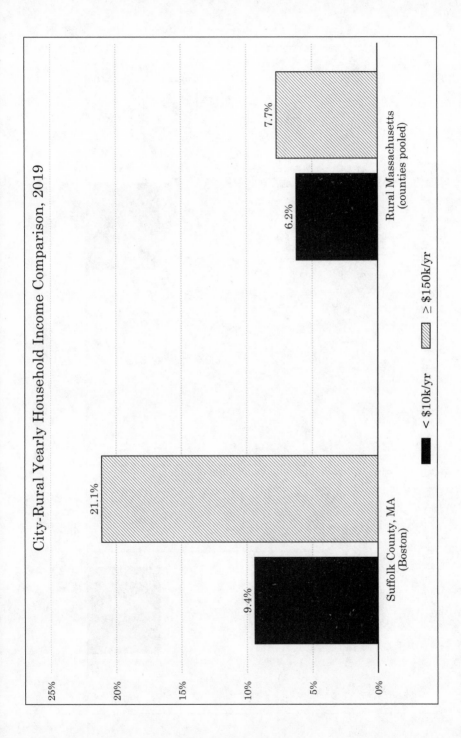

City-Rural Yearly Household Income Comparison, 2019

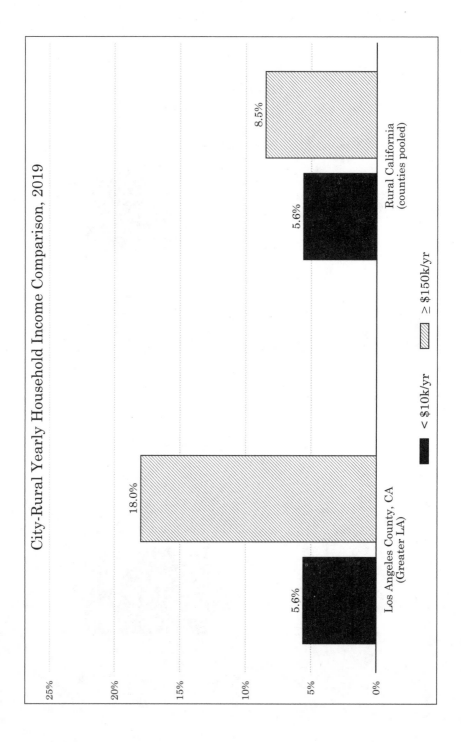

City-Rural Yearly Household Income Comparison, 2019

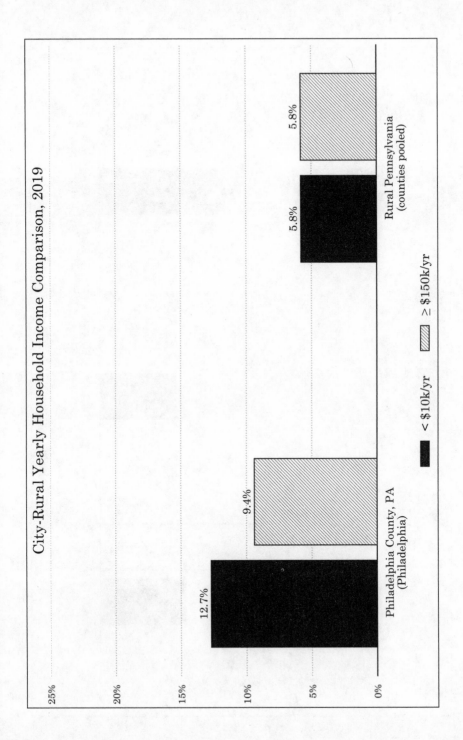

City-Rural Yearly Household Income Comparison, 2019

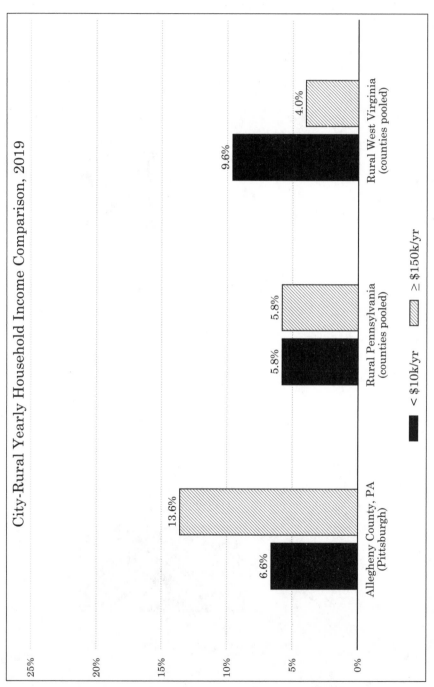

City-Rural Yearly Household Income Comparison, 2019

Allegheny County, PA (Pittsburgh): 6.6%, 13.6%
Rural Pennsylvania (counties pooled): 5.8%, 5.8%
Rural West Virginia (counties pooled): 9.6%, 4.0%

< $10k/yr   ≥ $150k/yr

Source: American Community Survey, 2019

rich or poor. Moving to New York City, despite the wealth and opulence, I saw more poverty in my first year of graduate school than I had seen in my entire life in rural Pennsylvania.

It is the same sense I get when I talk to people across the United States. They are not living profligate lives. They do not have everything that a New York City partner in a law firm might have. Their kids are not likely to go to private school. They don't fly first class, drive a new Audi, or get weekly manicures. They like their lives, and they do not express any need for more. When I asked one woman from a small former coal county about what she would do if she had all the money in the world, she replied, "Oh wow. I can't answer that. I have everything I need or want. If I want something, I go out and buy it, I guess. As a matter of fact, I drive Toyotas most of the time, a Prius. I've had it for ten years." Another woman from the same part of the country laughed and said, "Oh. I haven't a clue. Boy, I don't know. Elizabeth, I don't know." This is a question I asked of all of my interviewees, and these two women's answers were more or less what most people said. Perhaps they would donate the money, get something for family or friends, or help solve world problems. What they did not want was extravagance or more for themselves. Wayne from Wisconsin responded, "My wife drives a 2000 Lexus with sixty thousand miles. I have a 2006 Chevy pickup truck with a diesel engine, and that's it. We don't spend a lot of money on new things unless we need a new thing." Or, as my friend Craig from Iowa said in his typical easygoing style, "I don't know. You know, buying isn't my thing."

Craig personifies the data I studied on the Midwest. Because this region in many ways provides the archetype of Americana, it is often almost fetishized, for better and for worse. When I hear stories of the desperation of the Midwest, I find them hard to square with the economic and social indicators of a much more vibrant place. The rural Midwest has the lowest poverty rate, highest median income, lowest inequality, lowest unemployment rate, and

second-highest homeownership rate of all rural regions in the country. While the Midwest's fortunes have certainly improved over the
last thirty years, it has never been worse off than other rural places.
This is not a tale of woe but a story of prosperity. Despite the lack of
knowledge-economy jobs and college degrees, the Midwest, decade
after decade, is a place with a good quality of life.

Certainly the data and my interviewees, many of whom live
in this region, suggest as much. There are of course hardships for
some. Sarah Smarsh's book *Heartland* documents her own experience growing up in poverty in Kansas and fighting against a tide of
teenage pregnancy, abusive relationships, and lack of education. I
don't question that this was her reality, but the statistical data suggests, very hopefully, that most others in this part of the country
may be living better lives than what she experienced growing up.
After studying the fortunes of the various regions, I have come to
find that by romanticizing the woes of the heartland, we lose sight
of other places that really require economic development and social
interventions.

The region with the greatest need is the South. Far from a
portrait of rural prosperity, the South is the most economically
depressed region of the country and has been for decades. In both
urban and rural areas, the South has the lowest rate of college
degrees, the lowest median household income, the second-highest
unemployment, and highest poverty levels. Comparing country-
wide rural and urban poverty, 7.19 percent of all rural households
made less than $10,000 annually in 2019, while 5.83 percent of urban
households did. If the South is removed from this analysis, the difference between rural and urban poverty for the rest of the country
is less than half a percent. In short, the South explains an enormous
amount of the poverty and lack of social mobility in this country.
The South is also home to the greatest rural inequality.

It is a region in desperate need of intervention to enable greater
mobility. Just over 10 percent of rural southern inhabitants have a

bachelor's degree. The median rural southern county has a household income of just over $41,000, compared to the median household income for the United States of just below $70,000. Median home value, at less than $93,000, is over one and a half times less than median home value for the rural Coastal West and just over half the value of houses in rural New England. As Michael Storper and Dylan Connor find in their study of intergenerational social mobility from 1920 to the present day, the South remains a place of consistently depressed levels of opportunity compared to the Northeast, Midwest, and West, despite an increase of industry and jobs. They conclude that persistent levels of both social and economic oppression in the South, particularly for the Black population, explain the stagnancy of the region. "In the early and late 20th century, the average adult income attainment of children born to parents at the 25th percentile in the South has often failed to exceed the 40th percentile," write Storper and Connor. "Thus, low-income children across much of the South have faced particularly severe constraints on upward mobility throughout the 20th century."[10] They find that discrimination, inequality, and poor schooling persist and impact intergenerational mobility far into the twenty-first century.

While we don't focus nearly enough on problems affecting the entire region, we have heard the stories of opioid addiction that have ravaged parts of the South and the extreme poverty and lack of industry and jobs that further perpetuate this cycle of despair.[11] In Vance's *Hillbilly Elegy*, he outlines the recursive nature of poverty and dysfunction in the Appalachian community. "People talk about hard work all the time," writes Vance. "You can walk through a town where 30 percent of the young men work fewer than twenty hours a week and find not a single person aware of his own laziness." In another passage, Vance observes, "We talk about the value of hard work but tell ourselves that the reason we're not working is some perceived unfairness.... These are the lies we tell ourselves

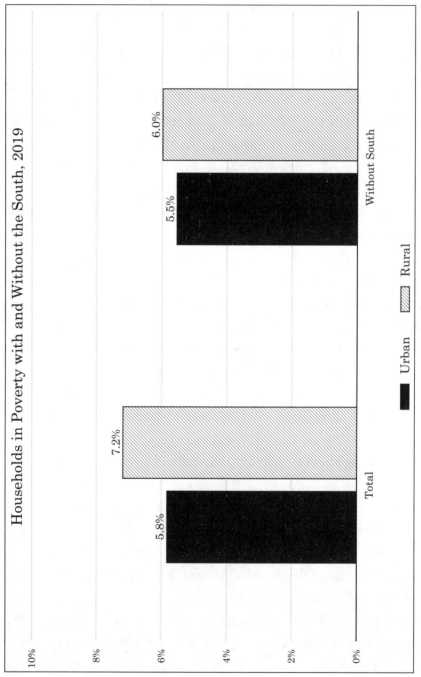

Households in Poverty with and Without the South, 2019

Source: American Community Survey, 2019

to solve the cognitive dissonance—the broken connection between the world we see and the values we preach." Vance's portrait of his hometown is not entirely unsympathetic; he criticizes elites and the "othering" of working-class white people. He also opens up about the self-consciousness he feels as both a Yale graduate returning to his hometown and a kid from Appalachia in the highest echelons of society.

Vance doesn't have a lot of time for people who aren't willing to have higher expectations of themselves. But I'm not sure how we can expect people to have these high expectations when there is quite literally nothing in their world that would show them such possibilities or, more practically, provide a ladder to reach them.

THE SOUTH's SOCIOECONOMIC profile is an outlier compared to most of rural America, and it is a place that I will return to in these pages. But its hardships capture an underlying truth of most regions: that the economic structure of a place explains many of its outcomes, from prosperity to inequality. For example, the inequality of New York City can be seen through the disproportionate rewards to those who work in the financial industry and the poorly paid service industry that upholds it. The rising unemployment rates in the 1970s and 1980s in many Western industrialized cities can be explained by the hemorrhaging of the manufacturing sector. The concentration of an educated population in Northern California is due to the draw of Silicon Valley. As an economic geographer and urban planner, my initial line of inquiry when I am studying a place is to understand its economy and to identify the internal and external resources that enable it to thrive or that limit its possibilities. Given that rural America seemed to be doing better than I had assumed with regard to employment, homeownership, income, and inequality, I wanted to understand what drove its economic development. I was particularly intrigued because I had thought that many of the sectors that had powered small towns (manufacturing, agriculture, mining) were in great decline. And of course, much of the activity of the world economy (technology, finance, professional services) is concentrated in our cities. I could not square the fact that rural America seemed to be a place where many people were doing quite well. What were the economics that explained such a paradox?

My research assistants and I set to work studying broad sectors—finance, manufacturing, agriculture, real estate, health, professional services, and technology—along with specific industries from banking to newspaper publishing to forestry. We studied employment and growth changes in these sectors from 1990 to 2020, and we looked at these results by urban and rural geographies in each region of the country. What we found surprised us in two important ways. First, some of the sectors that are thought to be dying in this country are actually doing well. Second, regardless of whether the global economy's home is in our cities, much of rural America greatly benefits from its spillover into the hinterlands.

When I was in graduate school, I was assigned *Nature's Metropolis* by William Cronon. Spanning six hundred pages, this tome of a book won the Bancroft Prize and was a finalist for the Pulitzer Prize in history. In a vast historical analysis of the emergence of the city of Chicago and its relationship to its rural and frontier hinterlands, Cronon argues that cities and rural towns are not discrete entities but rather part of a larger economic system on which they both depend. "The urban-rural, human-natural dichotomy blinds us to the deeper unity beneath our own divided perceptions," writes Cronon. "We also wall ourselves off from the broader ecosystems which contain our urban homes." The rivers, fields, and livestock are "first nature," and nineteenth-century Chicago relied on them: fields that generated grain, rivers for transport, and land for animals. But cities offer a "second nature": they are the centers of economic life, how the family farms are able to sell their animals and grain. Chicago essentially commodified the frontier, but it also allowed the frontier to expand by opening up markets and increasing demand for the farmers' goods. Cronon's overarching point is to document the symbiosis between urban and rural, city and frontier. They need each other. His view challenged the widely accepted "central place theory," which put a much greater emphasis on the primary role of the city.[12] Instead, Cronon saw cities as the place where natural resources became commodities.

Earlier theories of economic development aligned with Cronon's analysis. Prior to the creation of an economy driven by stock markets and information, places thrived as a function of their natural resources and the ability for those assets to develop into a market economy. In the 1950s, the economists Douglass North and Charles Tiebout engaged in a now-famous debate on the essential nature of economic growth. In his 1955 article "Location Theory and Regional Economic Growth," North argues that a region's livelihood ultimately rests on its ability to export goods. He describes how this process starts with a region becoming self-sufficient through its local assets, such as fields and a climate to grow wheat or forests that provide wood for building houses. Only after establishing self-sufficiency can investment and specialization occur: a region focuses on corn, or cows for beef, or fields of citrus trees. Thereafter, a region can expand to a secondary market that allows for export. It is in those exports—converting a natural advantage into a commodity—where rural and urban intersect.

In an influential rejoinder to North's argument, Charles Tiebout argued that this view was too simplistic.[13] In his 1956 response, "Exports and Regional Economic Growth," Tiebout argues that myriad forces, many of them a function of municipal governance, were responsible for economic growth outcomes. Labor and capital are mobile, after all. Thus economic growth is also related to other factors that lure or repel labor, firms, and resources. By combining North's and Tiebout's understanding of economic growth, economists came to understand growth as a mix of production, exports, labor pools, resources, and capital.[14]

This understanding made sense when natural and physical resources played a dominant role in the economy. One might understandably assume that if one industry was in decline, there were other jobs and sectors that needed eager workers. Tiebout's understanding of labor and capital moving together in lockstep makes sense if people and resources are able to move wherever they choose. But, in the latter half of the twentieth century, huge industries within the manufacturing economy pulled out of the United States, and American workers weren't able to follow.

Many people, both rural and urban, had benefited from the rise of the manufacturing economy in the mid-twentieth century, a time when a college degree was not essential to attaining a middle-class life. Factories offered unskilled, steady work and paid well. But advances in technology allowed firms to access cheaper resources and labor in the developing world and transport their finished goods back to the United States (and other Western countries) at lower costs. As a result, many cities from Buffalo to Cleveland to Pittsburgh, along with small towns across the country, lost jobs, tax revenue, and, ultimately, the means by which middle-class folks could live a good and decent life. From 1990 to 2000, the manufacturing sector lost two million jobs, and even more were lost in the coming decades.[15]

At the same time that the decline of the manufacturing economy dealt a terrible blow to American workers, something else was afoot. The cities that were home to a more diverse set of industries, places that dealt in information and skills, continued to prosper.[16] While the work of making things shifted from Western cities to developing countries and automation replaced factory workers, people still had to run these companies, and those people resided in our major metropolitan areas. In addition, financial markets began to dominate the world economy, and as a result, accountants and lawyers needed to be nearby. By this logic, cities transformed into great centers of educated people who engaged in the exchange of capital, ideas, and information.[17] Saskia Sassen's "global city," Manuel Castells's "information city," and Richard Florida's creative class do not deal in the currency of corn, slaughterhouses, or car parts. Nor do they deal with unskilled workers.[18] Instead, these scholars argue that human capital and the generation and sharing of ideas is the fundamental underpinning of the global economy, and the places that offer the possibilities for such knowledge exchange are the most prosperous.

Regions still export as a part of economic development, but it's a more complicated dynamic. Increasingly, the exports from our global cities are not physical products but ideas and knowledge, which then spin off one another to create new products and ideas.[19] This is what the economist Paul Romer calls "increasing returns" to technological growth. Unlike a machine or a forest, ideas do not depreciate; rather, they evolve and multiply over time.[20] One only has to think of the iPod to see Romer's theory applied: over the course of twenty years, this little box of music evolved into far more sophisticated versions, including the colorful hand computer that many of us now own. On the macro level, we can also see this evolution of economic growth from natural resources to ideas and their applicable goods and services. In 2021, agriculture generated just 0.8 percent of the United States' GDP. Contrast this figure with the financial sector at 22.3 percent, professional and business services at 12.8 percent, and retail at 5.7 percent.[21] Today, our primary economic generation comes through the trade of knowledge, intangible capital, and technological innovation, all of which are concentrated in our urban centers, what the Nobel Prize–winning economist Paul Krugman calls the New Economic Geography.[22] Unlike what Tiebout's model assumes, people who live in Appalachia or the poor neighborhoods of the South Bronx aren't able to simply pick up and go where they choose. They can't go to China or Brazil when their factory moves there, and they can't just land on Wall Street or in Silicon Valley. Not to mention, there's not an enormous amount of financial capital flocking to these less competitive parts of our country.

Today, as we deal in a market of information and software, one might think that the symbiosis between urban and rural is no longer possible. Because all these people and jobs are in our cities, the understanding is that those who are not educated would be left behind in a "skills mismatch"—the jobs on offer do not align with workers' skill sets.[23] Indeed, that was and remains the case for many. The factory jobs that supported a middle-class life in America were replaced with part-time service industry jobs that paid half as much. This erosion of jobs also affected the tax base and took away funding for schools and basic public works. The departure of manufacturing from the United States siphoned away the American Dream for millions of people. The most dramatic decline occurred from 2000 to 2010, when the sector shrank by almost 34 percent, affecting both urban and rural areas and all regions almost equally.

Source: BLS Quarterly Census of Employment and Wages 2000 and 2010

But despite these losses that suggested manufacturing would never recover, from 2010 to 2020, the sector experienced an overall 5 percent growth across the country, with the Southwest and South growing 20.2 percent and 8.6 percent, respectively. To put that in perspective, the South's manufacturing sector grew by almost three hundred thousand jobs. More broadly, from 2010 to 2020, across the United States, both urban and rural areas benefited from the increase in manufacturing. In fact, the only region that continues to experience manufacturing decline, and indeed was the hardest hit overall, is the Northeast. Both the Mid-Atlantic and New England regions lost over 6 percent of their manufacturing jobs from 2010 to 2020, while most other regions gained by at least that much.

Despite this moderate recovery of manufacturing in the past decade, Saskia Sassen's concept of the global city and her observations about the dominance of highly professionalized services and finance were on point. The industries that have grown dramatically over the past thirty years include financial and insurances services of almost all

Manufacturing Job Gain, 2010–2020

■ 2,001 or greater
▨ 1,001 to 2,000
▦ 1 to 1,000
□ Job loss or no gain

Source: BLS Quarterly Census of Employment and Wages 2010 and 2020

types; professional, scientific, and technical services; and some industries within the information sector. Since 1990, financial and insurance
services have grown almost 16 percent overall for the country, while
professional and technical services have grown 87 percent.

While information services—which includes newspapers, radio,
film, and television—has overall declined by 5 percent over the last
thirty years, some industries within this sector have grown sharply
over the past ten years, including software publishing and data
processing. Almost all of the growth in the information sector has
occurred in the West, particularly the Pacific states of California and
Washington. With the rise of smartphones, many of our previous
forms of information—print newspapers, radio, and magazines—
have become obsolete, with local newspapers experiencing some of
the biggest declines.[24] The rise of streaming services has further created a new way for people to watch movies and television. Many of
these new forms of social media, news, and streaming entertainment
are located on the West Coast, emerging from the region's historical
and seemingly untouchable position as the leader in technology.

The most remarkable part of this story is that, where our cities have
benefited from the changing nature of our economy, so have our rural
areas—perhaps even more so. It's important to remember that regional
is not the same thing as urban versus rural. Superstar cities like San
Francisco and Los Angeles can hide a thousand sins, and even in the
most prosperous cities, poverty is still present. And the converse is true
as well: in almost every sector where the country—and our cities—has
experienced growth, rural America has as well. The following graphs
document the change in growth over time for jobs within information,
finance and insurance, and scientific and professional services. These
are the very sectors that power the global economy and are most associated with the urban professional-managerial class. In every area, rural
America has mostly been in lockstep with urban America. From 1990
to 2020, while urban growth in knowledge-worker jobs was 87 percent,
rural areas experienced a growth rate of 82 percent.

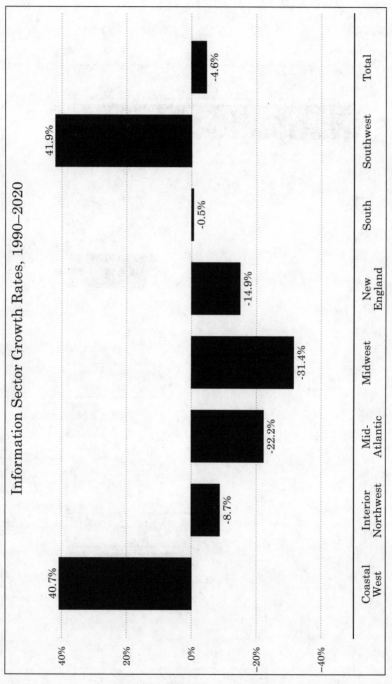

Information Sector Growth Rates, 1990–2020

Source: BLS Quarterly Census of Employment and Wages 2010 and 2020

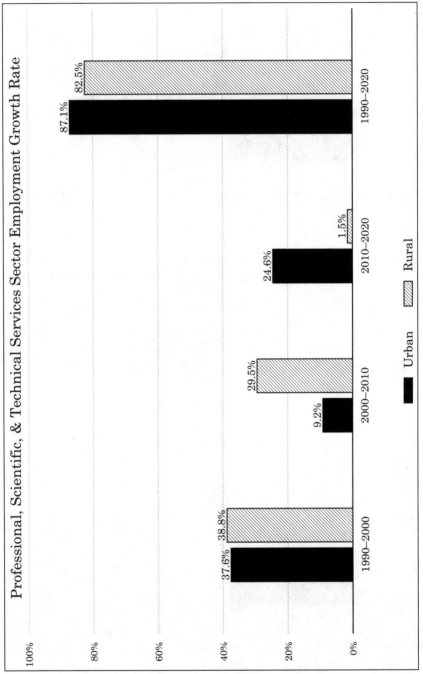

Professional, Scientific, & Technical Services Sector Employment Growth Rate

Source: BLS Quarterly Census of Employment and Wages 1990, 2000, 2010, and 2020

Turning to the information sector, if we look strictly at growth percentages, we can see that rural and urban America experienced similar trajectories over the thirty-year period. From 1990 to 2000, both geographies experienced growth in the information sector, with rural America growing at almost 10 percent and urban America at 30 percent. From 2000 to 2020, however, both experienced an overall decline, with a greater negative impact on rural America. However, these numbers are misleading. While almost all of the United States experienced significant contraction in the information sector, Coastal West cities—where Hollywood and Silicon Valley are located—drive much of the expansion in information jobs.

While rural America has experienced the greatest overall decline in the information sector, the opposite is true when it comes to the finance and insurance sector. Rural America has experienced significantly greater growth in this sector than urban America. From 2000 to 2010, rural American finance and insurance jobs grew by almost 33 percent, while this same sector contracted by approximately 2 percent for American cities. Even coming off of the global financial crisis, from 2010 to 2020 rural America experienced just a mild contraction in job growth in finance and insurance. Overall, over the thirty-year period, financial jobs grew in rural towns by over 25 percent, compared to urban America's more modest 16 percent.

When I first saw these sectors' explosive growth, I guessed that highly skilled jobs would be located in cities and the remaining auxiliary support jobs would be in small and rural towns. In other words, the growth of highly skilled jobs would benefit rural communities through the creation of support jobs. To test my hypothesis, I looked at jobs on a more granular level to see exactly which parts of each sector were located in cities versus rural towns. I was surprised to see remarkable overlap in the types of jobs in both areas. In 2020, for example, almost 40 percent of rural jobs in the technical services sector fell under computer system design; another 14 percent were in management consulting. Over 10 percent of rural professional

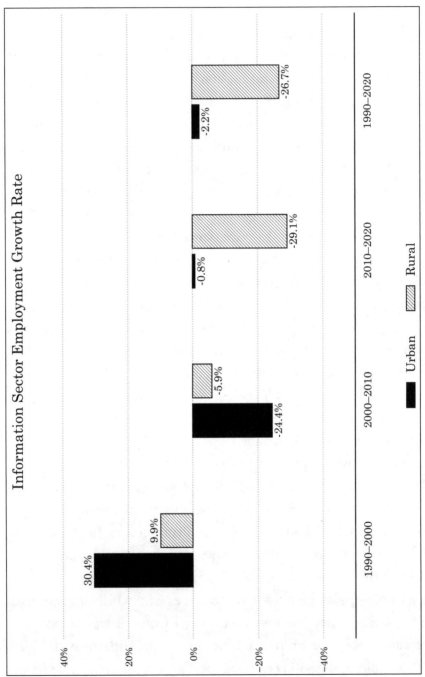

Information Sector Employment Growth Rate

Source: BLS Quarterly Census of Employment and Wages 1990, 2000, 2010, and 2020

Urban   Rural

1990–2000   30.4%   9.9%

2000–2010   -24.4%   -5.9%

2010–2020   -0.8%   -29.1%

1990–2020   -2.2%   -26.7%

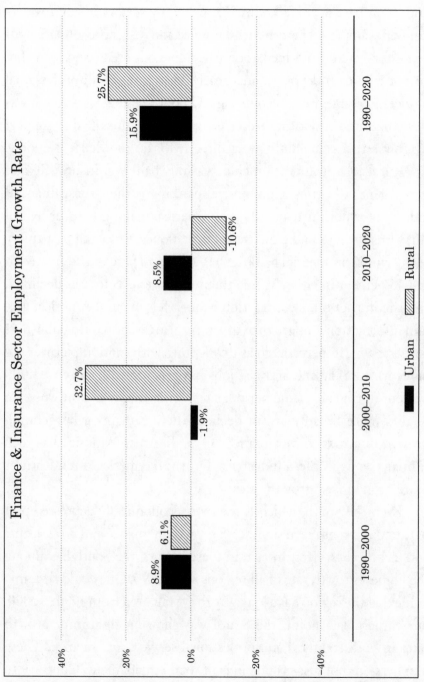

Finance & Insurance Sector Employment Growth Rate

Source: BLS Quarterly Census of Employment and Wages 1990, 2000, 2010, and 2020

services jobs are in engineering. Auxiliary support did make up an important part of these knowledge-economy sectors in rural America. For example, 14 percent of all finance and insurance jobs are non-depository credit intermediation (they give out credit and loans but do not take cash deposits), and nearly 15 percent of all professional services jobs are within accounting and bookkeeping. However, it was clear that rural Americans weren't working only unskilled or support jobs but rather contributing very directly to the knowledge economy.

Rural jobs in finance include various banking, insurance, and investment industries. Commercial banking is the largest financial industry for both urban and rural America, making up over half of rural finance jobs and a quarter of urban ones. Over the past thirty years, rural commercial banking has grown 50 percent, compared to just 16 percent in cities. While the information sector has declined, and the impact of its contraction is most felt in rural America, certain information jobs are thriving in rural areas. Software publishers have grown 316 percent since 1990, along with motion pictures (71 percent). Library and archival jobs have increased by almost 1,000 percent during this time period, suggesting that while information sectors more broadly are in decline, there remains a burgeoning growth in access to information. Overall, urban America has seen similar trends in these industries, but rural America often features more pronounced growth rates.

Even the South, which is the most economically depressed part of the country, has seen significant growth in finance and professional and technical services. In fact, in these sectors, the South has among the highest growth rate of all regions since 1990. One could certainly argue that the region has a long way to go, but even from 1990 to 2000, our earliest data point, the South was showing significant growth rates in both technical and professional services and finance. These numbers are not just proportions of total employment. Contrary to the popular myth that Boston, New York City, and Connecticut are the center of the financial sector, the South has the greatest number of finance jobs in the entire country. In 2020, the South had almost 750,000 more finance and insurance jobs than the Northeast. When I saw these numbers, I was stumped, given the higher rates of poverty and lack of education in the South. But within the region, there are states thriving in the finance industry, including Florida, Georgia, North Carolina, and Texas. Even in the interior of the South—in states with historically lower education levels and higher poverty, such as Alabama, Mississippi, and Tennessee—I saw growth. Since 1990, this region has grown by 34 percent in finance and 92 percent in technical and professional services, and declined 20 percent in the information sector, a decrease that is still less than in the Mid-Atlantic and Midwest.[25] These findings gave me hope. The growth in the South suggests that the industries that drive the global economy are coming, albeit more slowly, to the parts of the country that need them the most. The burgeoning growth found on the southern Atlantic coast could most certainly spill over to nearby states with some government intervention and encouragement.

Additionally, the Midwest, which has also been thought of as a region in decline, shows remarkably stable numbers that follow the general trend of the economic fortunes of the country. Although it has seen greater declines in the information industry than other regions, the Midwest has experienced growth in finance and professional and technical services and a lesser decline in manufacturing than other regions. I also solved the mystery of why the Midwest is home to some of America's most prosperous rural folks. I had always been under the impression that the Midwest was struggling because agriculture had gone by the wayside. On the contrary, not only is the Midwest doing well, but agriculture is still a crucial component to the region's economy.

While there are pockets of decline in agriculture, as there are with any industry, overall, the Midwest shows tremendous growth of over 130 percent in agriculture over the last thirty years. In 1990, American agriculture was dominated by the Coastal West and South, but by 2020 the Midwest had emerged as a major center of agricultural productivity.

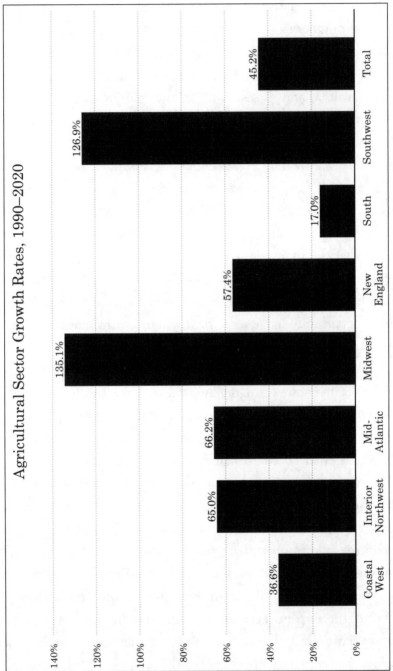

Agricultural Sector Growth Rates, 1990–2020

Source: BLS Quarterly Census of Employment and Wages 2010 and 2020

While the numbers can bog us down, there is an important trend to observe. The global economy that resides in our cities exists across America. When you look at the maps and charts of urban versus rural America, you see that both are greatly benefiting from the fortunes of technology, science, and finance and have been hit equally hard by declines in manufacturing and parts of the information sector. Within these sectors, particular industries are growing and declining. For example, from 1990 to 2020, as we can observe in our daily lives, newspapers have declined by 50 percent. In 1990, almost half of all information jobs were within wired telecom (that is, landline telephones). By 2020, these jobs had completely disappeared. On the other hand, we see the booming growth of software, the internet, film production, and music publishers, particularly in the Coastal West. Rural and urban America are experiencing these changes similarly, sometimes even down to the same exact share of employment within an industry. What is remarkable is how much rural America benefits from the upswings. It also feels the downswings the same as—and at times less than—our cities. What is clear to me when I look at rural America is that, as a whole, it is doing fairly well on almost all indicators, despite the data indicating lower education levels for its population. Many industries require hardworking people, irrespective of their college degree, and in rural America that often means one can hold a job, own a home, and have a reasonably good quality of life. That may not be the case in the urban United States, where a college degree may be much more necessary given the higher cost of living.

The other important element of this story is that your fortunes are not determined by whether you are urban or rural. There are rich and poor people in both of these geographies. Rather, our fortunes are more determined by where we live regionally.[26] If you live in the Northeast, based on the data, you are more likely to be educated, own a house that is worth more than in most other places, and have a higher median income. The opposite is true if you live in the

South. The information industry has ballooned in the Coastal West and declined everywhere else. "Can the United States truly prosper when 90% of its R&D- and STEM-intensive 'innovation sector' employment growth takes place in just five 'superstar' tech hubs?" ask two senior scholars at the Brookings Institution.[27] I understand their concern, but I have spoken to many people who live good lives without working in the technology sector. Looking at the United States as a whole—just like lumping all cities together and comparing them to all of rural America—hides the underlying dynamics of particular places and regions. This really matters when it comes to policy. We can't undertake economic development, increase education, and figure out how to attract industry if we don't understand the specificity of place.

My results corroborate work done by Harvard economist Raj Chetty and his colleagues in their Opportunity Atlas project, where they also find contradictions across the rural and urban divide. As Chetty and his colleagues write, "First, opportunities for upward mobility are not necessarily better for children growing up in cities rather than rural areas. Second, the sharply divergent patterns of opportunity across the country suggest that the underlying drivers (as well as potential policy solutions) may also vary greatly from place to place."[28]

What Chetty is writing about and what my research here shows is what has come to be called "regional divergence." In the early half of the twentieth century, there was a "convergence," essentially the gap between rich and poor was closing.[29] But the latter half of the century brought a decline in unskilled manufacturing jobs and a perceived imperative for a college education. By the early 2000s, discussion of superstar cities, the creative class, and, more recently, the "great inversion" began to inform how we understood the economic geography of the United States.[30]

But I want to push this further and challenge the conventional wisdom. There are places within America that are really struggling, but these differences in fortunes vary by region and scale. In San

Francisco, a supposedly superstar city, there are people as poor as Clay's friends in Kentucky, and there are extremely prosperous people living in the Midwest. We must really understand scale when we consider these differences. Superstar cities look great from thirty thousand feet, but they often house the most acute forms of inequality, irrespective of their college-educated population. Industry-wise, there is no question that some parts of the country are reaping most of the rewards of technology and agriculture, for example. However, regional divergence masks a thousand inequities within our prosperous regions. Our interventions to address these inequities must be more specific: certain states like Kentucky and certain neighborhoods like Compton need intervention, and they need it in different ways. Our blanket observations about rural versus urban and South versus Northeast do little to help the people within these geographies trying to make a life for themselves and their families.

I would also like to say something that is controversial but gaining momentum, particularly in the post-Covid era. I am not sure the answer is for everyone to get a college degree. I have long thought too many middle-class kids are pressured down that track only to prefer a job that involves artistic creativity or craftsmanship, and I know too many kids who aren't able to afford the education at Yale or MIT or NYU through which they would thrive and triumph. In this conversation around college, we lose sight of the many people in this country who do not have a college degree and are doing just fine. Yes, a third of Americans hold a college degree, but that means that two-thirds do not. They are not all in poverty; they are certainly not all to be pitied. Much of my analysis suggests that people in rural and small-town America, many of whom are not college educated, make the same if not better money than the median income in our cities, they own homes, they hold down jobs, and, from my experience talking to them, they are satisfied with their lives.

The median economic numbers in the urban and rural United States look similar because most people do not exist in the highest income bracket. Most people, irrespective of where they live, do not attain graduate degrees or work in technology. Even in cities, most people are not members of the creative class, and most people are not financial titans. The median household in urban America experiences many of the same types of economic constraints as the median household in rural America. There may be more one-percenters residing in our cities, but that's not the same as every urban resident being a member of the elite. The fever-pitch discussion of the importance of global jobs and top-tier cities sounds as if the rest of the United States didn't exist and every American wished they were part of the urban vortex. Rural America has problems, and this chapter has identified some ways we can understand them more fully. But it also has a lot more prosperity and greater economic and social contentment than the headlines might imply. People in America are suffering, but not everyone is, and not necessarily the people we think. There are many ways to embrace a life in this country. Being educated and rich is one way, but so is being middle class and finding stability in one's community.

3

LIFE CHANCES

There are many boys, and men too, who ... have never had a fair chance in life. Let us remember that, when we judge them, and not be too hasty to condemn.
—HORATIO ALGER[1]

This is what I would say if I could, to all smart people of the world with their dumb hillbilly jokes: We are right here in the stall. We can actually hear you.
—BARBARA KINGSOLVER, *Demon Copperhead*[2]

WHILE MUCH OF RURAL AMERICA IS DOING FINE BY MANY measures, there is a part that runs against the positive social and economic statistics. Appalachia and some of the Deep South—including Alabama, Arkansas, and Mississippi—are struggling economically and have been for decades. They lack access to what many people in the United States take for granted: fruits, vegetables, nearby stores, and hospitals. They are not beneficiaries of the spillover effect I have found in other parts of rural America. There is also an undeniable link between particular rural areas and negative health outcomes. This is not by any means the story of all of

131

rural America, but the situation for some states is so acute, I would be remiss to not address it.

The most salient of these stories is the opioid epidemic, of which most people living in this country are aware. Despite the many headlines and memoirs on the topic, just one of my rural interviewees mentioned opioids directly without prompting. Shannon from Kentucky discussed her work with two organizations; one of them helps prevent drug use and the other encourages recovery. The latter, Celebrate Recovery, is a national, twelve-step, Christian organization that employs religion to help with addiction recovery. Shannon met her third husband, to whom she remains married, at one of these meetings. While Shannon herself was never an addict, she volunteered with Celebrate Recovery to help with her depression. As she mentioned many times to me, she finds caring for others to be her calling and it gives her deep joy. Shannon also helped start Project Daris, a local organization she established with two friends, where they go into schools and talk to children about staying away from drugs, particularly prescription drugs, which have been a scourge to their local community. Project Daris is named after one of the cofounders' young boy, who died of a drug overdose. The women hand out brightly colored rubber bracelets to the students with "Say no to drugs!" written on the band. While the pandemic has prevented them from making visits to the school in the last few years, Shannon and her cofounders have worked with local University of Kentucky pharmacy students to develop a website that parents and kids may access at home.

Given how involved she is in the issue, I call Shannon up to try to understand the lived experience of opioids in her hometown. As always, she graciously agrees to speak. I ask her how she is doing, and she warmly says she is fine and asks about my book, telling me she has been praying for its success. I start to ask her about Project Daris and Celebrate Recovery. I explain I am looking specifically at opioid addiction in rural America. Shannon begins to talk about her organizations, but then she pauses. "Remember when you asked me how

I am and I said I was fine?" she asks me. "And I put a big smile on my face?" My stomach starts to feel uncomfortable as she goes on. "Two, three weeks ago, my husband started acting funny." She explains that she had a sense he may have been back on drugs. While he denied it, Shannon felt sure and gave him a choice: either he would go to rehab or she and their young daughter and older son would leave. Within days, she told me, he checked himself into a local rehab center.

I know how hard this must be for Shannon. She had met her husband at Celebrate Recovery when he was a recovering addict. He was now involved in their local chapter. "My suspicion is Suboxone," a drug used to help get people off of opioids, but which (like methadone for recovery from heroin addiction) can become a source of addiction itself. "What the doctors will do is give patients ninety pills for a month," she explains. "But patients need only a quarter of a pill, so what do they do? They sell it, or they don't swallow it. They crunch it up, snort it, or inject it. A man at Celebrate Recovery who's been clean for five years said to me that every day he wakes up and has to make a commitment to stay sober. Every day." Shannon remarks that drugs are omnipresent in her town, and so for recovering addicts the temptation to slip up is constant. "It's at the grocery stores. It's at the gas station. It's everywhere."

I know Shannon is a stay-at-home mom, and outside of her work babysitting, I'm not sure how she will make ends meet. "So my husband paid all the bills, which is why I realized spouses never send their partner off to rehab—because they can't pay the bills. [But] I'm not jumping ship because I can't pay. I need $216 a week to pay my bills," she explains matter-of-factly. She then recounts how money is coming in. First, a friend who hears of her plight wants to give her money, but Shannon won't accept it. "I said if you want to buy my artwork you can. She sends me $46 on Apple. On Friday, I get paid $70 from the mother who I babysit for, and I am working with another woman to help her lose weight, [which earns me] $100." She pauses, then reveals why she feels hopeful despite how tough life is right now. "If you add $46 to $170, what do you get?" she asks me.

I answer. Shannon concurs, "That ends up as $216. It's like God wanted to say, 'Gotcha girl. I gotcha,'" and she laughs with delight. I laugh too. Shannon remarks that had she made $500, it wouldn't have had the same meaning as the fact that somehow the exact amount of money she needed came together at the exact right time. Still, I am deeply saddened by Shannon's situation, and I express my worry for her. "My husband and I run Celebrate Recovery together. How can I help a wife whose husband has relapsed if I haven't gone through it myself?" she says with a frankness and tenacity I will come to admire as our conversations continue over many months. "I feel God is helping me learn how to take care of others who are in this situation. When people have personal experience, this is how you can help someone. I'm going to be okay one way or another." When I talk to Shannon in early October 2022, she tells me joyously that her husband is out of rehab and working with someone to stay that way.

As concerning as Shannon's story is, hers is not the archetype for rural America. One would think from the headlines and sensational books that opioid addiction plagues most rural towns. But that is not the case at all. From the statistics I have seen, the opioid epidemic is devastating but highly concentrated in a few rural states, which means that there are many small-town places and people who haven't experienced the tragedy firsthand. Opioids are everywhere, people are addicted in our cities and small towns, but a high concentration of addiction and death is the scourge of just a few rural states, often the same places with less resources, less education, perhaps more exploitative doctors, and more depressed economic conditions.[3]

But it isn't the story of all of rural America, far from it. According to the Centers for Disease Control and Prevention, in 2015 the rural death rate from overdoses surpassed that of urban and suburban areas, but Kentucky, Ohio, Tennessee, and West Virginia are disproportionately impacted (Louisiana, New Mexico, and Pennsylvania also witnessed more overdose deaths than the national average).[4] The rural Midwest is one of the least affected regions of the country, with overdose rates less than those of coastal states like California and New York.[5] The CDC's most recent data shows the same concentrated pattern of opioid mortality rates. While to some extent every state experiences drug overdose mortality, the same handful of predominantly rural states overwhelmingly drives the rate of opioid overdose deaths, with West Virginia remaining by far the highest. In 2022, 81.2 per 100,000 people in West Virginia died from a drug overdose. That's 40 percent more than Kentucky, the state with the second-highest overdose mortality rate. Contrast this with Iowa, where the overdose mortality rate is 14.3 people per 100,000.

It's no surprise to me that Shannon and her friends started Project Daris in Kentucky. Even in my hometown in rural Pennsylvania, opioid addiction is a presence; one of my mother's friends lost a child to an overdose. To be sure, the quotidian reality of addiction, accidental overdoses, and suicide hit rural America the hardest—but far from all of rural America. My interviews reaffirm these trends. Almost none of the interviewees even mentioned opioid addiction.

Over the past couple of decades, the opioid epidemic and its impact on rural America has commanded our attention. Books like *Hillbilly Elegy* have fixated on Appalachia and conflated its very specific problems with the rest of rural America, to the benefit of neither. The opioid crisis has in fact targeted very specific types of rural communities. Just like all of rural America is not filled with poor, angry Trump supporters, all of rural America is not filled with opioid addiction and death. But perhaps these tragic stories are more interesting to tell, even if they aren't the whole truth. I wanted to know the real story of opioids in rural America, and I knew just whom to ask.

I WAS AT A small Charleston newspaper," the Pulitzer Prize–winning reporter Eric Eyre begins when I call him to discuss

West Virginia's opioid crisis. "It was 2013, obviously the opioid epidemic had been going on for twelve or thirteen years. [At the time,]
I was writing mostly about meth labs. Obviously I had dropped the
ball. I had not seen what was going on right under my nose." As
Eric documents in his 2020 book *Death in Mud Lick*, he soon started
to run into information that ultimately uncovered a terribly corrupt
operation for distributing opioids, seemingly unregulated and with
government officials turning a blind eye. "In 2013 we had a new
attorney general [Patrick Morrisey], and I got tips that he had an
inaugural party," Eric explains. "We looked down the list of people
[paying for the party]. There were the usual oil and gas, grocery
stores, and then there was a company called Cardinal Health." Eric
was stumped by this organization. What was it doing supporting
Morrisey's inaugural ball? Cardinal Health, it turns out, is a drug
giant and one of the leading suppliers of opioids in West Virginia. As
Eric traces in his book, over the course of a decade, Cardinal Health,
in collaboration with McKesson Corporation, worked with regional
distributors to deliver 16.6 million pain pills to a single drug store in
Mount Gay, West Virginia, population 1,700. "Those same companies, along with AmerisourceBergen—ranked twelfth in the Fortune
500—shipped 20.8 million prescription opioids to two pharmacies
four blocks apart in Williamson, a town with twenty-nine hundred
people and only twenty miles from Kermit," Eric writes in his book.
Kermit, population 382, was the recipient of nearly nine million opioid pain pills, which went to the town's one pharmacy, Sav-Rite.[6]

Operating clinics, which often didn't even have a doctor present, would dole out prescriptions for opioids like a McDonald's
drive-through, and then the prescriptions would go to a handful of
pharmacies. As Eric writes, the line at Sav-Rite for those pills went
all the way down US Route 52, which runs through Kermit. Jim
Wooley, part-time used car dealer and owner of Sav-Rite, actually
set up a hot dog and chips stand to keep waiting opioid customers
entertained. Federal investigators began to look into Wooley's and a

nearby medical clinic's dealings. "One undercover agent noted that the cash drawer at the Sav-Rite was so full the assistant couldn't close it," the *Guardian* reported.[7] In 2009, they arrested Wooley, who pleaded guilty to conspiracy and selling prescription drugs illegally.[8] An FBI press release dated November 15, 2012, reports that James P. Wooley pleaded guilty and was sentenced to six months in a federal prison along with a $5,000 fine and one year of supervised release "for conspiracy to acquire or obtain controlled substances by misrepresentation, fraud, forgery, deception, and subterfuge."[9]

The previous attorney general, who had been in the role for twenty years, had sued Cardinal Health on behalf of the people of West Virginia as a part of the wider, large-scale effort to stop excessive opioid distribution in West Virginia. And yet despite this history, as Eric Eyre discovered, Cardinal Health was supporting the then-new attorney general Patrick Morrisey's campaign. What was going on? "Turns out his wife was [a] lobbyist in DC for Cardinal Health," Eric tells me. According to federal disclosures, Denise Morrisey was one of a number of lobbyists representing Cardinal Health.[10] "That year, he [Morrisey] inherited the lawsuit against Cardinal Health," explained Eric, and Eric believed that Morrisey may have been trying to get it to go away. According to Eric's book and other sources, prior to his work as attorney general, Morrisey worked for the drug industry as well.[11] "As a lobbyist, Morrisey was paid $250,000 to represent a pharmaceutical trade group funded by some of the same distributors West Virginia is now suing," CBS News reported in 2016.[12] According to multiple sources, Cardinal Health contributed $8,000 to his campaign.[13] After this information came to light, Morrisey recused himself from the lawsuit against Cardinal Health, along with the state case involving Amerisource-Bergen and McKesson.[14]

While as attorney general Morrisey has filed multiple lawsuits against opioid distributors, Eric Eyre and others have suggested that these historical relationships may have posed potential conflicts of interest.[15] "The allegations were that he was sort of trying to settle pennies on the dollar," Eric explained with regard to the original Cardinal Health lawsuit, although these allegations have not been proven.[16] Morrisey has denied any conflict, and his Senate election campaign (he ran in 2018 and lost to Joe Manchin) dismissed any accusations of conflict of interest.[17] According to his official attorney general website, Morrissey has brought multiple lawsuits against drug companies and distributors of opioids, reaching settlements of $380 million to date.[18] In August 2022, in a "landmark" settlement, Cardinal Health, McKesson, and AmerisourceBergen agreed to pay $400 million to West Virginia over allegations that they played a role in the opioid crisis.[19] It's worth noting that Cardinal Health, McKesson, and AmerisourceBergen, along with Johnson & Johnson, also agreed to a $26 billion national settlement on an opioid lawsuit, although they have denied any wrongdoing.[20] In July 2022, a federal judge ruled that Cardinal Health, along with McKesson and AmerisourceBergen, was not liable for the opioid crisis in West Virginia's Cabell County and the city of Huntington (these locales were not included in the aforementioned $400 million settlement).[21] As I write this, Patrick Morrisey remains in his position. He and his wife have not been personally charged of any misconduct or legal violations.

Why West Virginia? Weren't there people in despair everywhere? Weren't there corrupt people looking to capitalize on human weakness everywhere too? What Eric found was that the counties with the most overdoses were also those with the fewest jobs. "Here's the weird thing," he says to me, almost as an afterthought. "When I was looking at the top twenty counties for drug overdose, twelve are in West Virginia, a couple in Kentucky and Tennessee and the Ozarks of Missouri, and then one in Utah." He was initially surprised by this last entry, but it "turns out it's called Carbon County, and it's their biggest coal producing county." By Eric's account, people get injured doing mine work, they take painkillers, they become addicted, and they may not be able to find another job that requires less manual labor—and the cycle continues. As one can see in this map, mining is also a sector with less uniform growth, less ubiquity, and significant decline compared to finance, agriculture, and technical and professional services.

The specifics of this data can help us better understand the full impact of the mining sector's growth and decline in particular parts of rural America. From 2000 to 2010, the mining industry grew sharply throughout the United States, especially in Appalachia and other non-coastal regions. Kentucky, for example, effectively doubled its number of mining jobs during this period, as did Arkansas. West Virginia and Tennessee increased their mining workforces by over 75 percent. Yet, directly on the heels of this growth came a steep decline. Myriad forces—stricter environmental regulations, advanced technologies and automation, and competition from elsewhere—collided to depress the growth of the industry, particularly in Appalachia.[22] Between 2010 and 2020, the US mining industry declined by approximately 19 percent overall, but the South was hit particularly hard. Kentucky led all US states in share of jobs lost with an 85 percent decline, Arkansas followed with 60 percent, Mississippi third with 58 percent, and West Virginia seventh at nearly 46 percent. In terms of total jobs, Louisiana lost the most at over 19,000, Kentucky ranked second at over 14,000, and West Virginia lost over 8,700 jobs.

Because mining is a scattered industry, examining the decline on the county level provides an even clearer picture of the targeted impact on Appalachia. Between 2010 and 2020, out of the 285 counties that lost at least 75 percent of their mining jobs, Kentucky, Ohio, and West Virginia counties rank as the top three. The decline of an entire industry can impact a state and even a nation, but these effects are even more destructive on the local level, particularly in the case of mining, with just a few states highly dependent upon it. For most of the United States, however, mining has not been an important part of the regional economy, and thus its decline was hardly noticed, if at all.

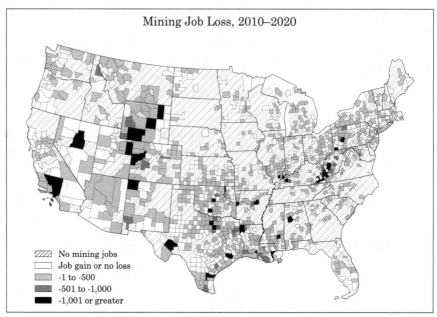

Source: BLS Quarterly Census of Employment and Wages 1990, 2000, 2010, and 2020

Given the link Eric Eyre makes between mining injuries and opioid addiction, the statistics on Appalachia explain why it is at the center of the prescription drug crisis. Eric goes on: "[The opioid epidemic] affected families. We had OxyContin dealers living next door. I know plenty of people who died. We all carry Narcan or naloxone. One of the biggest effects is there are so many grandparents raising kids because somebody died." He explains that the huge homelessness problem has only increased. He points out that while needle exchange programs are not popular, at least they provide a point of interaction where addicts can find out about treatment. At one point, he remarks, "I can never understand why we are the second-highest voting state for Trump." I say that I thought it was because, as Arlie Hochschild has observed, Trump was their "great salesman of hope."[23] He did not forget the miners and he promised to bring their industry back, even if he didn't succeed.[24] Eric replies, "I 100 percent agree with Arlie."

Jason Doctor, a health economist and colleague of mine at the University of Southern California, points out the recursive cycle of addiction and poverty. "Studying opioid prescriptions by zip code, we can see a 25 percent reduction in people looking for work in the quarter afterward." Jason explains that 25 percent of discouraged workers (people who are unemployed and not looking for a job) can be explained by opioid use. He also zeros in on the discreteness of the opioid epidemic. "That whole Appalachia area is its own whole problem," he explains to me. "Rural counties. There is definitely a big issue there."

Jason attributes the incidence of opioid addiction in Appalachia to potentially ignorant and unethical doctors. "I think there's a sorting effect, where physicians who do not keep up with the literature end up [in rural America]. They're not striving to keep up and be a top doctor in a big city." Even from my own childbirth experiences in Los Angeles, I knew that urban doctors were increasingly reluctant to prescribe painkillers. By the time my third son was born, I was no longer offered a prescription to manage postpartum pain and was given lots of Advil instead. (As someone who is scared of drugs, I was fine with that.) From this perspective, while doctors in big cities, aware of the ramifications of painkillers, have become far more careful with their prescriptions, doctors in rural America either may have been unaware or perhaps didn't care. Citing Eric Eyre's work, Jason continues, "These doctors in West Virginia and Tennessee and all those bordering states [like] Kentucky, they would be chased out of town by county law enforcement [for overprescribing].... But they would hopscotch across county borders."

Jason's observations chilled me to the bone. They reminded me of what Shannon had said as she talked about her own hometown and the significant but seemingly futile efforts of her local sheriff to stop opioid distribution: "It's just everywhere." But the mystery was unresolved. I wanted to understand why some people and some places were driven to addiction and overdose deaths while other parts of the country were thriving. Poverty wasn't the only explanation; there were plenty of poor people in the United States. The mining injuries didn't explain it entirely; people get hurt in all sorts of places and recover without becoming addicted to prescription drugs. Rurality also didn't explain it; many rural areas were not demonstratively impacted by opioids. There was something bigger, something more existential, at stake.

In 2014, married economists Angus Deaton and Anne Case stumbled across an alarming statistic. As a 2020 *New Yorker* profile of the couple reports, Case had been suffering from chronic back pain and, like any good researcher, looked to understand the phenomenon in the wider population.[25] She collaborated with her husband, and what they found shocked them. While life expectancy was rising in almost all Western countries, the United States had observed a significant drop. As their story goes, this finding collided with what Deaton had found in his previous work: America had become healthier and wealthier but more unequal.[26] From 1999 to 2017, over six hundred thousand more people had died than expected, and this jump was dramatic in comparison to other countries.

As they probed more deeply, Deaton and Case found that the drop in life expectancy was not equally applied. Most of these six hundred thousand additional deaths came from one demographic: white, middle-aged, and lacking a college education. By this point, the opioid crisis was well established and understood. Deaton and Case wondered if it might be driving the numbers. However, while many people are prescribed opioids for pain, particularly after surgery, most people stop using them eventually, even if they develop a short-term dependence. In fact, abuse by non-white Americans and Americans with a college degree is rare, so it wasn't the opioids themselves that explained everything. Nor did obesity, another ubiquitous health problem that doesn't immediately lead to death. Instead of looking at the specific cause of death, Deaton and Case began to look at what context might enable the use of opioids (and firearms) to kill oneself, by either accidental overdose or suicide.[27]

The researchers coined the term "deaths of despair" to describe these mysterious deaths. They stem from a loss of jobs, loss of personal agency, and loss of faith that the situation will ever change. Eric Eyre, when discussing West Virginia, describes it as a loss of hope. Deaton and Case refer to the great French sociologist Émile Durkheim, who observed that suicide and despair were a result of one's life failing to meet one's basic expectations. For Deaton and Case, this captured what was going on for the uneducated, middle-aged, white working class, whose wages had stagnated since 1979, who were often deep in debt and unmarried at greater rates than their educated counterparts, and who had lost their sense of being part of the nation's social fabric.[28]

While opioids are only one of the conduits by which people consciously and accidentally killed themselves, these drugs made it really easy. Not everyone who dies of opioid addiction commits suicide, but desperate people in an uncontrolled market may find temporary respite in these drugs, and sometimes they take too much. This is the haunting story that has come to the surface through billions of dollars of lawsuits against Purdue Pharma, the maker of OxyContin. Patrick Radden Keefe's book *Empire of Pain* is a devastating account of the complicity of Purdue Pharma in the opioid crisis and the owning Sackler family's role. Purdue Pharma admitted to wrongdoing in two separate plea agreements with the Department of Justice. While the Sacklers have not been charged with anything, they separately agreed to pay $225 million to the Department of Justice.[29] The Sackler family also agreed to pay $6 billion to eight state attorneys general along with the District of Columbia in exchange for immunity from opioid lawsuits.[30] But high-profile lawsuits distract from the daily loss of life brought on by these drugs. According to the *Lancet*, from December 2019 to December 2020 opioid deaths were up almost 30 percent from the previous year.[31] While the

Sacklers have never admitted to any wrongdoing and have not been personally charged, Keefe argues that they do bear responsibility. In an interview with NPR, Keefe remarks, "I believe that the Sacklers do bear significant moral responsibility for having initiated—you know, not intentionally—right?—but carelessly a series of events that got us to where we are today."[32]

As important as the work on deaths of despair is, the phenomenon is not geographically ubiquitous but rather highly concentrated, specific to areas with high unemployment and a lack of financial and social resources. The depth of the damage caused by the opioid crisis is unfathomable, even if it has been limited to very particular types of communities. I began to wonder more broadly about the day-to-day existence, beyond the headline-grabbing tragedies, of people living in poor rural areas. I was curious about how they made sense of their situation.

I talk about it with my new friend Clay. When we first spoke, he was living near his mother in Kentucky and working at a coffee shop. When we speak about a year later, he is living in Ohio. He has just gotten a job at a record store down the street and will be

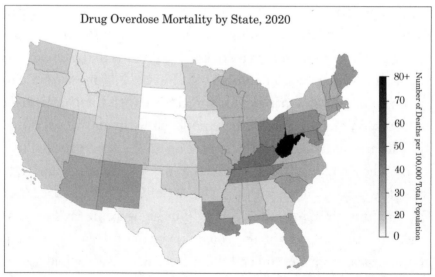

Source: Centers for Disease Control and Prevention, National Center for Health Statistics NCHS

starting work the very next day. As he was the first time we chatted, Clay is soft-spoken and kind. He is close with his mother, which is the reason he had stayed in rural Kentucky for so long. Clay tells me she was supportive of his move away for better opportunity.

At this point, I had reviewed all of the data that I share in this book, and I ask Clay about his thoughts on my findings. I rattle off statistics on Appalachia and the South, and I want to know how these numbers play out in real life, what it felt like to live in a region beset by economic decline. Clay is quiet for a moment. "I've grown up hearing something like ten of the top poorest counties in the nation are in Kentucky, including Clay County where I grew up," Clay says, offering a statistic he's shared with me before. "People don't really have [choices]. For instance, where I was living, I could go to a gas station for food, that means [the options for groceries are] what's on the aisles, that's chips or candy bars. . . . A fun cultural statement about Kentucky is how wonderful their gas station food is, but that doesn't make it healthy. I mean, there would be a forty-five-minute wait to get pizza and onion rings, but that's because there isn't a grocery store," Clay continues. "I could drive a twenty-five-mile road in the mountains to get to a grocery store. It's a very basic grocery store [with no fresh vegetables, just canned food]. If I drove another fifteen minutes, I might be able to make it to a Walmart, a dollar store with the same offerings. . . . If I drove another hour, I would get to a Kroger, where I could get vegetables." Clay then sighs. "So to get a complete diet is a pretty inaccessible thing."

I am haunted by Clay's description of the lack of resources and access to healthy food in his community. I keep thinking about the bright fluorescent lights of the gas station's convenience store, the standing in line to get food that would satiate hunger but not nourish, that to get a vegetable would require an hour's drive through the mountains. How different this world is from Instacart and farmers' markets and Whole Foods—the very trappings of urban affluence. I like junk food like everyone else, but it struck me that

Clay's community doesn't have the option to choose onion rings one night and a salad the next. We talk about food deserts in the city, of course—neighborhoods with very little produce and lacking any decent grocery store. We don't talk enough about rural food deserts. At least a city benefits from the clustering of all types of goods and services. It may be extremely difficult to get from one part of the city to another in search of healthy food, but it's feasible with public transportation and, in some instances, walking. In rural America, even such time-consuming trips are impossible.

While his story feels frustrating and desperate, Clay does not see it that way. "It's not difficult to see poverty when living in Kentucky, but the myth that that's everything available is not [accurate]." He is not despondent about his community by any measure. "Poverty doesn't necessarily mean you are without culture. This isn't to undermine the tragedy of poverty, but those things are true. I don't think it makes it an awful place to be.... It's not overlooked or unseen by those there. It's just hard to garner ways to successfully combat it." Clay points out that reading about an impoverished community from afar rarely gives an outsider a true sense of the place, and he observes that poverty can coexist with a positive cultural identity. "People just want to be seen as people, and I think that's a great way to combat poverty," Clay says, bringing tears to my eyes. "It's very easy to understand where you're from and the resilience and ability to be human."

I ask Clay what he means by community. I wonder if his version feels like mine, which includes the people who live on the same street and my collection of family and friends. But as I speak to Clay, it becomes clear that he has a much more broad and open definition that includes not just those he has selected but all who have entered his life. "I think mostly when I speak of community I mean of each other, and lives that connect, and anything we do with those lives and having one another," Clay says. "This isn't to push back on poverty, but rather the two-dimensional [view of poverty]. People have lives; they know their neighbors. If they didn't know [you], they wanted to know who you are. People have lives that are fully formed and three-dimensional, and there is a web between them called community."

I understood then what had been implicit in many of my conversations with rural Americans. Theirs was a version of community that transcended their class position. If you live in New York City or Los Angeles, your neighbors likely won't want to know you in the way that Clay speaks so warmly about his own community. The cities are stratified by class, and anonymity is the rule. Even if life can be difficult for some rural Americans, the nature of rural towns is that they provide a greater sense of community and class interaction, which manifests in religious organizations and the small-town phenomenon of everyone knowing everyone. These types of diverse community ties are often missing in cities, where people are siloed by socioeconomic group and organized by neighborhood.

I need to clarify that poverty is prevalent in Appalachia, and it is dire in some instances. That fact is not to be minimized. What I am trying to say is that, rather than fetishize or romanticize or apologize for or blame poverty, we must see that being poor economically and yet rich in social capital can coexist. Clay talks about the ordinary life of rural poverty. The community is ordinary too, but I think it is the best conduit for making change. What is absent in our societal conversations about rural America is often that fuller, more complex view that Clay describes.

Like Clay, other rural Americans described the importance of their close ties and community in navigating the hardships of their lives. Jane, the woman from rural Pennsylvania who lost her granddaughter to cystic fibrosis, spoke of how lucky she was simply to have people in her life who support her and give her joy, helping her through difficult periods. Many spoke of the role of the church in forming community. Some lived in the towns they grew up in and so had family nearby. None of these experiences of closeness could be explained by education or income. They had everything to do with a sense of community and friendship.

I remember how, after one of my calls with Shannon, she wrote me an unsolicited and kind email, expressing how happy she was that we had made contact. She wrote, "Before I had EVERYTHING money could buy. My parents had always taught me that as long as I had money I would be fine. They might not have actually said those words, but it is obvious from the direction I was given." Shannon then alluded to her diagnosis of breast cancer a few years back: "When cancer came, money could not buy me out of that problem. No amount of money could fix it." Shannon and Clay share a similar perspective on where money sits on their hierarchy of needs. Even amid poverty and struggle, they have found comfort through the community of their towns—not through psychotherapists or shopping or other trappings of urban life. This is not to discredit these other salves but to say that rural America finds its own way to get through the difficult times of being human.

I knew from the data that the extreme poverty Clay spoke of was not the majority experience in America. Where it does exist, it is everywhere, not just in rural areas. And I knew for the people I spoke with that poverty does not define their existence, even if for some it is always present. These were two pieces of information that made me hopeful. But I could never shake the stories Clay had told me about daily living in his part of Appalachia. Those gas station florescent lights kept coming back to me. Driving over an hour to get vegetables. I cannot pretend to understand the subjectivity of another person's existence but, to me, this is truly unacceptable in a country with so much to give, and where so much goes to waste.

IN MY DISCUSSIONS with rural Americans, I realized it didn't have to be deaths of despair that muted their existence and health. I looked at my friendship group in Los Angeles, London, and New

York, where everyone exercised most days, ate salads, and saw their doctors for every little malady. The ability to engage in any of these activities required money, time, information, and, most importantly, access. Rural America, for all of its surprising prosperity, didn't strike me as a place focused on preventative health—it just wasn't mentioned much in my interviews. Happy as people were, they had less than many of the people I knew in cities. I wanted to know how the daily living and health habits of rural Americans differed from urban America. I didn't know if and how they might matter, but I wanted to find out.

I began working with two economists at USC, Bryan Tysinger, a researcher at the Schaeffer Center for Health Policy and Economics, and Jack Chapel, a doctoral student in the economics department. Using data from the University of Michigan's Health and Retirement Study, Bryan and Jack are working on what they call "the forgotten middle," analyzing cohorts of Americans in their midfifties at various stages from 1994 to 2018.[33] They looked not just at deaths but rather at quality of life, using a measure called the quality-adjusted life expectancy, which they translate to quality life years. "You hear so much about deaths of despair and how that is causing this stagnation in life expectancy," Jack explained. "When you look closely it's not the driving story, even if it is a part of it." He continued, "There is this area-level inequality that is observable, [and] understanding the unevenness might help us understand what is driving the decline in life expectancy."

"My perspective is that deaths of despair are tragic," said Bryan. "But we also have a set of 'diseases of despair' that will have long-term consequences and impact many more individuals."

Jack agreed. "I don't think the deaths of despair work is wrong, but I think it's just part of the story for explaining the general stagnation of life expectancy and rise in health inequalities." He explained that a life expectancy divergence between the United States and Europe could be observed back in the 1980s. Around that time, geographic inequality in life expectancy also started to occur within the United States. As Jack put it, there are wider patterns that are exacerbating health inequality and pulling down health in the United States. "Deaths of despair are a worrying new part, but I think the long-term trends in general health, like rising obesity and slowing/reversing progress in heart disease, are just as important and we shouldn't forget about them."

When we first met, Bryan and Jack were working on what broad conditions and factors influenced these outcomes. As we talked about my book and discovered that we were all studying populations that had been "forgotten," we decided it would be useful to look more closely at comparisons between rural and urban America. Bryan and Jack looked at the current state of health for urban versus rural Americans. When they showed me the results, I didn't like what I saw. In 1994, the gap between urban and rural America was indiscernible. By 2018, however, rural folks had between one and two fewer quality life years than their urban counterparts, and the gap was growing at a faster pace. While this may be partially explained by concentrations of mortality in opioid-afflicted areas, due to confidentiality issues, it is impossible to untangle the specific locations of individuals. Bryan and Jack also looked at pain, smoking, education, and chronic conditions like diabetes and heart disease, and they compared these variables across geographies. On all measures, the urban and rural gap was widening, and the rural population was doing worse.

Bryan and Jack wondered if that could be changed. One of the unique aspects of their analysis is that they can simulate what outcomes might look like if we could change some of the inputs—that is, change people's lives a little bit, all other things being equal. They set up a series of alternative scenarios or simulations by looking at health outcomes if certain variables were altered slightly. In particular, they wanted to see what health outcomes for rural Americans might look like if their starting point (for example, the level of obesity or education) was the same as urban folks. In reality, these two groups have very different starting points. But if they were the same, would their quality life years be equal as well? First, Bryan and Jack looked at if simply living in rural America in older age could explain the reduction in quality life years. They found that rural living had no meaningful impact; it wasn't geography that was driving different health outcomes. Then, Bryan and Jack evened out the chronic conditions people had in midlife so that the urban and rural populations had exactly the same distribution. Although this had a growing impact over time, it did not come close to fully explaining the total gap in quality-adjusted life expectancy.

Bryan and Jack went through all of the health factors that were different and tried to find which ones, if changed, would have the biggest impact on rural outcomes. They found two. Even though body mass index (BMI) is more or less distributed the same in rural and urban America, the peak rural BMI is higher by a few points than urban America's, which may make a difference in health outcomes. However, BMI on its own does not create a large effect, only improving quality life years by a few months at most. Nor does smoking, which is also significantly higher in rural America. But simulating the combination of the same BMI and smoking rate in urban and rural America closes the gap in their quality life years by almost a year. What this means is that if rural females smoked at the same rate and had the same BMI distribution as their urban counterparts, the life expectancies of these two groups would be the same. If rural males smoked equal to their urban counterparts and had the same BMI distribution, they would close the gap with urban males by 50 percent.

With both of these issues, much comes down to prevention. It's easier to stop someone from starting to smoke than it is to convince them to stop at age fifty-three. More practically, Clay and his community need options that don't just include processed and fried food from the gas station. Access to fresh food will help people stay within a healthy BMI their whole lives.

Bryan and Jack found something else interesting: that education offered something bigger than a college degree. When they created an alternative scenario where college education rates for non-Hispanic whites in rural America were the same as in urban America, the quality life years gap closed by almost a year for males and six months for females. Bryan, Jack, and I talked a lot about this finding. BMI and smoking rates were obvious; I was unsurprised that if we could reduce them for the rural population, we would see better health outcomes. But education in and of itself didn't make sense. I couldn't believe that it had a greater effect than minimizing pain and chronic conditions, yet it did. In fact, education had a greater health benefit than quitting smoking for men, and a bigger effect than only reducing BMI for both men and women. What could be made of this finding? "I've been thinking about people's different reactions to the pandemic and how the rural and urban plays out there, how education plays out there," Bryan says when I ask him. "And it seems to come down to trust. Trust in experts plays a lot into health, more than I thought it did. It's not when you go get your BA, you learn how to eat well. We learn that in fourth grade. But maybe when you get your BA, you learn how to value expertise on those matters." It became clear to me that this particular form of cultural capital drove decision-making about masks during the pandemic, about exercise, about food moderation, and even about those vegetables that were so out of reach for Clay's community.

A college degree wasn't driving these results so much as shaping one's perspective on other life experiences. The pandemic became a new lens to understand what seemed to be a rural wariness toward science: the science of masking, the science of vaccines, and the science of virus transmission.[34] We weren't the only ones who'd arrived at this conclusion.[35] Economists David Blanchflower and Andrew Oswald find that, from 1993 to 2019, the share of the US population in "extreme stress" rose from 3.6 percent to 6.4 percent overall. Yet among low-educated, middle-aged white people, the proportion of those in extreme stress jumped from 4.8 percent to 11.5 percent.[36] Related, Deaton and Case find that Americans with less than a bachelor's degree are far more likely to experience pain, despair, and emotional distress and commit suicide than those who are educated.[37] Conversely, scholars at the National Bureau of Economic Research suggest that increases in education levels across the general population have contributed to 7.5 percent of increased longevity since 1940.[38] As they write, "The benefits of education, as shown by a large body of literature, can go beyond its labor market returns."[39] Or as Deaton and Case remark, "We are also not primarily concerned with the (contested) question of whether education directly causes better health. Our own causal story is not about the treatment effects of education on an individual but about the broader social and economic processes in which the BA degree is increasingly used to separate people."[40] In short, higher education provides more than just knowledge; it offers many benefits that extend beyond degree qualifications. Perhaps most importantly, it shapes one's perspective on experts, science, and trust in authority. Like Bryan said, we learn about healthy eating in fourth grade, but what matters is the ongoing, fundamental belief that medical advice on food and exercise is credible.

I wasn't sure what to do with Bryan and Jack's findings on the importance of education to health outcomes, particularly since my data suggested many people in rural America didn't want to be a part of the professional-managerial class and were doing very well without a college degree. This is not to say they wouldn't do better with one—they might with regard to income—but it was clear many people did not seek to be in the top 10 percent, 5 percent, or 1 percent. They didn't want to be masters of the universe. But the health numbers troubled me a lot. Access to good food was the story for some. For others it was understanding the health risks of smoking and the benefits of going for a walk a few times a week. We know what needs to change, but what remains a great source of concern for me is how to change it. Some of it, as Bryan points out, is about whom we trust and what we believe in. Part of these health discrepancies, which may be linked to education, come down to differences in culture and value systems.

If experts and meritocrats want rural America to embrace healthier choices, they must learn how to better communicate with rural Americans and understand what their desires and fears are. For me, that's the biggest issue plaguing America today. Our understanding of who rural people are and what they want is painfully insufficient. Most rural Americans are not dying of deaths of despair. The communities that are facing this plight deserve our urgent and acute focus. But for the vast majority of rural Americans who suffer chronic conditions and practice unhealthy habits—whether they smoke too much, are overweight, or are uninformed about preventative health measures—we need a different intervention.

While deaths of despair and lack of preventative health care are not mutually exclusive, they are two different problems facing rural America. From a policy perspective, respecting urban and rural areas' different forms of cultural capital would do a lot of good. Rural Americans wary of scientific authority will not embrace technocratic expertise if it is fed to them in a condescending manner. People who are scared of vaccines or who are unaware of the virtues of daily exercise or who have lost all hope deserve our empathy and understanding, not our scorn. We need to treat rural Americans as fellow human beings, worthy of dignity. Giving that grace to people so different from us isn't always easy—and it can be uncomfortable, as I've come to find out—but it is the crucial point of connection that erases the "us" and the "them."

4

COGNITIVE DISSONANCE

The test of a first-rate intelligence is the ability to hold two opposed ideas in mind at the same time and still retain the ability to function.

—F. Scott Fitzgerald[1]

I was wondering where you got to!" Shannon exclaims when I call her in late July. We had last spoken a few months before in May 2021. I smile, touched by her concern and interest in my well-being. I am already looking forward to talking to her again. Every time I email Shannon, she responds that she is so happy I am writing a book about America. She promises she will pray to God that I find the time to write, acknowledging my three young children and blessing me for the work I am doing. Shannon's email signature always ends with a series of proverbs and Bible verses, including one that she reiterates through the course of our conversations: "Commit your work to the Lord and your plans will be established."

At this point, I had hoped I would be in Kentucky interviewing Shannon face-to-face. I had grown fond of her tinkling laughter, her drawl, her emphatic "absolutely" and "absolutely not" to various questions. Unfortunately, in July 2021, as coronavirus infection rates were climbing again nationally, the vaccination rate in Clay

County, Kentucky, was just 30 percent, and Shannon herself was not vaccinated. It seemed safer to just check in by phone.

Shannon is an avid Trump supporter who questions the results of the 2020 election and believes there is an "army rising up" to bring Trump, or at least what he stands for, back to the forefront of American politics. "I'm kind of a conspiracy person," she admits during our first call when I ask her whether she feels left behind with regard to national politics. She is angry that Trump was banned from various social media apps and feels he has been misrepresented and mistreated by the media. I ask her if she hopes President Trump will run again in 2024. "Hoping for more than that," she says matter-of-factly. "You know what's happening in Arizona?" she asks, referring to the ongoing recount of ballots. "If fraud is found, then what?" (The conclusion of the recount showed no proof of fraud.)[2]

When I ask Shannon whether she believes in climate change, she replies, "Absolutely not." When I ask her if she supports gay marriage, she replies, "No. I live by the word of God." When I ask her about getting the Covid vaccine, her response is, "Absolutely not." When I ask her about immigration, she says, "If it's legal, it's great. If it's not, it's terrible," comparing illegal immigration to just walking into someone's house without knocking. She goes on, "Well, it may seem harsh, but I have a wall around my house. The pope, who says there should be no wall, I couldn't see him. There's a wall [around him]. If people who say they don't want a wall believe that, then they should take down their walls and unlock their doors."

When I call Shannon again, we circle back to a few of these issues. I am particularly interested in discussing her stance on marriage equality. Her reasoning for not supporting gay marriage has to do with her strict observance of scripture. "I am completely against it," Shannon says. Well, okay, I say, acknowledging the role of the Bible in her view, but I push further. Shannon has shared that she's been divorced twice and is on her third marriage, and I point out that is certainly not allowed if you're adhering strictly to the Bible.

Her anti–gay marriage stance feels à la carte to me, and I say so. Shannon laughs, taking my challenge in stride. "I'm saying that as a divorced person. I've been divorced two times, and I would be divorced three times if not for God. We were married January 2013, and by June 2013 I was ready for my third divorce!" Shannon and her husband had a huge fight over whether he would attend a family reunion, and when he declined she felt certain they were on the path to separation. Then she talked to God. "I drove three hours [to the family reunion], and God and I were arguing the whole time. God won the fight. [As the Bible says], you submit to your husband."

Shannon explains that her two divorces were prior to her becoming deeply religious, and that her religion is what keeps her married. "You should submit to your husband," she reiterates. There is consistency in this response, but it still doesn't jell for me. Shannon strikes me as a kind and fairly reasonable person, so I want to really understand the root of her position. She explains, "I have many friends who are gay, but it doesn't matter. We have to do it God's way." I find this part of our discussion particularly difficult because of my own pro–gay marriage beliefs and also because public opinion regarding same-sex marriage has become more and more accepting in recent years. Shannon is truly in the minority. More perplexing is that contact with others usually enables us to become more tolerant of their differences. Shannon clearly knows gay people, calls them her friends, and likes them. I remain unable to resolve this part of our conversation.

During this part of our exchange, I agree with Shannon quite literally 0 percent of the time. I support marriage equality completely. I have been vaccinated against Covid-19 and vacillate between anger and concern toward those who choose not to do so. I do not equate undocumented immigration with an open door to my house, because I feel those poor people are desperate and running to the United States for help. I believe President Biden won the election fair and square (and I voted for him). Shannon embodies the opposite of my worldview. If you wrote her beliefs down on paper with no association to her, I would find her views misguided and intolerant. And yet I like her. A lot. We should have nothing to say to each other that is relatable. But I find it no struggle at all to connect with her, and I truly value her as a human being.

At one point, Shannon says to me, "You live in California, and I feel we are already friends." I feel that way too. My conscience is confused. My heart likes Shannon. When I see her name in my inbox, I smile. When we get on the phone, I could talk to her for hours. You might think I like Shannon because she's sweet and funny, which she is, and that charisma can lure us into liking people we shouldn't, whatever that means. Nevertheless, my affection and admiration for Shannon go deeper than her charm and our general rapport. Yet I feel significant discord about her anti–gay marriage, anti-vaccine, and climate denial stances, to name only a few. I don't know where to put my feelings about her, partially because the media we each consume would imply that we shouldn't get along. From the pages of the *New Yorker* or *New York Times*, my favorite news outlets, you would think people like Shannon are exactly the problem with this country: anti-vaxxer, right wing, anti-intellectual. But these caricatures do not align with what I know as a researcher, a mother, a person on this planet—that Shannon is full of contradictions, but the truth is, we all are.

I WOULD ACTUALLY BUY a couple of things. An orphanage to put on my property," Shannon says. "I would buy a home called Potter's Wheel for men who graduate from rehab, a place for them to go. And for anyone who has had teeth removed due to drug addiction, I'd buy them new teeth. On my vision board, I have [a note]: 'Buy teeth.' Because not having teeth keeps them from smiling." Shannon's response is to the question I ask all of my interviewees: *If you had all the money in the world, what would you buy?* From the dozens of people I've interviewed, answers range from a new car to a new house to a ranch with llamas. Some people's ideas are vague; others don't really know how to respond. Some are materialistic; others reveal deep dreams. A woman from Berkeley says, "Lots of housing for others." One young man said he'd buy his mom a house. A seventy-four-year-old woman from Pennsylvania simply said, "I don't want money. I have what I need." But Shannon's reply overwhelms me with emotion, which I swallow best I can. It is the specificity of her dream, so concise and immediate and detailed. She has clearly thought about these plans a lot, and they are beautiful and reveal beauty in her.

The next time I call Shannon, I ask her for specifics on her dream, and she elaborates. "These people, they can't have their teeth fixed. We have a lot of drug addiction here and a lot of kids who are neglected [as a result]. Just want to give them their home. I hope the Lord helps me achieve this dream." She explains that before she discovered God, she was making very good money as a pharmacist: "I had all the money in the world, swimming pool, fancy car, fingernails, a thousand pairs of shoes. I was not happy. I was sad and depressed. Then when I got cancer and I called out to God and he answered and called on me to be a stay-at-home mom and take care of others. That's when I became happy, when I started taking care of others. That brings such joy and peace and things money can't buy." She goes on, "Now we are living in a modular home. Some people call it a trailer. We bought land for people so we can build an orphanage and a place for recovery and we are waiting for God to open those doors." Shannon then talks about her work with Project Daris, the local organization she cofounded to help schoolchildren stay away from drugs, and Celebrate Recovery, the Christian addiction recovery group she runs locally.

After our chat, Shannon sends me a Facebook photo of young wrists held out, proudly displaying colorful Project Daris bracelets. Shannon also sends me a video of her husband, daughter, and herself singing as a part of a virtual Celebrate Recovery event. Immaculately groomed, Shannon is wearing a soft, pink-and-white sweater and several glittery necklaces, one of which holds a giant cross made of crystals. Her kid, wearing a long-sleeved T-shirt with a jack-o'-lantern cutout, is adorable. Her husband, hair in a ponytail, with a small goatee, is off to the side playing guitar. Shannon's long, shiny, dark auburn hair sways and her silvery gray eyes sparkle as she sings. Prior to this point, I had no idea what she looked like and had only a vague sketch of a person in my mind. Shannon is both nothing like and exactly what I expected all at once.

I think about my friend Shannon a lot. On my jogs around the hills of my Los Angeles neighborhood, during dinner conversations with family and friends, and sometimes staring out my home office window. I often sit in silence trying to find the through line in her contradictions. My cognitive dissonance lies in the fact that I feel removed from Shannon's cultural universe and at times deeply disconcerted by her views, and yet I am completely connected to her as a human being. It feels to me, in the current political climate, that to like someone different, perhaps even someone who holds antithetical views to my own, is no longer acceptable.

As I thought about our conversations and my feelings toward Shannon, I realized that what I was really questioning was not how I felt about her but why I was so shocked that I felt warmly about her despite her politics. Since when did disliking another person's politics supersede loving their kindness, their generosity, and their sense of humor? These character traits are far deeper and more important than their views of presidential races or whether they watch Fox News or Rachel Maddow. The idea that political differences are the most important divide is essentially orchestrated by parts of our media. Left-leaning outlets have depicted conservative America as stereotypically backward and out of touch, even joking that their skepticism toward liberal values is akin to being scared of extraterrestrial invasion.[3] Conservative news sources are equally guilty of creating a stereotype of coastal urbanites as out-of-touch elites, fueling skepticism toward vaccinations, blaming crime on the Democrats running cities, and minimizing the very real grievances of minorities that have been championed by Black Lives Matter and other social justice movements.[4] But why are we so susceptible to this messaging? Why would we "other" another person, let alone a whole demographic, geography, or political party? Surely we can find more in common than not.

THE OTHER IS everything that lies outside of the self," wrote Edward Said in his groundbreaking and controversial book *Orientalism*. "Familiar" is "us"; "other" is "strange," argued Said, and thus maligned and ostracized. Published in 1978, *Orientalism* challenged the West's view of the East as primitive, illogical, zealous, and lesser than Western culture and society. In Oriental studies (that is, the study of the East), scholars endorsed and exaggerated the differences between Europe and "the West" versus the Orient and "the East," Said argued. "Arabs, for example, are thought of as camel-riding, terroristic, hook-nosed, venal lechers whose undeserved wealth is an affront to real civilization," he writes. "Always there lurks the assumption that although the Western consumer belongs to a numerical minority, he is entitled either to own or to expend (or both) the majority of the world resources. Why? Because he, unlike the Oriental, is a true human being."[5] Said's work was not without its critics, who found his account of Western hegemony to be careless and geopolitically inaccurate. The fact that the Ottoman Empire had ruled and posed a legitimate threat to Western Europe was in itself an indication to some critics that Said's portrayal of East and West was not entirely accurate.[6] The great public intellectual Bernard Lewis accused Said of politicizing the study of the Middle East and unnecessarily creating a negative association with the word "Orient."[7]

Despite the criticism, *Orientalism* put into sharp relief the damaging effects of establishing any group as the "other." I read the book in graduate school, and its notion of how society constructs a view of the "other" remained with me as a powerful lens through which to challenge my own ideas about people who think, look, and speak differently than me. In light of the recent perception of a divided America, this frame has become an especially useful tool. Not so long ago, I was reading an interview between the sociologist Robert Wuthnow and *Vox* media journalist Sean Illing.[8] Wuthnow's book *The Left Behind*, which details the resentment of rural America but also illuminates its diversity and multitude of perspectives, had recently been published. I'd read the book, and felt that he was trying to understand the disenfranchisement of rural America and the anger he was finding in some of his interviews. At the time, I had begun doing my own interviews, and I was not encountering the rage that Wuthnow documents. However, I knew we were coming at our work from the same place: an effort to understand without judgment.

Throughout the *Vox* interview, Illing grills Wuthnow about the intentions of the people he'd written about in his book. At one point, Illing says, "It seems to me that many of these people haven't been left behind; they've chosen not to keep up. But the sense of victimization appears to overwhelm everything else," to which Wuthnow deflects, "I make it very clear in the book that this is largely a choice. It's not as though these people are desperate to leave but can't....Maybe they're making the best of a bad situation, but they choose to stay....In that sense, they believe, quite correctly, that they're the ones who stayed in these small towns while young people—and really the country as a whole—moved on." Later Illing appears to mock a woman in Wuthnow's book who laments America's moral decline and misguidedly uses "the government intervening" in spanking one's child as her example. "Am I supposed to take this seriously?" Illing asks. A few beats later, he says, "I guess I just don't know how to respond to these sorts of complaints," again seeming to belittle rural America's concerns.[9]

Reading and rereading this interview, I was struck by what I felt was Illing's complete lack of even trying to understand rural Americans from their vantage point, despite Wuthnow's many delicate efforts to humanize his subjects. "It's important to understand where they're coming from and not simply dismiss them as disconnected or out of touch with reality," Wuthnow says at one point. "If they feel threatened by racial diversity or homosexuality or abortion or whatever it might be, I want to understand why they feel that way." As Said writes in *Orientalism*, "The more one is able to leave one's cultural home, the more easily is one able to judge it, and the whole world as well, with the spiritual detachment and generosity necessary for true vision. The more easily, too, does one assess oneself and alien cultures with the same combination of intimacy and distance."[10]

As I try to understand how society makes sense of and resolves differences across cultures, I need some help. I meet with my colleague Peter Redfield, chair of the anthropology department at USC. I explain this tension between the two versions of Shannon and how I'm struggling to reconcile them in my head. "Most ordinary people are full of cognitive dissonance," he laughs. "Only academics get upset about it." I laugh too. Peter may be right, but the discord I feel will not be unique to me, and it has become increasingly problematic in America.

The liberal media and elite social groups, I'm confident, would relegate Shannon to the "other," using coded language to depict a stereotyped and oversimplified version of a rural, conservative American.[11] By doing this, we lose sight of the extent to which we create and exacerbate divides rather than seek to understand commonalities. We are not, as Arlie Hochschild writes in her book *Strangers in Their Own Land*, climbing the "empathy wall." I am not so sure most people in my world would even bother to get to know the kind, generous

Shannon if they first learned about her political and cultural beliefs. They certainly wouldn't climb any walls to understand her.

Anthropologists have found that different societies at different times have more similarities than differences, even if it wouldn't seem so at first blush. As UCLA anthropologist Akhil Gupta writes, "In what way is the daily routine of commuters who leave their home at dawn and return at sunset any less rhythmic than the circular path traversed by the Nuer shepherd taking his herd out to pasture?"[12] Gupta posits that we construct ways—in this instance, Western and Eastern conceptions of time—to establish differences between self and "other." He argues that these differences could easily be inverted into a similarity: the observation that both Eastern and Western societies construct a cyclical mechanism by which to measure time (the Western clock versus the Eastern rising and setting sun). But often we ignore the common themes of human experience, falling prey to what Sigmund Freud termed the "narcissism of small difference." As he argued, we focus on and amplify differences, thus feeding into feuds and boundaries, in particular ethno-nationalism.[13]

This framework for understanding how we construct and vilify difference brings me back to what's going on in America. My cognitive dissonance is a choice, even if it presently feels out of my control. It is my own worldview that stops me from being able to make peace with the different aspects of Shannon; she feels consistent to herself. I also reflect on how my beliefs might be viewed by Shannon, a devout Catholic who lives her life by the Bible. To her, my support of marriage equality, my acceptance of divorce if two people feel it is necessary, and my rejection of the existence of hell must seem heretical and morally wrong. I cannot imagine believing in what Shannon believes, but surely she cannot imagine believing my truths either.

I started to wonder why we have created these different territories and cultural boundaries. On the one hand, America is hardly a cohesive, single culture, even though we are joined by our flag, language, democracy, and popular foods—whether hot dogs or pizza or Coca-Cola or Heinz tomato ketchup. But in creating the distinctions of "urban" and "rural" and "coastal elite" and "hillbilly," or even by exaggerating the differences between "Democrat" and "Republican," we may draw unnecessary boundaries. As Ezra Klein writes in his book *Why We're Polarized*, we have cohered into tribes of people with whom we identify culturally, economically, socially, and demographically, eschewing those who are different. Klein argues that this process is almost Darwinian, that we care more about winning and sticking it to our political enemies than about the greater good or even our own tribe's outcomes.[14] We create territories that may not be necessary. We focus on the Freudian small differences rather than the things most of us believe in: democracy, freedom, equality, family—the values that were mentioned by whomever I talked to, from San Francisco to rural Missouri.

Why are we not questioning the need to create such separation in the first place? In a world of instant communication, social media, and online news, we have the ability to find information about and from all political and religious systems at any time. My friend Shannon and I can find roughly the same information on the internet. As Shannon rattled off the names of public figures to whom she listened, I was able to look them up simultaneously. We can share the same world and information, if we choose. As Akhil Gupta and Stanford anthropologist James Ferguson write, "The irony of these times, however, is that as actual places and localities become ever more blurred and indeterminate, ideas of culturally and ethnically distinct places become perhaps even more salient."[15] What we see, then, is how our media and by extension our tribes construct an "other" that is both spatially and temporally distant.[16] Rather than using these instant forms of communication and information to find commonalities, they become easy ways to exacerbate differences.

Through easy stereotypes of "red America," "latte liberals," or "Orwellian liberal cities," the media—whether CNN or *Breitbart*—is able to draw these boundaries and allow each of us to connect to what the political scientist Benedict Anderson called "imagined communities."[17] When Anderson first coined the term, he focused on the way nationalism, across many countries and cultures, was established through a shared sense of belonging and the role of the newspaper in the formation of this sense of identity. In the case of the United States, these communities are imagined because we do not personally know most other Americans. Yet through, for example, the Super Bowl, baseball, the national anthem, Fourth of July, and summer barbecues, we establish a shared sense of being. The media has long been a space for establishing community and understanding our collective progress and sense of national identity.[18] But today, that community is more fractured: Fox News rallies around conservative culture, the *New York Times* around liberal culture. NASCAR is conservative and watched by more rural fans, HBO by liberal urbanites. Today's imagined communities are not shared nationally but rather divide our nation into a series of fractured cultural worlds of "self" and "other."

MORE PRACTICALLY, "OTHERNESS" can become the root of prejudice. Those who are different but with whom we do not mingle or engage become people we judge. In a 1946 *Journal of Psychology* article, psychologists Gordon Allport and Bernard Kramer set out to find the "roots of prejudice." "But it is neither the benevolent minds of the unprejudiced fifth of the population, nor the pathology of the rioter, that interests us in the present investigation," they write. "We are concerned rather with the correlates of prejudice in a rank-and-file group of college students.... It has been said that prejudice stems from insecurity, from religiousness (or its lack), from early traumatic experiences, from poor intercultural education."[19] Studying several hundred students from Dartmouth, Harvard, and Radcliffe, Allport and Kramer find that prejudice

against others is a social response. "The young child undoubtedly
starts his life without prejudice," the authors observe, "and during
pre-school years seems almost incapable of fixating hostility upon
any group as a whole." Yet by elementary school, students attain a
"great bulk of prejudiced attitudes." Allport and Kramer conclude
that many Americans hold some form of racial, religious, or "other
group" prejudices. While the authors make a whole host of asser-
tions based on their research, they ultimately conclude that people
are not even fully cognizant of how prejudiced they are (i.e., implicit
bias) and are often unaware of the root of their judgments.[20]

Given the dissatisfying conclusions drawn from this study, it
is unsurprising that Gordon Allport went on to find out how, if we
cannot be self-aware about the source of our prejudice, we might
learn to mitigate it. In 1954, he published *The Nature of Prejudice*, one
of the most influential books in social psychology ever written. Allport argues that we stereotype and make assumptions about others
as way to be efficient, and that on some level this process is a part of
"ordinary cognitive function," even if our stereotypes are not based
in fact or personal experience.[21] He proposes the "intergroup contact theory," which, he believed, would mitigate prejudice under certain conditions.[22] If people with differing and potentially opposing
views, religions, or lifestyles came together equally, with common
goals, cooperation, and support by others, they could reduce stereotyping and prejudice. If prejudice is about generalizations based
on only partial information, then contact would provide more data,
reducing fear and anxiety and encouraging empathy. Some critics
of Allport's theory have argued that contact only increases hostility,
and others have said that those who benefit from and seek out contact with different people are already less biased to begin with.[23] But
overall the book has stood the test of time as a framework for reducing prejudice and stereotyping.[24] We can become more tolerant people, regardless of whether we come from intolerant backgrounds, if
we try to meet people somewhere along the empathy wall.

Getting close to people is how we begin to climb that wall. That walk toward an "other" is how I got to know a version of Shannon that didn't fit the stereotype. The more I spoke to her, the more I liked her, and the more our differences fell into the background. While Allport's study had great implications for race, the overall mechanisms he identifies are applicable to all forms of prejudice. In our current political and cultural milieu, this effort could not be more urgent. Our imagined communities have become a way to stereotype others and become stereotypes ourselves. While many Americans tend to be more in the middle, the political climate is polarized and thus produces polarized depictions of various parts of our country. We have the snotty coastal elites and the uneducated and intolerant rural voters. The heartland is for Trump in some versions of the story, and distinctly not for Trump in others.[25]

Recent political science research puts these stereotypes in sharp relief. "Affective polarization" is the phenomenon by which people who possess true "out-party animus" embrace policies and behaviors primarily because they are in direct opposition to the political group they dislike.[26] This phenomenon was clearly evident as we watched various states and localities respond to the Covid-19 pandemic.[27] Despite the fact that Covid-19 is a terrifying disease that has killed a million Americans regardless of their political affiliation, it became a leitmotif in the supposed culture wars. So much so that highly politically polarized people (in this case, Republicans) did not engage in preventative behavior to stop the spread of Covid-19, even if cases were climbing in their locality.[28] On national TV, Fox News's most popular host, Tucker Carlson, with a viewership of 2.9 million people, accused the director of the National Institute of Allergy and Infectious Diseases, Dr. Anthony Fauci, of "creating Covid."[29] (He also called the Biden door-to-door vaccine program "the biggest scandal of his lifetime.")[30] When President Biden instituted a national mask mandate for federal buildings and public transit, it was red states such as Florida and Tennessee that barred local mask requirements. The increase in Covid-19 mortality in Republican over Democratic counties only occurred after vaccinations were widely available and in counties with low vaccination rates.[31] The most vaccinated US cities are liberal enclaves like San Francisco, Portland, and Seattle.[32]

Another example of this phenomenon is the pushback to Black Lives Matter with the rallying cry of "blue lives matter." Critics have argued that it is evidence of conservative and far-right groups rejecting the premise of the Black Lives Matter movement. "Who doesn't think cops' lives matter?" writes one angry *Los Angeles Times* reader. "Only criminals and some on the far, far left. Black Lives Matter is about the disproportional violence African Americans meet at the hands of the police. 'Blue lives matter' implies that Black people do not care about cops."[33] In *HuffPost*, USC professor and chaplain Jonathan Russell writes, "Blue lives have always mattered, present and past. Their experience of social space is (again, for the most part) one of profound privilege and deferential treatment....It is profoundly misrepresentative and disrespectful to develop an analogous hashtag as if blue lives have an analogous experience of social life in America as Black lives have."[34]

Part of the disproportionate reaction to those on the other end of the political and cultural spectrum has to do with our perceptions of the "other." When it comes to American politics, our sense of the "other" is misplaced and misconstrued on even the most basic facts. In a 2018 study of political stereotypes, the researchers found that people think 32 percent of Democrats are LGBT, when in reality that number is just 6 percent. People surveyed think that 38 percent of Republicans earn over $250,000, when the figure is close to 2 percent. The authors conclude, "People's perceptions of party composition contain large, systematic errors. In particular, people overestimate the share of party-stereotypical groups in the parties. On average, respondents overestimated these groups' prevalence by 342%."[35] While people tend to misconstrue members of their own party, the biggest gap between stereotype and reality is associated with the other party. But stereotyping is not the same as hate, and it is in this space that I feel we can actually make a change for the better for all of society.

Polarization needs to be seen for what it is. There might be two polarized political groups out there in America, and there are people who are angry and hate the "other"—whoever that is for them. However, most Americans are political moderates, and my experiences talking to dozens of Americans for many hours shone a bright light on this truth. Political scientists have sought to understand what polarization really means. In a recent article, two researchers studied the amplified hostility between Democrats and Republicans to find out the extent to which this applies to the typical citizen. They found that moderates feel pretty frustrated with both parties, but they do not feel a greater divisiveness or distance from either one—a true case of the mean obfuscating the mode. Polarization increases the average distance people feel from Democrats and Republicans, but modal data indicates that the typical person actually feels the same as ever about each party. The outliers raise the average.[36] In another article, scholars found that the real division in this country was between those who care about politics and those who don't. Most Americans—that is, 80 to 85 percent—don't follow politics or only engage casually. The great polarization is occurring with just 15 to 20 percent of the population.

In fact, most people don't easily fit a Democratic or Republican mold. Many people in both parties care about increasing hourly wages. While the moral decline of America has often been associated with Republicans, the more casually engaged Democrats name it as an important problem for the country. These results square pretty well with General Social Survey data, which indicates that the divisions between Americans on major social, government, and economic issues are far less than the concerns and beliefs we have in common. These findings hold up with my own experience. Most people I spoke to talked far less about animus toward a political party and far more about the issues they cared about and their broader worries. Poring over pages and pages of my interview transcripts, "hate" and "polarization" are not words that came up to describe anyone's feelings.

Which brings me back to Shannon. Shannon is not homophobic. Homophobia, if you look it up in the dictionary, is dislike or prejudice toward gay people. Those are not Shannon's feelings. While most people I spoke with were supportive of gay marriage, those who were not didn't speak in a language of hatred or fear. They are following the truth as they see it written in the Bible.

Others who were wary of government involvement in racial issues (whether social justice or affirmative action) were not racist. As Hochschild argues, racism is about hierarchy and believing you are better than someone else because of their skin color. As was the case with Hochschild's interviews, my interviewees never expressed superiority over others due to race or gender or sexuality. Many were swift to say America is a deeply unequal place that discriminates against Black people, even if they were uneasy about government involvement in rectifying these issues (they tended to express suspicion in many matters of government intervention). I cannot say that this conclusion is satisfactory or makes me any less inclined to keep pushing Shannon and others to clarify their perspective. When hearing these more detached views, I often thought that it was hard for those in rural America who live in almost entirely white communities to fully understand the vast discrimination that many minorities face in this country. For many rural Americans, these stories are abstract headlines, far removed from their homogenously white towns. I thought many times how painful it would be for a person of color to hear the perspective of those who are so distant, both racially and geographically, from some of the most pressing racial issues in our country. This felt like an important place for rural Americans to also climb the empathy wall.

I do hold on to an important fact: most people do not come from bad places; they come from different places. Their point of origin and truth may be different from mine or yours. Sometimes it is helpful to remember that all of us want empathy and the benefit of the doubt, so we might start with giving it to appreciate how important it is to receive. I never had to ask Shannon; she was always quick to give the liberal Californian professor all the benefit of the doubt I could ever ask for. After our first conversation, Shannon wrote me, unsolicited: "I know you were busy trying to type and didn't really get to speak as much as you could have but I could tell you are a very kind person. Thank you for your time today! God bless you and I look forward to our next meeting!!"

WHY DO WE have such distorted views of each other's opinions and beliefs, if in reality many of us have fairly understandable political perspectives? One reason that a number of my interviewees mentioned was the media. As Debbie, a seventy-four-year-old woman from Pennsylvania, put it, "I think some of the newscasters make people more divided." Another woman remarked, "Because of my South Dakota roots, I think [rural folks] for the most part are good and hardworking. I don't think they are exposed to what city dwellers are exposed to, and so depending on their [rural folks'] news source they are misinformed." These comments illuminated something I already saw myself. A scroll through any news outlet reveals an awful lot of polarization. A hop between Fox News and the *New York Times* feels like a jump between two different versions of reality. The opinion sections are wildly different, but so is the reportage of important events of the day.

The public is also ricocheting from a twenty-four-hour news cycle dependent on constant crises and dramatic developing events, many of which are steeped in a polarized narrative. Blazing headlines proclaim that Americans see a "major" threat to democracy. After the January 6 attack on the Capitol, increasing numbers of public intellectuals shrilly discussed the end of democracy in liberal newspapers, despite the fact that most Democrats are feeling positive about this country. Case in point: at the same time that two-thirds of Americans think democracy is under threat, a full 87 percent of Democrats and 47 percent of all Americans feel the country is going in the right direction—a positive outlook not seen in almost fifteen years. And yet the headline of a July 2021 PBS article about this survey does not highlight the positive outlook.[37] One needs to read half the article to get to this news. Rather, the two-thirds who feel there is a threat to democracy lead the story.

Not unrelated, despite the fact that it is assumed and reported that many Republicans supported the January 6 insurrection, a recent survey by the political scientists Yanna Krupnikov and John Barry Ryan found that conservative support for the riot depended on the order of the survey questions.[38] If January 6 was asked about first, 23 percent of Republicans expressed support. If asked after a question on protests in general, just 5 percent of Republicans supported the insurrection. In both instances, Republican support is strongly in the minority. This survey indicates that conservatives overall supported the protests far less than popular perception suggests, and yet the negative reputation remains. In fact, as Krupnikov and Ryan show, setting up January 6 in comparison to other social protests makes Republicans far less willing to support it.

Regardless of the headlines or how people respond to inflexible or biased questions asked by pollsters, when we actually sit down and talk to Americans, most of them are far more preoccupied with their own lives than worried about the state of a democracy that is, despite all of the anxiety, actually working. As I write this, many observers lament pandemic fatigue as the reason why Americans can't find the will to care about these big issues. Americans are worried about getting sick, grieving someone they have lost to Covid-19, concerned about the economy, depressed, and burned out. All of this is factually correct, and yet I also believe that many Americans don't meaningfully see the threat to democracy that they are told to be scared of—except when they are point-blank asked by an anonymous pollster and need to pick something, and "no concern" is likely not the right answer.

One might say the media is just reporting the news as they see it, but communications and political science research suggests otherwise. In a 2021 review of almost one hundred articles on media and political polarization, two German psychologists found polarization in both traditional (newspapers, TV, radio) and social media.[39] What is particularly compelling about their analysis is that selective exposure to media—that is, actively choosing to go to a liberal or conservative website because one is liberal or conservative—increases one's political and affective polarization. In fact, the very use of social media is predictive of polarization, whereas traditional media is more mixed in its effects.[40] While reading a newspaper or watching TV does increase political polarization, it can also—if presenting a view from the other political side—sometimes mitigate it.

While the present moment suggests polarization is at a fever pitch, concerns regarding polarization have been present for over a quarter of a century. In a 1996 article in the *International Journal of Public Opinion Research*, the authors Matthew Mendelsohn and Richard Nadeau studied 1988 data from the Canadian National Elections Study. They hypothesized that more media exposure would reduce "social cleavages," with the exception of Quebec, where residents consume more "narrowcast"—that is, biased and selective—media. Mendelsohn and Nadeau's hypothesis was correct: generally broadcast media muted social cleavages, but those who were exposed to narrower media reaffirmed their opinions rather than expanded their viewpoints. Exposure to broadcast media may reshape a woman's view of the military to be more favorable, or a native-born Canadian's view of immigration to be more positive. Mendelsohn and Nadeau conclude, "It seems that by providing a 'common source of everyday culture [to] an otherwise heterogeneous population'…increased exposure to the mass media has minimized preexisting sociodemographic cleavages and encouraged opinion convergence across groups."[41]

The media has become far more segmented since Mendelsohn and Nadeau's study. A 2018 article in the *Journal of Media Psychology* reports on an experiment where a sample of three hundred Democrats and Republicans read a news story in which it was reported that the public believes society is in either a high or low state of conflict, or they did not receive a story to read at all. The study finds that news coverage reporting greater political conflict leads to (surprise!) greater political identification, affective polarization, and ideological polarization.[42] If we internalize what we read, watch, or listen to as fact (which is understandable), then that influences how we view society and each other. The media thus plays a paramount role in our understanding of the world.

This may seem an obvious statement, but it underlines media's responsibility to society. As the media scholar John Fiske observes in his book *Media Matters: Race and Gender in U.S. Politics*, most Americans have little direct engagement with major news events, and thus media and the public discourse it cultivates become essential to their understanding of an event, whether the Rodney King riots and Bill Clinton's election (Fiske's examples) or Black Lives Matter and the January 6 insurrection. Media events may not have tangible impacts on people, but the way the media disseminates information does impact the "structures of feeling" about living in America in a particular moment in time.[43] Think of Benedict Anderson's imagined communities. What did it feel like to be American under the Trump administration? The Biden administration? This is a very different question than how the presidents' different leadership styles, ideologies, and cultural movements materially impact your life.

The media plays an important role in our emotions. As studies suggest, it can exacerbate our feelings of conflict, and it can report news to a biased audience in a biased way. The reality is that, increasingly, almost all media is overtly biased. Even prior to 2016, media began engaging in what scholars have called "outrage discourse," which is an effort to produce visceral responses of anger, fear, and sanctimony. We may take it for granted that the media engages in emotionally charged and divisive language, but scholars compared present-day media to newspaper columns from 1955 to 1975 and found that such outrage was almost entirely absent in the middle of the twentieth century.[44] The authors also found that fully embracing a polarized approach increases audience size, as was the case when MSNBC became more obviously liberal.[45]

While this is the case on both sides, a number of studies suggest that conservative media is more biased than liberal media.[46] I have chosen, however, to focus on liberal media because it is the side that is misrepresenting, demonizing, and mocking rural America. It is widely understood that conservative media is biased, and this is partially due to the sensationalism of many of its leading news outlets: Fox, the *New York Post*, and *Breitbart*, to name a few. Headlines like "HAPPY BIDENFLATION ANNIVERSARY" (*Breitbart*) and "POLLUTER IN CHIEF" with regard to John Kerry's use of a private jet (Fox News) are so obviously slanted that they need little explanation. But liberal media also, perhaps in more subtle ways, contributes to the bias against conservatives, whether it is Sean Illing seemingly sneering at rural Americans in *Vox*, or writers lumping together all Trump supporters as MAGA, or Democratic politicians' notion that wearing camouflage and flannel shirts is an important strategy for getting rural Americans' votes.[47] Even factual stories about rural America cherry-pick statistics to depict complete despair, even if the data, as this book has shown, can portray a far brighter outlook.[48] Conservative media may be more brazen in its scorn of the "other," but liberal journalism is doing plenty of damage on its own.

Media polarization has a demonstrative effect on our perceptions and reinforces our political stereotypes. The question is why

does it occur? There is no doubt there's a chicken and egg phenomenon: the media influences our political polarization, and politically
polarized people want more polarized media. There is also an economic reward: the media engages in polarization because consumers of media may seek out more polarized media, and because bias
creates simplicity that is understood as accuracy.[49] Consumers of
media want to read, watch, and listen to messages that reflect and
reaffirm their point of view, and media appears more accurate if that
messaging is clear and uncomplicated. Regular news does not have
time to present subtle differences, and to simply say something is
wrong or right may come across as more precise even though, para-
doxically, such messaging is more likely to be biased.

The media also rewards polarized behavior by covering extreme
politicians, whether Alexandria Ocasio-Cortez or Ted Cruz, more
than moderates.[50] This may work for those who are polarized and
seek out politicians that reaffirm their worldview. The problem is
that moderate, everyday folks from Nebraska to Florida to California turn their televisions and radios on too, and what they see are
extreme politicians and outrage. To draw from John Fiske, their
structure of feelings about being American becomes associated with
division and polarization rather than any of the good things that
also may be occurring in society.

Liberal and conservative media are both to blame. Both create
an "othering" of the opposing side's political leaders and constituents, which leads to greater affective polarization and keeps us in
our ideological silos. Given that conservatives make up a majority
of rural America, it's unsurprising that conservative media shapes
the opinions of those who live there. The same is of course true of
liberal media and cities. Part of this has to do with cultural capital,
but essentially media is an important currency in our communication with others. Podcasts, columnists, and our perceptions of the
news of the day become the ties that bind us in modern society. We
engage in the public discourse as a part of fitting in.

There are consequences to polarization beyond the fact that regular Americans feel our country is divided. On big issues like climate change, scholars have found that most people get their information and views from the media, which means political slant can have a profound effect on whether one takes climate change seriously or sees it as a progressive ruse. Wildly different views on these issues often ricochet within conservative and liberal echo chambers, stymieing societal efforts to establish consensus around what to do.[51]

Even the perceptions of rural America as predominantly farmland or steeped in traditional values are drawn from popular stereotypes circulated in the media rather than the lived experience of small-town residents.[52] Not all of rural America is dependent upon agriculture; not all rural Americans wear hunting gear in blaze orange and own guns. Not all of rural America, by any means, supports what happened on January 6. When these ideas of what rural America is or isn't become maxims, it becomes almost impossible to climb the empathy wall. We aren't seeing rural Americans as multifaceted and complicated. We don't get to see Shannon or Craig in full, and then we feel divided from them and from a whole swath of the country. The same, of course, is true the other way around: had Shannon leaned on the stereotype of who I am rather than getting to know me, we would barely have made it through our first conversation.

As I've made clear, I really like Shannon. What has always perplexed me is how she can be a deeply kind and wonderful person yet hold views that can negatively impact her health and that of those around her. Toward the end of one of my last conversations with Shannon, I bring up the Covid-19 vaccine again and hope her position has changed since we last spoke. "I did not get the vaccine," she confirms. "I am a pharmacist," she declares, then clarifies that prior to giving up work she was an inspector for the Kentucky Board of Pharmacy. "Let me rephrase this: I am a stay-at-home mom and God called me to be a stay-at-home mom. [If I were still a pharmacist,] I would believe everything. But I know it is not FDA approved. There is not a chance I am taking anything that's not FDA approved. I am going to play it out and see what happens." I ask Shannon if she questions the existence or seriousness of Covid-19, to which she replies, "I do believe Covid is real. We had a revival in our church and sixteen people got sick. My good friend is in the ICU. I was fasting for her today. I do believe it's real. I just don't know if the vaccine is the answer."

I push Shannon a bit more. She is an avid supporter of President Trump, who really supported the development of the vaccine under his Operation Warp Speed program, so I want to get at her hesitancy. Is her concern political? Will she get the vaccine once it's FDA approved? At this moment, Shannon becomes very serious and candid with me. "I did a lot of research. There is a religious aspect to this. Mother Miriam and Father Altman and maybe a few more made me aware that it [the vaccine] was tested on aborted baby cells. For me, I don't care. I want to follow God, who says abortion is wrong. I will not better my life by using a vaccine that was developed on aborted baby cells." I do not say anything, but my lips are pursed together and I am nodding my head in acceptance of her position.

I am pretty sure Shannon has received misinformation, but when I do my own research, I see she is not entirely wrong. Fetus cell lines from elective abortions from decades ago were used in the proof of concept for the mRNA vaccines and in the development, confirmation, and production of the Johnson & Johnson vaccine. While this is not the same thing as using aborted fetuses, as they are grown in a laboratory, the cells are descended, thousands of generations removed, from cells from an aborted fetus.[53] Despite this lineage, even the Vatican has permitted Catholics to get the vaccine, calling it a "moral obligation."[54]

While this feels like a very abstract and removed process to me, how can I argue with Shannon's view? As a deeply religious

Catholic, she is strongly anti-abortion. Her stance on the vaccine is, by extension, not irrational for her. I am worried about her and wonder when she will tell me that she's sick with Covid-19. I wish I could change her mind on the vaccine, and indeed I try. Shannon follows up with an email a little bit after we end our call. Subject line "covid," she discusses the medications being used to treat severe disease that she believes are very effective: Zithromax, hydroxychloroquine, and zinc. I reply, "Please stay safe (and consider getting vaccinated—better to stay healthy and not need any medications!) and we will talk again soon as I continue to write."

Shannon writes that she got her information from America's Frontline Doctors, an organization of which I'd heard the name but nothing else, so I look them up. The first line of their Wikipedia entry is as follows: "America's Frontline Doctors is an American right-wing political organization.... Founded by Simone Gold and promoted by the Tea Party Patriots, it has opposed lockdowns and social distancing mandates during the COVID-19 pandemic by citing alleged and unapproved treatments for COVID-19."[55] Simone Gold was arrested for her role in the January 6, 2021, Capitol insurrection. In March 2022, she pleaded guilty to violent entry and disorderly conduct on restricted grounds, and in June 2022 she was sentenced to sixty days in jail.[56] I then look up the other two sources of coronavirus information that Shannon mentioned, Mother Miriam and Father Altman. They are both popular conservative Catholic media figures. Mother Miriam does not support the Covid vaccine.[57] Father Altman denounced Covid restrictions as "Naziesque" and said that anyone who supports Democrats would burn in hell.[58] He was subsequently removed from his position by his bishop for an "undetermined length of time."[59] Father Altman has denied any wrongdoing.

Shannon means no harm, and even though her sources of information are political, I never get the sense she has a political stance regarding Covid. After all, President Trump, whom she very much admires, was instrumental in the vaccine development, and he himself announced on national television that he got his booster shot.[60] When I press Shannon on her news sources, she does not cite Fox News or *Breitbart* but rather people she follows on YouTube, Facebook, and Telegram, corroborating a *New York Times* analysis that found that almost all misinformation around Covid-19 was linked to just twelve people, the "disinformation dozen," who primarily reside on social media.[61] Shannon is skeptical of CNN, which she can watch for free, but says she would be just as unconvinced by Fox News.

As an interviewer, it would not be appropriate for me to tell Shannon her views are based on false information, that the people she is paying attention to are essentially making things up. But I feel incredibly uncomfortable, and I see the damage polarized media can do. I can only softly press her to get vaccinated. The truth is, I cannot convince her to get the vaccine, and that doesn't feel good. I have learned to make peace with Shannon's views about election fraud and climate change. While I think she is entirely incorrect, I do not believe her views change the outcome of our country or world. But, practically speaking, her choice to not get vaccinated does. What I've realized is that if there is any chance that Shannon will change her view, it will be in what information she gets. Her media consumption is drawn from a few extremely biased sources that package their message about Covid as fact. I'd imagine that's true for her views on election fraud and climate change too.

Shannon's perspective on vaccines is a stand-in for a number of the conversations I have had with her and others. These people gave thoughtful and carefully reasoned responses for their perspectives; they were not ignorant, glib, or unthinking, as left-leaning media might presume. One might hypothesize that my interviewees are guarded with what they say, as with very little homework they can find out my likely political and cultural views. But the truth is, no one pulled back on their views about anything—immigration, marriage equality, race, the media, the other political party.[62] They were respectful and kind. For the most part, people mean well, and sometimes they, too, are not aware of how to square their contradictions.

THIS WAS THE case with Keith, a man I interviewed in the fall of 2020. A bit older than me, Keith grew up in the same town as I did in rural Pennsylvania, but he stayed. He is from a family of six. "We were like *The Brady Bunch*," he laughed. "Three boys and three girls." I ask Keith whether he has kids. He laughs again, "Oh boy. Well, Kim is my second wife, and she had three kids when we got together. I had two when we got together, and we had two together—so there's seven kids total."

Wow, I think. I have three boys and find my life exists in a constant state of chaos. His children were a good bit older than mine, and I was interested in how things had turned out for them. Keith clears his throat, "Oldest to youngest: My oldest did not go to college. He's living in Illinois. He works for the train company out there. He's a conductor on a train service, CDX, I think it's called." The next oldest, Keith felt, hadn't done much with his life. "There's Keith Jr. He went to IUP [Indiana University of Pennsylvania] and did four years of family sciences. He graduated, came home, couldn't find anything in his field and so started working at Geisinger Medical Center," Keith explained. "Nicole would be the next one. She's doing online courses now. She's twenty-eight years old. She works for LEER Truck Caps, and she's doing well for herself at the moment. Nicolas, he went to Job Corps, graduated from Job Corps, and has his own business as a truck driver." Keith explained that his youngest son was still in school and was bright but faced some learning difficulties. "He was writing his own computer codes at ten years old. He taught himself how to do it," Keith said. "Then there's Dakota, my fourteen-year-old daughter. Let's see…she is very artistic. She does online schooling. She does all her schooling online. I really didn't like the idea of it, but my wife talked me into it. It's really working for her."

I marvel at Keith's descriptions of his kids and how he has managed to feed, shelter, and support their education and path toward adulthood. Keith himself never went to college and works hourly lawn-mowing and handyman jobs around the town, along with helping with property management for various landlords, including my own father. We talk for some time, and I get a picture of a family that is, despite a lack of resources and parental education, emotionally close and making it work.

Over the course of an hour or so, Keith and I talk about all sorts of things: democracy, immigration, marriage equality, organic food, and his favorite holiday. Keith has a refreshingly philosophical view on many of these issues. When I ask him about equality and whether it exists in America, he takes a wide view. "No, I think there's a whole lot of prejudice. There's a whole lot of everybody thinking they're better than everyone else. As far as I'm concerned that's not the case. We all get up in the morning and put our pants on one leg then another. Some people think they're better because they're rich. You still breathe the air I breathe." Then Keith tells me a story of his own experience of being on both sides. "There are people out there who have less than me," he begins. "[But I remember] when I've been at Weis [the local grocery store] where my card's been denied, and the lady behind me paid for my food, and in the same way I've been out to dinner and paid for the old ladies' dinner because it's a nice thing to do. I believe everybody should help everybody else. There shouldn't be anyone left out because of what they have or don't have or the way they look." There's a kindness to Keith that feels big and broad. We tiptoe toward politics, and I am curious where he stands. Keith says he is a Democrat. "Hillary had the popular vote but didn't have the [electoral college] vote. I think that's ridiculous. If she had the popular vote, she should have been president." When I ask Keith about the future of this country, he says, "If Trump gets reelected, we're screwed."

Keith feels both familiar and alien to me. We can laugh about the mayhem of having multiple children and the difficulty of balancing work and family (the latter of which we both really value). We share a view that equality and quotidian kindness toward others are essential parts of a functioning society. These aren't Keith's words, but they are the themes of many of the topics we discussed and the sentiments he shared with me. And yet, Keith and I are also so different: He has not three children but seven. He seems relaxed about issues that would send me into a tailspin. He doesn't express financial concern even though I don't know how he pays the bills for his large family.

What is the through line in these contradictions? How do we make sense of people who are, in the very same moment, so similar and so different from us? What does it mean to really know what someone else's life is like? To know their favorite food and favorite holiday and their saddest and happiest moments? Even then, we are left wondering. What I have come to realize is that we are all subject to these contradictions within ourselves. It is how we deal with and accept our opposing feelings about others that matters.

In a book review of *Deaths of Despair and the Future of Capitalism*, the stunning portrait of opioid addiction in working-class America written by Angus Deaton and Anne Case, Hochschild observes the phenomenon of "splitting." She remarks that it is hard for us to square what we feel are conflicting ideas of the same person. "Faced with a coal miner suffering black lung disease, or a laid-off factory hand, liberals feel compassion," writes Hochschild. "Faced, on the other hand, with a man in cowboy boots and red MAGA hat, arms defiantly folded, who dismisses climate science and insults overeducated 'snowflakes,' many see—and hate—'the enemy.' Yet what if these are one and the same man?" The noise of politics and value-laden beliefs obscures another person's humanity. We fail to understand why someone is so different from us or, perhaps a bigger loss, where we have deep commonalities.

We are all talking past each other until we are talking to each other. In July 2021, I called Hochschild to talk about my interviews, given her own work on "the Great Paradox," as she called the strange contradiction of Louisianans' support of the Tea Party despite its anti-environmental stance. Hochschild found that Louisianans care about other things, both cultural and practical, and they are able to mentally separate the pollution companies produce from the fact that the companies offer jobs, productivity, and a sense of pride for the community. They hold these two truths separate.

Like Hochschild, I don't want to apologize for views that are racist, anti-immigrant, anti-gay, or anti-vaccine. Outside of a few instances, I did not observe explicit bias from my interviewees. However, I came to appreciate that rural Americans' views on all sorts of matters were shaped by the information given to them, just as my views are shaped in the same way. By stripping away the public discourse, we established a more important truth and understanding between us. Through my interviews with dozens of Americans and hundreds of pages of transcripts and data, I have found that if we can ignore the noise and focus on what we actually share, the through line within seemingly contradictory people is the same one that connects us to them: our shared sense of humanity. Rather than making us the "other," our differences are simply a part of our lived experience. The contradictions are there, but they matter less. We are all just living and being human.

I found that with Keith, and I still hold on to the feeling. To this day, the moment where we understood each other as humans fills up my heart with warmth and love. At one point in our conversation, I ask Keith about the happiest moment in his life. He pauses, taking the question seriously. "My favorite time in my life was when my kids were born," he says. "Because I made something that was, you know what I mean…" Keith stops and laughs softly, self-consciously, but with a gentle pride. "I made that. Now I'm responsible for that." I did know what he meant, because I felt that exact way, at the exact moment when my kids were born too.

5

THE MERITOCRACY BIAS

The choices people make are framed by the
opportunities they are given.
—Raj Chetty[1]

COURTNEY FOWLER WAS NOMINATED TO BE BOTH PROM AND homecoming queen in 1993 at Danville High School. Her boyfriend, Damon Fitt, the Ironmen's quarterback and local heartthrob, was her escort for homecoming. "I did not win either," Courtney explained to me via text, followed by an LOL emoji. She and Damon broke up a couple of years later. "We didn't end up like the fairy tale ending," she wrote me. While Courtney was a few years older than me, I remember vividly her rarified position in the high school pecking order. We both grew up in the small town of Danville, Pennsylvania, and outside of both being members of the cross-country team and National Honor Society, we did not exist in the same social and cultural world. As a high school student, Courtney was pretty by any measure, with long, curly, auburn hair, sparkling blue eyes, a smattering of freckles across her nose, and a big, beautiful smile (to this day, she looks the same). She graduated fourth in her class, a "strategic move," Courtney says with a light jingle of a laugh. A natural introvert who doesn't like public speaking,

Courtney explains to me that the top three students would speak at graduation and "I was not going to let that happen [to me]." She went on to study behavioral science at Pennsylvania State University in State College, Pennsylvania.

Courtney had always dreamed of going to Penn State. "My entire childhood is infused with memories of PSU football and visits to State College. I remember being a PSU cheerleader for Halloween." It wasn't an easy school to get into. Many students who wanted to go to Penn State ended up at one of the branch campuses that had varying degrees of selectivity. "I only wanted to go to PSU, and it was the only college I applied to. My dad went there, and I was determined to go from an early age."

At the time, all of this seemed hard but doable. "I was strategic about what I did in high school as it pertained to getting into college," Courtney texted me in response to my question about how aware she was of the college preparatory process. "Keeping my grades high, National Honor Society, cross-country, cheerleading, all the things you were supposed to do in high school to increase chance of college acceptance. I felt I was on the right path in my choices, and it appeared to have paid off as I got into main campus." At the end of senior year, with prom and homecoming court accolades, graduating at the top of her class, and a new boyfriend, Courtney felt on top of the world. She was off to Penn State to become a math teacher. She was not just beautiful and popular but also really smart, and she seemed to be going places.

Courtney knew it too. "I was a big fish in the small Danville school. Learning came so easy to me." She doesn't explain her situation with any braggadocio. "Then I went to Penn State. My first day [was] in a chem class with over two hundred other students. The professor asked everyone who had been high school valedictorian to raise their hand. All these hands went up all around me as I slouched lower in my auditorium seat. Then it began to dawn on me: in my math classes I could not keep up with the others in my class." At that point, Courtney no longer felt she could be a math teacher, and she ultimately majored in behavioral studies instead. She now works in mid-level administration for the local hospital. She describes herself as "lower middle-class."

There is nothing inherently wrong with Courtney's choice to switch majors. What troubled me was that she felt she had to do it, and that despite graduating fourth in her class at a strong rural public school, she felt completely out of her league when she attended college. How could a woman so accomplished, so hardworking, and so smart ultimately feel she was not capable of pursuing her dream? There was something extremely unfair about Courtney's story, and it bothered me a great deal.

What's worse, her story isn't unique. In the autumn of 2020, I helped a dear friend's daughter with her college applications. Emma, who also went through Danville's public school system, is a talented artist. She participated in Black Lives Matter protests in the middle of rural Pennsylvania, painted portraits for the movement, and donated other artwork to the Biden election headquarters in Danville, all the while getting good grades and good SAT scores. From my perspective, Emma had enormous potential to go as far as she wanted, and I encouraged her to do so.

We first spoke about her college application process in late summer 2020, and I was not pleased that her guidance counselor was intent on her attending an uncompetitive local university. Why wasn't she talking to Emma about the Ivy League? Or Parsons School of Design? Instead, her guidance counselor pushed her toward a number of nearby colleges. When I heard this, I worked with Emma to generate a list of top universities to which she should apply. I read her college essays and provided feedback. I felt her SATs were good but not terrific and encouraged her to retake them and to take a few practice tests in the meantime. I wrote her a recommendation letter. In October, we discussed her applying to Brown, and she realized she had just missed the early decision deadline. I told her to email the admissions office and ask if they were accepting late applications. The admissions officer wrote her right back and said they'd be happy to give her a week's extension. In the end, Emma applied to Bryn Mawr, Carnegie Mellon, Brown (early decision), Wellesley, Kutztown University (her guidance counselor's suggestion), and the School of the Art Institute of Chicago. Emma did not get into any of the schools except Kutztown and SAIC. She accepted a slot at SAIC with a scholarship. In the end, Emma found a good school, but I remain mystified as to why she didn't get into any of the other very selective universities she applied to.

Emma shouldn't have just landed on her feet; she should have soared. She ranked in the top 15 percent of her class, and her SAT scores were in the ninety-fifth percentile. While she wasn't a star athlete or member of the Honor Society, she did other interesting things with her time. She produced genuinely remarkable artwork, which had been recognized with gallery shows, and independently engaged in social justice issues. She did all of this despite living in a very conservative part of rural America, with a single mom who was a nurse working many, many hours to support her family. Why didn't she have more choices? Why didn't Emma get into Brown? Or Wellesley? Isn't she exactly what these universities want? Doesn't she deserve to be there too?

I ATTENDED THE SAME public school system as Courtney and Emma. However, I went on to Carnegie Mellon as an undergrad and for my master's and Columbia University for my PhD. I was only a few years behind Courtney, so the competitive landscape would have been more or less the same. I was not a talented artist like Emma, and while I engaged in some social causes outside of school, my efforts were not as remarkable as hers. I certainly did not graduate fourth in my class like Courtney. The difference, I realized, was not so much that we had different capabilities as we had different parents. My parents, Irish immigrants who had worked desperately to get through higher education—my mother medical school and my father an MBA and PhD—instilled a belief that my education mattered more than anything. By high school, getting into a world-renowned university was a nonnegotiable top priority. My parents and I were thinking about college for many years before the application process even began. My father had a college tome, bigger than the Bible, on his office bookshelf. I knew the names of Vassar and Harvard and Northwestern and Rice years before making any effort toward being accepted at these institutions. The difference between Emma and Courtney and me was not our aptitude but rather our horizons.

At the time, I did not realize that my parents' ideas were unusual in rural America. Their long view of education would have been far more suited to New York City or San Francisco, places where parents have college expectations before their children even attend kindergarten. Because my parents were immigrants from Dublin, their view was very different from other parents in our small town. What did my parents do differently? They always assumed I would leave, that I would go far away, and that I would try—and sometimes fail—to achieve the most I possibly could. There was always the expectation that I would attend university and that it would not be down the street or in the next town over. Courtney did go to her dream school, but what surprises me is that her dream was Penn State, rather than Stanford or Columbia or University of Pennsylvania. Students like Courtney are desirable to many of the country's elite educational institutions. But one only needs to take a look at the general aspirations of Danville High School students to see why Courtney's decision made complete sense at the time.

The website Niche has a database of kindergarten through twelfth grade public and private schools that offers overall state and national rankings, as well as a breakdown of various educational outcomes, from Advanced Placement enrollment to SAT and ACT scores. I wanted to know how Danville High School students' scores and graduation rates stacked against those at other public schools. As rural high schools go, Danville is strong. The school offers AP classes, good sports teams, and a vast campus nestled on top of a hill with fields for soccer games, cross-country races, and football practices. Just down the hill, visible from the high school and perhaps a five-minute walk away, is the local YMCA where the swim team practices and holds meets. The high school is clean, textbooks are aplenty, sports teams have the equipment they need, and the school musicals are well performed and well attended.

According to Niche, the school's average SATs are 1220, and the school boasts a 95 percent graduation rate, similar to other highly ranked high schools like those in Mount Lebanon outside of Pittsburgh and San Marino in suburban Los Angeles. While these latter two schools have better SAT scores (1270 and 1370), they are not wildly different. What is notable, however, among Danville, Mount Lebanon, and San Marino is the difference in the aspirations of their students. While just 22 percent of Danville students enroll in AP courses, over a third of San Marino and Mount Lebanon students are taking these advanced classes. La Cañada High School, also in a suburb of Los Angeles, boasts a 99 percent graduation rate, and over 50 percent of the student body enrolls in AP courses.

Niche also tracks the colleges and universities that are of interest to students at each profiled high school. While students at San Marino and Mount Lebanon are interested in local universities (which happen to be very highly ranked), the students tend to have a more expansive list of colleges. Danville students, on the other hand, are almost entirely interested in local—and often middling— places of higher education. San Marino's list of top interest schools starts with UCLA, USC, and Berkeley and ends with NYU and Stanford. Mount Lebanon's list starts with University of Pittsburgh and Penn State, but includes University of Pennsylvania, NYU, and

University of Michigan. Danville students' list starts with Penn State and includes University of Scranton, Bloomsburg University, Lock Haven University, and Susquehanna University. It's not that these latter institutions are terrible, but they are also not, rank-wise, in the same league as the universities that comparative students at San Marino and Mount Lebanon are considering. That these are the places to which Danville students aspire strikes me as the problem.

This observation brings me back to Emma. Not until three months before the admissions deadlines did Emma engage seriously with the prospect of attending somewhere really extraordinary. But, as any book on the college rat race will tell you, by then it's far too late. Emma needed to be thinking about Brown over a year before she applied, not a month before. She needed to be prepping for her SATs not just here and there but diligently, for months—and taking the test at least twice. For Emma, the pandemic made it especially hard, but this is why the path to elite higher education starts so early.

Urban meritocrats know this reality only too well. They are extremely stressed out about their kids' academic fortunes starting in ninth grade, or even earlier. They expect their students to end up at a top university. Educational consultants are hired for thousands of dollars, prep for standardized tests starts in tenth grade, and all the while activities—lacrosse, volunteering, chess club, debate team—are scrupulously chosen. Are these parents craven? Are they too obsessed? Perhaps. But what they really are is conscious of how difficult it is to get into a top university and the steps that are necessary to make it happen. While at least 50 percent of colleges and universities have become less competitive since the middle of the twentieth century (though not by much), the top 10 percent of universities have become even more selective during the same time period.[2] Those aware of this competitiveness—almost entirely affluent urban and suburban parents—start as early as possible to make sure their kids are in position.

In the first half of this book, I challenged the myth of a divided America. In statistics and interviews, it's clear that this country is far more cohesive than we are led to believe. On matters of income, homeownership, employment, and other socioeconomic metrics, rural America is largely doing as well as urban America. Appalachia and the South are the exceptions to this success story, and they need to be dealt with separately. On matters of values, Americans share a fundamental human connection. This is true in both my conversations with Americans and the data from the General Social Survey. If we ignore the headlines and the supposed reasons to feel divided—our politics, our news sources—we can find a closeness. This is not to say Americans are all the same and that there aren't differences between rural and urban. Of course there are. In education, religion, and other areas of cultural capital, we find that there are very different approaches to how these aspects of life exist and manifest differently across geography. Those differences do not make us less able to connect, but they do produce vastly different life outcomes and social connections.

My interviews with both urban and rural parents regarding education reflect this divide. One of the questions I asked all parents was, *How important is it that your kids get into a particular college?* I elaborated that I didn't mean to name a specific place but a broad grouping of universities or colleges, such as the Ivy League, the top twenty-five as ranked by *US News & World Report*, highly competitive universities, or state schools. When I first went through my transcripts, there was a sense that everyone said the same broad generalities: they wanted their kids to be happy; they wanted them to follow their dreams. However, the outcomes for urban versus rural students are so different that I knew there was more to these answers.

I went through my transcripts more closely. I divided my interviews into urban and rural respondents and then three piles within: parents who definitely expect their children to attend university and/or have expectations of where their children will go to school;

those who are not overly concerned with whether their children attend university; and those who were upset their children didn't go to college. (Only one parent, a mother living in small-town Pennsylvania, expressed dismay at her children's choices to not attend college. One works at a local diner, and the other is on disability.) With rural parents, it was evenly divided as to whether they cared if their children attended college. As one rural mother explained, "It's not important to me. If they want to [attend college], I would want them to." A parent from Kentucky responded, "Not really [important]. We mainly wanted them to be happy and learn what they wanted to learn." Another parent from Wisconsin said, "As long as they find a path that is something that they care about, and a job that is meaningful to them, I wouldn't be upset if they worked in a factory or as a librarian or a chef. It just doesn't matter." While some rural parents did expect their kids to go to college, they had a relaxed approach to the issue, and they didn't indicate that they expected their children to attend a top university. There was a consensus among rural parents that finding happiness and choice (with no preordained constraints) was the most important thing.

Urban parents are far more complicated. Well over half of the parents unequivocally expected their kids to attend college, and those with older children expressed far more concern that they specifically attend a top university. As one father in New York City put it, "How much did college selectivity matter to me? If I'm honest, a lot. You know, for the football coach, athletics permeates their household. I'm a professor; the value of education and thinking in general matters most to me. In theory, I know I shouldn't care about rankings of institutions. I should care more about what kind of education and what they are extracting from that institution, but unfortunately I fall prey to the rat race of education." His daughter went to Princeton, and his son is now attending graduate school at Columbia. A Los Angeles mother of a high school senior explained, "Would I be disappointed if Andrew went to Ohio State? Hell yeah."

Even those who said it wasn't important where, or even whether, their children attended college still went through the motions of touring schools, considering gap years, and anchoring their expectations. A gap year, for example, is a highly privileged chance to travel the world and improve one's prospects for universities after finishing high school. This year is often spent retaking the SATs or volunteering or interning for free—not an option if you have to start making a living right away. Even the most relaxed urban interviewees were cognizant of what it took to get into a top college. One San Francisco mother said, "I don't need them to go to Harvard," but of course that's hardly a low bar. A father from Nashville said, "I didn't get caught up in that. I wanted them to go where they wanted to go. We did all the college tours and all that, but I had no expectations." These parents did not demand that their child attend an elite university, but rather used phrases like "a good fit" and "intellectual curiosity." But from my perspective, I did not see any real difference between them and the more competitive parents when it came to the outcomes for their children.

All of these responses reveal a deep awareness of how the process works and the subtle but important difference between attending college (almost a given) and attending a top-tier university. When I spoke to urban parents, I also wondered if it was easier to say they didn't care where their kids ended up because they were so clearly secure that it would be somewhere decent. One mother, a Harvard alum herself, shared with me that "it's [just] knowing they are engaged and trying their hardest. The school is not that important." Of course, this response indicates that the mother assumes her child will attend a university of sorts, but it may also indicate a quiet confidence. If you attended Harvard, the chances seem low that your child will end up skipping out on college altogether. Another mother from San Francisco expressed similar sentiments: "I think what's important to me [is] that they are a really good fit with whatever path they might be interested in." I pushed her a bit further and asked how she might respond if her child announced she wanted to attend Murray State, a public university in Kentucky that accepts over 80 percent of applicants. The mother, a graduate of Cornell (acceptance rate 10.9 percent), paused. "I think I would ask them, 'Why?' I would like to think I'd be open-minded." But even this response reveals that Murray State would be questioned, and this university wasn't what she expected for her kid. Conversely, among many rural parents this choice likely would not be viewed as a bad decision. (In fact, one rural parent I interviewed did happily send her child to Murray State.)

The rich are far more careless with money than those who have none. Is the same true of education? That those educated at the finest institutions offer some performative insouciance because the social net for their children is in place and always will be? Or because in reality the deck is already stacked in their favor? For years, affluent parents have been enrolling their kids in AP classes and extracurricular activities. As one Los Angeles mother shared, "Both of my boys wanted to attend a four-year college. Education was instilled in me by my parents, and so I instilled it in my children. Now Ryan is at Berkeley. Everyone asks what he is majoring in. Honestly, I don't know yet. I've done my job. He's at Berkeley." These subtle and not-so-subtle signifiers positioned these parents and their children in a world where their baseline was attending college.

As a Los Angeles mother of two boys, one of whom just began college and another who is in high school, candidly explained to me:

Anything perceived as a not desirable school was problematic to me. But I was super cognizant of what happened to me and how I felt. I went to Harvard for undergraduate, and I was miserable. Tulane [where her eldest son attends]—I was not crazy about it. The university was not aligned with "academic excellence." It was perceived as a party school, but I also recognized that it was a good school, competitive and hard to get into, so that made it tolerable. I don't know if I lived in a vacuum if I would be feeling this way. But it's very hard to live in my family and have a kid go to a subpar university. Somehow, it's the ability to be able to tell people where my kids go to school and that it reflects well on me.... Like, I feel badly for parents whose kids go to a community college.

This mother's response is complicated. She means well, she wants the best for her kid, and she wants him to attend the university he wishes to attend. And yet the social pressure of her family and friends means that she also wants him to go to a school with the appropriate status and competitiveness. While on the surface almost all of the parents I interviewed expressed the same sentiments of wanting the best for their children and caring about their future happiness, urban parents had children who ended up at the very best universities in the country, and rural parents—barring a few exceptions—did not. Rural parents were not any less concerned about their children. Among them, however, there was less of an expectation that their children would attend college, let alone a top-tier institution. There was far less of a belief that elite education was the only ticket to meaningful work.

These broad expectations were true of my interviewees and in general statistics. As one study found, while almost 50 percent of high school students in cities and 43 percent of those in suburbs attend college, just a third of rural students enroll in higher education—and the gap is widening.[3] And it's not just that they go to college less; they also are less likely to graduate.[4]

In many ways, the difference between the urban and rural responses about their children attending college comes down to *They can do what they want* versus *They can go where they want*. These two phrases seem almost identical, but they express a chasm in expectations. Rural parents are far more open to their children doing various things with their lives, which *may* include attending college, but also could mean vocational or technical school. Most urban parents I interviewed are open to various permutations, but within their framework is the expectation that their child *will* attend college. For rural parents, college is met with ambivalence. Hard work and a meaningful life in rural America is not entirely focused on individual academic and professional achievements. Family, faith, and connection to community often take precedence over getting into a top college. This is a stark contrast from urban and suburban America, where college admissions is approached with laser-like focus. The expectation may not always be Harvard, but it is always college and usually what anyone would consider a good school. The father from Nashville who ostensibly didn't get involved in the pressures of college admissions still ended up sending his daughter to Vanderbilt, which in 2021 was ranked fourteenth in the country, tied with Brown University. Or, as one father from Milwaukee remarked, "They were both expected and both understood that college, that we required that—that we expected that to happen."

Some of these differences are undoubtedly a result of something that almost every urban parent I interviewed experienced and almost no rural parents mentioned: competitive parenting. Competitive parenting—almost a meme in contemporary culture—is the practice by which parents compete in subtle ways to demonstrate the superior style of their parenting and in turn their children. This type of parenting has been parodied in novels like *Gifted* and *Such a Fun Age* and captured in tell-alls like *Primates of Park Avenue*. Almost always, the central players are urban, affluent parents engaged in one-upmanship regarding their children's sports, acceptance into gifted and talented programs, playing of musical instruments, and attendance at top universities. In real life, this type of behavior manifests in bumper stickers announcing that one's child is attending a particular elite private high school or is an honor student. A few years ago, I was standing in line to pick up one of my sons from school, and the parents in front of me were trading stories about their children's coding acumen. At the time, our children were in first grade—six years old. When I ended up in the conversation, I had to admit that my son was not coding but still very much involved in elaborate games of make-believe. I wasn't sure whether I should laugh at the absurdity or feel anxious that my child hadn't yet started learning Python (years later, he still hasn't).

Still, in other ways, parents themselves show their superior parenting through excessive volunteering, endless school fundraising, and general involvement in all aspects of their children's lives. As Madeline Mackenzie, one of the central characters of HBO's *Big Little Lies*, remarks to a fellow stay-at-home mom, "I only do twenty hours a week max. Between you and me, I try to maintain my full-time mommy status so I can lord it over Renata and other career mommies." While once relegated primarily to sports, the phenomenon of competitive parenting has permeated all aspects of child-rearing, even breastfeeding. "For us Anglophone mothers, the length of time that we breastfeed—like the size of a Wall Street bonus—is a measure of performance," writes the journalist Pamela Druckerman. "We all know that our breastfeeding number is a concrete way to compete with one another."[5] Or, as the philosopher Matthew Stewart remarked of competitive parenting in a *Vox* interview, "Generally, I don't think it's terrible for the kids. It's just a model of parenting that is a) insane and b) cannot conceivably be emulated by most of the population."[6]

This orchestrated style of parenting upholds the almost singular goal of many affluent urban parents: the secured entrance of their children into the meritocracy. The peer pressure around attending a top university is the first part of this process. The term *meritocracy* was coined by Michael Young in the late 1950s in his futuristic satire *The Rise of the Meritocracy*.[7] Taking place in 2034, the book was a warning against the notion of a ruling class whose members ostensibly attained their position through this formalized structure of education, intelligence, and high-level social skills, or as Young defines it: "IQ + effort = merit." Fast-forward to the twenty-first century and Young's novel has more than a hint of prescience. Gone perhaps are Thorstein Veblen's idle aristocrats and their social status based entirely on birthright. In their place arose a group of people who, perhaps initially by dint of their own hard work, attained their top position through credentials and highly paid professional jobs as lawyers, medical doctors, professors, and, later, tech executives and hedge fund managers. Young never thought meritocracy was a good thing, though. Society remains every bit as unequal as under an aristocracy, yet seemingly more justified.

D ANIEL MARKOVITS IS a card-carrying member of this meritocracy and also one of its most scathing critics. Born in England, Markovits attended Yale for mathematics and won the prestigious British Marshall scholarship, which allowed him to study in England, where he received a master's in mathematical economics and econometrics from the London School of Economics and a doctorate from Oxford University. Upon returning to the United States, Markovits obtained a law degree from Yale University, upon which he clerked for Guido Calabresi, senior judge of the US Court of Appeals for the Second Circuit, and then returned to Yale, full circle, as the Guido Calabresi Professor of Law. As a shockingly impressive and educated man, chaired law professor and author of multiple books, Markovits may reap the benefits of his perch among the meritocratic elite, but he is also deeply troubled by this now entrenched system of social mobility, a topic he writes passionately about in his book *The Meritocracy Trap*. A widely read and reviewed polemic against the elite, Markovits's book describes the meritocracy as "a mechanism for the concentration and dynastic transmission of wealth, privilege and caste across generations."

I emailed Markovits in autumn 2021, hoping that we could talk about the implications of the meritocracy for rural America. He immediately replied and scheduled a time to talk the following week. Despite his pedigree and impressive career, Markovits is a very unassuming and kind person. The Friday before our meeting, he sent me a lovely note saying he was looking forward to our conversation. His email was dated in the message box, almost mimicking a handwritten letter. Being just five minutes late for our Zoom meeting, which I would consider on time, Markovits profusely apologized for his tardiness.

What is not lost on Markovits is that to acquire the credentials needed to become a meritocrat, you must both know what you need to do to get them and have the money to do so. This criteria is exactly why Markovits doesn't believe America's meritocracy is so different from an aristocracy. As a professor at the most prestigious law school in the country, he sees this up close. In order for their child to end up at Yale, parents must be thinking about what it takes to get there far before any application is submitted. Years, or even a decade, before an application is begun, parents are enrolling children in private preschool and then funneling them into private primary school, private secondary school, and extracurriculars like fencing, soccer, martial arts, and piano. All of these engagements are taxing in terms of time and money, and they require the parents—often members of the meritocracy themselves—to know how to groom a child into the type of applicant that an elite university might consider. Markovits argues that, for those who can afford this investment in their children, it really pays off. Such education endeavors result in lifetime earnings of $10 million.[8]

If it's so exclusive, I asked Markovits, playing devil's advocate, why should we even care? For example, I don't spend any waking moment lamenting that I'm not a multimillionaire. I recognize that, income-wise, the ultra-wealthy are a rarified class and I would do better to focus on the things in my life I can control: being a good mom, teaching my students well, and writing on issues I care about. "First of all," Markovits responds, "if you think about meritocracy as a regime under which people get access to advantage based on their own accomplishments, then there are lots of ways in which that regime is better than alternatives—better that way than based on race or gender or ethnicity or anything like that." He continues, "But every meritocracy has to fill in the frame of what counts as an accomplishment at school and an accomplishment at work, based on superiority, not based on who can do something well enough. The way in which we fill out meritocracy is hierarchy." Markovits explains that the first great example of meritocracy was the Chinese system of exam performance, but, as he points out, "pretty soon that became the people who did well were those who [already] had the resources to do so."

The problem, then, is not with the meritocracy's navel-gazing but its existence's impact on other groups. "The kind of extreme meritocratic inequality we have is harmful to everyone else. " Markovits pauses. "This meritocratic class is taking away from the rest of society—opportunity, income, dignity—from everyone else. We're running law in a way that disempowers ordinary consumers. We're running corporations that do away with middle managers. We are doing away with local businesses." Markovits then tells me a personal story about a good friend who owned a local yoga studio, which was ultimately overtaken by a major company. The corporate chain opened a yoga studio with the veneer of being local. Local consumers were none the wiser, and eventually the better resourced national chain outcompeted the locally owned studio, forcing it to close. "It's the meritocratic manager," sighs Markovits, "who put my friend out of business."

On a broader level, Markovits worries about the precariousness of the middle class, urban and rural, who are not members of the meritocracy. "I think a lot of people are doing fine. The thing that you want is not that your position is fine now, but that it is secure for the foreseeable future. There is the fear, both felt and rational, that things might now be good, but they might not be ten years from now." For meritocrats, Markovits explains, there is a much greater safety net. I talked to him about an acquaintance in Los Angeles, a graduate of Yale, who lived in a small rental and worked on acting, supplementing her income by tutoring kids for the SAT. Markovits points out that, at any point—like his own friend with a degree from Harvard, which he calls the "Harvard cushion"—this woman can find better-paying work by virtue of their meritocratic credentials.

The other problem Markovits laments is how we value work. America has all but mechanized good-paying manual jobs like plumbing. In Germany, Markovits explains, plumbing involves an apprenticeship, skill, and bespoke work. In America, plumbing has become more standardized and prefabricated; the innovation is at the top with design and distribution. This is the case with plenty of vocational careers that were once viewed as artisanal and valued for their craftsmanship. The same is true of workers at Swiss petro-chemical companies, Markovits explains. "They don't have college degrees. The way these organizations are run they don't require a college degree, [which offers] more choice for everyone." In the United States, however, we tend to value careers without merito-cratic credentials less and continue to pay homage to those careers and jobs that are a function of the meritocracy.

The truth of the matter is that both the money and the knowl-edge needed to attain meritocratic jobs is mainly out of reach for everyone other than rarified elites. But I will go further: this pro-cess of grooming one's children to be members of the meritocracy does not demonstratively exist in rural America. The meritocracy is, for the most part, geographically bound, and this should be of no surprise. The jobs in the highest echelons of the global economy tend to be concentrated in big, coastal cities. The very people work-ing those jobs are the parents of children applying to the very best universities. Because fewer meritocrats live in rural America, and because access to the accoutrements of the meritocracy is absent, students in rural areas rarely are in position to gain entry.

E MMA NEVER ATTENDED college admissions tours. While Covid-19 halted in-person tours, she didn't attend any virtual events either. She practiced for her SATs somewhat. However, none of the adults in her life pressured her to do so routinely, and few of her peers studied rigorously, lessening the pressure she felt. Emma's experience is a far cry from that of many high school students in Los Angeles, where I live. Parents spend hours going over essays with their children. They shuttle them to SAT tutoring, buy them elaborate SAT testing programs, pay for practice exams, and spend hundreds more dollars a month on piano, tennis, guitar, or any other extracurricular interests. Students are very clear about where they will apply early decision because they know it will greatly increase their odds of acceptance. I do not judge these parents in the slightest. My children are young, but if I am fortunate enough to be able to support them fully as they approach the college application process, I certainly will. Why wouldn't I do as much as I possibly can to help my children reach their potential, to get into the college of their dreams? But I am aware of how this process is alien to most American families. So much so that Richard Reeves calls the meritocratic elite "dream hoarders."[9] Reeves argues that the entire system is set up such that social mobility remains among a rarified echelon of American society (his cutoff is the top 20 percent, although the band could be even narrower).

More than anything, these disparate outcomes boil down to differences in cultural and social capital, which drive the fortunes of rural students and their ability to access the meritocracy. In their book *No Longer Separate, Not Yet Equal*, Thomas Espenshade and Alexandria Walton Radford observe that lower-social-class white students (who often herald from rural America) are the least likely to be accepted to an elite university. Using National Survey of College Experience (NSCE) data representing 79,222 applications of students from both public and private high schools who applied to highly selective colleges, Espenshade and Radford wanted to understand the impact of race-based admissions preferences and affirmative action on college acceptance rates.[10] To do so, they statistically modeled the probability of particular students' admittance by their racial and ethnic background and translated that probability into the equivalent of increased SAT scores. From their study, Black students received a boost that is the equivalent of 310 SAT points (out of 1600), and Hispanic students received the equivalent of 130 SAT points. While low-income students receive an admissions advantage of up to 130 SAT points, this advantage only pertains to non-white students.

It goes without saying that these increases in admissions for minority students who have historically been left out is unquestionably a good thing. As Espenshade and Radford write, "But in our judgment, it is more likely that a proper assessment of these data is that the labels 'black' and 'Hispanic' are proxies for a constellation of other factors in a candidate's application folder that we do not observe." Overcoming disadvantage, limited resources, and challenging socioeconomic circumstances may be qualities associated with acceptance rates. "It is these other aspects of race and ethnicity that matter, not race itself," Espenshade and Rosen speculate.[11] The problem is obviously not that minority students receive a boost—they certainly should—but that working-class, underprivileged white Americans remain excluded. Within the NSCE database, the greatest admissions preferences are for low-income minority students. Eighty-seven percent of Black and 65 percent of Hispanic students in this category are admitted to the nine highly selective colleges in their study. Twenty-eight percent of middle- and upper-middle-class whites at private schools are accepted. But lower-class white applicants are the least likely to be accepted of all social classes and racial and ethnic groups, with just 8 percent accepted.[12] Upper-middle-class white students are three times more likely to be admitted to a selective college than poor white applicants, even when their qualifications are similar.[13] Another study found that social class is twice as impactful as race or gender on the selectivity of a students' college decisions.[14]

Why might this be? In the bluntest of terms, the cultural capital of rural America is not interesting to the meritocratic class and their elite educational institutions. As Espenshade and Radford found, community service, extracurricular activities, and the quality of participation in those extracurriculars (holding office or receiving awards) were all associated with increased chance of admission. However, when these activities were associated with career-oriented and rural activities, chances of admission were reduced by 60 to 65 percent. Reserve Officer Training Corps (ROTC), Future Farmers of America, and 4-H clubs are associated with students that "are somewhat undecided about their academic futures."[15] Rural students tend to have lower standardized test scores, which makes them less attractive applicants because their scores impact the college's national ranking.[16] Another study found that thousands of poor rural kids with high standardized test scores and high grades were being overlooked and ultimately funneled into state schools or community colleges.[17] When it comes to rural white students in particular, they fall between two stools. They do not tend to possess the cultural and social capital of their upper-middle-class urban and suburban counterparts, and they also do not fulfill the goal of racial diversity sought after by admissions officers.[18]

These statistics fit the story of both Emma and Courtney. No one sat them down as juniors in high school and told them to dream big. It's hard to blame the guidance counselors. For many rural guidance counselors, their horizons are also hemmed in. They do not have connections to elite universities, their schools do not offer

AP courses and enrichment, and they don't know the various subtle but important signals to send in applications.[19] For a majority of
their students, technical or vocational school or community college
makes the most sense.

There is also a wariness about the best talent leaving small-town
America. As Thomas Espenshade wrote to me poignantly when we
corresponded about his research, "All students need to form aspirations to attend college and elite colleges in particular. This may
be more difficult for lower-income students or for those who are
the first in their family to attend college. Occasionally, high school
counselors may actively discourage students from aiming too high,
fearing that students will not succeed, or may not return to their
home communities if they do succeed."

"I taught a Princeton student some 20 years ago who was from
West Virginia," Espenshade continued. "She told me that her high
school counselor refused to write her a letter of recommendation
to Princeton, because going to Princeton would mean her talents
would be lost to her home community." It is no surprise then, that
Fox's Tucker Carlson can say that "college diminishes you" and
everyone should "get out" and this sentiment resonates with some
in rural America. Carlson even argued that he tried to deter his own
children from attending college, and people believe him.[20] The deep
irony of course is that Carlson himself went to private secondary
school and attended Trinity College, a private institution ranked in
the top fifty colleges in the United States. It is highly unlikely that
Carlson would have his current job if not for his meritocratic pedigree. When we corresponded about the Princeton student many
months later, Espenshade shared that she did ultimately return to
West Virginia.

I think back again to my own experience as a student in rural
Pennsylvania. I took the SAT, and when I wasn't thrilled with my
first scores, I studied, took the test again, and got the score I wanted.

I tried out a number of different sports, but I stuck with cross-country because I was fast and ended up on our state-ranked varsity team as the second runner. I worked on the school newspaper as a writer, and I volunteered at a local soup kitchen. I was not, at the time, aware of these choices as strategies, but my parents' approach that everything done ought to be done well meant that I tended to gravitate toward the things I was good at—and, thus, I looked like the type of student a competitive college might want. In addition, by the time I applied to college, I had been to a dozen different countries, from Israel to Mexico to Denmark. I was able to write about these experiences in my essays and reveal my cultural capital in a way that most rural students can't. My parents just happened to live in rural Pennsylvania. In reality, because of their education, the way they cultivated my talents was no different than that of their meritocratic urban counterparts.

I asked my parents about the extent to which they were cognizant of their behavior. The truth is that not only did I never feel pressure, but they never felt they were exuding it. They had a philosophy that supported this way of child-rearing, but it came naturally to them despite the lack of peer pressure in the community. My safety school was Penn State, and my parents expected me to aim higher and be accepted to a top-notch place. I did not get in everywhere I applied by any means, but because I applied to many selective and highly selective universities, I did have plenty of choices. My parents said that one of the only regrets they had about moving to rural Pennsylvania is that they always knew their kids, all three of us, would, without question, move on to bigger places far away.

The difference between Courtney, Emma, and me is what the Stanford economist Caroline Hoxby finds in her study of "achievement-typical" and "income-typical" behavior.[21] For students like Emma and Courtney, it was not that they were necessarily poor with regard to resources (although they were far from wealthy), but that they lacked the "critical mass of high achievers" in their peer group and regular interaction with those who had already attended a highly selective university. They weren't fully aware of their potential. While Emma engaged with these possibilities (due to our very last-minute conversations), she did so with little time to fully prepare herself to be the candidate highly selective colleges were looking for. "We show that the vast majority of very high-achieving students who are low-income do not apply to any selective college or university," write Hoxby and Harvard economist Christopher Avery.[22] What happens then is that students are "undermatched," meaning that they are qualified to attend a much more selective university than they end up attending. As other scholars have found, over 40 percent of students are undermatched. While this is a somewhat widespread problem, it is most common among low-income families, those whose parents did not go to college, and those living in rural America.[23]

There is also the reality that even if a rural student does end up at a selective university, they may be culturally mismatched, a phenomenon the Princeton sociologist Shamus Khan documents in his book *Privilege*. In this ethnography of the private school Saint Paul's, Khan describes how the rich students know how to fit in and those on scholarship feel like fish out of water. "Since colleges and universities often normalize white, middle and upper-class cultural capital," writes Appalachian State professor Sonja Ardoin, "college knowledge can be a barrier for rural students from poor and working class backgrounds who will be the first in their families to pursue higher education.... Many of them [rural students] described talking about 'going to college' with their parents, but shared that they never had a real conversation about what it takes to get there— academic qualifications, applications and corresponding documents, financial aid, etc."[24] Or as Emily Ritchey, who grew up in a small town of 345 in Pennsylvania, remarked of her initial days at Franklin and Marshall College, a selective private school, "I looked around at all these kids wearing Patagonia and Vineyard Vines, clothes I'd never seen before, and I just felt way out of my league."[25]

"YOU KNOW WE—BOB and I—felt from the very beginning of our discussions about having children that we wanted to bring them up to have more advantages than we had," Maryanne Randolph says during an early autumn phone call from North Carolina. "Absolutely, they were to understand they were given a lot of privilege," she continues emphatically. "Those who are given much, much is expected. We wanted them to have an education that had sports, arts, and academics, and that was how we proceeded through their early years." Despite their meritocratic educational philosophy, Bob and Maryanne were newcomers. Both grew up in small-town Pennsylvania; neither of them came from families with an elite education. "We grew up in the 1960s and 1970s. We went to Penn State. To me," Bob laughs, "the idea of going to an Ivy League would be like going to Mars. [It was] go to school, get a job, and get out of the house." For Maryanne, no one saw (or perhaps was equipped to see) the capabilities she later demonstrated. "I mean, neither of my parents went to college. I wanted to be a doctor, and they were not supportive of that, so I did that late 1970s thing and 'went into business.' Twenty years later, I went back and got a second degree in nursing and then had a career as an oncology nurse at UNC."

Bob and Maryanne may not have been offered the road map for how to raise a child to enter the meritocracy, but they were fastidious in following their children's education. They had two sons, Danny and Greg, and a younger daughter, Charlotte. Initially, Maryanne and Bob enrolled them in the local public school in North Carolina. When that didn't fit, they enrolled the boys, and later Charlotte, in Catholic school. "But it was clear at that point that Danny wasn't being challenged," Maryanne explains. While she was concerned, she also felt lucky to have a friend who happened to be the founder of a nearby charter school, where Maryanne decided to enroll the boys. "It was this magical moment," she says, "with teachers who were passionate. It lit the boys on fire."

Danny and Greg attended the charter school from fourth to eighth grade. At that point, with their increasing demonstration of aptitude and talent, the boys were accepted into an International Baccalaureate program at a nearby high school, which had historically been a draw for old southern families, not interlopers like Danny and Greg. "He [Danny] comes in, and there are a lot of really gifted people coming in under this IB program, so you're going to self-select some really good students," Maryanne explains. "So we went to the guidance counselor at the end of freshman year to plan out what Danny would take the next year. She kind of dismissively says, 'We kind of know now who will be in the top five and ten of the class,' and Danny wasn't in that list." Maryanne, ever so diplomatic, goes on, "To her credit, she knew all the old southern families, and their children who would be on that list. Until Bob and me—the carpetbaggers—said, 'Wait one minute, you may not know Danny's background and educational aspirations. Danny wants to get into Duke, he wants to be a lawyer, and he has aspirations to be on the Supreme Court, so you need to work with us.'"

In the end, "Danny got into Yale and Harvard but went full ride to UNC with a Morehead scholarship. As Gregory did too," Maryanne finishes this remarkable story of achievement with matter-of-fact pride. The Morehead-Cain scholarship is University of North Carolina Chapel Hill's most prestigious fellowship. It offers a full ride, plus an initial international gap year and summer support. When I ask Greg about his fellowship, he explained that his parents could afford to send him for three years to Yale or Harvard, but he would have had to take out loans for his last year, something he was wary of doing given the prestige and resources offered by the Morehead scholarship. Greg laughs, "Unlike most people who leave college in debt, I actually left college with a savings account." As I write this, Danny is now a successful lawyer in Washington, DC, and Greg is a twice-awarded Fulbright fellow and my doctoral student at University of Southern California, writing a book on India. Charlotte, while she did not follow the same path as Danny and Greg, ended up studying textiles at North Carolina State and now works for the North Face.

Maryanne reflects, "We had already been negotiating education waters for eight to nine years at that point. Public school isn't going to work, Catholic school is okay, but that's now not going to work. Now charter school. But our eyes were already open. Where I was caught off guard was, 'We already know who the top five will be.'" While Maryanne is talking, I am listening in awe of her courage and tenacity in supporting her children, her ability to understand what it took despite not having the experience firsthand. As Maryanne revisits her first interaction with the guidance counselor, she puts the meritocracy into a most apt metaphor: "Really one of those moments where the bus was leaving the terminal and I didn't even realize there was a bus."

I am also impressed with Maryanne and Bob's ability to read the subtle codes of the meritocracy and figure out a way in for their children. Once they were on the bus, it was clear what had to be done. "Things that need to happen for your kid to have those opportunities," Maryanne explains. "We were all working on that and experiencing that together. It was kind of formulaic: athletics, you have to hold offices, be nice if you started a club or two of your own, have to have some volunteer activities. They did it all and they seemed to have the capacity to do it all," Maryanne says, almost still astonished. "There were long days sometimes."

For Bob, there was an absurdity to the process. "I remember standing in our driveway having an intense conversation with Gregory about whether he should stay editor of his newspaper and be fifth in his class versus quitting and aiming for valedictorian or salutatorian," Bob chuckles almost incredulously. "And I thought, this is ridiculous! Be head of the newspaper, who cares if you're fifth or second?"

Bob's observation is in tune with the dominant criticism of the meritocracy and competitive parenting in particular—that it has become a treadmill on which participants completely lose sight of the actual point of learning. "For affluent, white-collar Americans, higher learning is something close to sacred. We bask in the sunshine of enlightenment that prestige universities radiate, and we speak of them in the language of dreams, of religious veneration," writes Thomas Frank in the *New York Times*. "They are the foe of much that is evil and the source of a lot that is good. More and better education, we like to believe, will solve climate denialism, overcome bigotry, and even mitigate our grotesque income inequality." But ultimately, the quest for credentials—the right school, the right job—interferes with the very process of learning.

The dark side of meritocracy is most stark in its inequities. That Maryanne and Bob were able to meet this system head-on and help their children gain the footing they deserved is exceptional. That they had the tenacity and wherewithal to educate themselves as to what needed to happen is rare. Most small-town parents would get a whiff of the barricaded fortresses of the International Baccalaureate program and, being understandably intimidated, sit back and let things play out. The meritocracy is so fixated on credentials that they become the barrier between its members and everyone else. Or, as the Harvard philosopher Michael Sandel, author of *The Tyranny of Merit*, observes, "Credentialism has become the last acceptable prejudice."[26]

THE MERITOCRACY EXCLUDES, but rural kids don't always want to be included. For children growing up in rural America, elite universities hundreds if not thousands of miles from home are not necessarily where they want to be. One clear explanation is that rural students and their parents feel intimidated. They are out of touch geographically, they do not possess the same social and cultural capital, and many of them will be in a demonstrably lower income group than their collegiate peers. As such, college is not a natural fit for them. They are not just being pushed out; they do not want to be pulled in. Maryanne and Bob are the exception to this phenomenon. Whatever intimidation they felt, they rose above it. Whatever cultural capital cues didn't come with their own life experience, they learned them quickly.

One might think it is not in rural America's self-interest to deprioritize college and eschew the path toward the meritocracy. However, it is more complicated than simple disinterest. Rural students tend to be very tied to their communities. They grow up in families where members stay nearby, so childcare is more likely to be kept within the family than it is in cities. Religious practice is also more frequent, and church often plays an important role in the social lives of rural students. In short, they are looking at life through a different lens than urban and suburban students. There is a clear choice between learning to leave and learning to stay. The belief for some in rural communities is that leaving home means "leaving the ways of living in which one is raised."[27] In a study of rural Canadian youth, scholar Michael Corbett found that this decision was traumatic. Leaving for college was "for some students...liberating, for others unthinkable and for most it is problematic and conflicted."[28] Part of this stress has to do with the act of leaving their communities and the fear that, once educated, they will no longer be able to return and assimilate. The community is also often concerned that they won't return, as highlighted in Thomas Espenshade's observation about his student from West Virginia.

In addition, rural students are influenced by the values espoused by their parents and community. Rural life in general deemphasizes the importance of intellectualism and book learning while making more of practical knowledge and skills. When rural students think about future jobs, they rarely think of being a hedge fund manager,

stock trader, fashion designer, or literature professor. Instead, farm-
ing, factory work, some health care occupations, and blue-collar and
service jobs are more likely considered.[29] As Ardoin writes in her
book on rural students and higher education, "Children in rural
and working-class areas are taught information and behaviors that
prepare them for blue-collar work."[30] Reading this research made
me wonder what, when I asked my interviewees whether they "valued education," they thought I meant. I realized that as a professor
with a PhD, when I ask about education I'm talking about books
and exams and statistics and, yes, credentials. With so many rural
parents telling me they value education and yet so few of them being
truly focused on their child attending a top university, I came to
realize our definitions of education and its outcomes were likely different. Education may mean a trade, vocational school, or learning how to run a farm, but it did not necessarily mean getting a
bachelor's degree. In relation to urban and suburban America, rural
Americans' ambivalence toward higher education suggests a very
different conception of meaningful work and a good life.

At a USC Family Weekend event in the autumn of 2021, I was
seated at a table with a diverse group of parents, and two of the
mothers had come from the heartland. The woman next to me ran
a research and policy center in the University of Wisconsin system.
I was describing the book and the differences between rural and
urban parents. She explained that rural students are pushed toward
vocational and technical training far more than toward a degree in
anthropology or law. Another woman at the table, who was getting
her doctorate in education at the University of Iowa, elaborated on
what seems like an almost ossified path that rural students are compelled to take. She discussed a study looking at how rural and urban
students respond to college essay questions, which found that the
two groups expressed vastly different responses.

It's clear that rural students possess different cultural capital and social norms than many of the students applying to top

universities. This observation aligns with what Ardoin calls "college knowledge." In its most literal form, college knowledge is understanding how to apply, knowing people who can help, and so forth. In its more complicated interpretation, it is about how one communicates oneself to the world. Using the sociologist Pierre Bourdieu's concept of cultural capital, Ardoin makes the point that language is the slipperiest part of a person's social position. "Higher education institutions," she writes, "also favor linguistic and cultural competences that can 'other' rural students and create barriers for them." Jargon, she explains, becomes another element of the college experience that rural students find difficult to interpret.[31]

While these women I met at USC's Family Weekend did hark from the very places I am writing about, they, too—with doctorates and careers in research—were the exception. Because of their own education and understanding of college knowledge, they were able to help their kids end up at a school like USC. They had the confidence that their kids could do it, and they were able to instill in their children the belief that a college education was a valuable path.

A CCORDING TO *US News & World Report*, less than 0.5 percent of all students attend an Ivy League university. Less than 10 percent attend a flagship or research-intensive state university, which would include the University of California system and the University of North Carolina system, where Danny and Greg attended. Just 16 percent of students attend a private, nonprofit college or university (places like Stanford, MIT, or USC).[32] When we look at these numbers, it's hard to wonder how anyone—regardless of geography—could possibly enter one of these venerable educational institutions that pave the way into the meritocracy unless they were already part of it.

But maybe it doesn't matter that elite education remains by and for elites. In a number of recent studies, researchers have found that while attending an Ivy League institution certainly doesn't hurt, it also may not do much good. Two famous studies by economists Alan Krueger from Princeton and Stacy Dale from the think tank Mathematica show that Ivy League graduates do not necessarily make more than students who attend less selective schools. In the first study, Krueger and Dale found that students who were accepted to an elite university but went to a less selective one ended up in the same income tier as they would have had they attended the more prestigious school. This suggests that it is other qualities, not the university, that determine a student's future success. In the second study a decade later, Krueger and Dale were able to observe that even students who'd been *rejected* by an Ivy League school (which is between 90 and 95 percent of all applicants) made just as much money as those who attended one of these elite institutions (controlling for SAT scores). As Krueger and Dale write in the *Quarterly Journal of Economics*, "Students who attended more selective colleges do not earn more than other students who were accepted and rejected by comparable schools but attended less selective colleges." The researchers find that tuition cost is a much more explanatory variable associated with greater pay down the road, which they explain as a function of the ability of "higher cost schools [to] devote more resources to student instruction."

This research corroborates a number of other scholars' efforts to unpack the qualitative differences in colleges and their subsequent impact on students' futures. In general, the research suggests that the importance of attending an elite university really depends on who you are. As the Harvard economist Raj Chetty and his colleagues find, students coming from households in the top 1 percent are seventy-seven times more likely to attend an Ivy League school than those in the bottom 20 percent. In and of itself, this does not change their outcomes. After all, if you start in the top 1 percent, it's a bit academic to fret about which tenth of a percentile you end up in. In the same paper, looking at thirty million students between

1999 and 2014, Chetty finds that the biggest gains are to be had by poor students who attend elite universities such as the Ivy League. Not only that, but low-income students who attend elite universities make as much when they graduate as their high-income counterparts, suggesting that the idea of a "mismatch" (that poor students are out of their depth at an elite university) is inaccurate; they do just fine.[33] Case in point, 60 percent of Columbia graduates end up in the top 20 percent income bracket, regardless of whether they come from a high or low household income.[34]

Chetty and his colleagues also find that it may not be the top universities that provide the greatest social and economic mobility but rather less selective, mid-tier institutions. In their "Mobility Report Card," they find that Cal State Los Angeles, Stony Brook University, and the City University of New York (CUNY) system are the most likely to offer mobility to low-income students. Over half of all Stony Brook students coming from households in the bottom twentieth percentile end up in the top fifth income group. This makes sense: Even if Ivy League colleges admit low-income or minority groups who would stand to gain from the social and cultural capital offered, they still only give out a very limited number of slots. On the other hand, mid-tier colleges have much greater acceptance rates. What surprised me about the results was not that bigger universities with less selective admissions might offer greater mobility but rather which universities were critical to this process. Chetty and his colleagues do not list smaller private universities like Pepperdine or all of the big state schools. Instead, outside of CUNY and the State University of New York system, the list includes places that wouldn't necessarily seem to be obvious engines of mobility, including Cal State Los Angeles, Pace University in New York, and University of Texas Pan American.

Another paper, written by National Bureau of Economic Research scholars, finds that college selectivity matters for women's labor force participation. Their study focused on selective and highly selective colleges and the schools' average SAT scores. For every hundred SAT points, women experienced a 4.8 percent increase in probability of attaining an advanced degree, a 2.3 percent increase in probability of working, and a 15 percent increase in earnings.[35] In another study that looked at UT Austin and Texas A&M compared to non-flagship universities, the scholars found that students did achieve a wage premium for attending, but who received these advantages differed based on background. Minority students did not benefit particularly from attending UT Austin as opposed to a less elite university, while their postgraduation income was consistently high if they attended Texas A&M (a less prestigious university). It is worth noting that at the absolute top of the earnings distribution UT Austin did positively impact income, but for most students Texas A&M offered the most reliable opportunity for higher earnings.

Quality may matter, but what these studies suggest is that the student matters more, in terms of both aptitude and background. Students who attain high SAT scores, a proxy for ability, and attend a mid-tier college seem to do as well as students of similar ability attending more elite universities. It turns out that many students benefit from going to mid-tier colleges. The experience may not catapult a low-income student into the top 1 percent, but it will often move her into the top 20 percent. In addition, elite education seems to matter most for those students who enter college on the back foot: low-income students, women, and minorities who do not have the initial endowments of social capital offered to their wealthier, white, male peers. In fact, for this latter group, elite colleges don't move them up at all, because there is not much room when you're already at the top. While this data suggests that elite universities should open their doors to those who are disadvantaged in any number of ways, it seems that those same students can also thrive at mid-tier colleges.

This gets me to the point of how much we should care about the meritocracy and the top 1 percent. "In the Ivies and their ilk," reports an article in the *Atlantic*, "there has been almost no overall growth in students whose families are in the bottom 20 percent."[36] While this is a distressing statistic, the work done by Chetty and his colleagues suggests that many students are able to gain social mobility without ascending to the heights of the meritocracy.[37] If the meritocracy is a recursive loop that every once in a while lurches and helps a person of color or a woman or a low-income, first-generation college student, then great, but it's hardly going to promote the profound social change that we need education to catalyze. As a National Bureau of Economic Research paper entitled "Old Boys Clubs and Upward Mobility Among the Educational Elite" reports, "We conclude that social interactions among the educational elite mediated access to top positions in the post-war United States but did not provide a path to these positions for underrepresented groups." For the most part, elite institutions provide and affirm rarefied social networks and access to other institutions (whether social clubs or finance jobs) to those who are already, well, elite.

Rich people stay rich, elite people remain elite, but I'm not sure that it's a good use of our time as a society to care about their outcomes when there are far bigger issues of equality and mobility in rural America's educational system. I am not apologizing for the elitism of our finest educational institutions. However, from talking to rural parents and reading about rural schools, I believe we must take a more Benthamite approach where we focus on the greatest happiness of the greatest number. If Ohio State or Texas A&M can move more low-income students into the middle or upper middle class, then I would argue we need to spend less time worrying about the small percentage of such students who might enter the top 1 percent if they go to Yale.

I WONDERED WHAT THE fortunes of rural America looked like even without the trappings of the meritocracy. I knew from my interviews that many rural Americans were content and doing well. I also wanted to know how the life outcomes of children growing up in rural America compared to those growing up in America's biggest cities, especially in the affluent, upwardly mobile neighborhoods in New York, San Francisco, and Los Angeles. Is geography really destiny? And what would that mean in the twenty-first century, anyway?

Opportunity Atlas is Raj Chetty's database of socioeconomic and demographic variables for almost all the zip codes in America. Chetty and his colleagues have tracked twenty million Americans from childhood to their midthirties, looking at how the environment of a particular place affects their education, income, marital status, and other outcomes. I started looking at Chetty's data by plugging in the zip codes of the rural towns where people I interviewed lived. I started with Jesup, Iowa, where Craig (a farmer I spoke to a number of times) lived. At the time I looked at the data, the adult household income for a child growing up in a middle-income family was projected to be $59,000.[38] I thought that was pretty high and that Jesup must be an exception, so I plugged in the zip code of Neenah, Wisconsin, the location of a pastor and his wife: $39,000 to $48,000. Then I plugged in 17821, Danville, Pennsylvania, where I grew up: $41,000.

I then wanted to see what upper-middle-class urban neighborhoods' projected income looked like, so I typed in the zip codes for Los Feliz (Los Angeles), Silver Lake (Los Angeles), and Yorkville (Manhattan): $34,000, $44,000, and $46,000 respective projected adult household income for those who grow up in middle-income families. I then looked at what percentage of the population of future thirty-five-year-olds who grew up in middle-income families would be in the top 20 percent of income. For Jesup, Iowa, the number is 29 percent. For Silver Lake, 27 percent. For Danville, Pennsylvania, it's 18 percent. For 10128 in New York City, it's 27 percent. This happened over and over again. These numbers didn't initially make sense to me. How is it possible that the outcomes for middle-income rural America are largely the same as for those growing up middle-income in largely affluent neighborhoods in our cities?

Here's how I make sense of this data. We—the academics, the media, the coastal elites—spend an enormous amount of time talking about Ivy Leagues, the meritocracy, and the top 1 percent. Yes, these very narrow bands of people and qualifications are rare; they're rare in our cities and significantly rarer in rural America. We also know that, qualitatively, if we unpack where rural kids go to college, we find that more of them go to less selective community colleges, and very few are able to follow the path to a flagship state school or Ivy equivalent. This data is reversed for the kid who grows up on the Upper East Side of Manhattan or in Brentwood, Los Angeles, where it is almost assumed he will attend a highly selective college and ultimately remain within the top 1 percent income bracket into which he was born.

After looking at this data, I wondered why we cared so much.[39] If rural Americans coming out of middle-income families were projected to make a living and gain a foothold in the middle class at a similar rate as many of their urban counterparts, I wasn't sure it was so important for incomes to be higher, particularly given that the cost of living is so much less in rural America. My interviews and other research suggested they were pretty happy already. Far more so than their urban counterparts who were fretting, striving, and feeling the pressure of existing in an expensive global city, trying to raise children in the vortex of competitive parenting, awash in $40,000 tuition fees, multi-thousand-dollar summer camps, violin lessons, and nannies.[40]

I think this was more a question I needed to answer myself, because, truthfully, I cared so much. I had gone to school in small-town America, and my life now is much different from most of my classmates' lives. But I failed to appreciate that these may be more active choices than I had thought. My life is not better than those in my hometown. I am not necessarily happier. Our lives are different but should not be placed in a hierarchy. Living in Los Angeles and teaching at a major research institution can make one blind to the idea that many people don't want to be a part of the meritocracy. Many people don't care about the top 1 percent because, well, 99 percent of people don't belong to it.

This is particularly true for rural Americans, who are physically removed from the major cities at the center of the world economy. What they care about, as I came to learn so profoundly in my interviews, is their family, holidays with their loved ones, God, and the other stuff of their lives. There is a qualitative difference in their aspirations. On paper, their income and class position were not meaningfully worse than most of America. In fact, by some measures, they were better. In the rural Midwest and the Interior Northwest, collegiate education levels are fairly on par with cities. Rural Massachusetts boasts a higher median rate of bachelor's degrees than the state's urban counties. But rural America is not a place with an abundance of fancy graduate degrees where the top 1 percent resides. Indeed, the data is unequivocal that those populations are in our urban centers, the very nexus of the global knowledge economy and home to the lawyers, researchers, media professionals, and other members of the managerial and meritocratic elite.

But if you live in rural America and you are told only 0.5 percent of people attend an Ivy League and the top 1 percent includes, tautologically, just 1 percent of the population, do these feel like issues that concern you? You've got a house, your kids live nearby, you see them and your grandchildren almost daily, food is reasonably priced, you don't pay for private school, your kids don't attend $70,000 per year private universities, and everyone is doing alright. How much can you really care that you're not a member of an elite class? No one I spoke to felt left out or left behind. They didn't express the angst that so many urban meritocrat parents experience as their kids apply to top universities. The rural Americans I spoke to conveyed a contentment that none of my friends in coastal cities with meritocratic jobs and pedigrees ever express. Rural Americans wanted something different for their kids, not something worse. That gave me something to think about.

I WILL NOT CONCLUDE by saying none of this matters. Of course it does. The meritocracy runs the global economy, and those within it are shaping the fortunes of the world. While the global economy isn't directly centered in rural America, its reverberations can be felt everywhere. The meritocracy's obsession with sending their children to Ivies and other elite universities has come to dominate American culture, and as a result we're not nearly as receptive as we should be to trade or vocational schools. The assumption that every child ought to attend a four-year, elite educational institution loses sight of the differences in abilities and passions. Alternatively, the idea that a young woman from rural Arkansas has no possibility of attending Princeton to study sociology should she want to is equally tragic. In each of these instances, the child may miss out on their chance to live life the way they want to. For me, this is the crux of the problem with the ossified educational system and how it impacts rural America.

The meritocracy rightly has many critics. It is a pressure cooker. Parents are driven by anxiety and fear to ensure their children's future. And it has become apparent that, after all of that preparation, our children are not necessarily happier for it. Nor are they, riddled with tens of thousands of dollars of debt, making a success of life (and they sure are in the hot seat to do so, given all of the resources thrown at them). There are other ways to make money, to be socially mobile, to make a life.

And thus, I had unanswered questions. If Princeton didn't matter to one's life chances, then why did many kids feel a pressure to apply and be accepted? If elite education wasn't worth the stress, then surely the influence and competitiveness of the Ivies would have diminished years ago. I wondered, as those of us in the more qualitative side of social science often do, if there was more to the story than the numbers. Were there other factors that were hard to capture from income levels and mobility from one quintile to another? How was job and life satisfaction measured through these outcomes? Did those who followed the path of mid-tier university to top 20 percent have the same types of lives as those who went to a top twenty-five university? Did these graduates end up in flexible jobs that allowed them to pick their kids up from school, participate in an exercise class, make meaningful career changes? Do numbers ever allow us to capture the most important aspects of life? Even if rural Americans were happy living their lives outside of the meritocratic rat race, was it good for society? Was it good for them? These were definitely questions for Raj Chetty.

While I have mentioned Chetty's work already, the man himself is worth an introduction. Harvard professor, MacArthur genius grant awardee, and John Bates Clark medalist (the second-most prestigious award in economics after the Nobel Prize), Chetty is known as one of the greatest economists in the world. As the economist Edward Glaeser, his colleague, remarked in an *Atlantic* profile, "The question isn't *if* Raj will win the Nobel, but *when*."[41] Naturally, if I wanted answers to these questions, Chetty was the person to ask. I did not assume that he would have time to chat, but I figured it was worth giving it a try—so I wrote him an email.

I got a reply. I was beyond thrilled. We arranged to speak a few weeks later in mid-October 2021 by Zoom. Chetty showed up on time from a simple, clean office with no frills. I had done my background reading, and I knew that despite his many accolades he was a man of little fanfare. At the time of his 2019 profile in the *Atlantic*, his house was devoted to his young daughter's artwork and make-believe, and he drove the journalist, Pulitzer Prize–winning writer Gareth Cook, around in an old Acura as he picked up takeout. In

every photo I've ever seen of him, Chetty is wearing an unpretentious Oxford button-down shirt, sometimes a tie, and dark pants. In
one photo for an article in *Bloomberg* magazine, Chetty's shoes are
actually a bit worn in, which is normal for every day, but endear-
ingly unpretentious for a major profile in a magazine.[42]

There is no question that Chetty's uncontrived and genuine
demeanor is part of his appeal. Even when speaking over Zoom,
he is quiet and careful. He explains his data matter-of-factly rather
than bragging or presumptuously assuming he definitely has the
answer. It is clear in his work that he is constantly thinking and
rethinking whether he's got it right and whether the solutions he
and others have applied are actually helping. There is no sense that
he ever thinks his work is done.

His worry for low-income people with limited opportunity is
not whether they go to law school or medical school (a distinction
he finds irrelevant for upper-income kids too). Rather, Chetty wants
to make sure that those with less opportunity and less chance for
mobility don't end up incarcerated or dead. His center at Harvard,
Opportunity Insights, has found different outcomes for children
who grow up on one street versus one two blocks over. This research
suggests policy interventions that meet urban planning by looking
at how to improve outcomes on a granular level. Many have looked
at Chetty's work as an intervention that may allow for the American Dream to become a reality, but it is also an existential lesson in
Sliding Doors–type chance: that any of us, having been given a little
more or a little less, could have a vastly different life.

What makes Chetty's work so powerful is that he is interested
in lost opportunity—what could have been and the potential we for-
sake when we don't intervene as a society. He and his team have
found that access to education and resources plays a huge role in
determining whether kids are successful. Chetty and his colleagues
coined the term "lost Einsteins" to explain how being good at math
in third grade is linked to being an inventor when one grows up.

However, this doesn't hold true for everyone, as can be seen in the number of patents. For children coming from top 1 percent families, there is a rate of 8.5 patents per one thousand people. For those coming from families making less than the median income, the number is 0.85 patents per one thousand people. Men are more likely than women to generate patents for their work. Chetty and his colleagues find that for those children in the top 5 percent of math scores who are also in the top 20 percent of income, there is a rate of seven inventors per one thousand people. For those equally gifted young mathematicians in the bottom income quintile? Only three per one thousand. When children are in eighth grade, this "gap in innovation" can be explained by test scores because, by that time, the lower-income students have fallen behind—not from lack of aptitude but rather lack of resources and good schooling that would capitalize on their giftedness. "Children at the top of their 3rd grade mathematics class are much more likely to become inventors, but only if they come from high-income families," the researchers conclude. "High-scoring children from low-income or minority families are unlikely to become inventors. Put differently, becoming an inventor relies upon two things in America: excelling in mathematics and science and having a rich family."[43]

The economists zero in on what might drive these discrepancies. Money is part of the story, but so is the cultural and social environment. A consistent family life, a good school, and exposure to the possibilities to be something else. For example, children who grow up around inventors, say in Silicon Valley or near the Jet Propulsion Laboratory, are more likely to become inventors themselves, even down to the type of technology they were exposed to. We know money matters, but there's more that enables some kids to become the next Steve Jobs while others become "lost Einsteins." "You would think," Chetty remarks to me with a quiet intelligence, "talent is uniformly distributed across different places, but if you look at career paths people chose to pursue, they are incredibly influenced by what happens to be going on in their own families, or what happens to be going on in their neighborhood, et cetera."

Chetty only knows this too well. His own young life reflects the variables he studies today. "My own personal experience, one generation back," Chetty tells me. "My parents both grew up in poor Indian villages. There wasn't enough food for the kids, really extreme poverty." There was no reason to believe at the time that his parents' lives would be any different. As it turned out, a series of random events transformed their lives. "In my mom's case, there just so happened to be a girl's school that opened up right near her house that allowed her to go to complete high school and then college, which was very unusual for women at that time in south India," Chetty explains. "She went on to become the first female doctor in our community." As the story goes, Chetty's mother, Anbu, supported his father, Veerappa Chetty, as he acquired his degree. "And similarly my dad had the option to come to UW Madison to do operations research and an economics PhD," Chetty says. "He would describe how he got this letter in the mail, and at that time in India, he went to an astrologer to ask if he should go, and she said, 'No you shouldn't. I've read my…'" Chetty fills in, "whatever," "'and I predict that the boat is going to sink!'" He is smiling as he goes on. "And my dad was like, 'I don't know. I'm just going to go,'" Chetty laughs out loud. Very quickly, though, he gets serious again. "That obviously had an enormous impact on the opportunities for me and my sisters, but we've also seen the generational impact on our cousins, with a dramatically different set of opportunities."

Chetty was born in India as well, and at the age of nine he immigrated with his parents to America, where he went on to enroll in a prestigious independent secondary school and then Harvard for his undergraduate and graduate degrees in economics. Even at a young age, Chetty showed an affinity for numbers. There is a photo that has appeared in a couple of profiles of him where he is standing next to a chalkboard, wondrous smile on his face, gangly, with a piece of chalk in his hand. Despite the fuzziness of the photo, one can make out the summation symbol and a series of variables and sequences. Chetty, aged nine, is working out calculus problems. "I've always been interested in statistics and math," he tells me, laughing quietly and self-effacingly.

Chetty explains to me that his grandparents on both sides just didn't have the money to support all of their children's educational aspirations. By luck or potential at the time, they educated Chetty's father and mother. "They had this dramatically different life because they had this opportunity to get more education and come to the US," Chetty explains to me. "But then when we look at our uncles and aunt and their kids. One is working in Singapore to support his family in India and doesn't get to see his kids. Another has a tough manual-labor job." Chetty pauses. "They're doing fine but a totally different set of opportunities, and so that has been with me since I was a kid."

Chetty's life's work has been to understand this counterfactual, how we are all either victors or victims of our circumstances. "To put it another way," as Chetty remarked in an interview with the *Atlantic*, "who are all the people who are not here, who would have been here if they'd had the opportunities? That is a really good question."[44] Chetty's work offers solutions. He finds that a mid-tier college can bump a low-income student into the top 20 percent, questioning the worth of an Ivy League degree. He has also found that kindergarten teachers play a significant and disproportionate role in a child's success: a good teacher at this age can help promote a lifetime of higher earnings for their pupils.[45]

Chetty's work left me feeling better about the state of rural America and other parts of the country that do not have access to the resources necessary to get into a top university. But I was still nagged by the unobservable benefits of an elite education, because clearly on some level going to one of these universities still matters. I ask Chetty what a rural kid might gain from going to Harvard rather than just aiming for a mid-tier university. Why would the Ivies be so desirable if there weren't some real benefit to attending? Chetty surprises me, because he doesn't dismiss my concern, despite all of his data suggesting elite universities are overrated. "That kind of thing is extremely important, something that gets less attention than [income levels]," he begins. "Previously I've certainly had the view that you can think about social mobility broadly by reaching the upper middle class, and the Ivy League is basically irrelevant. It's too small in terms of numbers. Very few kids attend these colleges, and if that was your ambition then the clear goal is you have to attend Harvard or Stanford or wherever." Chetty stops for a moment. "But I think it's a very different story when you're thinking about the upper, upper tail, and the reason that I think this matters is not because we are helping people become billionaires but because the people who are in positions of influence—obviously politicians, Supreme Court justices—they exert a great influence on everybody else's life and you have a particularly un-diverse set of folks in those positions. The elite are left catering to their own group."

Chetty explains in detail that every elite sector of society that has an influence on America as a whole is composed of Ivy League or "Ivy plus" colleges. Seventy-five percent of Supreme Court justices went to an Ivy League. Pan out to MacArthur genius award winners like Chetty, Nobel Laurates, CEOs, and writers for the *New York Times*, Chetty argues, and you can see that these super-special, highly influential sectors of our society and economy are run by those educated at Stanford, Yale, Duke, and the like. "A huge fraction of them come from a tiny number of colleges, these elite Ivy League–type of colleges that account for something like half a percent of college enrollment [overall]," Chetty says. "Then you essentially have the propagation of the elite through these elite institutions, and that is something that the average American in rural America ought to care about as well, because they are going to be affected by the Supreme Court justices." Chetty's explanation echoes the study of social clubs at Harvard. The most elite kids—those from the most prestigious private high schools—remained part of a group that kept them elite when they arrived: joining private social clubs, living in "high priced" housing, and, upon graduation, going into high-paying careers in finance.[46] Yet, the benefits of social interaction at Harvard did not spill over to underrepresented groups; they simply reinforced the elite status of those already in position.

CHETTY'S DESCRIPTION REVEALS why we as a society should be concerned about elite universities and who they choose to enroll, and why, in particular, rural America should care too. Membership in the meritocracy is more than just the degree. Chetty and my conversation implicitly touches on C. Wright Mills's damning indictment in his book *The Power Elite*. Written in 1956, *The Power Elite* articulated the key sectors—government, the military, members of the most elite families, and giant corporations and their leaders—and makes the case that these people are, most famously, "the Ones Who Decide" about many aspects of society. Wright argues that these people tend to emerge from particular realms, most notably Ivy League schools, which demonstrates the reproduction of privilege and elitism among the rare few. If rural Americans don't attend these schools, then they will not be represented in some of the most important institutions in American society, and they should be.

In a more quotidian way, those who attend elite universities—the meritocracy—have a strong belief in what they can do with their lives. Whatever we say about the "cultural elite," their careers and schedules are flexible, and they can pursue whatever they'd like.[47] Much of the good of the meritocracy is about options and access, things that are unobservable in college graduation rates and income statistics. Members of the meritocracy live in cities with world-class museums, poetry readings, the opera, and diverse cultures. Professional-class jobs offered remote work and flexibility far before the pandemic hit. If you have a degree from Yale or MIT or Berkeley, you will land on your feet again and again and again, another version of Daniel Markovits's "Harvard cushion." And in some careers, attending a name-brand institution really matters a whole lot. Craig, the Iowa farmer, has a son with a PhD in English literature from a branch campus of the University of Illinois. At the time of my interviews with Craig, his son was working as a janitor at a university, hoping for a way into a tenure-tracked position. As I write this, Craig's son landed a one-year teaching position in literature and writing at the University of Iowa. Craig's update gave me much joy, but his son's path was long between degree and securing a job that matched his credentials. Such misfortune isn't likely to happen if you go to Stanford.

Nevertheless, in general, I think the obsession with the meritocracy and the top 1 percent or the top 10 percent is the navel-gazing of its members. People in rural America live good, meaningful, and happy lives without being part of the rat race. But what is problematic is the lack of opportunity to join the elite should they so desire. The meritocracy may or may not truly matter to one's happiness and sense of a meaningful life, but rural America is certainly excluded from it. Worse yet, the exclusion only goes in one direction. I can, at any moment, decide to up sticks and move back to my hometown and buy a house and live that life. Additionally, rural Americans may feel culturally out of place even if the opportunity to be a part of the meritocracy arises. It's not so easy to assimilate into a major metropolitan city and assume an upper-middle-class life if you don't already have its accoutrements. Most importantly, rural Americans, because they are not represented in elite education, are excluded from the institutions that shape American society: the Supreme Court, major newspapers and radio programs, and the halls of government.

But, as my interviews suggest, rural Americans aren't paying much attention to being excluded. They don't seem particularly upset that they weren't invited to the party because meritocratic culture doesn't matter to them. Partially, this is because their definition of meaningful work and achievement is different, and as such their culture is different too. And maybe, for most people living in rural America, that's okay. When I asked one young woman from Kentucky what was the most important thing she could pass on to her kids, she simply responded, "I want them to be kind and to be brave and to feel like they are good enough to exist in the world." When she said that, I thought, *That's what any kid wants from their mother.* That sense of belonging matters more than any piano competition or admission to a top twenty-five university. But even so, personally, I want more for our rural children. I still want that kid from Appalachia on the Supreme Court. I want that girl from Arkansas writing for the *New York Times.* Because their voices matter in shaping this country too.

6

MYTHOS AND LOGOS AND
THE SEARCH FOR TRUTH

I don't care what you call it. I care that you call upon it.
—Gabby Bernstein[1]

I was diagnosed with cancer in 2013 after my second routine mammogram," Shannon begins when I ask her about the saddest moment in her life. "I was forty-four when I was diagnosed. I was working as a single mom with a young son. I didn't know any-one who had cancer, so it was really eye-opening. I didn't know if my son would have a mother. I didn't know what the answer would be, whether I would live or die." Shannon speaks clearly and evenly, almost clinically, despite the scariness of what she is discussing. "At that point I'd been married and divorced twice, had one son, and was out in the bars, going to church rarely. [When I was diagnosed,] I just called out to God and said, 'If you are real, show me.'"

Shannon continues, "I ended up getting surgery Friday, September 13, 2013. It was a seven-hour surgery. It had not spread, I did not have chemo, and my son's father was able to take care of him for my surgery and recovery. The full recovery was about six weeks. I had one complication. They'd taken away so much breast tissue that it turned my skin black. It was so overwhelming." Shannon sighs in defeat. I can almost see her shaking her head. "The nurse said take some aspirin, cold compresses. The doctor said, 'I'm sorry there is nothing I can do.' I went home." As Shannon tells this story, I am struck by her steeliness and her ability to hold her nerve. I feel so sorry for her. What an awful situation to face alone.

"I live in a small town, and I put on Facebook that this had happened, and right then it turned black to blue to just a bruise," Shannon goes on. "I asked my small community—it's like the Bible Belt—and everyone was praying. My Facebook was blowing up, everyone was so interested in helping me." I can hear the enthusiasm reentering her voice. "But it gets better. At that point I'm still getting what I want from the Lord. He's answering all my prayers. But during that week it was really hard, being on pain medication, coming out of surgery. One night I had this really bad night. I couldn't breathe, hyperventilating. Next day, a lady comes with a Bible verse saying, 'You will not die.' I said, 'Why would you bring this to my house?' and she said, 'The Lord told me to bring this to you.' I had been brought up in church, don't get me wrong, but I had never had faith like this." Shannon chuckles.

"I was still seeing the doctor for reconstruction, but I'm going back to my old lifestyle, going to the bars, not going to church. Next spring, I felt I was going to commit suicide. There are a lot of coal trucks here. And one day I was driving to work, and this coal truck was coming toward me and I thought, 'I could end this right here,' and I looked down, for some reason, at my dashboard, and there was a Bible verse that said, 'Lead me your way everlasting,' and life was breathed into me and I never thought of it [suicide] again." I can hear Shannon's relief and sense of an enormous journey completed as she retells this story. I am equally transfixed, and I understand why she believes in God's personal intervention in her life.

In subsequent conversations with Shannon, she almost always refers to the ways God, often through Jesus, intervenes in her life.

We are in the midst of the pandemic as I am interviewing her, and, as always, I begin our conversations asking if she has been vaccinated. I have come to care about her, and I do not want her to get sick. She remains unvaccinated and also certain that God will protect her. She tells me the story of how she was at a Pentecostal revival in the summer of 2021. Thirty people got sick with Covid-19, and one thirty-year-old mother at the event was hospitalized. The very next day, Shannon attended a play at her church. "[I was] sitting next to a woman whose whole family gets it." Shannon didn't get it. Even the young mother took a dramatic turn for the better after their pastor made a trip to the hospital to which she had been transferred. Shannon believed that the pastor's visit might be the reason the woman recovered. Whether helping her avoid Covid-19 or ameliorating her marital woes, Shannon sees one clear reason, as she says confidently, "God just keeps showing up around me."

CONTEMPORARY FORMS OF religion are often marked by God "just showing up around me." What people mean by this is that God intervenes in their personal lives and that they have a direct line of contact with their deity. I was listening to an episode of the podcast *Dolly Parton's America* where the singer shares her own experience contemplating suicide. As she sat in bed and held a gun in her hand, her dog Popeye ran into her bedroom. In an interview with the *Daily Mail*, Parton says, "I kind of believe Popeye was a spiritual messenger from God." In the podcast, she goes further, observing that "dog" is "God" spelled backward. Parton laughs when she says this, but it's clear in her voice there's meaning to her in that connection. At the height of the pandemic, with no vaccines yet available, a Wisconsin woman I interviewed shares the story of her whole family getting together for Christmas. When I mention Covid-19, she laughs and tsk-tsks me. "Oh Covid, who cares?" Then she tells the story how her six-month-old granddaughter sang "Silent Night" underneath the Christmas tree, almost possessed by the spirit of Jesus, as those in attendance gathered round.

God showing up is perhaps most associated with religions marked by "immanence," or the belief that God exists within our earthly world as opposed to being a distinct deity far away from everyday life, the latter of which can be termed "transcendence."[2] While immanence is a salient characteristic of contemporary evangelical Christianity, it is not new. The cosmos of Greek mythology is a historical example of the notion of immanence, as are many Eastern religions.[3] As the Oxford religious historian Alan Strathern observes of the immanent point of view, "The world plays host to supernatural forces and beings with whom we must interact in order to flourish." The key here is "to flourish": immanence is notable for the benefits felt on earth bestowed upon those who worship.

I called the religious scholar Philip Gorski to ask him about how this might play out in contemporary America. Gorski, the chair of the sociology department at Yale University, has studied modern American Christianity in depth. Given his work on evangelicalism and white Christian nationalism, I wanted to get his view on this particular cultural divide. I was surprised that he didn't start with evangelicalism but rather with the ancient Greeks. As he explained, if we hearken back to the Greek gods, it was not so much that one particular god was worshiped or even thought of as an all-holy deity (the gods were powerful but not all good). Rather, engagement with a particular god resulted in good outcomes needed at that time. "This sort of practice looks weird to us in a culture [that tends toward monotheism], but it does not look weird at all through the lens of late antiquity Rome or the Khmer Empire in Cambodia," he explains. "Polytheistic gods, meta-persons all around you, and, you know, you're very pragmatic. Your feeling is, 'Oh this worked for a while, trying something else now.' [There was] no reason to devote yourself to one particular practice—dieting, sexual—to engage in to be happy or well or prosperous. [There were different needs and different gods,] some big gods, but some little ones too."

As Christianity is monotheistic, the description of the Greek gods does not match precisely. But, as Gorski points out, the way worship emerges as beneficial to daily life in evangelicalism is not dissimilar. This relationship between worship and earthly flourishing broadly started with Christian religions of the early twentieth century. As Richard Hofstadter documents in his book *Anti-intellectualism in American Life*, the inspirational or self-help literature of the 1930s and 1940s assured that religion was the path to wealth and mental and physical health. Hofstadter cites one inspirational writer from this time as stating that "God is a twenty-four-hour station. All you need to do is to plug in."[4] Older versions of self-help linked faith to character building, while these newer forms were marked by "self-manipulating" for greater earthly outcomes. As I read Hofstadter, I found myself thinking of contemporary evangelical Christianity, which places great emphasis on the personal interventions of God in our quotidian existence. Shannon shared a story of when she was furious with her husband one night because he wouldn't make dinner for their daughter. Just as she was going to express her anger, she looked down on her desk and there was the psalm, "Let peace flow like a river." "It was like God was speaking to me," Shannon explains. "I got up, I made her food, I didn't say a word, and guess what? I woke up and everything was fine. He is so real. It's not just some God high in the sky."

I SEE A PARALLEL explanation for these events. Shannon was getting routine mammograms, which remain the single most important means of catching breast cancer early and minimizing its possible spread. In passing, Shannon mentioned that she and her husband may have had Covid-19 in the winter of 2020. They both lost their sense of taste and smell, but nothing else. When Shannon says she didn't get Covid-19 from the revival or from the church play, I immediately thought that either she had natural immunity or she clearly weathers this virus better than many others. The poor woman who was hospitalized could equally have gotten better because she was getting good medical care and the virus ran its course; the timing of the pastor's visit could be spurious. Even looking down at the verse on the dashboard in her lowest moment required Shannon to receive it as a message to not take her own life. I shared Shannon's story with one of my interviewees who lives in Los Angeles. In response, he opened up to me. "In the last year, [I quit taking my anti-depressant] and was just on Wellbutrin. I got so low and so depressed. My psychiatrist says, 'Why not try going back on your Lexapro?' That's my psalm on the dashboard. Take your fucking Lexapro."

I hope it's obvious that I like Shannon tremendously. I honor where Shannon is coming from and understand why she has formed her opinions. There is a rich literature on the sociology of miracles.[5] We can see miracles everywhere if we choose to interpret the world through something metaphysical rather than through scientific fact. Our perception of reality—what is miracle, what is science, what is coincidence—is shaped by those around us. If our community sees miracles and reinforces our view of a higher power's intervention in our lives, we are inclined to see and believe all the more.

In order to understand this phenomenon more deeply, I wanted to talk to someone who was very engaged with the sociology of religion. I contacted the religious scholar Robert Wuthnow, who also wrote *The Left Behind* and was the recipient of *Vox* host Sean Illing's seeming disparagement of rural America. Wuthnow, who is the former director of the Princeton University Center for the Study of Religion and is now professor emeritus, has written many books on the topics of both rural life and religion. His book *The Restructuring of American Religion* documents the transformation of religion in this country since World War II.

When I called Wuthnow early in 2022, we talked about all sorts of things relating to religion and rural America, and I shared

Shannon's story with him. I also shared my alternative view. When you speak to Wuthnow, you perceive his lack of judgment of others, something that is clear in his writing too. "One of the things that is useful on miracles, [one of the] important things to look at, is the miracle story. There is a story that gives attribution to what happened, how the healing happened or if it didn't why not," Wuthnow explains. "The way that religious congregations work is that they provide the occasion for miracle stories to be told. It happens in small groups, and people get up and they give their miracle story and that defines their reality. Other people there know there are mammograms, and science, and all that, but what they are doing is attributing the healing to God. And as they share these stories, these stories influence how we perceive reality. After hearing one of those stories [in your congregation], you go to the doctor and you are in remission and [you think], 'It's just like that woman at church.'"

Miracles are not, of course, isolated to contemporary forms of Christianity. They run through the Bible, starting with Moses in the Old Testament and later those performed by Jesus in the New Testament. Catholicism, Judaism, and older forms of Protestantism teach of such events that transcend science and rationality. But these religious sects still see miracles at a distance, and certainly not as something that occurred with alacrity in day-to-day life. Older, more orthodox religions are marked by transcendence, which is the notion of a God outside and external to our daily lives.[6] They tend to worship God but not with the belief that God will offer wealth or prosperity or intervene regularly. Instead, older forms of Judeo-Christianity are about a quest for an ultimate truth and a quiet respect for a higher power, something that transcends human society. "Isn't religion precisely to do with what is *not* present in this plane of reality," writes Alan Strathern, "with that escape from the world that we know as salvation?" Part of this journey is self-reflection, discipline, and a path toward deep theological understanding.[7] So stark is the difference between immanence and transcendence that the fractures within contemporary Christian religions can be partially explained by these fundamentally different views of religion as part of our daily lives.

T HE PURITANS THEMSELVES were perhaps America's first intellectual meritocracy. As Philip Gorski argues in *American Covenant*, at the formation of the country, Christianity was not seen as threatening to the new government but rather as harmonious with it. Both religion and government, Gorski argues, were fused with the influence of the Hebrew prophecies.[8] One of the most prolific public intellectuals of the early American colonies was Cotton Mather. Say what we may about his part in the Salem witch trials, but Mather was educated at Harvard and one of the early advocates of smallpox inoculation. He applied a scholarly rigor to his sermons and was an essential part of the Puritan development of New England as the epicenter of American intellectual life.[9] Toward the end of Mather's life, there was a burgeoning revolt against established churches. Churches had ceased to connect with their congregations, and this was evidenced in the decline in attendance. The Enlightenment, embraced by Benjamin Franklin, Thomas Paine, and, in its early days, Mather himself, focused on reason, evidence, and science and de-emphasized the importance of religion.[10] While the extent is debatable, the Enlightenment influenced how religion was understood and practiced.[11]

During the Great Awakening of the early 1700s, revivalists— including Jonathan Edwards, a major figure in the early Enlightenment in America—argued for religious reform. Christian revivalists prioritized emotion and personal salvation in the religious teachings of the day, as well as an entirely new style of preaching that directly engaged the congregation.[12] They also challenged settled churches. Puritans and Protestantism up until that point revered educated and professional clergymen because knowledge and rationality were thought critical to religious understanding. Up to that point, "civil religion," to use Gorski's term, dominated both intellectual and religious life.[13] Church services were solemn and controlled.[14] Revivalists, on the other hand, had a whole new approach. In the eighteenth and nineteenth centuries, one can see the roots of contemporary evangelicalism, even religious nationalism, and immanence.[15] There was a rise in the practical over the esoteric, an eschewing of intellectualism in favor of charisma and enthusiasm. Emotion mattered more than rationality, as did direct, personal access to God. While such tensions had always existed in Christianity, in early America revivalism became the more favored approach.[16]

This transformation of religion and the generalized eschewing of intellectualism went hand in hand. This disengagement between intellectualism and religion contributed to the decline in religion's cultural influence in American life. The emergence of anti-intellectualism is not due to the decline in the value of knowledge but rather precisely because of the elite position that intellectuals hold, even in American society.[17] Rationalism prevailed as a framework that employed evidence and fact over faith, resulting in a decline of public religion.[18] Liberal Protestantism faded, and liberal secularism took its place. As Gorski observes, highly educated Protestants who might have been clergymen in a different era turned away from religion and instead pursued more professional careers in law, medicine, and academia. The rise of a more mainstream professionalized class uplifted secular fields' social, economic, and cultural capital and eroded religion's cultural capital.[19]

The distinction between older, transcendent, and increasingly secular Protestantism and more contemporary, immanent forms of Christianity may help explain the rise in opposition toward any form of intellectual elitism among the religious, and the simultaneous disdain toward overt religiosity displayed by secular liberals. Gorski describes the darkest forms of these two sides: on the one hand, religious nationalism, which he defines as "a toxic blend of apocalyptic religion and imperial zeal that envisions the United States as a righteous nation charged with a divine commission to rid the world of evil and usher in the Second Coming" and, on the other, radical secularism, "an equally noxious blend of cultural elitism and militant atheism that envisions the United States as part of an Enlightenment project threatened by the ignorant rubes who still cling to traditional religion."[20]

Radical secularism embraces nonreligious forms of intervention, whether wealth or wellness or science.[21] Its adherents possess their own religion in the form of meditation, organic food, exercise, progressive politics, and scientism.[22] Part of the tension that grew into what would now be called anti-intellectualism—and to a certain extent "anti-science"—was the fact that the upper and professional classes embraced rationalism and eschewed immanent religions while the working class leaned toward emotion and religion.[23] Today, for example, 40 percent of white evangelicals have a high school degree or less.[24]

There are many other religions and forms of religious expression that I do not engage with in this book, and all of them are important as well. Churches provide a safety net for minority and immigrant communities, offering both social capital and physical resources.[25] As Henry Louis Gates Jr. documents in his book and documentary *The Black Church*, the church has been instrumental in the Black community's political activism, cultural production, and local organizing.[26] Judaism has played a central role in the intellectual and cultural life of America, along with being a critical safe haven for post–World War II immigrants and reform movements.[27] Islam is gaining increasing prominence in the United States and is the third largest religion following Christianity and Judaism.[28] Religion and its physical institutions matter a great deal to a lot of people and play an important role in the cultural, social, and economic development of America. For pragmatic reasons, I am focusing on

Christianity and the rise of liberal and radical forms of secularism, because I believe these are where we see the supposed fault lines of the urban-rural divide.

W HEN I SPOKE to Americans about religion, it seemed clear that rural Americans were more interested in discussing faith as part of their identity and lives. This aligns with the common perception of rural folks being very religious. However, the statistics tell a contradictory story. Using the General Social Survey, I took a look at how questions on religion and spirituality shook out across rural and urban geographies.[29] The data indicates that Americans are cohesive in their belief in a God. Most Americans—urban and rural—are Christian. While there are more nonreligious people in cities, the difference between these geographies is not extraordinary.[30] Rural Americans do have greater reservations toward non-Christian religions than urban Americans, which is reflected in the fact that they are more likely to believe being Christian is "very important." Despite the ostensible secularism of city culture, both urban and rural people pray. Over 27 percent of urban dwellers pray several times a day compared to 34 percent of rural inhabitants. Approximately 40 percent of both urban and rural respondents describe themselves as somewhat religious, while approximately 15 percent of both groups call themselves "very" religious. Urban and rural respondents are equally likely to call themselves spiritual, with urban dwellers slightly more likely to define themselves as "very" spiritual, and approximately 65 percent of both groups agree or strongly agree that they are able to connect with God without a religious institution. In terms of the actual engagement with religious services, 14 percent of urban and 19 percent of rural respondents go to church every week. Four percent of both groups attend more than once a week, while roughly 30 percent of both groups never attend church services.

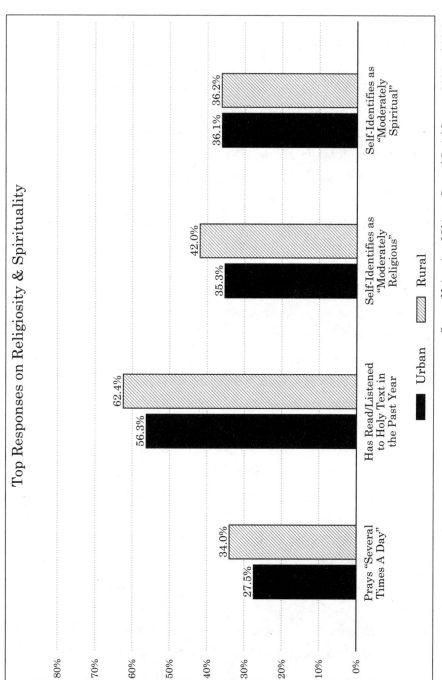

Top Responses on Religiosity & Spirituality

Prays "Several Times A Day" — Urban 27.5%, Rural 34.0%

Has Read/Listened to Holy Text in the Past Year — Urban 56.3%, Rural 62.4%

Self-Identifies as "Moderately Religious" — Urban 35.3%, Rural 42.0%

Self-Identifies as "Moderately Spiritual" — Urban 36.1%, Rural 36.2%

Urban Rural

Source: University of Chicago General Social Survey, 2014 and 2018

Why do I share this blur of statistics? Because when it comes to numbers, when asked point-blank about their religious and spiritual beliefs—an approach that captures observable and quantifiable differences—Americans are fairly similar in how they approach religion. When it comes to numbers, rural Americans are not meaningfully more religious than urban Americans, they do not pray significantly more, and they do not even go to church that much more.

When we look at religious or spiritual affiliation by education, rural people with a high school degree or above are more likely to be "moderately religious," while city dwellers with a college degree or above are more likely to be "spiritual" than their rural counterparts. Overall, these numbers are not remarkably different, with the exception that educated urban respondents are 35 percent more likely to be "moderately spiritual" than their rural counterparts, and rural Americans with just a high school education are also almost a third more likely to call themselves "moderately religious" than high school graduates in cities. These numbers show a largely similar relationship to religion and spirituality across these different groups. In fact, to put these similarities into perspective, the top result for each group is "moderately" for both religion and spirituality, with the exception of educated rural Americans, whose top response is "very" spiritual (40 percent of those surveyed gave this response, versus 30 percent of urban educated respondents). However, when I looked more closely at this group, I saw that exactly 68 percent of urban and rural educated respondents said they were either very or moderately spiritual, again showing a consistency across these ostensibly different places.

Why, then, did I see such a different response among my urban and rural interviewees? If most people ostensibly share a similar degree of religiosity and spirituality, why is it not evidenced when we speak to them? Further, why is there a common perception that rural America is so much more religious than the rest of the country?

248

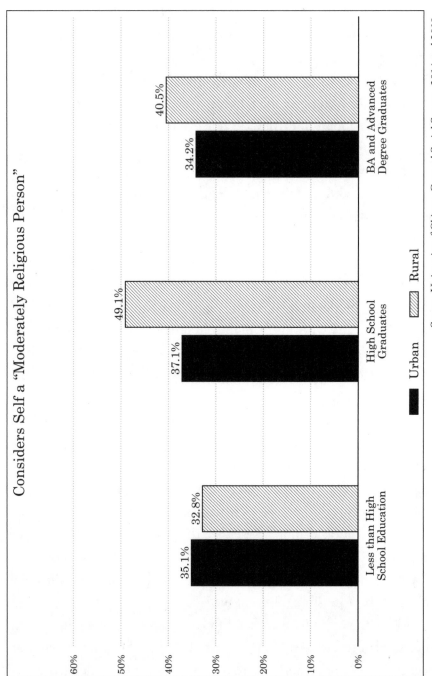

Considers Self a "Moderately Religious Person"

Source: University of Chicago General Social Survey, 2014 and 2018

■ Urban ▨ Rural

BA and Advanced Degree Graduates: 34.2%, 40.5%

High School Graduates: 37.1%, 49.1%

Less than High School Education: 35.1%, 32.8%

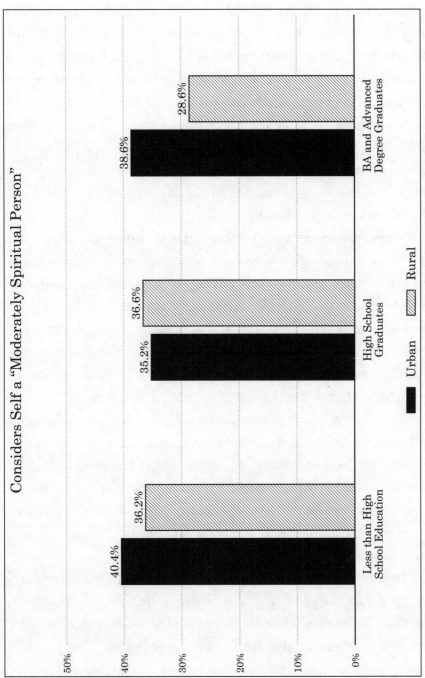

Considers Self a "Moderately Spiritual Person"

Source: University of Chicago General Social Survey, 2014 and 2018

Surveys and interviews provide different lenses through which we study human society. While surveys may give us some version of quantifiable data, they do not provide the context of why people say what they say, and they do not offer the freedom for people to share their view in an open-ended, nuanced way. Interviews can be seen as a window into people's priorities or what might first come to mind on a topic. The choice to bring up religion versus other values or interests reveals a cultural and social emphasis. As the political scientist Laura Olson writes, "In any culture, individuals pick and choose which values to espouse on the basis of their favored social characteristics or relationships."[31]

From this perspective, these qualitative differences come back to cultural capital—that is, our sum of formal and informal knowledge, behaviors, and style of speaking. Cultural capital is different in rural and urban America, as is social capital. Our social capital amounts to the advantages and benefits that our personal and professional networks might provide. A letter of recommendation, a referral to a great doctor, or an invitation to a big party are all examples of how social capital plays out. The church is the center of life in small communities, where Christmas fairs, bake sales, and after-worship donuts and coffee are instrumental community builders. In these environments, both social and cultural capital are present. While urban Americans are similarly religious according to the numbers, they do not necessarily arrange their identity or social lives around a church. For rural Americans, it offers the fabric through which small-town social life is woven.

Because Robert Wuthnow has studied both religion and rural life for decades, I asked him how he saw social and cultural capital intermingle and how they might explain my incongruent findings. "They are different, of course," Wuthnow begins. "But in small towns the social capital and cultural capital overlap. Not entirely, of course. Their social capital consists of who they need to be in contact with, who they need, but the cultural capital then is the local aspect, the local identity and the sense of pride. Cultural capital [then] is helping people get what they need in the same way social capital does."

This was my thinking, too, and it reminded me of Shamus Khan—also a Princeton sociologist—and his view on cultural capital as more than just an elitist tool. "Everyone has culture," Khan had remarked to me in conversation. I ask Wuthnow what he thinks. "We sociologists like to say, Who has cultural capital?" Wuthnow responds. "People who have a college education, people who read, people who go to museums. That's fine, but it doesn't capture cultural capital in small towns."

Growing up in small-town America and returning year after year, I found that my cultural capital had become more urban and educated, defined by my increased knowledge of books and newspapers and world events, and subsequently less valuable for assimilation with my former high school classmates. I'll never forget my Columbia University dissertation adviser remarking that she needed to have read the opinion section of the *New York Times* prior to any conversations with colleagues that day. From the moment she shared that perspective to this very day, the first piece of outside information I glean from the world is from the *New York Times* opinion page. But this is not cultural capital in Danville, Pennsylvania. For most of my former classmates and neighbors, this knowledge is at best irrelevant and boring, and at worst pretentious.

Wuthnow and I talk at length about what cultural capital means in small-town America. Knowing the history of the town and the local high school sports teams, even the cadence of one's voice and turn of phrase are part of showing cultural capital. "It's being able to say in church or at a community meeting, 'Anne told us such and such,'" Wuthnow explains, "and everyone knows who Anne is. Cultural capital is that local knowledge." In cities, it is almost impossible for such knowledge to count. We often don't know our neighbors, let alone share a large set of contacts with people who live in our apartment building or on our street. "Anne" could be anyone. My Anne is probably a fellow professor or mother at my children's school, which is probably not the same school that kids two blocks away attend. Urban, educated folks with less community roots tend to connect over more global points of shared knowledge: newspaper articles, podcasts, a new exhibition at the museum. For this group, that is local knowledge.

Social activities are equally important as a point of shared cultural capital. There are not so many options in small-town America, whereas in cities many people are doing many different things. When I was a teenager, everyone went to the same football game; everyone went to the annual fair and the holiday parades. Many civic events were organized at local churches: craft fairs, winter performances, and so forth. We were always bound to see each other, irrespective of our income, education, profession, or age. One interviewee explained of his life in a small town in the Midwest: "Everything in my parent's life revolved around the church. I don't think there was a single person in their life that wasn't connected to the church. So I mean, Sunday was church day but there were often things during the week—potlucks, so forth—any socializing on a Friday night was always from church. I don't think they had one friend outside the Episcopal church. Certainly that would affect your worldview," he said, almost introspectively. "Interestingly, there was a wide range of wealth. We lived in a town where Kimberly-Clark was significant, so we'd have a bigwig from Kimberly-Clark and [my parents] were also friends with the janitor. I think the church was a great equalizer of class."

Wuthnow echoes this point in his own examples: "The USDA divides rural America into an amenity index. If you live in a high amenity area, you go less to church. Churches in small town[s] are so much a part of the civic culture that churches are visible, they're early on, and they are still close to downtown, surround the town square if there is one. They are important to people's families. They've been Catholics, Methodists, Baptists forever. They know one another. 'That gal, we went to school together.' They have that knowledge. They've lived there very long."

Wuthnow goes on to talk about what I found in my own research: that churches are a critical node for civic activities. In the smallest of towns, schools may be consolidated, and there may not be a local football team. Churches provide social and cultural capital outside of their position as places of worship. "Because people know each other, and know each other across generations, there are a lot of funerals," Wuthnow explains, "so people go to the funerals. The pastor being a respected person—the pastor is one of the better edu- cated people in town, although that varies, but generally the pastor is a respected person." He then chuckles. "One thing I found was that, methodologically, they were great informants. If I wanted to know what was happening, I'd go to the clergy."

In most places, the clergy possess high-status social and cultural capital. Phil, a man I interviewed, grew up as the son of a small- town Wisconsin pastor. While he left the church and Wisconsin and moved to Los Angeles to become a successful screenwriter, he recalled a childhood that was marked by the social influence of sim- ply being the pastor's son. "We were obviously poor. At one point there were three kids in college, my dad on a preacher's salary, my mom didn't work. My dad didn't ever make more than $30,000 a year. And yet, even though we weren't moneyed people, we were hanging out at the country club," Phil recalls. "There was another guy who was a very wealthy man. He also had homes in Lake Tahoe. And he wanted my dad to be the bishop of Tahoe—I guess the dio- cese of Reno. I remember flying out to Lake Tahoe, and staying at one of this man's big houses on the lake." For Phil, this juxtaposition between his low income level and high social status as the son of a preacher caused him great cognitive dissonance. Even to this day, he has trouble making sense of it.

The cultural capital of religion in small-town America mani- fests in a number of important ways. First, religious institutions and their events offer important opportunities for people to establish social networks and social capital. For example, Wuthnow finds that simply being a member of a congregation, irrespective of church attendance, provides status and social capital.[32] Wuthnow also finds that while wealthy and urban people tend to have more high-status friends, small-town religious folks have strong connections to elected officials. In small-town America, where some of the more high-status occupations and the ultrarich are scarce, local elected officials become important high-status public figures, and many of their constituents connect with them through church.

Second, the currency of religious cultural capital in small-town America may be a function of the limited number of other outlets that compete with the church. As one scholar put it, from the lens of Pierre Bourdieu, religion is a "positional good" in flux within a symbolic economy, competing with other cultural goods.[33] In New York City, for example, one might belong to a congregation but also be a member of the Museum of Modern Art, attend the opera, or be an alumnus of Columbia or New York University. All of these entities possess institutionalized cultural capital that shares the same space with religious organizations.

Fundamentally, the cultural capital of religion is deeply related to local and civic life. As political scientist Robert Putnam and his colleagues found, religious people may also feel an obligation to engage in more do-gooder activities such as volunteering, donating money, and general neighborliness. This finding is not limited to the United States. In a comparison between the United States and Germany, research shows that religious networks drive civic behavior. "Religion is (at least potentially) a powerful and enduring source of social capital in this country, and indeed of social capital that has socially and ethically desirable effects," the author concludes. "Only the deliberately blind will continue to ignore religion as a source of social capital or deal only with its negative effects."[34] The connection is not simply between attending church and doing good things.

In fact, while religious attendance and affiliation are on the surface linked with civic engagement, Putnam and his colleagues argue that it is the social capital underpinning churchgoing that motivates people to volunteer and donate. Simply having a lot of religious friends strongly correlates with good citizenship. Even nonreligious people with religious friends engage in more civic activity.[35]

The question is why? Recall what Wuthnow said about the blending of social and cultural capital in rural America. In small communities with strong, overt religious identification and the values that often go with religiosity, one finds that their social network reflects these same values and activities. The quotidian setting of religion offers the dense, bounded networks that create and perpetuate cultural and social capital. In short, everything is local. People are far more influenced and shaped by local religious leaders than those on a national scale.[36]

"Sunday we go to my church, [my husband's] church, and then his church again on Sunday night," Shannon explains of her social life. "We have breakfast together after service [at the Catholic Church] and then Brad's [Pentecostal] church, they do a lot of things. Celebrate Recovery keeps me very busy. They have a Valentine's Day party, Christmas parties, and an Easter play." Shannon has been a volunteer with the Christian twelve-step group Celebrate Recovery for many years, and it is where she met her husband, Brad. Shannon's story of her civic work reminds me of the conversation I had with Arlie Hochschild as I was beginning my research for this book. As she had traveled deep into the Bayou to places with strong religious history, I asked her what she made of the community in these small towns. "Cosmopolitans talk about community, but these folks are local. They practice community," Hochschild said with a profundity that I associate with most all of her observations on humanity. "A beat-up old car with cracks in the leather would have walnuts in the back for someone, plastic cups in the trunk for the community drive [to raise money] for Afghanistan. It's community."

I am not overtly religious, nor do I see the Bible as literal. But I understand how in a changing world, with so many things beyond their control, many underprivileged communities find security in religious cultural capital. It is not that I have control over macro social changes, but economically, socially, and culturally, the global tides flow with me rather than against. Rural Americans are often out of position: they lack access to the meritocracy and its social networks, changing social and sexual norms feel anomalous in their hometowns and in conflict with all they've ever known, and they lack elite cultural capital, which may not be something they personally want but nevertheless has benefits. The departure of educated liberal Protestants from religion and the rise in nonreligious beliefs and practices has eroded the value of religious capital.[37] Scientific knowledge has been embraced by mainstream America and is increasingly dominant in public life.[38] As their religion is challenged, secularism and scientific authority sweeps the country, and meritocrats—not preachers—become the most respected leaders, the religious faithful hold on to their Bibles all the more.

In that respect, I understand the desire for consistency, for something that has always been and always will be. In their small towns, they are not "othered" because they believe in the Bible. Instead, they belong. Institutionalized religious cultural capital becomes a safety net, a comfort, a North Star. The donuts and coffee will be there every Sunday after Mass; the pastor will always offer something to hold on to; their community, often tied to their faith, has remained the same for decades. These are truths in this world when everything else seems to shift, all of the time.

THERE'S ANOTHER PROBLEM that religion faces, particularly evangelical Christianity. Evangelicalism has long been derided and castigated by the Left and liberals—and for unsurprising reasons.

It is thought to prioritize miraculous intervention over science, eschew intellectualism, and embrace very conservative politics.

In 2020, 80 percent of evangelical Christians voted for incumbent President Trump, and there is no question that some evangelicals played a role in the January 6 riot protesting Trump's loss.[39] Some evangelical churches have recently witnessed scandals and division over their handling of critical race theory.[40] "Evangelicalism is a populist movement. It has no hierarchy or central authority, so you might think it would have avoided the abuses of power that have afflicted the Roman Catholic Church," writes David Brooks in the *New York Times*. "But the paradox of decentralization is that it has often led to the concentration of power in the hands of highly charismatic men, who can attract enthusiastic followings. A certain percentage of these macho celebrities inflict their power on the vulnerable." More broadly, as Philip Gorski and Samuel Perry write in their book *The Flag and the Cross*, white Christian nationalism has been strongly linked to white supremacy under the guise of preserving liberty and democracy. Gorski and Perry argue that white Christian nationalists believe that the nation should be defined by their ethnicity, their religion, and their way of life. Other forms of religion, leftist politics, and secularism are ruining the great experiment of America.[41] It's important to clarify that not all white evangelicals subscribe to white Christian nationalism. Far from it. One can be a devoted evangelical and not adhere in any way to the values upheld by white Christian nationalists.

In addition to the threat of white Christian nationalism, evangelicalism has seen a decline in membership: in the last fifteen years, white Americans who identified themselves as evangelical dropped from 23 percent to 14.5 percent. Despite this overall declining trend, in 2019 32 percent of rural Americans identified themselves as evangelical, representing the greatest share of all religious denominations within this geography.[42]

Indeed, evangelicalism has become the poster child for the division between religious and secular America, despite the fact that overall religion is in decline and secularism is on the rise. While evangelicals witnessed the greatest drop, all religious groups studied have seen a decline in white members, while secular white Americans have jumped from 16 percent to 23.3 percent.[43] Some attribute this decline to a backlash against the religious right, resulting in both the rise of "nones" (those who believe nothing) and a rise in spirituality.[44] Traditional religion has been eschewed for other forms of faith: faith in science, wellness, mysticism, and secular spirituality. These new forms of faith are scary for religious folks, who already feel disdained by cultural elites and, as a result, have been building anti-intellectual and anti-science momentum for decades. While I am troubled with the idea of "anti" toward reason, rationality, and fact, it's important to take a moment and understand why such feelings might come about. Understanding people's perspective is the first step in alleviating their concerns, correcting misinformation, and finding a connection.

For some time, intellectuals themselves have been a part of the problem. As Susan Jacoby writes in *The Age of American Unreason*, intellectuals have historically misused science to propagate their own values. With the Gilded Age of the mid- to late nineteenth century came an emphasis on ideas, lectures, and intellectualism as a part of the social milieu. The increase in literacy and the introduction of adult education in cultural centers spread important knowledge and ideas to the general public, including an awareness of biological evolution.[45] However, the misuse and misconstruction of Darwinism by intellectuals to advance their own social beliefs had profoundly negative consequences. One such example is Alexander Winchell, who was hired as the president of Vanderbilt for a brief stint in the late 1800s. Winchell used Darwinism to bolster the white race: he argued that evolution must be true because Black people did not come from a white Adam; therefore, the human race must be older than Adam. This idea of something before the Bible angered many of the southern Methodists supporting the university, and so Winchell was fired. He promptly took his racist, white supremacist ideas up north to the University of Michigan. Winchell is a template of what happened with other evolutionists in the South. The problem was that people like him, who were held in such high esteem in the scientific community, were able to create a "social pseudoscience" as a veneer to justify their own racism.[46]

Perhaps the most famous propagator of this idea is Herbert Spencer and his concept of social Darwinism, which drew from the notion of natural selection and suggested that people's position in society was a function of where they ought to be.[47] Society, like biology, rested on natural selection. It was Spencer, not Darwin, who coined the term "survival of the fittest." By his distorted reasoning, the rich deserved their positions, and the poor, sick, or discriminated against deserved theirs too. This ignorant view—which disregarded the myriad political, social, and economic forces that shape our outcomes—was steeped in classism and racism.[48] Social Darwinism allowed a "biological justification for racial discrimination," writes Jacoby. It should come as no surprise, then, that "the leading American social Darwinists of the late nineteenth century were, almost without exception, upper-class, white Anglo-Saxon Protestants," she writes. "The class-based bias of leading social Darwinists against any evidence that contradicted their philosophical views is startling, because they were all men who, on an intellectual level, revered rationality."[49]

This is an important element in the story of how intellectualism alienated people of faith. That intellectualism became more respected than religion and ever more dominant in society was already a difficult reality for believers. That evolution, despite running against biblical teachings, became accepted as fact was met by outcry. The final betrayal was the dishonesty of members of the scientific community who created a pseudoscience and called it the truth. Social Darwinism thus was "a metaphysical creed disguised in scientific plumes."[50] People of faith—already disdained by an increasingly secular hegemony—had every reason to dismiss not just evolution but the very intellectuals propagating it. As Jacoby points out, pseudoscience did not end with social Darwinism. Eugenics, Ayn Rand's objectivism, laissez-faire economics, and, I believe, Charles Murray's *The Bell Curve* are all examples of how beliefs can be wrapped in a gauze of science and served as facts.

In twenty-first-century America, we see the same disturbing phenomenon with the rise of what the Pepperdine University political scientist Jason Blakely calls "scientism." Blakely's argument is that scientific authority loses ground if it is inconsistent and abused for social and political purposes. "In particular," writes Blakely, "specialist claims of scientific authority in matters of governance and social organization have come to be seen by more and more Americans as a bid for power by elite cliques contemptuous of the broader public."[51] To be clear, scientism is not science. Science is a methodology to study nature and organisms. Natural sciences—biology, physics, chemistry—are rooted in evidence, fact, and reason. Scientism, on the other hand, is a philosophy in which people believe all truth comes through science.[52]

At its worst, scientism is quackery (unproven drugs to treat Covid-19, crystals to cure depression). In a more general way, scientism gives science too much authority, which for some is not warranted, as scientific views evolve and sometimes contradict themselves. Not to mention, there are many unobservable types of human connection and expression that can't simply be explained by hard science. Scientism emerges from authorities like Richard Dawkins, who, as he writes in *The Selfish Gene*, sees scientific principles underlying even our most seemingly emotional and altruistic behavior.[53] While Dawkins calls the term scientism a "dirty word," in a scathing article in *Harper's* entitled "Hysterical Scientism," Marilynne Robinson deemed Dawkins's book *The God Delusion* overly simplified and arrogant, not allowing for diversity of thought.[54] "So bad science is still science," Robinson writes, "in more or less the same sense that bad religion is still religion. That both of them can do damage on a huge scale is clear."[55] But scientism exists as "pop science" as well, promoted by left-leaning sources from the *New York Times* to Goop. This is the form I would like to consider. Scientism and intellectualism may not be the same thing, but they are bedfellows that prize objectivity, facts, and expert authority above all.

As science progresses, sometimes what was accepted fact is rethought and a new approach is recommended. This may seem like a contradiction or a challenge to the legitimacy of science, but it is actually based on advancements in research and evidence. In my last book, I wrote about the evolution in medical thinking around breastfeeding, which at any moment in history is either the ideal form of feeding a baby or a far second to a wet nurse or formula. Even today, it is inconclusive as to whether breast milk is superior to infant formula, yet the medical and social pressure on mothers is to breastfeed.[56] While financial markets are not science, many of their leading defenders uphold their rationality as objective truth.[57] However, after the 2008 financial crisis, it was clearly exposed that the very proponents of a free market were rigging it to their benefit, wiping out the livelihoods of millions of unsuspecting Americans.[58]

Even Jane Brody, the *New York Times* personal health columnist from 1976 to 2022, remarked on the evolving view of "good" and "bad" fats in our diet. In 1977, a government report decried animal fats in favor of margarine and other vegetable fats. "Then studies found the trans fats in these hydrogenated vegetable products were even more damaging to arteries than animal fats," writes Brody. "But time will tell whether specific dietary fats, or the much-vaunted Mediterranean diet currently embraced by many doctors, will fall prey to future findings."[59] Most recently, Covid-19 has created new skeptics of science, as well as a distrust of experts. A *Nature* article documenting perceptions of Covid-19 shows a higher disregard of

Covid-19 news and mask usage with increases in an individual's anti-intellectualism. Those with less regard for the scientific community and for experts are more likely to possess Covid-19 misinformation, minimize risk perception, and disregard health protocols.[60]

I do not in any way support these views, but I do want to know their origins. Why do so many people challenge what people like me take for granted, that the CDC, the FDA, and those with medical degrees are speaking the truth? That sometimes experts' opinions evolve, but that's not reason to mistrust them? For Shannon, her decision to not get vaccinated is linked to her religious beliefs, but she also voiced skepticism about the vaccines themselves. For others, there is a sense of being chastised by intellectual elites and experts who have made a pastime of deriding them for where they live, their faith, and their life choices, and they don't like it.

Still others question scientific authority directly and see it as insular to itself and other elites. As Blakely writes, more than one thousand of the very medical experts who supported vigilant mask usage and social distancing signed a letter also supporting public protests in the name of Black Lives Matter.[61] As Black Lives Matter is a cause I wholly support, this letter does not seem to be a contradiction to me. Nor was I bothered by the follow-up essay in the *Atlantic* by two leading experts from Harvard and Yale, who argued that maximizing health must include all aspects of life, writing that white supremacy posed "too grave [a threat] to ignore, even with the potential for an increase in coronavirus transmission."[62] But, as Blakely points out, for those who are not progressives living in liberal, coastal cities, advocating for both social distancing measures and large public gatherings seemed like a big inconsistency.

From the perspective of these skeptics, once elites want to do something prohibited, there is a moral justification that makes it okay. Indeed, scandals have engulfed public leaders, including former UK prime minister Boris Johnson and governor of California Gavin Newsom. Both men stood alongside medical experts and scientists denouncing the public for socializing or not wearing masks, but then privately attended parties and fancy dinners indoors without masks. "People do dabble with bad theories because they feel something has gone wrong with scientific authority," Blakely explains to me in the spring of 2022. "They feel manipulated and controlled. Part of the sympathy I have for people who express this backlash, it's almost a methodological sympathy," he shares. "To understand people you need to listen to them and understand their self-understanding. That's crucial to understanding social reality." The hypocrisy in what elites say and what they do further erodes the trust of a public that is already wary of the way science challenges their faith and lifestyle. I do not agree with anti-intellectualism and anti-science sentiment, but I do understand where it comes from.

SCIENTISM MANIFESTS IN much of the intelligentsia's way of life. These approaches are all too evident in the burgeoning wellness industry. Oura Rings, fasting, meditation, yoga, keto, paleo, self-care, and Gwyneth Paltrow's Goop industrial complex—the wellness industry embodies the philosophy of scientism. Studies and evidence package many of these largely not-FDA-approved treatments. Even the *New York Times*' science section offers studies on how much coffee to drink, how much exercise to do, the importance of turmeric, and the number of hours to sleep a night. I've lost track of the number of my Ivy League–educated, professional friends who wear the Oura Ring (which collects data on sleep, heart rate, and skin temperature), sleep under weighted blankets, fill their bodies with various supplements, and get acupuncture. Parenting books, gobbled up by the meritocracy, turn bonding and nurturing into a formalized road map.

The problem, of course, is not the practicing of such habits nor the postulating of an idea or opinion (lots of people do that). It's that such perspectives are always in the name of science, and they ignore other philosophies worth considering. In many ways, wellness and health have replaced religion for today's secular meritocracy. Their religion is the highest form of physical well-being and spiritual centeredness. And yet, the idea that attention to self and connection to a higher power offers success and health is deeply rooted in immanent forms of religion. "In the '70s or '80s you'd have a cross on your neck or a Star of David," remarked Peloton founder John Foley. "Now you have a SoulCycle tank top. That's your identity. That's your community. That's your religion." He compares the Peloton instructor experience to "somebody talking to you from a pulpit for 45 minutes."[63]

Foley is not wrong, and I don't judge the Peloton evangelists. His remark applies to myriad practices within the wellness industry that have a spiritual element. Many people also embrace an articulated, contemporary spirituality alongside scientism and wellness. As Philip Gorski remarked to me, "They can no longer engage evangelicalism with religious language. They are in essence no longer religious. But they have their own practices and norms that are a religion of sorts." I understood what Gorski was saying, and it rang true. Lacking traditional religion, many progressive Democrats, coastal elites, and secular intellectuals long for spiritual fulfillment, like any human being. They embrace the rituals of wellness, scientism, and spirituality while in the same breath critiquing evangelicals' belief systems as unhinged and irrational.

In the fall of 2020, I interview Kathleen, a woman from Nevada, and I ask her what makes her happy. She responds, "Many times, my faith in God. If things are going badly or I am disappointed, I know he's in control, and I will learn from it. He's going to get me out of it, or I'm going to learn from it. Happiness...it's more like peace. Things in life are going to change—stock market going to go down, dishwasher is going to break. Horses in Reno. People get upset about the horse poop, but it dries and blows away." If one substituted "universe" for "God," Kathleen's response reads akin to a zen philosophy of life. Her view of life is not specific to religion. As the spiritual leader Gabby Bernstein said on a recent episode of *The Goop Podcast*, "I don't care what you call it. I care that you call upon it....A prayer suspends your disbelief....Prayer is the medium for miracles. My logical mind doesn't really have an answer for me....I'm going to turn it over...show me."[64] Is this perspective so different from Shannon's belief that God shows up all around her or Kathleen's sense of peace in ceding control to God over the ups and downs of life?

So why, then, do so many people deride organized religion and yet find meaning in wellness and spirituality? "Religious people might put it down to God's work," observes a *Financial Times* writer. "Others might call it serendipity or luck. Sceptics might dismiss such happenings as pure coincidence."[65] Columbia University religious scholar Courtney Bender observes that ostensibly secular social institutions often draw from a long lineage of American religious life.[66] However we choose to explain our existence, these rituals and beliefs underpin the human need for a unifying faith that makes us feel part of something. Perhaps understanding that universal need can help make us a little less judgmental of others and their practices, irrespective of how they find their way.

THE NARRATIVE IS more complicated than simply a division between the secular and the religious. While religious extremists may embrace beliefs that can harm others or challenge the sacredness of our democracy, as we witnessed on January 6, most religious people do not share these values or behave in such a way. In the main, I came to see that the worlds of religion and secularism were not meaningfully different in their framework or desires, even if the content varied. For secular America, the difference may be thought of as that between mythos and logos: immanent contemporary religion draws from a myth, while secular belief systems are drawn from logic, rationality, and evidence. I'm not sure the division is actually so stark. Outside of the natural sciences and their application, all of us—bar the nihilists and existentialists—subscribe to our own, often shared, myth of the meaning of existence. Some may find meaning in Christianity, others Judaism or Islam, still others spirituality, Zen, transcendentalism, or mysticism. For the ancient Greeks, who came up with these frameworks, neither mythos nor logos was superior to the other. Logos enabled survival in the world: making weapons, producing food, protecting a community. Mythos provided a framework for life's meaning and emotions.[67] Myths were not falsehoods but rather lenses through which they could understand life's triumphs and struggles. Stories of brave heroes or fallen gods torn by jealously gave them a deeper understanding of the human condition. Both mythos and logos were essential to survival.[68]

As the popular account goes, the Enlightenment put these two worlds in opposition and gave logos more authority. Early Enlightenment thinkers such as René Descartes and John Locke considered human existence from the perspectives of rationality and empiricism, respectively.[69] This approach did not immediately remove the existence of God, but rather removed God from the center of the meaning of life. Other philosophers like Voltaire and Immanuel Kant did believe in God, but their view was that of deism or "natural religion"—that there was good and evil, morality, and a divinely ordered universe, but fundamentally the higher power was removed from day-to-day life.[70] In this respect, Enlightenment thinkers embraced a more transcendental approach to religion; religion was to be managed within a rational framework. Some scholars argue that Enlightenment thinkers had an underlying hostility toward religion, specifically Christianity.[71]

Among these thinkers, opposing views surfaced, and perhaps none greater than the animosity between Voltaire and Jean-Jacques Rousseau.[72] Voltaire, who introduced the ideas of John Locke and

Isaac Newton to France, believed in religious tolerance, and, like fellow Enlightenment thinkers, his view was that social progress was only possible through reason and rationality.[73] Voltaire's bête noire, the Swiss philosopher Rousseau, became a vocal challenger to secular rationalism and part of what came to be known as the "Counter-Enlightenment" and, later, Romanticism.[74] In his book *Discourse on the Origin and Basis of Inequality Among Men*, also known as the *Second Discourse*, Rousseau argued that the root of inequality was not "natural inequality" (for example, physical strength) but rather "moral inequality" as a result of human decisions made in a civil society. Natural man may have lacked reason, but he killed only for self-preservation and did not compare himself to others. For Rousseau, the establishment of a civil society meant comparisons to others and a desire for more, and thus the origins of inequality, which compounds as society progresses.[75]

The *Second Discourse* became one of Rousseau's most famous texts. What is compelling about this book for my purposes is that Rousseau does not see rationalism, the underpinning of the Enlightenment, as always a good thing. Rationalism lacks compassion and humanity and prizes reason over all other values. Logic may dictate how people attain private property, and then reason justifies such ownership. Thus, it becomes fact that one person owns a particular piece of property and someone else does not, but is any of this fair? Is any of it moral?[76] The Counter-Enlightenment challenged a society that felt hostile to religion, hostile to humanity, and lacking in sentimentality for suffering and injustice.[77] Rousseau's revolt against the Enlightenment resulted in great celebrity for him and great enmity from Voltaire. "Never has so much intelligence been employed in order to render us stupid," remarked Voltaire of the *Second Discourse*.[78]

Yet in 1755, a natural disaster occurred challenging both Voltaire's and Rousseau's worldview. On November 1, 1755, an earthquake of 8.5 magnitude struck the city of Lisbon, Portugal. Because it was All Saints' Day, the churches were full. The buildings could not structurally handle the earthquake, and many people died while praying and attending service. In all, over sixty thousand people died in Lisbon alone, and there was terrible damage to the city's port, major buildings, and over twelve thousand homes. The earthquake, caused by seismic activity along the mid-Atlantic tectonic plate, generated a tsunami that caused damage as far as Algiers.[79]

The earthquake became a flashpoint for the intellectual debates of the day. Voltaire and Rousseau both wrote about it, and their analysis has had a lasting impact on the contributions of the Enlightenment.[80] In "Poem on the Lisbon Disaster," Voltaire writes, "Defects and sorrows, ignorance and woe / Hope he omitted, man's sole bliss below." For Rousseau, this poem was an attack on religious faith, and he may not have been wrong. In 1759, Voltaire wrote *Candide*, which features Lisbon and many other places filled with suffering and poverty while ridiculing religion. The book became a global success and cemented Voltaire's position in the literary canon.

Voltaire was essentially questioning how one can make sense of such tragedy while holding the belief in the goodness of a higher power. Rousseau responded by writing, "Most of our physical ills are our own work." He places blame not on God but on man, who constructed "twenty thousand houses of six to seven stories there, and that if the inhabitants of this great city had been more equally spread out and more lightly lodged, the damage would have been much less and perhaps of no account." Rousseau concludes that Voltaire, who lived a life of opulence, found only malevolence on earth, which seemed hypocritical.[81]

I tell this story of Rousseau and Voltaire because, oddly, it is Rousseau who demonstrates reason and rationality. In his dissection of the earthquake through the structural, socioeconomic conditions and human choices that magnified the disaster, Rousseau offers a social science analysis.[82] Voltaire, the great rationalist, offers a poem that ultimately blames God, hardly steeped in evidence and rationality. This story, while hundreds of years old, shows us something important about humanity. We are rarely either-or, and we are rarely always rational. Our morality informs things we care about: our stories, sense of existence, and understanding of others are often a blending of mythos and logos. Which is to say that for secular America to disdain religious America is to ignore our own mythos and evidence-free beliefs, many of which play an important role in our sense of self and community. "Sociality and its practices are universal to human behavior no matter the presence or absence of sectarian affiliation," writes the Yale religious scholar Kathryn Lofton. "Whenever we see dreams of and for the world articulated, whenever we see those dreams organized into legible rituals, schematics, and habits, we glimpse the domain that the word religion contributes to describe."[83]

The through line of self-help, self-actualizing, pragmatism, and immanence dominates religious and secular life in America today. We are all Romantics and anti-rationalists when it comes to the values and morals we hold dear. We all use facts and evidence to push an argument we believe in. In the Enlightenment, Voltaire and Rousseau had equal footing. Today, we emphasize rationalism and its bedfellows—scientism, science, agnosticism, secularism—as a badge of intellectualism, without seeing the anti-rationalism that underpins many of our deeply held values and beliefs.[84]

While many secular Americans may see religious America— particularly evangelical America—as a cultural universe away, it is important to understand that the rituals and practices between these two groups overlap more often than not. Ultimately, we are looking for meaning and a way to be better people. When I asked Wayne— an almost eighty-year-old man who lives in Wisconsin—what he wished he could teach his children, he responded, "Be honest. Have a faith in God. Be respectful. When you get opportunities, make the best of them." We all want to make sense of the world, somehow. Most of us strive to be good, decent people. We all want to belong. I am not so sure it matters how we accomplish that sense of belonging, so long as it is well-meaning, kind, and respectful. I think what is important is that we find a way to do it.

7

CULTURAL CAPITAL

*If you can't have empathy for a life that's different from
yours, you're not going to be able to look at your own life
from different points of view, which is what you're going to
need to do to make any change.*

—TARA WESTOVER[1]

SINCE WE LAST TALKED," CRAIG WRITES, ALMOST BEAMING
through the page, "we received approval of our 'Century Farm'
application and also a Certified Tree Farm." He shares a photo of
the sign indicating this designation. Over the course of our conversations, Craig sends me several photos of his land, which show
a breathtaking landscape of endless green, a winding creek with
swaying willows at its edges, and a watery, periwinkle-and-pink
sky with rolling clouds meeting the horizon. Craig also shows me
photos of his family, with lush greenery and farmland in the background. From our interactions, I discern that Craig is a low-key person, but despite his easygoingness, it is clear that his farm matters a
great deal to him. As we chat, he tells me that he went to Wartburg
College, a small liberal-arts college in Iowa, where he majored in
environmental support, and went on to work for the Iowa Department of Natural Resources. I ask him questions about sustainability

and environmentalism, but he barely engages on the topic, certainly not with passion. Something is going off in my head, but I'm not quite sure where to place it, so we continue and I put it in the back of my mind to think about later. In the meantime, we talk about his favorite holiday ("Easter. With family, as much as we can. Church and a big Easter dinner"), his favorite food ("Rib eye steak"), and his favorite time in his life ("I would say actually right now").

Our conversation follows the same path as I have had with many others discussing politics, equality, and the economy. Craig is a thoughtful, kind, and intelligent man, and his lack of self-awareness of these traits makes him very endearing. When I ask him if he buys organic food, he responds, "No. I grow my own. Most of my food is grown in the yard." I clarify my question, because it's not so much what he buys as what he chooses to eat. "I don't use pesticides, but I do use fertilizer. It's not certified organic, and I'm sure the organic people would have a cow that I used fertilizer instead of chicken manure." He then laughs and says he buys his chickens for $2 a pound, while his daughter, who lives in Los Angeles, gets $10 pasture-raised chickens. I didn't have the heart to tell him that, these days, pasture-raised chickens cost at least twice that amount. Craig believes in climate change, and when asked what he does to help the environment, he says modestly, "I try to be a good steward of the environment. We compost a lot of things here. We would like to recycle more than we do. I use wood [more than electricity], but 75 percent of my heat comes from wood harvested from my farm." But, Craig admits, "I still drive a car," almost intimating that this is an egregious act.

I also know from the photos that environmentalism is ever present in Craig's life, despite the fact that he doesn't label it as such. In one photo, he appears in overalls on a tractor with his grandchildren. Another features his multicultural and ethnically diverse family next to a sign that reads "Parker-Muncey Pioneer Park," which, he explains, is on land that he lends to the city for $1 per year. Another photo is of deer in his backyard. "I eat a lot of venison from the farm, and they eat my corn, soybeans, berries, and nuts, and that's just the cycle of life," he says.

Craig's sentiment echoed much of what others in rural America shared about their quiet lives. Many are content with their rural existence. While liberal elites shun rural people's religion and lack of education and often see their beliefs as backward, the rural Americans I spoke to rarely expressed reactionary responses to the questions I posed and were never contemptuous toward the coastal elites that often look down upon them. The media talks a lot about the culture wars, and, yes, there are vocal people on both sides— particularly secular liberals in cities and conservative evangelical Christians in small towns—but I increasingly felt that this view of the world was simplistic and based on a few strident voices, certainly not the majority of Americans. But even as most Americans seemed to get along well, I felt that the culture of rural America was valued less and taken less seriously by the nation at large.

It was urban, educated liberals' bias toward their own culture as superior that allowed them to denounce rural America as broken, to dismiss what goodness this part of the country may have to offer. Many of the signifiers of elite status are tied up in Hollywood, Wall Street, and our dominant media outlets and thus become the accepted form of culture.[2] Since rural America doesn't engage in the same habits and cultural practices, particularly regarding education and religion, they are somehow lesser than their big-city counterparts.

But I am reminded again of the Princeton sociologist Shamus Khan's remark that "everyone has culture." Khan observes that NASCAR fans possess a certain form of cultural capital and, as we know, so do those who listen to NPR and subscribe to the *New Yorker*. It's assumed in urban, elite circles that the latter form of cultural capital is better, but what if it's simply a function of super-imposed hierarchies? Khan writes, "Everyone 'has' culture. But some people's match institutions of power, and other people's exist in conflict with expectations of those powerful institutions. Those who match enjoy often invisible advantages, and those in conflict may well be punished."[3] Rural Americans have cultural capital; it's just different from that of urban America, not worse. People in cities are religious, but many of them gravitate toward secular forms of fulfillment. These channels are often far more overt and expressive, and so they dilute the power of churches in big cities. In the same way, religiosity in rural America is a concentrated form of cultural capital.

So where do we get this idea that rural cultural capital is of little value? Part of the superiority of urban, elite culture is that it is tied to institutions and social circles of power: top universities, major newspapers, museums, and film and television.[4] Elite education provides this type of cultural capital, even as cultural capital is often required to get into an elite institution. The story of rural America's less valuable cultural currency stems, at least partially, from the absence of elite education. This observation brought me back to my conversation with Raj Chetty.

At one point, Chetty and I are speaking about the importance of elite education. I doubted its influence simply had to do with history classes or learning statistics. That was knowledge one could pick up without attending Harvard. As Chetty found, just going to a decent university could enable the bottom 20 percent to move into the top 20 percent. But elite institutions help people get to the very top of the income, social, and cultural pyramid. I bring up the concepts of cultural and social capital. To me, these explain what an elite education gives someone, as well as the differences in how rural and urban Americans express themselves to the world. I wasn't sure if Chetty would buy this proposition, both because of the data he works with on income mobility and because, as an economist, he focuses on variables that can be clearly quantified. Social and cultural capital are nebulous and hard to track. But Chetty agrees with me. He was in fact looking at the role of social capital in a current research project.[5] "Studying social capital, and I think it's closely related to cultural capital," Chetty explains, "[we are] measuring contact through Facebook, different types of people are interacting. In broad brushstrokes, my big-picture takeaway is, social capital and who you're interacting with is hugely important in predicting economic mobility, probably the most important predictor we've found to date."

I don't really know what to say as I scribble notes furiously. Chetty has spent his life studying what impacts social mobility, and what he's come up with is that social and cultural capital are the magic bullet. Chetty was essentially isolating why elite universities matter—not because they are havens of the rich or tickets to the top 1 percent, but rather because they are the producers of the cultural and social capital that matters.

As ever, Chetty is interested in how this information can generate solutions. "Understanding how you get people from different backgrounds to connect to each other seems to be imperative in figuring out how you create broader paths to mobility, perhaps because it changes people's aspirations and the choices people make." As Chetty explains, if you've got no one around you going to college, you aren't as likely to consider it. However, if your social network values college, then this possibility becomes important to you too. "I think the fabric through which people are connected to each other and the choices they are making as a result are extremely important." It is through their rarified social capital that the elite continue to maintain their position at the top of society, making decisions for everyone else.

The flip side of this is negative social capital, which shows you norms that do not help with mobility or life expectancy.[6] "I personally feel it's not my job to make normative decisions," Chetty says when I ask him if rural kids should care more about going to elite colleges. "But if you see people getting addicted to opioids and with serious health issues, I think it's hard to make the argument that these people are happy in their own right. And we see in these places with low mobility, we also see lots of adverse health outcomes, see increases in incarceration, earlier mortality. There are tons of people who are happy and don't need to go to Harvard, but I do think there are sets of people being left behind—and it's not just that they are happy with the way things are going." Again, it is the cultural and social exposure we get, not simply our aptitude, that paves the road to mobility or, conversely, reinforces our current position.

Social capital and cultural capital are different, of course. If you're a sociologist, you would not think to blend these two concepts. However, as Robert Wuthnow pointed out, they are intertwined. Think about it like this: if your social capital is the sum of your networks and friendships—the people you spend time with and can call up for advice, a job, or to invite over to dinner—then your cultural capital is the thread that connects that network. Whether frequenting the same institutions, revealing the same material signifiers, or speaking with shared knowledge, cadence, or dialect, we tend to amass social capital with people with whom we share culture. We discuss the same sports and books. Our kids attend the same schools. We go to the same church. We share a set of cultural behaviors around mealtimes or lifestyle. Those of us in the same social class can share similar cultural capital and establish social networks with those who don't necessarily live down the street from us. As Chetty and his colleagues found in their study of twenty-one billion Facebook friendships, being friends with people in a higher socioeconomic class than oneself is one of the strongest predictors to date of income mobility.[7]

Education matters, then, not just because of what you read in textbooks, but because of whom you meet and the broader knowledge you gain about cultural norms and behaviors. Only a finite number of educational institutions offer a way to truly advance. This is not to say a good education, in and of itself, is not worth having. But rather it is social and cultural capital that distinguish

Yale from Cal State Los Angeles. Social networks are sustained due to their content, whether that's inventors trading ideas and creating patents, literary and art professionals determining the value of art, or members of Facebook connecting over a political issue.[8] In a global economy that prizes knowledge and the institutions that cultivate it, the cultural and social capital of the meritocracy has far greater currency than that of rural Americans. Elite education matters because it allows entry, providing the symbols, practices, and way of being to assimilate into this world.

While I was thinking about education through this lens, I became particularly interested in not what rural American kids could manage to accomplish without an elite education (a good-paying job, a nice house, and geographically proximate familial relationships), but rather what they were missing out on because they were excluded. Rural America did not need all of its students to enter top universities, gain access to the most influential jobs, and become the people who make big decisions about our country. But it needed some to do so. The problem, I realized, was that not only were rural Americans out of position to get into these universities, but their whole cultural universe did not align with what seemed to matter to the elite.

The French sociologist Pierre Bourdieu argued that culture produces inequality.[9] Bourdieu's point was that, as cultural capital is used to reinforce an elite position and exclude others, particular forms of cultural behavior become tacit symbols of one's social position or "habitus," which is simply one's way of being and way that one interacts with the world. Cultural capital, which shapes one's habitus, manifests in three ways: the things we own (clothing, cars), our behaviors (manner of speaking), and our affiliations and credentials (where we went to school, the organizations we join). Bourdieu called these objectified, embodied, and institutionalized cultural capital, respectively. It is not that elites determine all cultural capital but rather that they define what matters to institutions of power and thus to society. As a result, they become the social gatekeepers.[10]

Some of this cultural capital can be acquired, as Charles Dickens's Pip did with his fancy suits to become a gentleman in London society. If one gets into a top university or lands an elite job, one is tied institutionally to particular forms of cultural capital. What is perhaps most slippery is the embodied form of cultural capital: how to speak, what to order from a menu, what conversations are worth having. Cultural capital lays the groundwork for our social worlds and where we fit in. Recall that, often, rural students have different college essay topics and join different clubs than urban and suburban students. This wouldn't matter if all cultural capital were treated equally. The Harvard graduate who has lived in New York City all his life, scion to a wealthy financier, simply has different cultural capital than a rural Missourian does. But we know the cultural capital of the young man from New York is valued more.

As I thought about the role of cultural capital in achieving mobility, I realized that what we choose to display plays a large role in determining our success. Cultural capital, as the Australian economist David Throsby observes, is about cultural value, about what society values at a particular moment in time.[11] We possess many attributes, but some are dearer to our sense of self than others. Thus, while it's clear that some forms of cultural capital really are distinct to one social group over another, part of cultural capital is also about emphasis and how we assemble our image to the world. It is the manifestation of what we *think* matters. Attending a top university matters because it is representative of a good education and particular form of knowledge, overt displays of religiosity reveal membership in a local religious community and that God is part of one's identity, and "conspicuous consumption," to use economist Thorstein Veblen's term, emphasizes material goods as a way to establish social position. In all of these examples, we are making conscious choices to reveal some parts of ourselves over others, and often it is this outward expression that helps us form social networks.

I thought about this a lot as it pertains to God. I am, personally, a believer. Raised Catholic, for decades I've been fairly skeptical of the religious structure upholding faith in a higher being. I feel, quite strongly, that if there is a God, he/she/it is not Jewish or Catholic or Muslim or any other sect, so I do not engage regularly in the practice of a specific religion, even if my faith in something much bigger than me—whether a greater power or simply the awesomeness of the universe, what David Brooks, referencing the German Catholic priest Romano Guardini, calls "celestial grandeur"—runs deep.[12] But I do not talk about my spirituality to anyone except close friends in rare moments. It feels strange to be bringing it up right now. As an academic living in a major global city among meritocrats and bohemians, this facet of me is not part of my cultural capital, and with some of my atheist friends it would possibly be disdained. One Harvard-educated woman who lives in Los Angeles explained that while she believed in God, "there's a weird shame to it. Religion is still Marx's opiate of the masses." As I thought deeply about this issue I realized I didn't know the religious position of most of my friends. Some were Jewish, some were Protestant, and so forth, but these identities were largely cultural. I could not tell you fully where they stood on the actual existence of a deity.

There could not be a more opposite situation than in rural America. Time and time again, in my interviews with rural Americans, people brought up the importance of their faith. They were not self-conscious about their beliefs, and they were not private. Their faith was interwoven with all aspects of their lives and shaped their behavior and association with particular groups, especially the church. Their faith was regularly the answer to my questions *What do you value most?* and *What is the most important thing you could pass on to your kids?* "Faith, and love of family," said one man from Oklahoma. "The value of a personal relationship to the creator and savior of the universe," said a woman from Wisconsin. "My faith and my husband's faith," said a woman from Kentucky. "My faith and the knowledge of my faith," said a man from Missouri. "I value my relationship with Jesus Christ the most of everything," said another woman from Kentucky. "Faith and God and love for family," said another man from Missouri.

This got me thinking about how my urban interviewees responded to my questions on values and what they would like to pass on to their kids. Only two urban women mentioned faith as a response to one of these questions, and one of them also included "a lifelong love of learning." In the margin of one interview with a woman from San Francisco, I had jotted down by the question on values, "Many urban people struggle with this question. Rural people almost always say God or family." While a preponderance of urban interviewees respond with "family," as do many rural respondents, many also answer with "honesty," "love," "self-confidence," and some version of wanting their children to possess their own worldview and perspective. These answers align with the sense that urban America is more secular and thus does not prioritize faith as a value to pass on to their children. And yet, the General Social Survey suggests Americans—rural and urban—are far more similar in their religious views than different. In their book *American Grace*, Robert Putnam and David Campbell found, using different data, the same result: rural America was only modestly more religious than urban America.[13]

This discrepancy between survey and interview data reveals something important about what we externally prioritize. Cultural capital is entwined with how we define ourselves, what we choose to say about ourselves, and how we assemble our identity to present to the world. The cultural capital of religion—the institutionalized cultural capital of the church and the embodied cultural capital of talking about faith—is more significant in rural America than in urban America. What my interviews suggest is that rural Americans feel a strong sense of their own identity and value system within a religious frame; it is a part of how they form social networks and community life.[14] Rural Americans are not necessarily bigger believers than urban Americans, but religion plays a larger role in structuring their everyday lives, and it's unsurprising so many would see religion as an important part of their identity.

THE SAME OVERLAP in responses holds true for issues of race and gender. For example, according to the GSS, 70 percent of both rural and urban Americans believe it is somewhat likely or very likely that a woman will be passed over at work in favor of a man of equal or lesser competence. In fact, more rural Americans agree or strongly agree that women should be hired and promoted than do urban Americans (78 percent versus 73 percent, respectively). If we return to the data on racial issues, as discussed previously, the broad takeaway is that the difference between these groups is not so wide on most questions of race and racial equity.

And yet, I realized that for both urban and rural folks, their ways of expressing their views on race and equity are the inverse of how they speak about religion. Religion plays a crucial role in the social and cultural capital of rural towns and thus its expression is overt. The more complicated and diverse forms of social and cultural capital in our cities dilutes some of religion's more outward expressions. Conversely, while rural and urban folks express similar sentiments with regard to racial and gender equity, it is our urban centers where we see the greatest demonstrations for social justice, whether Black Lives Matter or the Women's March or #MeToo. These protests are participated in and often organized by minorities and women protesting for their own rights, but they are also attended by upper-middle-class liberal elites who are engaging in a cause that is far removed from their reality, even if they are ideologically aligned. This is so stark that many public commentators remarked upon the whiteness of BLM protests. "Black Lives Matter was once shunned by the white establishment. But now, it's chic. And that's a problem," comments the Black journalist Erin Logan. "BLM banners fly from homes in Silver Lake. BLM posters are taped to the windows of Portland coffee shops. BLM hashtags fill users' bios on Twitter and Tinder."[15] And why might this be? Like religion's role in small-town America, an embrace of social justice movements is part of liberal urbanites' cultural capital. I am not saying that overt religiosity and progressive politics are the same. What I am saying is that our identity often shows up in the same way. In these examples, both groups reveal themselves through embodied and institutionalized cultural capital. Thus, performative social justice is part of the larger amalgamation of NPR bumper stickers, *New Yorker* cloth totes, and organic food for this particular socioeconomic group. These are the signifiers that allow membership to the cultural elite.

As others have observed, for those who are privileged, there is a strong social element to engaging in these movements. For affluent coastal liberals, getting superficially involved in social justice movements can be beneficial, insofar as it makes others perceive them as progressive and socially aware. Fighting for social justice is a good thing, but, as some critics have argued, often elites' protest is superficial. Some have called this phenomenon "performative wokeness." "Performative wokeness is just that," writes a student in *Varsity*, Cambridge University's student newspaper, "performative, a superficial show of solidarity with minority and oppressed bodies of people that enables (usually white and privileged) people to reap the social benefits of wokeness without actually undertaking any of the necessary legwork to combat injustice and inequality."[16] When you think about it like that, it feels—if not nefarious—certainly self-serving.

In decrying performative wokeness, the historian Wilfred McClay argues that our use of "performative" is inaccurate. We use it to imply superficiality, rather than what performative actually means, which is the desire to do something. "Performative language is light-years removed from the virtue signaling with which we are awash," writes McClay, "the yard signs that assure us that 'hate has no home here,' even if we had never been curious to ask."[17] As one Black political organizer remarked with regard to white participation in the BLM protests, "Are you really in it? Do you understand the stakes? [Or] are you here for an Instagram picture?"[18]

Superficial is one way to describe the reappropriation of social justice as cultural capital for the meritocrats, but the Columbia University sociologist Musa al-Gharbi finds a more sinister meaning underpinning progressive, elite, performative wokeness. In a preview of his forthcoming book, *We Have Never Been Woke*, al-Gharbi writes, "The Americans who are the primary producers and consumers of content on antiracism, socialism, feminism, etc., also happen to be among the primary beneficiaries of gendered, racialized, and other forms of inequality—and not *passive* beneficiaries." He continues, "We are active participants in exploiting and reproducing inequalities. And yet, it is difficult for us to 'see' how we contribute to the problem—precisely *because of* our deeply felt commitments to social justice. So we expropriate blame to others... often people who benefit far less from the system than we do, and exert far less influence over it."[19] Indeed, as al-Gharbi goes on to keenly observe, it is the white, liberal elites who accuse poor, rural whites of "white fragility" precisely because they take offense. All of this is to say that, like other forms of cultural capital, wokeness has become a means by which one group wields power over another.[20] To be "woke"— to engage in issues of social justice not as an oppressed member of society demanding rightful change but as a privileged member engaging for the most part superficially with social movements—is to reveal your elite social position.

I REVISITED WHAT WAS nagging me in my conversation with Craig. That without ever calling himself one, Craig was a bona fide environmentalist. But Craig, like many of my rural interviewees, would not display his sustainable lifestyle as a badge of honor. Unlike the patrons of Whole Foods and local urban farmers' markets, the people I spoke to would not see their choices as something to brag about. One woman who lives in Warbranch, Kentucky, in the heart of the Daniel Boone National Forest, told me that she does organic gardening, uses solar power for as much as she can, and recycles. Emily, a woman also living in Kentucky, explained that she has a compost pile, recycles, and feels guilty every time she throws something away. The day after our interview, Emily emailed me, "Hey, Elizabeth, I thought of some other things I do to be environmentally conscious," she wrote. "We grow a garden, I buy a lot of clothes secondhand, and we have a subscription to a grocery service that sells imperfect or damaged produce and pantry items. I just got a worm compost farm, and we got three chickens for eggs."

I thought about Emily's response and was astounded with the conscientiousness of her choices. But what also struck me about Emily and Craig, and others, was that it took them a while to form the answers to my questions. They did not see their choices as a reflection of themselves. Rural Americans, while possessing little if any elite cultural capital, sometimes embrace similar practices as educated liberal communities, from environmentalism to shopping local. The difference, of course, is that rural Americans do these things without necessarily ascribing cultural value to their actions. In other words, small-town Americans' investment in sustainability was omnipresent but their consciousness of their position was less so. Craig does not ascribe social value to his farm or homegrown food; for him it is simply a way of life. Despite her great efforts to maintain a compost pile, recycle, and consume imperfect goods, only in retrospect did Emily connect her daily actions with the larger cause of environmentalism.

I thought about myself and my endless organic food and milk and my religious devotion to buying only humane meat and pasture-raised chicken. I knew these were good choices of mine and that many of my friends practiced the same consumer habits. We have a vegetable garden too, we recycle, and we buy compostable sandwich bags for our kids' lunches. I had to admit to myself that many of these behaviors, good as they may be, were partially acted out because they made me *feel* better. They were behaviors built into my own identity and the identities of many in my cultural world. While they were good for the environment, they were mainly good for my family. They came at an economic cost but not in the cost of time and effort put in by the likes of Craig. Luxury grocery stores like Whole Foods and Erewhon are built on how people like me create an identity around overt displays of sustainability and environmentalism. The cultural value increases the economic value of these goods.[21] Despite this sense of self I had formed, I was doing a lot less for the planet than Emily and Craig, who needed to be pushed to fully articulate all they did on a daily basis for the environment. They had not stored up their sustainability practices and environmentalism as part of their cultural capital.

That observation lines up pretty squarely with General Social Survey data on the environment, where urban and rural respondents share almost identical answers to questions on government spending on the environment, government responsibility for the environment, developing natural resources, and making consumer decisions for political and environmental reasons. When it comes to actually spending time in the natural environment, rural respondents are more likely to express frequency and satisfaction with their experience, perhaps unsurprising given how close many of them live to the natural world. Rural America's approach to environmentalism and food consciousness is parallel to what we see with urban America and religion. In both of these instances, urban and rural America do not offer significantly different opinions on these topics. And yet, rural Americans value the cultural capital surrounding religion, while urban Americans ascribe greater cultural capital to environmentalism and sustainability. For instance, many affluent urbanites frequent farmers' markets, which offer organic, humane, local food—often at ridiculously expensive prices. Farmers' markets, despite their ideologically good purpose, allow for virtue signaling— that is, expressions of piety and morality through overt actions—and an abundance of cultural capital for upper-middle-class urbanites. The markets thus become places of flânerie and display, replete with customers holding reusable grocery bags that shout some message or logo only decodable by the cultural elite.

The distinction between urban and rural perceptions of environmentalism also taps into what the cultural scholar Douglas Holt observes in his own study of "high cultural capital" (HCC) and "low cultural capital" (LCC) groups in State College, Pennsylvania. He found that HCC subjects spent enormous amounts of time discussing authenticity, connoisseurship, and individual choices that were reflective of their own social habitus. LCC subjects tended to respond tersely to the very same questions that HCC participants answered with "fine-grained sensibilities." Why? LCC respondents thought the questions were trivial: they didn't belong to a world where it mattered how deeply you thought about interior decorating or rap music. Exploring multicultural food was not a signifier of worldliness as it would be for those in the HCC group. While Holt's study does not track identically with my own interviewees, it offers insight into how the cultural capital ascribed to the same behaviors is radically different based on location and social class.[22]

Craig may practice the same types of sustainability as urban denizens aspire to, but he does not extract the same cultural value from his actions. He does not live in a world where talking about such things matters. Liberals misunderstand small towns, judging rural American culture by the standards of secularism and their own cultural capital, but this is the wrong lens. Maybe instead of focusing on how rural Americans engage with cultural artifacts or performance, it's worth actually looking at how they live, the values they espouse, and what they do.

W HAT WE HAVE seen is that, in reality, behavior and opinions are often not wildly different between rural and urban Americans, and yet the value we ascribe to expressing our religion, "wokeness," environmentalism, and sustainability—to name just the examples I've described—is vastly different when it comes to geography. Not because we necessarily feel things differently but rather because whether and how we express these values relates to our public identity and assimilation with our community. I wanted to understand why cultural capital plays out in this particular way. While it is hard to trace embodied forms of cultural capital, objectified cultural capital—that is, physical goods—would be a reasonable way to gauge what drives these differences. What we choose to buy is a reflection of how we want to display ourselves to the world.[23]

In order to understand the relationship between cultural capital and what we buy, I needed data on consumer items. In previous research, I have studied the Consumer Expenditure Survey put out by the US government. While this data offers patterns of what people spend money on—for example, the wealthy devote huge sums to education and low-income groups spend hardly anything on it—it does not offer two critical pieces of information: data for rural America specifically and data differentiation within a particular product. For example, we all buy milk, but what brand and what type can be revealing of more than just our consumption of dairy. For this type of granular data, I needed to go to Nielsen, the biggest tracker of consumer behavior in America. Nielsen consumer data tracks what people across the country buy at grocery stores, drugstores, superstores, and even convenience stores like 7-Eleven. Studying between forty thousand and sixty thousand people a year, Nielsen amasses a data set of millions of consumer products tied to particular demographic data: household income, educational attainment, race and ethnicity, and geographic location. Because they track purchases by universal product code, more culturally specific, qualitative data can be extracted.

My doctoral student Andy Eisenlohr and I got to it. We extracted data from 2004 to 2018 and focused on products that either enhanced elite cultural capital or detracted from it. For the former, we looked at organic milk, organic eggs, craft beer, foreign cheeses and wines, plant milk like almond or oat milk, fresh fruits, and fresh vegetables. These items were exalted as signs of being environmentally conscious, worldly, and culturally omnivorous, attributes thought to be high in cultural capital.[24] We then looked at items associated with negative cultural capital: frozen meals, soda and soft drinks, and tobacco products. Andy and I then divided the data into rural and urban, as well as breaking it out by income level and education level. We looked at this data descriptively, essentially just tracing how consumption of these items plays out across these different socioeconomic variables.

In this first analysis, Andy and I looked at areas of spending that suggested elite cultural capital (organic milk and vegetables) and negative cultural capital (tobacco, frozen meals, and soft drinks). The purchase of organic milk and vegetables suggests that you know they are good for you, good for the planet, and signify healthy living. The inverse is true of tobacco, frozen meals, and soft drinks. These worlds blend, of course. I buy organic milk and also frozen breakfast sandwiches for my kids. But the study here is to understand general trends in how particular groups divide up their expenditures across categories. What we find is disheartening but unsurprising. For negative cultural capital items, the people who spend the biggest proportion of their total expenditures on these items are those making less than $25,000 a year, followed by those without a bachelor's degree, followed by those living in rural areas. The rich and educated spend next to nothing on tobacco products, while, despite the high cost, the poor devote four times as much of their total expenditures on tobacco. Similar trends can be found with frozen food and soft drinks: the poor and least educated devote the greatest share to these items. In each of these instances, barring frozen meals, rural America spends more than the educated, the urban, and the rich on negative cultural capital purchases.

One might easily argue that share is deceptive: if you make less money or do not have a bachelor's degree (which likely means you make less money), then anything you buy takes up a greater

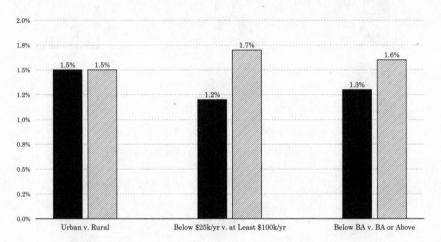

Fresh Vegetables Consumer Expenditure, 2018

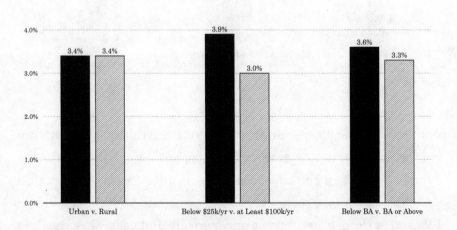

Frozen Meals Consumer Expenditure, 2018

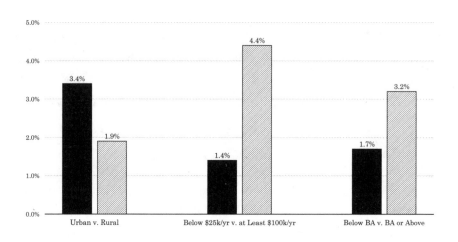

Organic Milk Consumer Expenditure, 2018

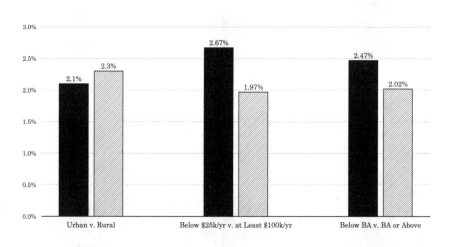

Soft Drinks Consumer Expenditure, 2018

share of your total expenditures than for the wealthy. But that's not true when it comes to elite cultural capital items. Those making over $100,000 and the educated (in that order) devote the greatest share of their total expenditures to organic milk and vegetables. As I looked at these charts, it was unsurprising and yet still astounding

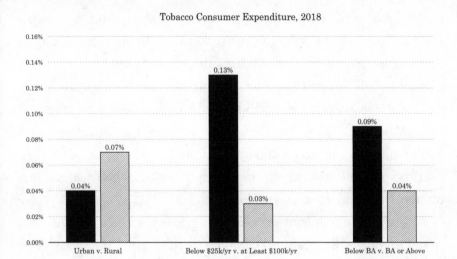

Source: *NielsenIQ Consumer Panel*

that it was always the rich and educated in diametric opposition to the poor and uneducated in their consumer habits, some of which (soda and tobacco) have dire consequences.

While this data reveals an overarching sense of trends, it does not unpack the underlying cause of consumer choices around cultural capital. In our second analysis, we expanded our collection of consumer goods reflective of different forms of cultural capital: imported cheeses, domestic and imported wine, and craft beer, along with organic eggs and milk, fresh fruits and vegetables, and, on the other end of the spectrum, tobacco, frozen meals, and soft drinks. To get at what might drive a person to purchase a particular item, we controlled for race and ethnicity, income, age, education, and geographic location.[25] What social, economic, and cultural forces might drive our consumer behavior?

Whether a household is in an urban or rural zip code is significantly associated with particular consumer habits. On all measures of elite cultural capital, with the exception of fresh vegetables, rural households spend less than urban households, including on goods like imported cheeses, organic eggs and milk, fresh fruits, wine, and craft beer. Rural households do, however, spend more on fresh vegetables, which may be reflective of access due to living in a more agricultural environment. Age mimics the effect that rurality has on consumption. As one gets older, they are less likely to spend money on organic milk, plant milk, and organic eggs, along with craft and foreign beer. At the same time, older folks tend to spend more on fresh fruits and vegetables and domestic and imported wine. In addition to spending less on organic food, older households spend less on items with negative cultural capital.

Education and income level are the greatest predictors of how we spend on objectified cultural capital. Corroborating the descriptive data, we find that having a bachelor's degree is significantly linked to spending on organic milk, plant milk, organic eggs, imported and specialty cheeses, fresh fruits and vegetables, domestic and imported wine, and craft or foreign beer. The educated also tend to spend notably less on tobacco, frozen meals, and soft drinks. These findings are almost identical for household income, where making $100,000 or more is significantly linked to elite cultural capital and not correlated with negative cultural capital items.[26] There are three interesting, related results. First, as household income shifts up or down, the expenditures toward particular products follow in lockstep. Second, the chasm in spending between the rich and poor is much greater than that between the educated and uneducated. Third, being rich and educated is far more impactful in determining spending choices than living in a rural location.

These results bother me in a profound way. I am not concerned about whether one can buy wine from Italy or cheese from France, but I am worried about the ramifications for those who do not spend on these items. These results hearken back to Shamus Khan's observation about cultural capital: we all have it; just some types are worth more than others. Indeed, some of the items we analyzed are more expensive, but some just have a high price in cultural knowledge and education. Is imported beer so much more expensive than domestic? When I looked it up, a six-pack of Budweiser is almost exactly the same price as six twelve-ounce bottles of Modelo. At the time that I compared prices of twelve-ounce Velveeta sliced cheddar cheese with ten ounces of Montchevre goat cheese at Vons, their prices differed by $2.50. These differences, even though they are expressed by wealth, are not necessarily about expense. Instead, it is that the wealthy and educated determine the goods that comprise elite cultural capital. Even though the cheeses cost the same, to know to buy the goat cheese and to eschew the sliced, processed cheese is to be part of a particular elite group. There's another concern I have with our findings. The expenditures associated with the poor and uneducated are linked to bad health outcomes. Smoking cigarettes (an expensive habit) and drinking Coca-Cola is a fast trip to lung cancer and diabetes. These are behaviors practiced by those with little money and little education but are all but nonexistent for the wealthy and educated.

As my exploration pertains to cultural capital, my concern moved from differences between rural and urban to differences between the wealthy and educated and everyone else. The wealthy and educated essentially decide what cultural capital matters through what they talk about, the institutions they are affiliated with, and, yes, what they buy. These elites do tend to live predominately in our cities. In and of itself, it doesn't matter whether someone goes to an Ivy League university, plays lacrosse, joins debate team, or drinks organic milk unless it is demonstrative of tangible differences in life chances and outcomes. If you aren't a member of the cultural elite, you are not becoming a Supreme Court judge and deciding the fate of the country's judicial system, you are not becoming a journalist at the *Wall Street Journal* or *New York Times* and shaping public thought and opinion, and you are not teaching in our universities where we educate the minds of tomorrow. If you are not educated or reasonably well-off, you are likely not consuming enough fresh produce, your milk may contain synthetic hormones, and you're more likely to smoke. This is where cultural capital becomes more than simply an urban and rural debate. There may, to be clear, be a greater number of uneducated people in rural America, but the problem isn't rural life itself. Craig Parker and many of the people I interviewed were doing just fine without possessing or identifying with elite cultural capital. It's the people without the other, more tangible attributes that go along with cultural capital—regardless of whether they live in small-town Missouri or South Los Angeles— that we must make our greatest priority.

CRAIG, STEWARD OF the land and conservationist, grows his own food and possesses the individualism of the average meritocrat. And yet, he values other things in life that don't fall within the progressive script. Craig values his family and his religion. He finds meaning in working hard and proudly views himself as self-made. Even though Craig engages in much of the same cultural capital that upper-middle-class urbanites cherish, he wouldn't use their words. He does not valorize these attributes as a part of his identity.

Cultural capital is everywhere, but it is also place specific: what helps you fit into a group in Arkansas isn't the same as in Marin County, California. Cultural capital represents much of how we identify ourselves in the world and to ourselves. For rural and urban Americans, the language used to convey knowledge and values is different, and what they choose to translate into cultural capital is different too.

Not all Americans today share the same vision of social mobility and the good life. In the mid-twentieth century, with new automobiles and suburban houses and the American Dream, we might have come close. But today, with increased multiculturalism, rising inequality, and political polarization, how we identify ourselves is more multifaceted. This difference is not simply a division of rural and urban. Organic food is bought everywhere, so long as people have money and are educated. Environmentalism and tolerance exist in the heart of rural Kentucky but lack the performative aspects we find in San Francisco or Portland. Many of us believe in God. For some, this faith is the foundation of social and cultural capital, while for others it is an internal relationship. What makes these ubiquitous behaviors, beliefs, and opinions translate into cultural capital is how we construct our identity around language, objects, and places. This process, often undertaken as a part of a social dynamic, is how culture becomes habitual and unconscious. We often do not realize that something we assume to be natural is actually a function of deeply embedded culture.[27]

For coastal elite America, it feels natural to eat organic food, to engage in progressive politics, to embrace scientism and judge those who do not. All of these behaviors—and I am no innocent here—are simply signs of cultural capital that we assume to be the "right" choices, and they alienate much of America. Rural America doesn't see the same things as cultural capital: their lives revolve around religion, family, doing good deeds, working hard. Time and time again, the rural people I spoke to prided themselves on their faith, their family, and being decent. One might call their cultural capital "moral capital," but it has become less valued by the global economy and the increasingly secular nature of our public discourse. As Yale religious scholar Philip Gorski observes, secular cultural capital has triumphed over religious capital.[28] In the mid-twentieth century, religion possessed more currency in society as a whole. So much so that, in the mid-1950s, most people believed its import would increase over time.[29] As Gorski points out, in another time, our engineers might have become clergymen, but liberal Protestantism faded as liberal seculars emerged, which ultimately switched out religion for other value systems.

"Family values," religiosity, manual labor, trade, and vocation no longer have the same worth in society. But these values matter a lot to rural Americans, both because they hold them deeply and because religion and family are the dominant fabric of their social lives. Recall Robert Wuthnow's observation that religion performs an important role in small-town America: it is the source of institutions, gatherings, and communication in a way that is impossible in diverse, multicultural cities.

The data suggests that many Americans are still religious, but elite economic and cultural capital is tied to secularism and individualism. These qualities are what elites value, along with a relentless belief in the acquisition of knowledge and its accoutrements. Rural America possesses some, not all, of the cultural capital espoused by the global elite: environmentalism, shopping local, and equality were important to many of my rural interviewees. The difference between rural and urban is that rural folks didn't need or want the language to convert their actions into cultural capital. These actions were just a part of their lives, or what Gorski would call "civic ecology."[30] "I guess it's organic. I mean, I don't use pesticides," I recall Craig remarking with indifference.

Does it matter that rural Americans don't embrace elite cultural capital? I think it depends. After all of this, I am not sure I can safely say who has it better. There's no question that being poor and uneducated is terrible and that our social and economic policies to correct for these disadvantages are inadequate. However, that urgency is not specific to rural America. There are poor and uneducated people everywhere, and they need society's and government's interventions. But for everyone else, on a purely individual level, I wasn't so sure these rural folks had it wrong. Day-to-day, their lives were good, or as good as any of ours can be. No amount of organic milk or imported cheeses matters if one feels at home in the world and possesses a sense of familial and community connection. Those connections are vital regardless of how they are formed, whether through the church or conversations about the most recent Jonathan Franzen book. We find a place we can feel like ourselves, and it's hard to say, by that measure, that any form of cultural capital is superior. Liberals misunderstand rural America as backward and unsophisticated. Rather, rural Americans just value different qualities and connections in their cultural capital, and there is nothing wrong with that. It is only when one looks at the big picture—zooms out to the hierarchies of the global economy and the people who run society, the government, and the economy—that there is an argument for people like Craig and his children to care. It would be to the benefit of everyone if people like Craig and Clay and the other kind people I met in rural America have a part in determining what matters and why.

MORE BASICALLY, CULTURAL capital obscures the things about people we may really admire. We assume a lot about people based on where they live and what they do for a living. Therefore, we fail to see qualities that aren't necessarily on display. These superficial factors do not have to overlap with our own for us to connect with someone and learn from their experience.

Courtney Fowler did end up at Penn State University, graduating with a bachelor's degree. She had everything she needed to be anywhere but rural America. Yet, after she graduated, she remained in State College, where she waitressed at a local restaurant. "I wasn't even using my degree," she says, almost aghast at herself. At the time, she was dating a man who lived down the street. "I think I was drawn to him because he was a simple person, a hippie, really laid back and not interested in material things. A good person...but obviously..." Courtney trails off and sighs.

She continues, "I found out I was pregnant. I was like, 'Oh what am I going to do?' I had to change everything. I was subletting and soon to be out of an apartment, so I ended up going back to Danville, a nice, safe place where I could live with my parents. He said he would come to Danville as well and completely ghosted me, before ghosting was even a thing!" She laughs. "Then, he sent me a note six months, a year later, an apology. And I ignored that too. It was easy for me to separate at that point." In the early days, Courtney attempted to track down her child's father to legally file for full custody. While they found him under complicated circumstances, Courtney's child has since declined to make contact with their father.

From very early on, Courtney was consumed with her newborn child, who was soon diagnosed with a rare genetic disease, which causes the body to continue to grow tumors. It is a life-threatening disease, because if her child grows a tumor on a vital organ, it could kill them. "Devon was born prematurely. It was present at birth, but things happened the older he got. His first surgery was when he was about six months old. He's had thirty-six surgeries. It's going to be an ongoing thing." Courtney pauses. At this point, she discusses her child's other difficulties. Devon is transgender and became Emily during her young adult years. Courtney continues, "The last surgery was eleven hours, and she had her eye removed, and it was a lot of reconstruction, and the recovery was horrible." She pauses. "And thank you drug addicts, she was not allowed any pain medication. Talk about mamma bear, I was screaming on the phone [to the nurses]." Courtney's voice is soft and sweet, almost fairylike, even though I can sense the rage she is feeling.

Only at one point does Courtney's voice break, revealing deep sadness and anger. "She has severe facial deformities, so it's really hard to just be alive." Courtney pauses. "Along with being transgender, on top of that, Emily has a lot of mental health issues going on." In Courtney's response I heard no judgment. She simply embraced her child with love. Her soft voice returns. "But you know what, it's the same actually. Anytime your child hurts, it's the same pain, regardless of how big the issue is."

In other conversations I had with Courtney, she expressed huge support for gay marriage, vaccines, and organic food (although she admits she really can't afford it), and she voiced concern for what feels like a divided America. I asked what city-dwelling Americans might think of her, and she laughed. "I think that they probably would think I'm Amish, but it is [just] a more laid-back pace of living in rural areas."

As I listened to Courtney, I admired her for so many things I could barely keep track. She was as open-minded, kind, and tolerant as any of my friends in Los Angeles, maybe even more so. Life had dealt her enough blows that I wouldn't blame her for being bitter or cynical. But she wasn't either of those things. Her soul radiated in every conversation. Her child was transgender, but this was something Courtney neither judged nor broadcasted. It just was a fact that she approached with understanding and concern for her child's well-being.

Courtney is only one of the many people I met who diverged sharply from our stereotypes about rural Americans as backward and intolerant. She is a low-income mother with a child who has to face both a life-threatening disease and transphobia. Through it all, she was able to share openness and tolerance on every topic we discussed. Aware of the stereotypes directed toward her, Courtney laughed where another might be angry. Her cultural capital isn't the same as mine. Hers would not find acceptance in our global institutions of power or in our major cities, though it should. Maybe her cultural capital shouldn't matter so much. Maybe we need to look underneath, at something far more valuable. Courtney's ability to show tolerance, empathy, and openness—irrespective of culture and despite being judged herself—should give all of us something to strive for.

8

THE THROUGH LINE

Reality is more complicated than mankind
might ever have supposed.
—Olga Tokarczuk[1]

On the campaign I called it the forgotten man and the
forgotten woman. Well, you are not forgotten anymore.
—Donald Trump[2]

I**N 2021, JUST AFTER** C**HRISTMAS, OUR FAMILY WAS HEADING** down Interstate 5 back home to Los Angeles. We had spent the holiday in Tahoe with my brother and his children, my sister, and my parents. The first family reunion since the pandemic had begun had felt normal, which in those days was an alien sensation. We had just left Sacramento, where we had spent the night to break up the trip. As we headed off on our long journey south, my son Oliver, nine years old at the time, requested we play Bill Bryson's *The Lost Continent: Travels in Small-Town America*. Oliver had recently discovered Bryson and, with his English father, he found the satirizing of American culture hilarious. As Oliver and his father laughed and laughed, I looked out at this anonymous stretch of interstate. It struck me that much of America looked like the space between

Los Angeles and San Francisco, not like the rarified cities more connected to Tokyo and London than to this vast hinterland.[3] I also thought of how so many of those living in global cities disdain this landscape as endless and unremarkable, constructed of dull highways, chain stores, prefabricated houses, pickup trucks, and American-made sedans. Across the country, Red Roof Inn, Dairy Queen, McDonald's after McDonald's, the occasional diner, Safeway, Kroger, the dollar store, and the car dealership marked America more distinctly than its changing topography of mountains, fields, and plains.

As if the soundtrack to my observations, I could hear Bryson's sardonic commentary on what he saw as the absurdity of American small-town life. "I was heading to Nebraska. Now there's a sentence you don't want to say too often if you can possibly help it." "In the morning I awoke early and experienced that sinking sensation that overcomes you when you first open your eyes and realize that instead of a normal day ahead of you, with its scatterings of simple gratifications, you are going to have a day without even the tiniest of pleasures; you are going to drive across Ohio."

I wonder what Bryson would say about the Central Valley. Undoubtedly, he would express a similar horror toward its banality. And yet, as I took in this landscape, I thought to myself, *But this is someone's life.* These homes and stores—as identical and unremarkable as they all seem—are where people live their lives, which are remarkable to them. These are the places where people get groceries, where they celebrate special birthday dinners, where children are born, and where, upon adulthood, they buy first homes and new cars they've saved up for, where millions of people experience their "one wild and precious life," to quote the poet Mary Oliver.

And yet other people write books and essays satirizing, critiquing, or lamenting their very existence. With disdain or pity, the coastal media and their followers describe flyover states, hillbillies, deplorables, and other derogatory terms by which they choose to "other" people who are not meritocrats, who do not live in global cities, and who are not overtly liberal. And yet, dominant liberal culture does not acknowledge these Americans' experiences as meaningful; rural Americans are rarely even represented, except in hyperbole or parody, or as people living desperate lives in economic decline. Their real lives and landscapes seem too dull to bother. Inhabitants of these regions are dismissed as ignorant, racist, regressive. Their adherence to the Bible's teachings is mocked. I can't blame my son and his father for laughing at the witty caricatures Bryson sketches. After all, everyone laughs at the middle of America. But do we even know these people? What could we say about their hopes and dreams and aspirations? Do we even think for a moment that they might not be so different from ours?

Well, I know now. It's a lot easier to listen to people when you are not already in the position to judge them. It's a lot easier to listen when you are only listening, rather than taking in their style of dress, their car, their home. You hear the pauses, feel the discomfort of the silence that seems to go on too long, and then they speak again and what they say is not what you expect. (What did you expect? Should you expect anything?) What they say is perhaps something you might have said too. That's when you realize: maybe we're not so different after all.

I came to this conclusion both empirically and emotionally. After looking at pages and pages of data documenting income, homeownership, employment, industries, and jobs, it's clear that rural Americans are doing much better than the conventional wisdom suggests. They may not be millionaires, nor do they live in palatial townhouses, but most Americans, regardless of where they live, do not have opulent lives. Rural Americans by most measures are living prosperously and decently. They own their homes, they are employed, they make more or less the same as those in cities. Even on hot-button issues such as democracy, race, social policy, and religion, we find that most Americans feel fairly similarly to one another, irrespective of where they live. But it was the non-statistical aspects of their lives that compelled me the most. When I listened to rural Americans, I truly appreciated the extent to which they just want to be viewed as people. They don't want special treatment. They ask only that they be not judged because they fail to embrace the same ethos as the nation's coastal elites. They are not all angry or enraged; they do not envy coastal elites or the creative class. They want to live their lives with basic dignity. Rather than looking down on rural Americans and their culture, we ought to see them as human beings whose lives and belief systems are worthy of respect.

While simple, this message seems to be hard for coastal elites to fully embrace. Last spring, I gave a talk on the topics I discuss in this book. While my remarks were generally well received, a success I did not take for granted, one woman from the audience asked a question that evolved into a diatribe. What initially started as a personal story proceeded into an attack on rural Americans for not getting vaccinated. The main thrust of her argument was that we couldn't be open-minded with people who were jeopardizing public health by not getting the Covid-19 vaccine. At the time, I wasn't entirely sure how to respond, and I didn't have vaccine statistics in front of me. Her point about vaccinations was valid, but later that night I was still thinking and I looked some figures up.

The reality is that outside of places like New York City and San Francisco, plenty of Americans have chosen not to get vaccinated. And plenty of people in rural America have chosen to get vaccinated too. In Montour County, where Danville, Pennsylvania, is located, 80 percent of adults and 95 percent of those over sixty-five years old are vaccinated. In Los Angeles, those numbers are 73 percent and 87 percent, respectively. In San Diego, the numbers are 77 percent and 94 percent. So rural Pennsylvania is actually in better shape, vaccine-wise, than some of our most populous coastal counties. When I looked at vaccination status in rural counties in the

South (the least vaccinated part of the country), between 50 and 60 percent of the population is fully vaccinated. And while this statistic is not 80 percent, the vaccination rate for rural America is not a whole different world from our cities. Even in Silver Lake, the local handyman isn't vaccinated and was clearly offended when I asked. Afterward, he would no longer respond to my calls.

There is pretty significant vaccine resistance in our cities. Measles and whooping cough—once essentially eradicated by vaccines—are making a comeback in urban centers, not rural America. In fact, in 2019, prior to the pandemic, the World Health Organization named vaccine hesitancy as one of the world's biggest health threats. Cities are ground zero for anti-vaxxers, as the proponents of the movement are called. While lack of access explains some low vaccination rates (particularly in rural areas), the CDC has identified "hot spots" in major cities, propelled by cultural and philosophical beliefs of often well-to-do parents, including the now-debunked belief that vaccines cause autism.[4] An *Atlantic* article reported that the vaccination rates in some of Los Angeles' wealthiest neighborhoods are akin to those of the South Sudan.[5] As the article reports, "Vaccination rates in elite neighborhoods like Santa Monica and Beverly Hills have tanked, and the incidence of whooping cough there has skyrocketed." In early 2019, New York City experienced its worst measles outbreak in decades, partially due to skeptical ultra-Orthodox communities in Brooklyn, where vaccination rates are as low as 60 percent and schools overreport vaccination.[6]

Conversely, the highest vaccination rates are found in the very states ridiculed for being uninformed and unsophisticated. According to the CDC, Pennsylvania, North Dakota, and Nebraska top the list of most vaccinated children, while California's rate is similar to that of West Virginia and Arkansas. At the time that I was writing this book, New York was one of the biggest culprits, with just a 64 percent vaccination rate. Public health officials warn that, depending on the disease, 80 to 95 percent of the population must be vaccinated for it to be kept at bay, a phenomenon known as "herd immunity."[7] We've heard this discussion with regard to Covid-19, but the same threshold applies for lots of dangerous diseases.

These statistics suggest that, yes, parts of rural America are equally susceptible to a public health crisis as the rich pockets of Los Angeles; however, small-town America cannot be lumped together as some homogeneous entity or as a place solely responsible for vaccine resistance. As one rural woman whom I interviewed wrote to me of her choice to vaccinate her child, "I will admit that I am not an expert on vaccines. However, I do find it impressive that small pox and other diseases have been eradicated from the planet via vaccines. I feel like who am I to question their effectiveness? I also feel like it is my responsibility, as a parent of three healthy kids, to have my children vaccinated to protect the children who are unable to be vaccinated (e.g., immunocompromised [patients], [patients] receiving chemotherapy)." This remark, like so many I received, challenges the stereotypes of an ignorant, uninformed, and intolerant small-town America.

The same can be said of breastfeeding, which most recently has been associated with the mothering style of the educated, urban elite, a trend I chronicled in depth in my previous book *The Sum of Small Things*. Indeed, the correlation between wealth, education, and breastfeeding is significant, with education being the number-one indicator of whether a woman breastfeeds her child.[8] That said, state-level data suggests that while places like California show high rates of breastfeeding, women in extremely rural states like Vermont, Colorado, and Maine are even more likely than their urban counterparts to breastfeed exclusively at six months and through to twelve months.[9] In fact, as one rural woman remarked in one of our correspondences, while she is well aware of the benefits of breastfeeding (and breastfed her own children), she is equally aware of the constraints most women face. As she explained, "I think most people realize it is healthier for baby to have breast milk. I definitely think there is correlation with socioeconomic class and amount of education of the mom or parents with breastfeeding." She continued, "I will say that it is very difficult to be successful at it to the point of exclusively breastfeeding until 6 months. I have seen many women have to supplement or give up and it is because of it being too much to manage while working full time. I feel like it is a complicated topic and that it may be something like higher education that the elite have more access to than the average American."

What do statistics like these suggest? In short, places are different from one another but not along the conventional lines or for the reasons we assume. Rural America is no more culturally or socio-economically out of touch than any given place in the country, and many of our stereotypes do not hold up. Rather, different places have different value systems and, sometimes consequently, different problems. Some parts of small-town America may be more likely to struggle with prescription painkillers, but measles outbreaks at the local amusement park are unlikely. Similarly, myths about rural America being unaware of important aspects of parenting, education, and health are misplaced. They are no more and no less involved and caring than people living in other parts of America. They just might approach things in a different way. While small-town parents are not necessarily as fixated on their children attending an Ivy League college, there is an increased desire for students from rural America to attend elite universities, and acceptance rates can be significantly higher for rural states like Alaska, Mississippi, and Montana than for California and New Jersey.[10] Not to mention, many rural people have found satisfaction and happiness in their lives without joining the meritocratic rat race. Post-pandemic data suggests that urbanites—realizing the freedom of working from home and exhausted with high rents and congestion—are flocking to rural America, where many small towns have gained population.[11]

As a card-carrying member of the coastal elite who grew up in rural America, I can see firsthand that the piousness of the liberal wing of the Democratic Party alienates most of America, whether rural or urban. While this particular and noxious form of political culture is being embraced by dominant media outlets—many of which I read—it is alien to most Americans, who tend to be political moderates. The brunt of this stereotyping may be felt by rural Americans, but those who live in San Francisco, New York, and Los Angeles get caricatured too. Not because they don't understand or don't relate to some of the issues, but because they are made, seemingly intentionally, to feel left out of the exclusive circles of meritocracy.

As the late philosopher Judith Shklar wrote in *Ordinary Vices*, embedded in everyday life are some of our most pernicious inhumanities, one of which is hypocrisy, another snobbery. In a democracy, ostensibly sensitive to snobbery and hierarchy, we are supposed to be equal. We may not be exactly the same, but our differences are not supposed to be imbued with value. Meritocracy, as she observes, is the worst form of snobbery.[12] Because meritocrats are educated, their position appears more legitimate in all matters. Those in power—the highly educated managerial-professional classes—possess such a convincing false consciousness of their own worth and point of view that they completely overlook the fact that, for most of them, their educated parents and economic position gave them their place in the elite. Democracy and meritocracy are supposed to level the playing field. And yet we know that's not the case in America, certainly with regard to race and gender. But it is also not the case for those who do not conform to elite cultural norms or who have not been accepted by the meritocracy. For all of the good things that come of our social capital, there is a dark side too: when we trust too much in our own group, we trust less in others, and our society exhibits less unity and normativity as a whole.[13] "When it comes to people whose lives aren't going well, American culture is a harsh judge: if you can't find enough work, if your wages are too low, if you can't be counted on to support a family, if you don't have a promising future, then there must be something wrong with you," writes surgeon and author Atul Gawande. "We Americans are reluctant to acknowledge that our economy serves the educated classes and penalizes the rest. But that's exactly the situation."[14]

America, like monarchical England and aristocratic France, has its own hierarchy, even if it is obfuscated by talk of Horatio Alger (who wrote fiction) and the American Dream (for whom?). In a democracy, meritocracy and the belief in social mobility become the great means by which social hierarchy is justified. We try to explain our social organization with the fact that someone went to an elite college or plays piano or works in finance. And yet the educated, the meritocrats, are snobby and cruel to the rural folks, the uneducated, and those who live outside of their comfort zone on the coasts. But these snobs do not identify themselves as such.[15] They think their tastes are merely refined, woke, educated, and informed; the corollary is that other people's views are not.

But all of our efforts to mitigate cruelty with a capital *C*— progressivism, social justice, and other reckonings—may obscure our everyday cruelty toward those for whom we do not feel empathy.[16] Wokeism—the impulse toward social justice turned toxic— engages in the cruelty of judging those unaware of their own missteps and ignorance and canceling them for not being politically correct, irrespective of their intent. For Shklar, cruelty is the worst of the ordinary vices, and "moral cruelty"—the seemingly small acts of condescension and piety—is just as mean and alienating as more overt forms.[17] "Those who fight to eliminate the obvious cruelty of brutality and violence can be no less cruel in their own subtle and sinister ways," writes Blake Smith in *Tablet* magazine.[18] As Shklar observes, all cruelty feels the same because cruelty is where fear lives.[19]

"Why is America so divided?" the pundits ask over and over again. My follow-up question is, "Are we so divided?" Maybe not.

I believe we see divides because rifts of some sort always exist in society, and media and politicians dramatize them for their own aims. I believe we see divides because we fixate on differences in politics and culture more than we pay attention to the commonalities we have as Americans, as humans. I believe we see divides because once every four years we get, realistically, a choice between two major candidates, and we have to pick one. We don't get to write in our comments or fill out a chart where we "agree" or "strongly agree" or are "neutral" about our vote. People may be Democratic or Republican; some people are more Left or Right. But most people are not extremely Republican or extremely Democratic. As the political scientists Yanna Krupnikov and John Barry Ryan observe, the opinions of the average voter have not moved farther apart. Rather, the extremes within a party drive division. The real divide in this country is not between liberals and conservatives but rather between those who are hyper involved and those who are apolitical. In fact, Krupnikov and Ryan observe the rise of "intraparty polarization," whereby most people are increasingly disaffected with *both* parties. As they observe, most people are just living their lives, while 15 to 20 percent of people are extremely active in politics and drive what feels like a widespread division between Left and Right ideologies.[20]

Of course, we should not ignore the fifth of America who are very involved. These voters donate more, and they shape both the media and politicians' understanding of public opinion.[21] Rather, the point is to understand that this minority is not reflective of the typical American. The Left and Right extremes do not explain the middle. Rather, they distort our understanding of the whole. As John Barry Ryan observes, "It's when you get into that slippage of 'and this is what Americans thinks,' 'oh America is hopelessly divided,'" that our media and politicians go wrong.[22] As Ryan points out, we can make America seem divided if we portray this small group as a stand-in for the general populace, but calling America divided obscures most people's views. People don't always vote based on the big ideas but rather for what makes them feel comfortable. People don't want to feel bad about themselves. They don't want to feel looked down upon because of their lack of education or their belief in God, because of who they are and who they want to be. They don't want to be made fun of for not using the correct acronym. They don't want to be canceled for inadvertently saying something "unwoke." "Cruelty lies behind pious talk about nobility and justice," observes Oxford professor David Runciman in his discussion of Nietzsche. "We pretend that we are better than we really are."[23] Rural Americans feel the cruelty of the meritocracy. And it feels horrible.

Donald Trump offered rural Americans a chance to feel okay about themselves and their futures. It may have been a lie from a Weberian charismatic authority, but it sure felt better than the snobbery and sanctimony of the liberal elite. Donald Trump is no everyday American. Trump is a rich, Wharton-educated businessman from New York City, but he, too, felt left out and looked down upon by the coastal elites. Many rural Americans voted for Trump. And who could blame them? He was the one who told them, even if he may have been lying, that they were not forgotten. Trump is cruel on Twitter, to public figures, to women, but he isn't cruel to those whose vote he wants dearly. Democrats, take note.

But to focus in on Trump is to distract from the larger narrative of this country. I am trying to understand where people come from and how we've ended up here. I don't think it's politics. I think it is culture and the culture of politics that drives differences that may not even exist. "Without doubt," writes sociologist James Hunter, "public discourse is more polarized than the American public itself." Hunter's argument is that culture underpins what we perceive to be political divides. In a Rousseauesque way, culture is formed by our moral view of the world. American citizens are not being told to think one way or another from some top-down authority; this is actually how people feel. For the orthodox and traditionalists, morals stem from religion and family values. For the more progressive arm of society, morals are tied to inclusivity, sexual freedom, and equality. It would be fine to agree to disagree, but, as Hunter observes, progressive culture is tied to the elite institutions of society—top universities, Hollywood, highbrow media—while traditionalist views are marginalized to middling and lowbrow institutions—unexceptional conservative colleges, religious organizations—derided by the educated coastal elites.[24]

One of the implicit findings of my interviews has been that much of what seems like resentment and resistance from rural America is actually a reaction to the piousness and condescension in how the meritocrats, aspirational class, coastal elites, and the creative class—whatever we want to call them—express their values. Rural Americans aren't idiots, and they're not oblivious to racial oppression. They see the headlines of police brutality, and they are horrified. They know a white man is far less likely to be questioned by a police officer than a Black man, and they don't like that. Most of them, even many of those who adhere to Christian scripture, don't care whom anyone marries. The issue is how these messages are conveyed, wrapped up in the language of performative anti-racism, academese, and virtue signaling. Poor white people living in the foothills of Appalachia don't feel "white privilege," and they don't keep track of everything we can and cannot say according to the professional-managerial class. However, most of them sure do understand that people are treated unequally because of their skin color and sexuality, and they know that's a terrible thing.

People like Shannon feel estranged from white coastal elites' rigid constructions around race because their experience is different. These very coastal elites, mind you, often live in overwhelmingly white, affluent urban neighborhoods, even as they like to put signs in their front yard about ending white silence. "There is a danger—not just in California, but everywhere," writes Ezra Klein, "that politics becomes an aesthetic rather than a program."[25] Those who put out lawn signs in their predominantly white community will do very little to increase their neighborhood's actual socioeconomic and demographic diversity, even as they performatively say and demonstrate they are on the right side of things.

People like Shannon from Kentucky or Jason from Pennsylvania have diverse social networks and appear to understand the complexities of race relations better than many white coastal elites living in homogeneous, affluent urban neighborhoods. Shannon and Jason feel that their life stories and points of view aren't fully appreciated or understood. There are millions of Shannons and Jasons in America.

Understandably, those holding traditionalist, conservative values often feel dismissed by elites who don't seem to want to understand where they are coming from. Political scientists Ronald Inglehart and Pippa Norris are not surprised that we are witnessing a cultural backlash. In the cases of Brexit and the election of President Trump, Inglehart and Norris show that the backlash is not one of economic insecurity (the commonly held notion) but rather against progressive values. They find that since 1970 there has been a burgeoning of "post-material values," which include the environment, self-expression, gender fluidity, and secularism. Inglehart and Norris find that these values are almost uniformly embraced by the young and well-educated middle classes.[26] The relative prosperity and peace of the post–World War II period partially explains why later generations were able to embrace these post-material values: they were far less worried about starvation, bankruptcy, or dying in a war.[27] The problem, then, is not the emergence of progressive values per se, but the swift rejection of all others.

Culture is a nebulous thing that is imbued with so much value. Everyone has an identity they hold dear. What causes these differences in self to become fault lines is how the greater tides of society flow and what we have decided matters more. As David Brooks remarked in an interview with Oprah Winfrey, community is about connection with each other, and tribes are formed through an identity and culture that marks us against others.[28] Thus we get to a point in society where the question becomes, which culture do we value the most? What if the answer was "neither/both"? What if we decided to listen rather than tell people why they should feel one thing or another? Culture may feel superficial, fluid, and secondary, but there is nothing peripheral to the elements that comprise our sense of self. When we look at rural and small-town America and see people resentful of change, this wariness may not be their "white fragility" but rather the erosion of the value of their cultural and social capital. They sense their lives don't matter to society—at all. Family and religion cease to hold the same worth, or so we are told by the industries and media that scorn traditional views. What if we saw different views as not ours, but also not bad? What if we saw fellow Americans like we see our own children? So different from each other, so challenging at times to understand, and yet we love them and respect their differences.

Yes, as Katherine J. Cramer has observed, small-town Americans feel that political elites are sometimes out of touch and prescribe policies without being close to the problems they are trying to solve. But small-town America is also inhabited by people who are broadly supportive of gay rights, immigration, and equality. They may not always feel impassioned by these issues, they may have different suggestions when it comes to immigration policy, but they are not antagonists. The problem is that we don't take the time to appreciate this subtle but important difference. Instead, public leaders and the media cast Trump voters and white supremacists as one and the same, but, as I've argued, they're not. Rural Americans did not uniformly support Trump, and those who did supported him for a wide range of reasons that had nothing to do with economic grievance or racism. Many rural Americans are displeased with Trump's performance in office, many voted for him simply because he was the Republican candidate, plenty voted for the Democratic candidate, and many who voted for him are kind, tolerant, and open-minded people just the same.

Small-town America is not full of deplorable white supremacists, but rural folks are all too aware of this offensive stereotype. When I asked a few interviewees how they felt about the media's depiction of them as angry and intolerant, they were discouraged. "It's just wrong," explained one woman. As another woman put it, "Thank you for recognizing that we are not dumb, hateful people. We are, for the most part, hardworking just trying to earn an honest living while providing the best we can for our families." Some rural Americans expressed frustration, others were simply skeptical—not critical of progressive, elite America but rather wary of its implications for their lives. And I can't say they're wrong to have that feeling. "[A] huge cultural divide has emerged between highly educated professionals living in cities and residents of smaller towns with more traditional values," writes Francis Fukuyama. "And the desire to belong and have one's dignity affirmed are often more powerful forces than economic self-interest."[29] We lose track of the fact that our desire to be respected as human beings is often a greater need than our rational concerns.

I N THE 1920s the sociologists Robert and Helen Lynd embarked on a project to understand a town "as representative as possible of contemporary American life." The Lynds used Muncie, Indiana, as their place of study, conducting ethnography and interviews with the town's inhabitants to better understand the values, beliefs, and choices of most of America. Muncie, renamed Middletown in the Lynds' book, was a place that captured most of America. In Middletown there were Democrats and Republicans, rich and poor, working class and professionals. Middletown represents what America used to look like, rather than the isolated bubbles to which we have become so accustomed today. "Whoever touches this book touches the heart of America," remarked Stuart Chase in a review in the *Nation*.[30] This is not to say the book was not met with criticism. Indeed, the Black community, despite being 5 percent of the town's population, was almost entirely ignored in the Lynds' study. Others remarked that Middletown was a story of an idealized America, not the real one. That said, as a result of the Middletown studies, Muncie has been thought of as an important lens—even if symbolic—for understanding what we mean when we say America.

This is not to say that there is no inequity, no poverty, or no cause for concern today or in yesteryear. Extreme poverty and chronic unemployment, along with intolerance and economic and social resentment, exist in rural America (and always have), but these problems are in our cities too. They are evidence of a class divide that cuts across geography and demographics. Yet there are millions of people—the figurative Middletown dwellers of the twenty-first century—who do not fit this current paradigm. This America, an overlooked America, is a place that we have not looked at closely since the early twentieth century. This is an America in the shadows, and one that, if understood more deeply, might give us a greater sense of how we can build a more cohesive country. Rather than continuing to insist that the vast majority of Americans are hyperpolarized, we might try to better understand, to take that Tocquevillian tour of America to see what is actually going on, which is what I have tried to do in this book. What I found was a small-town America that is just as complicated and diverse as urban America. A place filled with goodness, generosity of spirit, tolerance, and care for others. These were people who became my friends. When I didn't focus on our political differences as paramount, when I saw our cultures as different but equal in value, when I allowed myself to hold those differences and discomforts without judging, I saw people with whom I shared profound commonalities in the human condition. Perhaps that first step and acknowledgment is the bridge we need to regain the common ideas, the "principle ideas" as Tocqueville put it, that once defined America.

As I was writing this book, I stumbled across the Polish writer Olga Tokarczuk's Nobel Prize acceptance speech. I began reading and could not stop.[31] Strange as it may seem, it captured much of what I was trying to say about America. Tokarczuk's speech has three important themes: As children we often are able to see the deep connectivity and possibilities of the world. Then at some point we begin to see the world in discrete ways. Our ability to see another person truly as themselves, what Tokarczuk calls tenderness, is a means by which we can rediscover that connectivity and closeness so lacking in the world today. She tells Hans Christian Andersen's story of the teapot thrown out simply because its handle is broken. The teapot has feelings and expresses that if only her owners had been less critical, they would have kept her. (The teapot does in fact find a better life repurposed as a pot for growing flowers.) As a child, Tokarczuk found this story deeply moving. "I listened to these fairy tales with flushed cheeks and tears in my eyes," she says, "because I believed deeply that objects have their own problems and emotions, as well as a sort of social life, entirely comparable to our human one. The plates in the dresser could talk to each other, and the spoons, knives and forks in the drawer formed a sort of a family.... The landscape surrounding us was alive too, and so were the Sun and the Moon, and all the celestial bodies. The entire visible and invisible world."

Tokarczuk's story resonated with me because I, too, as a child had this sense of everything being connected. One of my favorite stories was *The Lion, the Witch and the Wardrobe*, and though it is ridiculed by liberal secularists for its religious overtones, I never much cared about the plot around the White Witch and Aslan. For me, the most compelling aspect of the story was the wardrobe that

went to Narnia. As a child, I believed that somewhere in my own
house there was a place like that hidden behind a wardrobe or in a
closet. I would roam around my house looking for it. I can recall
one summer evening stumbling across a place past our backyard
and the fields beyond that felt as if I'd fallen into another world. I
remember upon discovering it that I needed to run home for supper,
and thereafter I tried to retrace my steps to this magical paradise of
a winding creek, hills, and flowers, never to find it again. Was it a
part of my imagination? Had I approached the same plot of land I
saw every day from a different perspective? Was it Narnia? I'll never
know, but I do remember that sense of fluidity between all places
magical and real.

Why do I tell you these stories of a teapot and my childhood?
Because I no longer even try to find this place that I assume was a
figment of my imagination. Because for Tokarczuk the forks and the
spoons and the knives no longer speak to one another. "I'm trying to
find the moment in my life when at the flick of a switch everything
became different, less nuanced, simpler," Tokarczuk says. "At some
point in our lives, we start to see the world in pieces, everything
separately, in little bits that are galaxies apart from one another, and
the reality in which we live keeps affirming it: doctors treat us by
specialty, taxes have no connection with snow-plowing the road we
drive to work along, our lunch has nothing to do with an enormous
stock farm, or my new top with a shabby factory somewhere in Asia.
Everything is separate from everything else, everything lives apart,
without any connection."

I have that same sense about the cultures and thus the communities of our country. It is happening all across Western societies, of
course, but I can only write of the United States and the Americans
with whom I have spoken. We have lost sight of our shared sense
of humanity, our belief in each other, our ability to accept someone who is totally different from us and to respect their point of
view. This is not to apologize for the racists, the xenophobes, the

homophobes, and the people who are hateful. They are, in the most egregious sense, unaccepting of others. I am speaking only of those who simply see the world differently from each other, and thus we see fragmentation and chasms where there needn't be.

We must actively try to move beyond the narrative that Americans are hopelessly divided from one another; we must try much harder to see the humanity in each of us. When I spoke to Americans for this book, I immediately liked every one of them. If you had asked me five years ago if I would have anything to say or understand about a pastor in Missouri or a young man living in Appalachia or an evangelical who subscribed to conspiracy theories, I would have laughed. *Of course not.* I would not have given myself or these people any credit. We confuse differences in culture with differences in the human condition. Fundamentally, the latter is what binds us and the former makes us think such connection is impossible.

I remember talking with Arlie Hochschild about this tension between our connections with people and the seeming fissures in our understanding. I told her about Shannon and Keith and the many others who challenged my view of people. Hochschild is an easy poet in her conversation. "Language is not complex enough to capture these differences," she says, smiling. "Hold on to the contradictions, hold on to the confusion." If we accept our cognitive dissonance, if we see those contractions as inherently human, then our differences do not feel so big.

Tokarczuk finishes her speech by talking about tenderness, the "most modest form of love." Her argument is that tenderness is a higher form of care than empathy. Tenderness is not about seeking to relate to another person's situation but rather respecting and listening to someone's feelings *despite* the fact that we may not relate. Tenderness, observes Tokarczuk, "is the kind of love that does not appear in the scriptures or the gospels, no one swears by it, no one cites it. It has no special emblems or symbols, nor does it lead to crime, or prompt envy. It appears wherever we take a close and

careful look at another being, at something that is not our 'self.'
Tenderness perceives the bonds that connect us, the similarities and
sameness between us." I think that is what I am trying to say. The
word we use these days is empathy. But empathy is seeking to understand someone vis-à-vis our own situation. Tenderness requires us
to just take someone for who they are. In that openness, we find
the fabric that weaves into our own lives. And that moment can be
sublime.

There is a line in bell hooks's *All About Love* that gives me a poignant ache anytime I recall it. She writes, "But it was love's absence
that let me know how much love mattered....At the moment of my
birth, I was looked upon with loving kindness, cherished and made
to feel wanted on this earth and in my home. To this day, I cannot
remember when that feeling of being loved left me. I just know that
one day I was no longer precious." There must be something in the
fact that I chose, quite accidentally, to write about two authors discussing the loss of love. For Olga Tokarczuk it is tenderness and the
deep understanding of connectivity all around us. For bell hooks it
is the loss of feeling truly precious. I think almost all of us can relate
to these sentiments in different ways. The United States, should
we personify it, must feel it too. This is a place full of real people,
humanity in all its forms, and yet we feel relegated to our cultural
and political silos. A country that has lost its sense of preciousness,
a place worthy of a deeper collective meaning that transcends the
culture wars, a place we hold dear because we share some sense of
decency, hope, and pride. I get lost thinking about America, but it's
very easy for me to think about my fellow Americans. Most of us
really do want to be loved and to love, to feel that our view, our
identity, matters. *That we matter.*

One of the last times I spoke to Shannon, she followed up with a
note to me that said, "What a blessing that God put us in touch with
each other. Truly I feel honored to share my story with you and to
have met you! You are so kind, and I find it so meaningful that you

would like my story so much." Just today, I received a note from her asking me if I would visit. "If it was a weekend, we could go to Catholic Church together. . . . I just wanted you to know I wanted to meet you in person." As always, Shannon signed with love and prayers.

Gosh, I thought, my heart so full. How much I wanted to drive to Kentucky in that very moment. I thought about Shannon's cozy sweater, her sparkling eyes, and her husband playing guitar. I thought about her warm voice and laughter and our authentic conversations. I thought about Clay's poetry and openness to all, even to those who looked down on him. I thought of Craig's passion for the natural world and willingness to speak to me anytime. I thought about Courtney's quiet resilience as a mother and unrelenting kindness in the face of profound adversity. I thought about how much time and care and openness all these Americans gave me with no preconceived notions of who I am and from where I hail. Shannon is well aware I am a liberal professor with a PhD living in Los Angeles. She doesn't care, and she doesn't judge. I am well aware that Shannon is an evangelical, a Trump supporter, partial to conspiracy theories, living in Kentucky. I don't care, and I don't judge. From the very first time I spoke with her, Shannon shared her tenderness with me, and I with her. Americans are not vacant of love. Look beneath the surface. Don't let culture obscure our basic humanity. From my experience, Americans are full of tenderness, of love, of an ability to understand and respect one another. We just have to listen.

Acknowledgments

MY GRATITUDE EXTENDS BEYOND WORDS FOR MY LITERARY agent David Halpern of the Robbins Office. The time between an email from me and his phone call in response regularly defied the laws of physics. Thank you to everyone at Basic Books, particularly Claire Potter, who acquired this book, and my dazzling editor, Michael Kaler. Michael's granular level of detail and engagement in my ideas and writing goes beyond the call of duty. Thank you to the entire production team for dotting the i's and crossing the t's, particularly Michelle Welsh-Horst, my production editor, and to Basic's publicity and marketing teams, particularly Liz Wetzel, Joanne Raymond, and Meghan Brophy, for working their hardest to make this book a success. Thank you to my publisher, Lara Heimert, for always being accessible and endlessly supportive.

Special thanks to the University of Southern California, where I work, and to my dean, Dana Goldman, and colleagues, who are steadfast champions of my research and ideas. Thank you to the Kluge Center at the Library of Congress, where I spent my final days writing and editing this book. Thank you to Susan Fainstein and Tim Sullivan for reading my book and providing careful notes that improved this manuscript greatly, and to my dear friend Cara Esposito for reading and reading...and reading many drafts of this manuscript and offering the most thoughtful comments and edits with patience and grace. I thank you all from the bottom of my heart.

To my brilliant and indispensable research assistants and doctoral students: Marley Randazzo, Andy Eisenlohr, Greg Randolph, and Kurt Wyatt. You will all do great things. I just know it.

To my glorious, bestest friends and family: there's a place in my heart bigger than the sky for each and every one of you. I can't name you all, but I'll try: Cara Esposito, Brooke Cutler, Laura Davidov, Marisa Christian, Eric Lovecchio, Lucy Halpern, Michael Storper, Jerold Kayden, Joe Bernath, Eyal Ben-Isaac, Tess Mordan, Susan Fainstein, Corinne Fowler, Sloane Crosley, Elizabeth Price, Quintin Price, Barbara Callas, Paul Gurian, Michelle Dean, the English Halketts (Charlotte, Angus, Georgina, Edward, Joan, and Bill), Gabriela Marquez, my brother Evan and sister Sarah, Mom and Dad. My beautiful boys, Oliver, Ezra, and Eliot, who teach me daily what really matters in life. Richard, always. And a very special thanks to Dr. Mendell, who gave me the immeasurable hope that allowed me to keep writing day after day.

My greatest thanks goes to the American people who gave me their time and opened their hearts and minds and shared them with me. You are the reason for this book, you are the hope for this country. You are a reminder that humanity, in all of its idiosyncrasies and differences, remains beautiful, wondrous, and kind.

Appendix

UNIVERSITY OF CHICAGO GENERAL SOCIAL SURVEY

Statistics on Americans' attitudes, opinions, stances, and behaviors come from the General Social Survey (GSS) published by NORC at the University of Chicago. The GSS is a nationally representative survey of American adults that touches on a wide range of social, political, and cultural topics relevant to American society. Since 1994, NORC has published the GSS on even-numbered years, apart from 2020 due to the Covid-19 pandemic. In this book, we rely on 2018, 2016, and 2014 GSS data (in that order of precedence) wherever possible to generate descriptive statistics. We also take advantage of the most recent 2021 GSS, although only when describing national-level issues, as respondents' geographic information is not provided in the most recent GSS.

The GSS employs a rotation design in which some questions are consistent across all questionnaires, while others are only shown to a portion of respondents. NORC uses three survey ballots in its rotation.* For each respondent, a response of ".i" for a question item denotes inapplicability, either for a structural reason (i.e., the question did not appear on the respondent's ballot) or a personal reason

---

* Please see the GSS's NORC.

(i.e., the respondent's demographic or life experience background rendered an item irrelevant). Inapplicable responses were removed from all descriptive statistical analyses.

GSS respondents also have the option to decline to answer a question item or say that they do not know how to answer. GSS reports these responses as ".n" (No Response) and ".d" (Don't Know), respectively. Where present for a question item, these responses were included in descriptive statistical analyses.

For all GSS items discussed in this book, descriptive statistics were generated for "urban" and "rural" groups. The geographic delineation strategy is outlined in the following section. Where necessary, we also parsed responses by educational attainment, race, and self-identified social class using the variables EDUC, RACE, and CLASS, respectively. The three delineation strategies are presented in Table 1.

TABLE 1

Parsing Category	Criteria	Classification
Educational Attainment	EDUC < 12 years	Less than High School
	EDUC == 12 years	High School Graduate
	ECUC > 15 years	Bachelor's Degree and Higher
Race	RACE == 'White'	White
	RACE == 'Black,' 'Other'	Non-white
Self-Identified Social Class	CLASS == 'Lower Class'	Lower Class
	CLASS == 'Working Class'	Working Class
	CLASS == 'Middle Class'	Middle Class
	CLASS == 'Upper Class'	Upper Class

URBAN VERSUS RURAL

In developing urban and rural categories, we use the size of interview place variable, XNORCSIZ. For each respondent, NORC determines the smallest civil division for the interview site and categorizes its size using 1970 Census population figures and its metropolitan classification based on the pre-1983 Standard Metropolitan Statistical Area (SMSA) system.* NORC, for consistency's sake, has not updated this question item to reflect population changes or the US Office of Management and Budget's updates to the metropolitan statistical area (MSA) system. This categorization is slightly undesirable in that it fails to capture the effects of recent US population dynamics.

MSAs and now-outdated SMSAs are both county-level metropolitan classifications that draw upon population statistics and connectedness to a "central" or "principal" city. Each SMSA classification is based on the presence of a central city with a minimum population of fifty thousand. Generally, the largest city in an SMSA is categorized as central, although some SMSAs have more than one central node where population size and commuting pattern criteria are met (e.g., Minneapolis-Saint Paul).† Unlike the current MSA system— which parses between metropolitan and micropolitan statistical areas formed around large- and medium-size principal cities—SMSAs can have either large- or medium-size cities at their core. SMSA counties designated around a larger city may also contain medium and small cities, but only the larger city will qualify as central.

The XNORCSIZ variable parses interview place size into ten categories described in Table 2.‡ For the urban classification, we

---

* Tom W. Smith, Michael Davern, Jeremy Freese, and Stephen L. Morgan, *General Social Surveys 1972–2018: Cumulative Codebook* (Chicago: NORC, 2019).

† US Census Bureau, "Chapter 13: Metropolitan Areas," in *Geographical Areas Reference Manual*, 1994.

‡ Tom W. Smith, *Size of Place Codes in the 1972–1977 General Social Surveys*, GSS Technical Report no. 4 (Chicago: NORC, 1978).

restricted our analyses to large central cities and their surrounding suburbs within the boundaries of SMSAs. Suburbs of large cities were included in our urban category, despite NORC's broad inclusion criteria (civil division with population greater than one thousand), because many suburban areas in SMSAs with large central cities closely resemble their central city both culturally and socioeconomically (e.g., the City of Santa Monica qualifies as a suburb of Los Angeles, a large central city, in NORC's categorization). Medium central cities and their suburbs, as well as small unincorporated areas within SMSAs were excluded from our urban classification to distinguish the category. They are designated as N/A in the following table.

Our rural classification is restricted to areas outside of SMSAs, excluding areas defined by NORC as "small cities" with populations between 2,500 and 9,999. The purpose of excluding small cities is similarly to distinguish rural places from urban places and places of cultural and socioeconomic transition. Likewise, many small cities in 1970 have grown to medium-city status over the past several decades, insinuating material and ideological shifts that render the NORC category too conceptually slippery for our purposes.

BUREAU OF LABOR STATISTICS

County-level employment statistics used in this book are sourced from the Bureau of Labor Statistics (BLS) Quarterly Census of Employment and Wages NAICS-Based Data Files from 1990, 2000, 2010, and 2020 annual averages.[*] The NAICS-based coding system classifies jobs in the United States using a hierarchical structure to denote nested relationships between items. The organization of

---

[*] "QCEW Field Layouts for NAICS-Based, Annual CSV Files," Quarterly Census of Employment and Wages, US Bureau of Labor Statistics, last modified September 24, 2020, www.bls.gov/cew/about-data/downloadable-file-layouts/annual/naics-based-annual-layout.htm.

TABLE 2

XNORCSIZ Categories	Urban/Rural Classification*
Large central city (population greater than 250,000), within an SMSA	Urban
Medium central city (population between 50,000 and 250,000), within an SMSA	N/A
Incorporated or unincorporated suburb (population greater than 1,000) of a large central city, within an SMSA	Urban
Incorporated or unincorporated suburb (population greater than 1,000) of a medium central city, within an SMSA	N/A
Unincorporated area (no recorded population parameter) of a large central city, within an SMSA	N/A
Unincorporated area (no recorded population parameter) of a medium central city, within an SMSA	N/A
Small city (population between 10,000 and 49,999), outside of an SMSA	N/A
Town (population between 2,500 and 9,999), outside of an SMSA	Rural
Small incorporated (population less than 2,500) and unincorporated (population between 1,000 and 2,499) areas, outside of an SMSA	Rural
Open country (no recorded population parameter), outside of an SMSA	Rural

* N/A categories are not included in the analysis presented in this book.

sector (two-digit codes), for example, can be parsed by subsectors (nested three-digit codes), industry groups (nested four-digit codes), NAICS industries (nested five-digit codes), and national industries (nested six-digit codes).* All analyses presented herein use two-digit sector data and five-digit industry data where deeper specificity is required. Analyses and visualizations were generated using the NumPy, Pandas, GeoPandas, and Matplotlib packages for Python.

Urban and rural classifications applied to county-level BLS data are derived from the US Office of Management and Budget's 2020 metropolitan statistical area system. Delineation files were obtained from the Bureau of Economic Analysis (BEA) statistical areas page.† BEA geographic delineation files feature combination areas (e.g., Maui and Kalawao, Hawaii), whereas Census Bureau delineation files will represent these counties as unique. For the purposes of this book, counties within metropolitan statistical areas are classified as urban, and counties that fall outside of metropolitan and micropolitan counties are classified as rural. Micropolitan counties are removed from both classifications as they are based around urban clusters with small-to-medium-size cities at their core. These counties differ conceptually from the notions of urban and rural discussed in this book. Puerto Rican counties are removed from BLS analyses regardless of MSA class.

To analyze fine-detail five-digit NAICS industry data, statistics from all NAICS industries within each two-digit sector are summed and aggregated into a common file. Doing so allowed for quick comparisons between related NAICS industries across

---

* "Economic Census: NAICS Codes & Understanding Industry Classification Systems," US Census Bureau, last modified August 19, 2022, www.census.gov /programs-surveys/economic-census/guidance/understanding-naics.html.

† "Metropolitan Statistical Areas (MSAs), Micropolitan Statistical Areas, Metropolitan Divisions, Combined Statistical Areas (CSAs), and BEA Regions," Statistical Areas, US Bureau of Economic Analysis, last modified March 6, 2020, https:// apps.bea.gov/regional/docs/msalist.cfm.

decades and helped to calculate the relative importance of each NAICS industry to the broader sector over time. The annual average of monthly employment levels are used as a proxy for employment for each year.

Two-digit sector annual average of monthly employment figures are used as the basis for all geospatial analyses in this book. Only states within the contiguous United States (including the District of Columbia) are considered when mapping and analyzing sector employment across regions. All counties were also assigned a region as shown in Table 3.

AMERICAN COMMUNITY SURVEY

All US Census county-level data was downloaded via Brown University's Longitudinal Tract Data Base.[*] Tables NH3, NH23B, NP10, NP57, NP80, and NP80A were used from the 1990 decennial Census. Tables NH004B, NP008A, NH076A, NP037C, NP052A, and NP053A were used from the 2000 decennial Census. Tables B03002, B15002, B19001, B19013, B25003, and B25077 were used from the 2010 five-year American Community Survey (ACS). Tables B19001, B25008, DP04, S1501, and S2301 were used from the 2019 five-year ACS. Table P2 was used from the 2020 decennial Census. US presidential candidate votes by county were downloaded via the Massachusetts Institute of Technology's Election Data and Science Lab.[†]

---

[*] John Logan, Zengwang Xu, Brian Stults, and Charles Zhang, "Census Geography: Bridging Data for Census Tracts Across Time," Diversity and Disparities Project, Brown University, https://s4.ad.brown.edu/Projects/Diversity/Researcher/Bridging .htm.

[†] MIT Election Data and Science Lab, "County Presidential Election Returns 2000–2020" (Harvard Dataverse, V10, UNF:6:pVAMya52q7VM1Pl7EZMW0Q== [fileUNF]; 2018), https://doi.org/10.7910/DVN/VOQCHQ.

TABLE 3

Region	State
Coastal West	California
	Oregon
	Washington
Interior Northwest	Idaho
	Montana
	Wyoming
Mid-Atlantic	Delaware
	District of Columbia
	Maryland
	New Jersey
	New York
	Pennsylvania
	Virginia
	West Virginia
Midwest	Illinois
	Indiana
	Iowa
	Kansas
	Michigan
	Minnesota
	Missouri
	Nebraska
	North Dakota
	Ohio
	South Dakota
	Wisconsin

New England	Connecticut
	Maine
	Massachusetts
	New Hampshire
	Rhode Island
	Vermont
Other	Alaska
	Hawaii
South	Alabama
	Arkansas
	Florida
	Georgia
	Kentucky
	Louisiana
	Mississippi
	North Carolina
	Oklahoma
	South Carolina
	Tennessee
	Texas
Southwest	Arizona
	Colorado
	Nevada
	New Mexico
	Utah

All counties were classified according to the same typology of urbanity—metropolitan, micropolitan, or rural—that was employed for analysis of BLS data.

Analysis of the above data focused on identifying differences or changes in populations' sociodemographic, housing, and political characteristics over the urban-rural continuum (i.e., metropolitan versus rural counties), region, and time. Not all characteristics could be easily pooled across multiple counties, such as median home value or median household income. To facilitate use of a consistent methodology across all statistics, comparisons were initially drawn by cross-referencing median counties' values for similar intersections of space, region, and time. For example, the median rural county's share of the population identifying as Latinx in the South in 2010 could be compared to the median metropolitan county's share in the same region and time. Counties were assigned to regions using the classification scheme in Table 3 to remain consistent with ACS analysis.

To provide more summative comparisons over space—e.g., all metropolitan counties versus all micropolitan counties versus all rural counties at a point in time—count-based statistics were also pooled across counties by level of urbanicity and then translated to shares. Comparing these pooled shares with the more spatially granular median values helped illuminate the extent to which particular sociodemographic, housing, or political characteristics were concentrated in particular locales of the United States.

NIELSEN DATA AND METHODOLOGY

Data To examine cultural consumption at the individual household level, we leveraged Nielsen's proprietary consumer panel data set for the years 2004 through 2018.* In each year, the data set contains

* Additional information on the Nielsen consumer panel data set is available at "Nielsen and NielsenIQ Marketing Data," Kilts Center for Marketing, University

information on purchases made by a panel of forty thousand to sixty thousand US households located throughout the contiguous United States. Household characteristics on file include sociodemographic traits (e.g., household income range, number of household members, age of household head(s), educational attainment, race, and ethnicity) as well as geographic location, the latter of which is specified down to the five-digit zip code level.

Detailed transaction data is available for the purchases these households make across all of Nielsen's retail channels: grocery stores, drugstores, superstores, club stores, convenience stores, etc. In other words, robust data is available on households' "daily essentials" shopping. Each recorded transaction includes the universal product code (UPC) for goods purchased, the number of units purchased under each UPC, and the price paid per unit. Having UPC data allows us to identify purchase characteristics at a granular level, including whether a given food item is organic. That said, the panel data does not identify where a transaction occurred, in terms of both a store's physical location and the company that owns the store.

We seek to understand the household characteristics that predict consumption of cultural capital. Therefore, we use the UPCs in the Nielsen data set to identify an array of products that either strongly align with or contrast with the notion of cultural capital. Those that strongly align are (1) organic milk, (2) plant milk, (3) craft/foreign beer, (4) organic eggs, (5) specialty/imported cheeses, (6) fresh fruits, (7) fresh vegetables, (8) domestic wine, and (9) imported wine. Those that strongly contrast are (1) frozen meals, (2) tobacco products (chewed and smoked), and (3) soft drinks.

Defining "Urban" Versus "Rural" Given the ambiguity in the extant research, as well as clear disparities in the structures of US

---

of Chicago Booth School of Business, www.chicagobooth.edu/research/kilts /datasets/nielsenIQ-nielsen.

metropolitan areas (e.g., polycentric versus monocentric), we employed a relatively simple definition to distinguish between "urban" and "rural" areas. Any five-digit zip code area whose centroid lay within twenty-five miles of the centroid of a Census-designated place (CDP) with a population of at least three hundred thousand was designated as urban.[*] Any five-digit zip code area that failed to meet that criterion was designated as rural.

The twenty-five-mile dividing line in terms of distance is quite conservative for identifying a zip code area as rural. It is twice the typical commute distance for residents of the Atlanta-Sandy Springs-Roswell metropolitan area in Georgia (12.8 miles on average), the longest typical commute reported for a US metropolitan area.[†] The determination of urban versus rural five-digit zip code areas was made using the "Near" function of ArcGIS. Shapefiles of zip codes and Census-designated place boundaries, generated as of 2019, were downloaded from the US Census Bureau's TIGER/Line Shapefile online repository.[‡] We note that the population of US CDPs with at least three hundred thousand residents has been largely consistent over the past twenty years—that is, the period for which Nielsen consumer panel data is available.

Disclaimer Researchers' own analyses calculated (or derived) based in part on data from Nielsen Consumer LLC and marketing databases provided through the NielsenIQ data sets at the Kilts Center

---

for Marketing Data Center at the University of Chicago Booth School of Business.

The conclusions drawn from the NielsenIQ data are those of the researcher(s) and do not reflect the views of NielsenIQ. NielsenIQ is not responsible for, had no role in, and was not involved in analyzing and preparing the results reported herein.

Bibliography

Agiesta, Jennifer, and Ariel Edwards-Levy. "Most Americans Feel Democracy Is Under Attack in the US." *CNN*, September 15, 2021. www.cnn.com/2021/09/15/politics/cnn-poll-most-americans-democracy-under-attack/index.html.

Ahler, Douglas, and Gaurav Sood. "The Parties in Our Heads: Misperceptions About Party Composition and Their Consequences." *Journal of Politics* 80, no. 3 (2018): 964–981.

Ahmed, Sara. "The Nonperformativity of Antiracism." *Meridians* 7, no. 1 (2006): 104–126.

Alger, Horatio. *Ragged Dick*. Boston: A.K. Loring, 1868.

Al-Gharbi, Musa. *We Have Never Been Woke: Social Justice Discourse, Inequality and the Rise of a New Elite*. Princeton, NJ: Princeton University Press, forthcoming.

Allport, Gordon, and Bernard Kramer. "Some Roots of Prejudice." *Journal of Psychology* 22 (1946): 9–39.

America Counts. "One in Five Americans Live in Rural Areas." US Census Bureau, August 9, 2017. www.census.gov/library/stories/2017/08/rural-america.html.

Anderson, Benedict. *Imagined Communities: Reflections on the Origins and Spread of Nationalism*. New York: Verso, 1991.

Anderson, Michele. "Go Home to Your 'Dying' Hometown." *New York Times*, March 8, 2019. www.nytimes.com/2019/03/08/opinion/sunday/urban-rural-america.html.

Ardoin, Sonja. *College Aspirations and Access in Working-Class Rural Communities: The Mixed Signals, Challenges, and New Language First-Generation Students Encounter*. London: Lexington Books, 2017.

Armstrong, Karen. *The Case for God*. New York: Knopf, 2009.

Associated Press. "On COVID Vaccinations, Pope Says Health Care Is a 'Moral Obligation.'" NPR, January 10, 2022. www.npr.org/2022/01/10/1071785531/on-covid-vaccinations-pope-says-health-care-is-a-moral-obligation.

———. "Wisconsin Priest Flouts 'Godless' COVID Protocols." *Catholic Reporter*, April 26, 2021. www.ncronline.org/news/coronavirus/wisconsin-priest-flouts-godless-covid-protocols.

Austin, Benjamin, Edward Glaeser, and Lawrence H. Summers. *Saving the Heartland: Place-Based Policies in 21st Century America*. Washington, DC: Brookings, 2018.

Axelrod, Jim, and Ashley Velie. "West Virginia AG's Past Work with Drug Companies Questioned." *CBS Evening News*, June 2, 2016. www.cbsnews.com/news/questions-raised-about-west-virginia-attorney-generals-past-with-drug-companies/.

Bean, Lydia. *The Politics of Evangelical Identity: Local Churches and Partisan Divides in the United States and Canada*. Princeton, NJ: Princeton University Press, 2014.

Becker, Howard S. *Art Worlds*. Berkeley: University of California Press, 1982.

Belkin, Douglas. "For Colleges, a Rural Reckoning." *Wall Street Journal*, December 1, 2017. www.wsj.com/articles/for-colleges-a-rural-reckoning-1512159888.

Bell, Alex, Raj Chetty, Xavier Jaravel, Neviana Petkova, and John Van Reenen. "Lost Einsteins: How Exposure to Innovation Influences Who Becomes an Inventor." *Vox EU*, December 24, 2017. https://voxeu.org/article/how-exposure-innovation-influences-who-becomes-inventor.

———. "Who Becomes an Inventor in America? The Importance of Exposure to Innovation." *Quarterly Journal of Economics* 134, no. 2 (2018).

Bell, Phil. "Book Review: The Meritocracy Trap by Daniel Markovits." *LSE Review of Books*, March 30, 2020. https://blogs.lse.ac.uk/lsereviewofbooks/2020/03/30/book-review-the-meritocracy-trap-by-daniel-markovits/.

Bella, Timothy. "Tucker Carlson Falsely Claims Anthony S. Fauci 'Created' Covid." *Washington Post*, July 29, 2021. www.washingtonpost.com/health/2021/07/29/tucker-carlson-fauci-created-covid/.

Bender, Courtney. *The New Metaphysicals: Spirituality and the American Religious Imagination*. Chicago: University of Chicago Press, 2010.

Bercovitz, Janet, and Maryann Feldman. "The Mechanisms of Collaboration in Inventive Teams: Composition, Social Networks, and Geography." *Research Policy* 40, no. 1 (2011): 81–93.

Bergengruen, Vera. "How 'America's Frontline Doctors' Sold Access to Bogus COVID-19 Treatments—and Left Patients in the Lurch." *Time*, August 26, 2021. https://time.com/6092368/americas-frontline-doctors-covid-19-misinformation/.

Bertrand, Marianne, and Esther Duflo. "Field Experiments on Discrimination." In *Handbook of Economic Field Experiments*, edited by Esther Duflo and Abhijit Banerjee, 309–393. Amsterdam: North Holland, 2017.

Best Places. "Economy in Danville, Pennsylvania." Accessed March 23, 2022. www.bestplaces.net/economy/city/pennsylvania/danville.

Big Think. "What Is Scientism, and Why Is It a Mistake?" December 9, 2021. https://bigthink.com/13-8/science-vs-scientism/.

Blakely, Jason. "Scientific Authority and the Democratic Narrative: How Did We Arrive at This Crisis of Scientific Authority?" *Hedgehog Review* 22, no. 3 (2020).

Blanchflower, David G., and Andrew J. Oswald. "Trends in Extreme Distress in the United States, 1993–2019." *American Journal of Public Health* 110, no. 10 (October 1, 2020): 1538–1544.

Bloom, Alexander. *Prodigal Sons: The New York Intellectuals and Their World*. Oxford: Oxford University Press, 1986.

Bobo, Lawrence, and Frederick Licari. "Education and Political Tolerance: Testing the Effects of Cognitive Sophistication and Target Group Affect." *Public Opinion Quarterly* 53, no. 3 (1998): 285–308.

Bolsen, Toby, and Matthew A. Shapiro. "The US News Media, Polarization on Climate Change, and Pathways to Effective Communication." *Environmental Communication* 12, no. 2 (2018): 149–163.

Boorstein, Michelle. "A Horn-Wearing 'Shaman.' A Cowboy Evangelist. For Some, the Capitol Attack Was a Kind of Christian Revolt." *Washington Post*, July 6, 2021. www.washingtonpost.com/religion/2021/07/06/capitol-insurrection-trump-christian-nationalism-shaman/.

Bourdieu, Pierre. "The Forms of Capital." In *Handbook of Theory and Research for the Sociology of Education*, edited by J. Richardson, 241–258. Westport, CT: Greenwood, 1986.

Bowes, Lizzie. "Performative Wokeness Needs to Stop." *Varsity*, December 21, 2017. www.varsity.co.uk/violet/14313.

Bowlin, Nick. "Joke's on Them: How Democrats Gave Up on Rural America." *Guardian*, February 22, 2022. www.theguardian.com/us-news/2022/feb/22/us-politics-rural-america.

Boxer, Sarah. "Truth Or Lies? In Sex Surveys, You Never Know." *New York Times*, July 22, 2000. https://archive.nytimes.com/www.nytimes .com/library/arts/072200sex-surveys.html.

Braunstein, Ruth. "A Theory of Political Backlash: Assessing the Religious Right's Effects on the Religious Field." *Sociology of Religion* (2021).

Brehe-Gunter, Emily. "1995 vs. 2020: How College Admissions Has Changed over the Past 25 Years." KD College Prep, June 26, 2020. https:// kdcollegeprep.com/how-college-admissions-changed-last-25-years/.

Bristow, William. "Enlightenment." In *Stanford Encyclopedia of Philosophy*. 2017. https://plato.stanford.edu/entries/enlightenment/.

Brody, Jane E. "Farewell, Readers, It's Been a Remarkable Ride." *New York Times*, February 21, 2022. www.nytimes.com/2022/02/21/well/health -advice-diet-smoking.html.

Brooks, David. "The Dissenters Trying to Save Evangelicalism from Itself." *New York Times*, February 4, 2022. www.nytimes.com/2022/02/04 /opinion/evangelicalism-division-renewal.html.

———. "How the Bobos Broke America." *Atlantic*, August 2, 2021. www .theatlantic.com/magazine/archive/2021/09/blame-the-bobos-creative -class/619492/.

Bump, Philip. "The Americans Who See Democracy Most at Risk? Republicans." *Washington Post*, October 20, 2021. www.washingtonpost.com /politics/2021/10/20/americans-who-see-democracy-most-risk -republicans/.

Butler, Jon. "Religion and Eighteenth-Century Revivalism." In *AP US History Study Guide*. New York: Gilder Lehrman Institute of American History, 2009. http://ap.gilderlehrman.org/history-by-era/religion -and-eighteenth-century-revivalism/essays/religion-and-eighteenth -century-rev.

Cambon, Sarah Chaney, and Andrew Mollica. "Rural Counties Are Booming, but Can It Last?" *Wall Street Journal*, June 28, 2022. www.wsj .com/articles/rural-counties-are-booming-pandemic-back-to-office -work-from-home-11656423785.

Carnes, Nicholas, and Noam Lupu. "The White Working Class and the 2016 Election." *Perspectives on Politics* 19, no. 1 (2021): 55–72. https:// doi.org/10.1017/s1537592720001267.

Case, Anne, and Angus Deaton. *Deaths of Despair and the Future of Capitalism*. Princeton, NJ: Princeton University Press, 2020.

———. "The Great Divide: Education, Despair and Death." NBER working paper no. 29241, National Bureau of Economic Research, Cambridge, MA, September 2021. www.nber.org/papers/w29241.

———. "Life Expectancy in Adulthood Is Falling for Those Without a BA Degree, but as Educational Gaps Have Widened, Racial Gaps Have Narrowed." *PNAS* 118, no. 11 (2021). www.pnas.org/doi/10.1073/pnas .2024777118.

Castells, Manuel. "The Impact of the Internet on Society: A Global Perspective." In *Change: 19 Key Essays on How the Internet Is Changing Our Lives*. Bilbao, Spain: BBVA, 2014.

———. *The Information Age: Economy, Society and Culture*. 3 vols. Cambridge, MA, and Oxford: Blackwell, 1996–1998.

———. *The Rise of the Network Society*. Hoboken, NJ: John Wiley & Sons, 1996.

CBHA. "Small Towns and Rural Areas Hit Hard by Opioid Crisis." August 2020. www.cbha.org/about-us/cbha-blog/2020/august/small-towns-and -rural-areas-hit-hard-by-opioid-c/.

CDC. "Breastfeeding Report Card: United States, 2022." Last modified August 31, 2022, www.cdc.gov/breastfeeding/data/reportcard.htm.

Chang, Ailsa, Noah Caldwell, and Christopher Intagliata. "'Empire of Pain: The Secret History of the Sackler Dynasty' Profiles Pharma Family." NPR, April 13, 2021. www.npr.org/2021/04/13/986929541/empire-of -pain-the-secret-history-of-the-sackler-dynasty-profiles-pharma-family.

Chaya, Doug. "The Threat from the Illiberal Left." *Economist*, September 4, 2021. www.economist.com/leaders/2021/09/04/the-threat-from-the -illiberal-left.

Chetty, Raj, John Friedman, Nathaniel Hilger, Emmanuel Saez, Diane Whitmore Schanzenbach, and Danny Yagan. "How Does Your Kindergarten Classroom Affect Your Earnings? Evidence from Project Star." *Quarterly Journal of Economics* 126, no. 4 (2011): 1593–1660.

Chetty, Raj, John Friedman, Emmanuel Saez, Nicholas Turner, and Danny Yagan. "Mobility Report Cards: The Role of Colleges in Intergenerational Mobility." Equal Opportunity Project, 2018. https://opportunity insights.org/wp-content/uploads/2018/03/coll_mrc_summary.pdf.

———. "Mobility Report Cards: The Role of Colleges in Intergenerational Mobility." NBER working paper no. 23618, National Bureau of Economic Research, Cambridge, MA, July 2017. www.nber.org /papers/w23618.

Chetty, Raj, Matthew O. Jackson, Theresa Kuchler, Johannes Stroebel, Nathaniel Hendren, Robert B. Fluegge, Sara Gong, et al. "Social Capital I: Measurement and Associations with Economic Mobility." *Nature* 608 (2022): 108–121. https://doi.org/10.1038/s41586-022 -04996-4.

———. "Social Capital II: Determinants of Economic Connectedness."
   Nature 608 (2022): 122–134. https://doi.org/10.1038/s41586-022-04997-3.

Chidi, Erica, and Gabby Bernstein. "The Power of Surrendering." In
   The Goop Podcast, February 15, 2022. Podcast. https://goop.com/the
   -goop-podcast/the-power-of-surrendering/.

Chotiner, Isaac. "A Political Scientist Defends White Identity Politics." *New
   Yorker*, April 30, 2019. www.newyorker.com/news/q-and-a/a-political
   -scientist-defends-white-identity-politics-eric-kaufmann-whiteshift
   -book.

City-Data. "Manchester, Kentucky." www.city-data.com/city/Manchester
   -Kentucky.html.

CNA Staff. "La Crosse Bishop Removes Father Altman from Ministry."
   Catholic News Agency, July 9, 2021. www.catholicnewsagency.com
   /news/248326/la-crosse-bishop-removes-father-altman-from-ministry.

Cohen, Patricia. "Even in Better Times, Some Americans Seem Farther
   Behind. Here's Why." *New York Times*, September 14, 2018. www
   .nytimes.com/2018/09/14/business/economy/income-inequality.html.

Colton, Emma. "Arrests in Chicago Plummet to Historic Lows as Crime
   Rises and Police Admittedly Pull Back: 'No Way.'" Fox News, July 19,
   2022. www.foxnews.com/us/arrests-chicago-plummet-historic-lows
   -crime-rises-police-admittedly-pull-back-no-way.

Coman, Julian, and Michael Sandel. "Michael Sandel: 'The Populist
   Backlash Has Been a Revolt Against the Tyranny of Merit.'" *Guardian*, September 6, 2020. www.theguardian.com/books/2020/sep/06
   /michael-sandel-the-populist-backlash-has-been-a-revolt-against
   -the-tyranny-of-merit.

Connor, Dylan Shane, and Michael Storper. "The Changing Geography
   of Social Mobility in the United States." *PNAS* 117, no. 48 (November 16, 2020). https://doi.org/10.1073/pnas.2010222117.

Conway, Richard S., Jr. "Economic Base Theory of Regional Growth." In
   Empirical Regional Economics, 3–21. Cham, Switzerland: Springer, 2022.

Cook, Gareth. "The Economist Who Would Fix the American Dream."
   Atlantic, July 17, 2019. www.theatlantic.com/magazine/archive/2019
   /08/raj-chettys-american-dream/592804/.

Corbett, Michael. *Learning to Leave: The Irony of Schooling in a Coastal
   Community*. Nova Scotia, Canada: Fernwood Publishing, 2007.

Coren, Michael. "When True Believers Become a Danger to Themselves and
   Others," *Globe and Mail*, August 13, 2021. www.theglobeandmail.com
   /opinion/article-when-true-believers-become-a-danger-to-themselves
   -and-others/.

Crabtree, J. "A Different Path for Rural America." *American Journal of Economics and Sociology* 75, no. 3 (2016): 605–622.

Cronk, N. E. "About Voltaire." Voltaire Foundation for Enlightenment Studies. University of Oxford. www.voltaire.ox.ac.uk/about-voltaire/.

Cronon, William. *Nature's Metropolis.* New York: Norton, 1991.

Currid, Elizabeth. "The Economics of a Good Party: Social Mechanics and the Legitimization of Art/Culture." *Journal of Economics and Finance* 31 (2007): 386–394.

———. *The Warhol Economy: How Fashion, Art, and Music Drive New York City.* Princeton, NJ: Princeton University Press, 2007.

Currid-Halkett, Elizabeth. *The Sum of Small Things: A Theory of the Aspirational Class.* Princeton, NJ: Princeton University Press, 2017.

Curtis, Justin. "The Effect of the 2020 Racial Justice Protests on Attitudes and Preferences in Rural and Urban America." *Social Science Quarterly* 103, no. 1 (January 2022): 90–107. https://doi.org/10.1111/ssqu.13105.

Damrosch, Leo. *Jean-Jacques Rousseau: Restless Genius.* Boston: Houghton Mifflin Harcourt, 2007.

Darrisaw, Michelle. "On SuperSoul Sunday, *Educated* Author Tara Westover Talks to Oprah Defining Love." *Oprah Daily*, May 4, 2019. www.oprahdaily.com/life/relationships-love/a27359653/tara-westover-oprah-super-soul-sunday-interview/.

Davern, Michael, Rene Bautista, Jeremy Freese, Stephen L. Morgan, and Tom W. Smith. General Social Survey 2021 Cross-section (machine-readable data file). NORC, Chicago, 2021. https://gss.norc.org/Documents/codebook/GSS%202021%20Codebook.pdf.

Dawidoff, Nicholas. "The Man Who Saw America." *New York Times*, July 2, 2015. www.nytimes.com/2015/07/05/magazine/robert-franks-america.html.

Dawkins, Richard. *The Selfish Gene.* Oxford: Oxford University Press, 1976.

Deaton, Angus. *The Great Escape: Health, Wealth, and the Origins of Inequality.* Princeton, NJ: Princeton University Press, 2013.

Deloitte and Datawheel. "Danville, PA: Census Place." Data USA. https://datausa.io/profile/geo/danville-pa.

De Rosée, Sophie. "The Case for Manifesting." *Financial Times*, January 3, 2022. www.ft.com/content/6fed8d95-1917-4e78-91c6-b0bacf04f03c.

Dickerson, Chris. "Jenkins Says Morrisey Has Conflict of Interest About Opioids." *West Virginia Record*, February 6, 2018, https://wvrecord.com/stories/511331505-jenkins-says-morrisey-has-conflict-of-interest-about-opioids.

Douthat, Ross. "Can the Meritocracy Find God?" *New York Times*, April 10, 2021. www.nytimes.com/2021/04/10/opinion/sunday/religion-merito cracy-god.html.

———. "Let's Not Invent a Civil War." *New York Times*, January 12, 2022. www.nytimes.com/2022/01/12/opinion/civil-war-america.html.

Dovere, Edward-Isaac. "Democratic Governors Worry About Threat to Democracy but Don't See It as a Winning Message for 2022." CNN, December 13, 2021. www.cnn.com/2021/12/12/politics/democratic -governors-2022-messaging/index.html.

Doyle, Céilí, and Sheridan Hendrix. "Trump Promised to Bring Back Coal in Appalachia. Here's Why That Didn't Happen." *Columbus Dispatch*, October 20, 2020. www.dispatch.com/story/news/environment/2020 /10/20/trump-promised-bring-back-coal-appalachia-has-he/586642 0002/.

Druckerman, Pamela. *Bringing Up Bébé: One American Mother Discovers the Wisdom of French Parenting*. New York: Penguin, 2012.

Druckman, James, Samara Klar, Yanna Krupnikov, Matthew Levendusky, and John Barry Ryan. "Affective Polarization, Local Contexts and Public Opinion in America." *Nature Human Behaviour* 5, no. 1 (2021): 28–38.

———. "(Mis-)Estimating Affective Polarization." *Journal of Politics* 84, no. 2 (April 2022).

Druke, Galen. "Americans Aren't as Polarized as the News Makes It Seem." In *FiveThirtyEight Politics*, February 10, 2022. Podcast. https://fivethirty eight.com/features/politics-podcast-americans-might-be-less-divided -than-you-think/.

Dyer, Owen. "Founder of America's Frontline Doctors Is Sentenced to Prison for Role in Capitol Riot." *BMJ*, June 22, 2022. www.bmj.com /content/377/bmj.o1533.

Dynes, Russell R. *The Dialogue Between Voltaire and Rousseau on the Lisbon Earthquake: The Emergence of a Social Science View*. Newark, DE: Disaster Research Center, 1999.

Encyclopedia Britannica Online, s.v. "Lisbon Earthquake of 1755." Accessed February 23, 2022. www.britannica.com/event/Lisbon-earthquake-of-1755.

Espenshade, Thomas J., and Alexandria Walton Radford. *No Longer Separate, Not Yet Equal: Race and Class in Elite College Admission and Campus Life*. Princeton, NJ: Princeton University Press, 2009.

Eyre, Eric. *Death in Mudlick: A Coal Country Fight Against the Drug Companies That Delivered the Opioid Epidemic*. New York: Scribner, 2020.

———. "Morrisey's Wife Lobbied on Opioids for Drug Firm, Disclosures Say." *Charleston Gazette-Mail*, April 28, 2018. www.wvgazettemail.com

/news/politics/morriseys-wife-lobbied-on-opioids-for-drug-firm
-disclosures-say/article_be3d9ee8-00e1-570c-b161-c7b59c7c31d0.html.

Fabian, Johannes. *Time and the Other: How Anthropology Makes Its Object*.
New York: Columbia University Press, 1983.

Feldman, Maryann P. "The New Economics of Innovation, Spillovers
and Agglomeration: A Review of Empirical Studies." *Economics of
Innovation and New Technology* 8, no. 1–2 (1999): 5–25.

Fiske, John. *Media Matters: Race and Gender in U.S. Politics*. London: Routledge, 2016.

Fitzgerald, F. Scott. *The Crack-Up*. New York: New Directions, 1945.

Fletcher, Jason, and Hamid Noghanibehambari. "The Effects of Education on Mortality: Evidence Using College Expansions." NBER
working paper no. 29423, National Bureau of Economic Research,
Cambridge, MA, October 2021. www.nber.org/papers/w29423.

Florida, Richard. *The Rise of the Creative Class*. New York: Basic Books, 2002.

Fox, Maggie. "Anti-vaccine Hot Spots on Rise Across U.S., Study Finds."
NBC News, June 12, 2018. www.nbcnews.com/health/health-news
/anti-vaccine-hotspots-rise-across-u-s-study-finds-n882461.

Frenkel, Sheera. "The Most Influential Spreader of Coronavirus Misinformation Online." *New York Times*, July 24, 2021. www.nytimes.com
/2021/07/24/technology/joseph-mercola-coronavirus-misinformation
-online.html.

Freud, Sigmund. *Civilization and Its Discontents*. 1930.

Fukuyama, Francis. "One Single Day. That's All It Took for the World to
Look Away from Us." *New York Times*, January 5, 2022. www.nytimes
.com/2022/01/05/opinion/jan-6-global-democracy.html.

Gallo, Carmine. "Brené Brown's Presentation Caught Oprah's Attention. The
Same Skills Can Work For You." *Forbes*, October 11, 2013. www.forbes
.com/sites/carminegallo/2013/10/11/brene-browns-presentation-caught
-oprahs-attention-the-same-skills-can-work-for-you/?sh=57a3f10653c1.

Gallup. "Islamophobia: Understanding Anti-Muslim Sentiment in the West."
N.d. https://news.gallup.com/poll/157082/islamophobia-understanding
-anti-muslim-sentiment-west.aspx.

Gallup and Knight Foundation. *American Views: Trust, Media and Democracy*. Washington, DC: Gallup, 2018.

Gates, Henry Louis, Jr. *The Black Church: This Is Our Story, This Is Our Song*.
New York: Penguin Press, 2021.

Gawande, Atul. "Why Americans Are Dying from Despair." *New Yorker*,
March 23, 2020. www.newyorker.com/magazine/2020/03/23/why
-americans-are-dying-from-despair.

Ge, Suqin, Elliott Isaac, and Amalia Miller. "Elite Schools and Opting In: Effects of College Selectivity on Career and Family Outcomes." *Journal of Labor Economics* 40, no. S1 (April 2022).

Gellner, Ernest. "The Mightier Pen? Edward Said and the Double Standards of Inside-Out Colonialism (Review of Culture and Imperialism by Edward Said)." *Times Literary Supplement*, February 19, 1993.

Gentzkow, Matthew, and Jesse M. Shapiro. "Media Bias and Reputation." *Journal of Political Economy* 114, no. 2 (April 2006): 280–316.

———. "What Drives Media Slant? Evidence From U.S. Daily Newspapers." *Econometrica* 78, no. 1 (January 2010): 35–71.

Getis, Arthur, and Judith Getis. "Christaller's Central Place Theory." *Journal of Geography* 65, no. 5 (1966). https://doi.org/10.1080/0022134 6608982415.

Giles, Ben. "Arizona Recount of 2020 Election Ballots Found No Proof of Corruption." NPR, September 25, 2021. www.npr.org/2021/09/25 /1040672550/az-audit.

Gilliam, Franklin D., Jr. "The 'Welfare Queen' Experiment." *Nieman Reports* 53, no. 2 (1999): 49–52.

Gimpel, James G., and J. Celeste Lay. "Political Socialization and Reactions to Immigration-Related Diversity in Rural America." *Rural Sociology* 73, no. 2 (June 2008): 180–204. https://doi.org/10.1526/003601108784514561.

Gjelten, Tom. "2020 Faith Vote Reflects 2016 Patterns." NPR, November 8, 2020. www.npr.org/2020/11/08/932263516/2020-faith-vote-reflects-2016 -patterns.

Glaeser, Edward L. *Triumph of the City: How Our Greatest Invention Makes Us Richer, Smarter, Greener, Healthier, and Happier.* New York: Penguin, 2011.

———. "Urban Colossus: Why Is New York America's Largest City?" NBER working paper no. 11389, National Bureau of Economic Research, Cambridge, MA, June 2005. www.nber.org/papers/w11398.

Glaeser, Edward L., and Albert Saiz. "The Rise of the Skilled City." *Brookings-Wharton Papers on Urban Affairs* (2004): 47–105.

Glaeser, Edward L., and Jesse M. Shapiro. *City Growth and the 2000 Census: Which Places Grew, and Why.* Washington, DC: Brookings, 2001. www.brookings.edu/wp-content/uploads/2016/06/whygrowth.pdf.

Glaze, Catherine "Dru," Leslie D. Edgar, Emily Rhoades-Buck, and Tracy Rutherford. "Visual Communications: An Analysis of University Students' Perceptions of Rural America Based on Select Photographs." *Journal of Applied Communications* 97, no. 1 (2013).

Gleiser, Marcelo. "Can Scientists Overreach?" NPR, April 6, 2011. www.npr .org/sections/13.7/2011/04/06/135160725/can-scientists-overreach.

Gorski, Philip. *American Covenant: A History of Civil Religion from the Puritans to the Present.* Princeton, NJ: Princeton University Press, 2017.

———. "The Long, Withdrawing Roar: From Culture Wars to Culture Clashes." *Hedgehog Review* 23, no. 2 (2021).

———. "The Return of the King: The Politics of Immanence and the Disenchantments of Liberalism." *Hedgehog Review* (Spring 2022).

Gorski, Philip, and Samuel Perry. *The Flag and the Cross: White Christian Nationalism and the Threat to American Democracy.* Oxford: Oxford University Press, 2022.

Great Book. "Binary Choice Questions: Compelling Findings About the Coronavirus." https://greatbrook.com/binary-choice-questions -compelling-findings-about-the-coronavirus/#after_section_1.

Greeley, Andrew. "Coleman Revisited: Religious Structures as a Source of Social Capital." *American Behavioral Scientist* 40, no. 5 (1997): 587–594.

Groenendyk, Eric, Michael Sances, and Kirill Zhirkov. "Intraparty Polarization in American Politics." *Journal of Politics* 82, no. 4 (2020).

Gupta, Akhil. "The Reincarnation of Souls and the Rebirth of Commodities: Representations of Time in 'East' and 'West.'" *Cultural Critique* 22 (1992): 187–211.

Gupta, Akhil, and James Ferguson. "Beyond 'Culture': Space, Identity, and the Politics of Difference." *Cultural Anthropology* 7, no. 1 (1992): 6–23.

Gyourko, Joseph, Christopher Mayer, and Todd Sinai. "Superstar Cities." *American Economic Journal: Economic Policy* 5, no. 4 (2013): 167–199.

Hagendoorn, Louk, and Shervin Nekuee. *Education and Racism: A Cross National Inventory of Positive Effects of Education on Ethnic Tolerance.* London: Routledge, 1999.

Hancock, Christine, Heidi Mennenga, Nikki King, Holly Andrilla, Eric Larson, and Pat Schou. *Treating the Rural Opioid Epidemic.* Washington, DC: National Rural Health Association, 2017. www.ruralhealth.us/NRHA /media/Emerge_NRHA/Advocacy/Policy%20documents/Treating -the-Rural-Opioid-Epidemic_Feb-2017_NRHA-Policy-Paper.pdf.

Handel, Michael J. "Skills Mismatch in the Labor Market." *Annual Review of Sociology* 29, no. 1 (August 2003): 135–165.

Hartman, L. M., and David Seckler. "Towards the Application of Dynamic Growth Theory to Regions." In *Regional Economics*, edited by Harry W. Richardson. London: Palgrave Macmillan, 1970. https://doi.org /10.1007/978-1-349-15404-3_8.

Harwood, Richard. "The Alienated American Voter: Are the News Media to Blame?" Brookings, September 1, 1996. www.brookings.edu/articles /the-alienated-american-voter-are-the-news-media-to-blame/.

Healey, Patrick. "What Surprised Us in Focus Groups with Voters About Jan. 6." *New York Times*, January 7, 2022. www.nytimes .com/2022/01/07/opinion/voter-focus-groups-jan-6.html.

Hernandez, Richard. "The Fall of Employment in the Manufacturing Sector." *Monthly Labor Review* (August 2018).

Hessler, Courtney. "West Virginia Files Lawsuit Against Kroger for Opioid Distribution Practices." *Herald-Dispatch*, August 25, 2022. www .herald-dispatch.com/news/west-virginia-files-lawsuit-against-kroger -for-opioid-distribution-practices/article_3979d24c-5ee7-5ce9-983a -738ffdda8fef.html.

Hinckley, Story. "One West Virginia City's Pioneering Approach to Opioid Crisis." *Christian Science Monitor*, May 22, 2017. www.csmonitor.com /USA/Society/2017/0522/One-West-Virginia-city-s-pioneering -approach-to-opioid-crisis.

Hirschman, C. "The Role of Religion in the Origins and Adaptation of Immigrant Groups in the United States." *International Migration Review* 38, no. 3 (2004): 1206–1233. doi:10.1111/j.1747-7379.2004.tb00233.x.

History.com Editors. "Great Awakening." History, March 7, 2018. www .history.com/topics/british-history/great-awakening.

Hobson, Theo. "For Rousseau, It's Humanity That's Divine, Not Reason." *Guardian*, January 27, 2014. www.theguardian.com/commentisfree/2014 /jan/27/rousseau-humanity-divine-not-reason#:~:text=Voltaire%2C%20 the%20most%20famous,religion%20is%20known%20as%20deism.

Hochschild, Arlie R. "How the White Working Class Is Being Destroyed." *New York Times*, March 17, 2020. www.nytimes.com/2020/03/17/books /review/deaths-of-despair-and-the-future-of-capitalism-anne-case -angus-deaton.html.

Hofstadter, Richard. *Anti-intellectualism in American Life*. New York: Knopf, 1963.

Holt, Douglas. "Does Cultural Capital Structure American Consumption?" *Journal of Consumer Research* 25, no. 1 (1998).

Hoxby, Caroline. "The Changing Selectivity of American Colleges." *Journal of Economic Perspectives* 23, no. 4 (Fall 2009): 95–118.

Hoxby, Caroline, and Christopher Avery. "The Missing 'One-Offs': The Hidden Supply of High-Achieving, Low Income Students." NBER working paper no. 18586, National Bureau of Economic Research, Cambridge, MA, December 2012. www.nber.org/papers/w18586.

Hsu, Spencer S. "Anti-vaccine Doctor Sentenced to Prison for Jan. 6 Trespassing." *Washington Post*, June 16, 2022. www.washingtonpost .com/national-security/2022/06/16/simone-gold-sentenced/.

Hsu, Tiffany. "Despite Outbreaks Among Unvaccinated, Fox News Hosts Smear Shots." *New York Times*, July 11, 2021. www.nytimes .com/2021/07/11/business/media/vaccines-fox-news-hosts.html.

Hunter, James Davison. *Culture Wars: The Struggle to Control the Family, Art, Education, Law, and Politics in America*. New York: Basic Books, 1991.

Illing, Sean. "A Princeton Sociologist Spent 8 Years Asking Rural Americans Why They're So Pissed Off." *Vox*, June 30, 2018. www.vox.com/2018/3 /13/17053886/trump-rural-america-populism-racial-resentment.

Inglehart, Ronald. "Globalization and Postmodern Values." *Washington Quarterly* 23, no. 1 (2000): 215–228.

Inglehart, Ronald, and Pippa Norris. "Trump, Brexit, and the Rise of Populism: Economic Have-Nots and Cultural Backlash." HKS working paper no. RWP16-026, Harvard Kennedy School, Cambridge, MA, August 2016.

Jackman, Mary R. "General and Applied Tolerance: Does Education Increase Commitment to Racial Integration?" *American Journal of Political Science* 22, no. 2 (1978): 302–324.

Jackson, Kenneth T. *Crabgrass Frontier: The Suburbanization of the United States*. Oxford: Oxford University Press, 1987.

Jacobs, Jane. *The Economy of Cities*. New York: Vintage, 1970.

Jacobson, Louis. "A Closer Look at Patrick Morrisey's Family Ties to 'Big Pharma.'" *Politifact*, March 28, 2018. www.politifact.com/article/2018 /mar/27/closer-look-patrick-morriseys-family-ties-big-phar/.

Jacoby, Susan. *The Age of American Unreason in a Culture of Lies*. New York: Vintage, 2008.

Jones, D. A. "The Polarizing Effect of New Media Messages." *International Journal of Public Opinion Research* 14, no. 2 (2002): 158–174.

Jones, Robert P., Natalie Jackson, Diana Orcés, and Ian Huff. *The 2020 Census of American Religion*. Washington, DC: PRRI, 2021.

Katz, Irwin. "Gordon Allport's *The Nature of Prejudice*." *Political Psychology* 12, no. 1 (1991): 125–157.

Kaufmann, Eric. "Americans Are Divided by Their Views on Race, Not Race Itself." *New York Times*, March 18, 2019. www.nytimes.com/2019 /03/18/opinion/race-america-trump.html.

———. *Whiteshift: Populism, Immigration, and the Future of White Majorities*. New York: Abrams, 2018.

Keene, Danya E., and Mark B. Padilla. "Race, Class and the Stigma of Place: Moving to 'Opportunity' in Eastern Iowa." *Health & Place* 16, no. 6 (November 2010): 1216–1223. https://doi.org/10.1016/j.healthplace .2010.08.006.

Kendi, Ibram X. *How to Be an Antiracist*. New York: Random House, 2019.

Keneally, Meghan. "Trump Tells Supporters: 'You're Not Forgotten Anymore.'" ABC News, January 20, 2017. https://abcnews.go.com /Politics/inauguration-festivities-officially-kick-off-dc/story?id= 44875711.

Keyes, Katherine M., Magdalena Cerdá, Joanne E. Brady, Jennifer R. Havens, and Sandro Galea. "Understanding the Rural–Urban Differences in Nonmedical Prescription Opioid Use and Abuse in the United States." *American Journal of Public Health* 104, no. 2 (February 1, 2014): e52-e59.

Khan, Shamus. "Capital Inequalities." *Hedgehog Review* (Summer 2021). https://hedgehogreview.com/issues/distinctions-that-define-and-divide /articles/capital-inequalities.

Khazan, Olga. "Wealthy L.A. Schools' Vaccination Rates Are as Low as South Sudan's." *Atlantic*, September 16, 2014. www.theatlantic .com/health/archive/2014/09/wealthy-la-schools-vaccination-rates -are-as-low-as-south-sudans/380252/.

Klein, Ezra. "California Is Making Liberals Squirm." *New York Times*, February 11, 2021. www.nytimes.com/2021/02/11/opinion/california -san-francisco-schools.html.

———. *Why We're Polarized*. New York: Simon & Schuster, 2020.

Klein, Ezra, and Barak Obama. "Obama Explains How America Went from 'Yes We Can' to 'MAGA.'" In *The Ezra Klein Show. New York Times*, June 1, 2021. Podcast transcript. www.nytimes.com/2021/06/01 /opinion/ezra-klein-podcast-barack-obama.html.

Klein, Ezra, and George Saunders. "Ezra Klein Interviews George Saunders." In *The Ezra Klein Show*, February 19, 2021. Podcast. www .nytimes.com/2021/02/19/podcasts/ezra-klein-show-george-saunders -transcript.html.

Klein, Ezra, and James Suzman. "Ezra Klein Interviews James Suzman." In *The Ezra Klein Show*, Jun 29, 2021. Podcast. www.nytimes.com/2021/06 /29/podcasts/transcript-ezra-klein-interviews-james-suzman.html.

Knauth, Dietrich. "West Virginia Cities Reach $400 Mln Opioid Distributor Settlement." Reuters, August 1, 2022. www.reuters.com/business /healthcare-pharmaceuticals/west-virginia-cities-reach-400-mln -opioid-distributor-deal-2022-08-01/.

Knauth, Dietrich, Jonathan Stempel, and Tom Hals. "Sacklers to Pay $6 Billion to Settle Purdue Opioid Lawsuits." Reuters, March 4, 2022. www .reuters.com/business/healthcare-pharmaceuticals/sacklers-will -pay-up-6-bln-resolve-purdue-opioid-lawsuits-mediator-2022-03-03/.

Koh, Adeline. "Imagined Communities, Social Media, and the Faculty." *Academe*, May–June 2016. www.aaup.org/article/imagined-communities -social-media-and-faculty#.YtbWcnbMJnI.

Kolstad, Charles D. "What Is Killing the US Coal Industry?" Stanford Institute for Economic Policy Research, March 2017. https://siepr .stanford.edu/publications/policy-brief/what-killing-us-coal-industry.

Kron, Josh. "Red State, Blue City: How the Urban-Rural Divide Is Splitting America." *Atlantic*, November 30, 2012. www.theatlantic.com /politics/archive/2012/11/red-state-blue-city-how-the-urban-rural -divide-is-splitting-america/265686/.

Krugman, Paul. *Geography and Trade*. Cambridge, MA: MIT Press, 1992.

———. "Increasing Returns and Economic Geography." *Journal of Political Economy* 99, no. 3 (June 1991).

Krupnikov, Yanna, and John Barry Ryan. *The Other Divide: Polarization and Disengagement in American Politics*. Cambridge: Cambridge University Press, 2022.

———. "The Real Divide in America Is Between Political Junkies and Everyone Else." *New York Times*, October 20, 2020. www.nytimes .com/2020/10/20/opinion/polarization-politics-americans.html.

Kubin, Emily, and Christian von Sikorski. "The Role of (Social) Media in Political Polarization: A Systematic Review." *Annals of the International Communication Association* 45, no. 3 (September 21, 2021): 188– 206. https://doi.org/10.1080/23808985.2021.1976070.

LaMacchia, Robert A., Robert W. Marx, and Joel Sobel. "Chapter 13: Metropolitan Areas." In *Geographic Areas Reference Manual*. Washington, DC: US Census Bureau, 1994.

Lamont, Michèle, Laura Adler, Bo Yun Park, and Xin Xiang. "Bridging Cultural Sociology and Cognitive Psychology in Three Contemporary Research Programmes." *Nature Human Behaviour* 1, no. 12 (December 2017): 866–872.

Lancet. "A Time of Crisis for the Opioid Epidemic in the USA." July 24, 2021. www.thelancet.com/journals/lancet/article/PIIS0140-6736(21) 01653-6/fulltext.

Lemon, Peter. "Fox Host Tucker Carlson Says College Education 'Diminishes You' and 'Everyone Should Opt Out.'" *Newsweek*, April 24, 2021. www .newsweek.com/fox-host-tucker-carlson-says-college-education -diminishes-you-everyone-should-opt-out-1586212.

Lenthang, Marlene. "These Cities Have Reached Biden's 70% Vaccination Goal—and Beyond." ABC News, June 11, 2021. https://abcnews.go.com /Health/cities-reached-bidens-70-vaccination-goal/story?id=78195531.

Lewis, Bernard. "The Question of Orientalism." *New York Review of Books*, June 24, 1982.

Lewis, Michael. *The Big Short: Inside the Doomsday Machine.* New York: W. W. Norton, 2010.

Lewis, Valerie A., Carol Ann MacGregor, and Robert D. Putnam. "Religion, Networks, and Neighborliness: The Impact of Religious Social Networks on Civic Engagement." *Social Science Research* 42, no. 2 (2013): 331–346.

Ley, David. "The Immigrant Church as an Urban Service Hub." *Urban Studies* 45, no. 10 (2008): 2057–2074. doi:10.1177/0042098008094873.

Lichter, D. T., and D. L. Brown. "Rural America in an Urban Society: Changing Spatial and Social Boundaries." *Annual Review of Sociology* 37, no. 1 (2011): 565–592.

Lleras-Muney, Adriana. "Education and Income Gradients in Longevity: The Role of Policy." NBER working paper no. 29694, National Bureau of Economic Research, Cambridge, MA, January 2022. www .nber.org/papers/w29694.

———. "The Relationship Between Education and Adult Mortality in the United States." *Review of Economic Studies* 72, no. 1 (2005): 189–221.

Lofton, Kathryn. *Consuming Religion.* Chicago: University of Chicago Press, 2017.

Logan, Erin. "White People Have Gentrified Black Lives Matter. It's a Problem." *Los Angeles Times*, September 8, 2020. www.latimes.com /opinion/story/2020-09-04/black-lives-matter-white-people-portland -protests-nfl.

Lombardo, Guy, and Linda Shahinian. "Letters to the Editor: We Need to Talk About Racism and 'Blue Lives Matter.'" *Los Angeles Times*, April 18, 2021. www.latimes.com/opinion/story/2021-04-18/racism-blue -lives-matter.

Los Angeles County Department of Public Health. *COVID-19 Vaccine and Fetal Cell Lines.* April 20, 2021. http://publichealth.lacounty .gov/media/coronavirus/docs/vaccine/VaccineDevelopment_FetalCell Lines.pdf.

Lurie, Julia. "He's Running as a Hero of the Opioid Epidemic. Here's the Catch." *Mother Jones*, July 13, 2018. www.motherjones .com/politics/2018/07/hes-running-as-a-hero-of-the-opioid-epidemic -heres-the-catch/.

MacGregor, Caroline. "West Virginia Reaches Landmark Settlement with 'Big Three' Opioid Distributors." West Virginia Public Broadcasting, August 1, 2022. www.wvpublic.org/government/2022-08-01

/west-virginia-reaches-landmark-settlement-with-big-three-opioid
-distributors.

Maher, Kris. "West Virginia Reaches $400 Million Opioid Deal with Dis-
tributors." *Wall Street Journal*, August 2, 2022. www.wsj.com/articles
/west-virginia-reaches-400-million-opioid-deal-with-distributors
-11659460919.

Mann, Brian, and Elizabeth Baker. "Black Protest Leaders to White Allies:
'It's Our Turn to Lead Our Own Fight.'" NPR, September 22, 2020.
www.npr.org/2020/09/22/913094440/black-protest-leaders-to-white
-allies-it-s-our-turn-to-lead-our-own-fight.

Mann, Brian, and Martha Bebinger. "Purdue Pharma, Sacklers Reach $6
Billion Deal with State Attorneys General." NPR, March 3, 2022.
www.npr.org/2022/03/03/1084163626/purdue-sacklers-oxycontin
-settlement.

Marcus, Julia, and Gregg Gonsalves. "Public-Health Experts Are Not Hypocrites." *Atlantic*, June 11, 2020. www.theatlantic.com/ideas/archive
/2020/06/public-health-experts-are-not-hypocrites/612853/.

Marema, Tim. "Rural Population Declines Slightly over Last Decade,
Census Shows." *Daily Yonder*, September 7, 2021. https://dailyyonder
.com/rural-population-declines-slightly-over-last-decade-census
-shows/2021/09/07/.

Marshall, Terence E. "Rousseau and Enlightenment." *Political Theory* 6,
no. 4 (1978): 421–455.

Mather, Cotton. *A Man of Reason*. Boston, 1718.

———. *Reasonable Religion. Or, the Truth of the Christian Religion, Demonstrated*. Boston, 1700.

Mathewes, Charles. "By Whose Waters We Wept…" *Hedgehog Review* 23,
no. 1 (Spring 2021).

McClay, Wilfred. "Performative: How the Meaning of a Word Became
Corrupted." *Hedgehog Review* 23, no. 2 (Summer 2021).

McClosky, Herbert. "Consensus and Ideology in American Politics."
American Political Science Review 58, no. 2 (1964): 361–382.

McDonough, Patricia. *Choosing Colleges: How Social Class and Schools Structure Opportunity*. Albany, NY: SUNY Press, 1997.

McGee, Patrick. "How Connected Fitness Became the New Obsession."
Financial Times, January 21, 2022. www.ft.com/content/8fe94eef-1077
-4eaa-8192-26013f7931ea.

McGreal, Chris. "Why Were Millions of Opioid Pills Sent to a West Virginia
Town of 3,000?" *Guardian*, October 2, 2019. www.theguardian.com
/us-news/2019/oct/02/opioids-west-virginia-pill-mills-pharmacies.

McLaughlin, Bryan. "Commitment to the Team: Perceived Conflict and Political Polarization." *Journal of Media Psychology* 30, no. 1 (January 2018): 41–51. https://doi.org/10.1027/1864-1105/a000176.

McWhorter, John. *Woke Racism: How a New Religion Has Betrayed Black America*. London: Swift Press, 2021.

Melzer, Arthur M. "The Origin of the Counter-Enlightenment: Rousseau and the New Religion of Sincerity." *American Political Science Review* 90, no. 2 (1996): 344–360.

Mencimer, Stephanie. "Doctor, Lawyer, Insurrectionist: The Radicalization of Simone Gold." *Mother Jones*, May 6, 2021. www.motherjones.com/politics/2021/05/doctor-lawyer-insurrectionist-the-radicalization-of-simone-gold/.

Mendelsohn, Matthew, and Richard Nadeau. "The Magnification and Minimization of Social Cleavages by the Broadcast and Narrowcast News Media." *International Journal of Public Opinion Research* 8, no. 4 (Winter 1996): 374–389.

Merica, Dan. "Trump Met with Boos After Revealing He Received Covid-19 Booster." CNN, December 21, 2021. www.cnn.com/2021/12/20/politics/donald-trump-booster-shot-boos/index.html.

Merkley, Eric, and Peter John Loewen. "Anti-intellectualism and the Mass Public's Response to the COVID-19 Pandemic." *Nature Human Behaviour* (2021): 706–715.

Metcalf, Stephen. "Ezra Klein's 'Why We're Polarized' and the Drawbacks of Explainer Journalism." *New Yorker*, March 11, 2020. www.newyorker.com/books/under-review/ezra-kleins-why-were-polarized-and-the-drawbacks-of-explainer-journalism.

Metropolitan and Micropolitan Statistical Area Tables. 2022.

Michelman, Valerie, Joseph Price, and Seth D. Zimmerman. "Old Boys' Clubs and Upward Mobility Among the Educational Elite." *Quarterly Journal of Economics* (2021).

Moretti, Enrico. *The New Geography of Jobs*. New York: HarperCollins, 2012.

Morin, Rich. "Behind Trump's Win in Rural White America: Women Joined Men in Backing Him." Pew Research Center, November 17, 2016. www.pewresearch.org/fact-tank/2016/11/17/behind-trumps-win-in-rural-white-america-women-joined-men-in-backing-him/.

Mother Miriam. "COVID Vaccines Have Been 'Designed to Kill Off the Population.'" In *Mother Miriam Live*, October 7, 2021. Podcast. https://play.acast.com/s/mother-miriam-live/covid-vaccines-have-been-designed-to-kill-off-the-population.

Muro, Mark, and Andre M. Perry. "Regional Divergence Is More than an Economic Dilemma—It's a Civil Rights Issue." Brookings, January 28, 2020. www.brookings.edu/blog/the-avenue/2020/01/28/regional -divergence-is-more-than-an-economic-dilemma-its-a-civil-rights -issue/.

National Center for Health Statistics. "Drug Overdose Mortality by State." CDC. Last modified March 1, 2022. www.cdc.gov/nchs/pressroom /sosmap/drug_poisoning_mortality/drug_poisoning.htm.

Nebraska Medicine. "You Asked, We Answered: Do the COVID-19 Vaccines Contain Aborted Fetal Cells?" August 18, 2021. www.nebraskamed.com /COVID/you-asked-we-answered-do-the-covid-19-vaccines-contain -aborted-fetal-cells.

Newport, Frank. "Affirmative Action and Public Opinion." Gallup, August 7, 2020. https://news.gallup.com/opinion/polling-matters/317006 /affirmative-action-public-opinion.aspx.

North Dakota Health. *COVID-19 Vaccines & Fetal Cell Lines.* August 17, 2022. www.health.nd.gov/sites/www/files/documents/COVID%20Vaccine %20Page/COVID-19_Vaccine_Fetal_Cell_Handout.pdf.

Ofosu, Eugene K., Michelle K. Chambers, Jacqueline M. Chen, and Eric Hehman. "Same-Sex Marriage Legalization Associated with Reduced Implicit and Explicit Antigay Bias." *PNAS* 116, no. 18 (April 15, 2019). https://doi.org/10.1073/pnas.1806000116.

Oliner, Samuel P., and Jerrald D. Krause. "Racial and Ethnic Attitudes in Rural America: Focus on Humboldt County, California." *Humboldt Journal of Social Relations* 26, no. 1/2 (2001): 11–55.

Olson, Laura R. "Religion and American Public Life: A Discussion of Robert Putnam and David Campbell's *Saving Grace: How Religion Divides and Unites Us.*" *Perspectives on Politics* 10, no. 1 (2012): 103–106.

O'Shaughnessy, Lynn. "20 Surprising Higher Education Facts." *US News & World Report,* September 6, 2011. https://www.usnews.com/edu cation/blogs/the-college-solution/2011/09/06/20-surprising-higher -education-facts.

Otterman, Sharon. "New York Confronts Its Worst Measles Outbreak in Decades." *New York Times,* January 17, 2019. www.nytimes.com/2019 /01/17/nyregion/measles-outbreak-jews-nyc.html.

Packer, George. "How America Fractured into Four Parts." *Atlantic,* March 26, 2022. www.theatlantic.com/magazine/archive/2021/07/george-packer -four-americas/619012/.

Parker, Kim, Juliana Horowitz, Anna Brown, Richard Fry, D'Vera Cohn, and Ruth Igielnik. "How People in Urban, Suburban and Rural Communities See Each Other—and Say Others See Them." Pew Research Center, May 22, 2018. www.pewresearch.org/social-trends /2018/05/22/how-people-in-urban-suburban-and-rural-communities -see-each-other-and-say-others-see-them/.

Parks, Casey. "The Tragedy of America's Rural Schools." *New York Times*, September 7, 2021. www.nytimes.com/2021/09/07/magazine/rural-public -education.html.

Parr, Jessica. "Guest Post: Cotton Mather and the Enlightenment in New England: Redefining the Holy Spirit." *Junto* (blog), June 26, 2017. https://earlyamericanists.com/2017/06/26/guest-post-cotton-mather -and-the-enlightenment-in-new-england-redefining-the-holy-spirit/.

Payne, B. Keith, Heidi A. Vuletich, and Jazmin L. Brown-Iannuzzi. "Historical Roots of Implicit Bias in Slavery." *PNAS* 116, no. 24 (May 28, 2019): 11693–11698. https://doi.org/10.1073/pnas.1818816116.

Pengelly, Martin. "Republican Party Calls January 6 Attack 'Legitimate Political Discourse.'" *Guardian*, February 4, 2022. www.theguardian.com /us-news/2022/feb/04/republicans-capitol-attack-legitimate-political -discourse-cheney-kinzinger-pence.

Pettigrew, Thomas. "Intergroup Contact Theory." *Annual Review of Psychology* 49, no. 1 (1998): 65–85.

Pew Research Center. *Conflicted Views of Affirmative Action*. May 14, 2003. www.pewresearch.org/politics/2003/05/14/conflicted-views-of -affirmative-action/.

———. "U.S. Muslims Concerned About Their Place in Society, but Continue to Believe in the American Dream." July 26, 2017. www .pewresearch.org/religion/2017/07/26/findings-from-pew-research -centers-2017-survey-of-us-muslims/.

Pigg, Kenneth, ed. *The Future of Rural America: Anticipating Policies for Constructive Change*. New York: Routledge, 2019.

Pinker, Steven. "The Media Exaggerates Negative News. This Distortion Has Consequences." *Guardian*, February 17, 2018. www.theguardian.com /commentisfree/2018/feb/17/steven-pinker-media-negative-news.

Pomeau, René Henry. "Voltaire: French Philosopher and Author." In *Encyclopedia Britannica Online*. Accessed February 23, 2022. www.britannica .com/biography/Voltaire.

Porter, Eduardo. "The Hard Truths of Trying to 'Save' the Rural Economy." *New York Times*, December 14, 2018. www.nytimes.com/interactive/2018 /12/14/opinion/rural-america-trump-decline.html.

Portes, Alejandro. "Downsides of Social Capital." *PNAS* 111, no. 52 (December 22, 2014). www.pnas.org/doi/full/10.1073/pnas.1421888112.

Posner, Sarah. "How the Christian Right Helped Foment Insurrection." *Rolling Stone*, January 31, 2021. www.rollingstone.com/culture/culture -features/capitol-christian-right-trump-1121236/.

Potts, Monica. "In the Land of Self-Defeat." *New York Times*, October 4, 2019. www.nytimes.com/2019/10/04/opinion/sunday/trump-arkansas.html.

———. "Why Being Anti-Science Is Now Part Of Many Rural Americans' Identity." *FiveThirtyEight*, April 25, 2022. https://fivethirtyeight .com/features/why-being-anti-science-is-now-part-of-many-rural -americans-identity/.

Purtill, Corinne. "If You Want to Get into an Elite College, You Might Consider Moving to One of These States." *Quartz*, April 4, 2016. https:// qz.com/653167/if-you-want-to-get-into-an-elite-college-you-might -consider-moving-to-one-of-these-states/.

Putnam, Robert, and David Campbell. *American Grace: How Religion Divides and Unites Us*. New York: Simon & Schuster, 2010.

Ramey, Corinne, and Sara Randazzo. "McKesson, AmerisourceBergen and Cardinal Health Not Liable for Opioid Crisis in West Virginia, Court Rules." *Wall Street Journal*, July 5, 2022. www.wsj.com/articles /distributors-not-liable-for-opioid-crisis-in-west-virginia-court-rules -11657036182.

Randolph, Gregory F., and Elizabeth Currid-Halkett. "Planning in the Era of Regional Divergence: Place, Scale, and Development in Confronting Spatial Inequalities." *Journal of the American Planning Association* (2021): 1–8.

Raphael, Marc, ed. *The Columbia History of Jews in America*. New York: Columbia University Press, 2008.

Ray, John J. "Acquiescence and Problems with Forced-Choice Scales." *Journal of Social Psychology* 130, no. 3 (1990): 379–399.

Raymond, Nate. "U.S. Drug Distributors Prevail in $2.5 Billion West Virginia Opioid Case." Reuters, July 3, 2022. www.reuters.com/world /us/us-drug-distributors-prevail-25-billion-west-virginia-opioid-case -2022-07-04/.

Reeves, Richard V. *Dream Hoarders: How the American Upper Middle Class Is Leaving Everyone Else in the Dust, Why That Is a Problem, and What to Do About It*. Washington DC: Brookings Institution Press, 2017.

Richmond, Todd. "Father James Altman, Who Said Democrats Would Burn in Hell and Called Covid Restrictions 'Nazi-Esque,' Removed by His Bishop." *America*, July 9, 2021. www.americamagazine.org/faith/2021 /07/09/father-james-altman-removed-wisconsin-bishop-241015.

Robinson, Marilynne. "Hysterical Scientism." *Harper's*, November 2006. https://harpers.org/archive/2006/11/hysterical-scientism/.

Roche, Darragh. "Priest Says COVID Rules Enforcers Will Burn in 'Hottest Levels' of Hell." *Newsweek*, April 27, 2021. www.newsweek.com/priest-says-covid-rules-enforcers-will-burn-hottest-levels-hell-1586634.

Rogers, Katie. "What Is a Constant Cycle of Violent News Doing to Us?" *New York Times*, July 15, 2016. www.nytimes.com/2016/07/16/health/what-is-a-constant-cycle-of-violent-news-doing-to-us.html.

Romer, Paul M. "Increasing Returns and Long Run Growth." *Journal of Political Economy* 94, no. 5 (October 1986): 1002–1037.

———. "The Origins of Endogenous Growth." *Journal of Economic Perspectives* 8, no. 1 (Winter 1994).

Rosin, Hanna. "The Case Against Breastfeeding." *Atlantic*, April 1, 2009. www.theatlantic.com/magazine/archive/2009/04/the-case-against-breast-feeding/307311/.

Rothstein, Richard. *The Color of Law: A Forgotten History of How Our Government Segregated America*. New York: Liveright, 2017.

Rothwell, Jonathan. "The Biggest Economic Divides Aren't Regional. They're Local. (Just Ask Parents.)" *New York Times*, February 12, 2019. www.nytimes.com/2019/02/12/upshot/the-biggest-economic-divides-arent-regional-theyre-local-just-ask-parents.html.

Rousseau, Jean-Jacques. *The Collected Writings of Rousseau*. Vol. 3, edited by Roger D. Masters and Christopher Kelly. Hanover, NH: University Press of New England, 1990.

———. *Discourse on the Origin of Inequality*. Cambridge, MA: Hackett, 1992.

Rubinstein, Mark. "Rational Markets: Yes or No? The Affirmative Case." *Financial Analysts Journal* 57, no. 3 (May–June 2001): 15–29. www.jstor.org/stable/4480313.

Rubio, Marco. "Abortion Decision Exposes How Woke Corporations Are Hostile to American Families." Fox News, July 19, 2022. www.foxnews.com/opinion/abortion-decision-exposes-woke-corporations-hostile-american-families.

Runciman, David. "Nietzsche on Morality." In *History of Ideas*, season 2, March 2, 2021. Podcast. https://play.acast.com/s/history-of-ideas/neitzscheonmorality.

———. "Rousseau on Inequality." In *History of Ideas*, season 2, February 2, 2021. Podcast. https://play.acast.com/s/history-of-ideas/s2-rousseauoninequality.

———. "Shklar on Hypocrisy." In *History of Ideas*, season 2, April 20, 2021. Podcast. https://play.acast.com/s/history-of-ideas/shklaronhypocrisy.

———. "Tocqueville on Democracy." In *The Confidence Trap: A History of Democracy in Crisis from World War I to the Present*. Princeton, NJ: Princeton University Press, 2018.

Russell, Jonathan. "Here's What's Wrong with #BlueLivesMatter." *Huff-Post*, July 9, 2016. www.huffpost.com/entry/heres-whats-wrong-with -bl_b_10906348.

Saady, Brian. "A Real Killing: How Greedy Corporate Pushers Caused the Opioid Crisis." *American Conservative*, January 23, 2019. www .theamericanconservative.com/how-the-corporate-pill-pushers-started -the-opioid-crisis/.

Sacks, Peter. *Tearing Down the Gates: Confronting the Class Divide in American Education*. Berkeley: University of California Press, 2007.

Sadarangani, Manish. "Herd Immunity: How Does It Work?" Oxford Vaccine Group, April 26, 2016. www.ovg.ox.ac.uk/news/herd-immunity -how-does-it-work.

Said, Edward W. *Orientalism*. New York: Pantheon Books, 1978.

Sassen, Saskia. *The Global City: New York, London, Tokyo*. Princeton, NJ: Princeton University Press, 1991.

Sayers, Freddie, and Richard Dawkins. "Richard Dawkins: 'Scientism' Is a Dirty Word." In *UnHerd with Freddie Sayers*, June 18, 2021. Podcast. https://unherd.com/thepost/richard-dawkins-scientism-is-a-dirty -word/.

Seale, Elizabeth. "Coping Strategies of Urban and Rural Welfare Organisations and the Regulation of the Poor." *New Political Economy* 18, no. 2 (April 25, 2012): 141–170. https://doi.org/10.1080/13563467.2012.664124.

Selingo, Jeffrey. "The College-Admissions Process Is Completely Broken." *Atlantic*, March 23, 2022. www.theatlantic.com/ideas/archive/2022/03 /change-college-acceptance-application-process/627581/.

Semega, Jessica, Melissa Kollar, Emily A. Shrider, and John Creamer. "Income and Poverty in the United States: 2019." US Census Bureau, September 15, 2020. www.census.gov/library/publications/2020/demo /p60-270.html.

Senna, Danzy. "Robin DiAngelo and the Problem with Anti-racist Self-Help." *Atlantic*, August 3, 2021. www.theatlantic.com/magazine/archive/2021/09 /martin-learning-in-public-diangelo-nice-racism/619497/.

Sherman, Rachel. "Conflicted Cultivation: Parenting, Privilege, and Moral Worth in Wealthy New York Families." *American Journal of Cultural Sociology* 5 (2017a): 1–33.

———. *Uneasy Street: The Anxieties of Affluence*. Princeton, NJ: Princeton University Press, 2017.

———. "'A Very Expensive Ordinary Life': Consumption, Symbolic Boundaries and Moral Legitimacy Among New York Elites." *Socio-Economic Review* 16, no. 2 (2018): 411–433.

Shinder, Richard J. "The Very Real Threat in the Rise of Anti-Rationalism." *Hill*, June 27, 2021. https://thehill.com/opinion/campaign/559764-the-very-real-threat-in-the-rise-of-anti-rationalism.

Shklar, Judith N. *Ordinary Vices*. Cambridge, MA: Harvard University Press, 1985.

Simon, Mallory. "Over 1,000 Health Professionals Sign a Letter Saying, Don't Shut Down Protests Using Coronavirus Concerns as an Excuse." CNN, June 5, 2020. www.cnn.com/2020/06/05/health/health-care-open-letter-protests-coronavirus-trnd/index.html.

Simonetti, Isabella. "Over 360 Newspapers Have Closed Since Just Before the Start of the Pandemic." *New York Times*, June 29, 2022. www.nytimes.com/2022/06/29/business/media/local-newspapers-pandemic.html.

Simpson, April. "Why Rural America Is Joining the Movement for Black Lives." *Stateline* (blog), Pew Charitable Trusts. June 12, 2020. www.pewtrusts.org/en/research-and-analysis/blogs/stateline/2020/06/12/why-rural-america-is-joining-the-movement-for-black-lives.

Smarsh, Sarah. "Dangerous Idiots: How the Liberal Media Elite Failed Working-Class Americans." *Guardian*, October 13, 2016. www.theguardian.com/media/2016/oct/13/liberal-media-bias-working-class-americans.

Smith, Blake. "Moral Cruelty and the Left." *Tablet*, June 7, 2020. www.tabletmag.com/sections/arts-letters/articles/judith-shklar-politics-of-fear.

Smith, Christian. *The Secular Revolution: Power, Interests, and Conflict in the Secularization of American Public Life*. Berkeley: University of California Press, 2003.

Smith, Jonathan, Matea Pender, and Jessica Howell. "The Full Extent of Student-College Academic Undermatch." *Economics of Education Review* 32 (2013): 247–261.

Smith, Tom W., Michael Davern, Jeremy Freese, and Stephen L. Morgan. *General Social Surveys, 1972–2018: Cumulative Codebook*. Chicago: NORC, 2019.

Sobieraj, Sarah, and Jeffrey M. Berry. "From Incivility to Outrage: Political Discourse in Blogs, Talk Radio, and Cable News." *Political Communication* 28, no. 1 (2011): 19–41. https://doi.org/10.1080/10584609.2010.542360.

Sorkin, David. *The Religious Enlightenment: Protestants, Jews, and Catholics from London to Vienna*. Princeton, NJ: Princeton University Press, 2011.

Southern District of West Virginia US Attorney's Office. "Mingo County Pharmacist Sentenced to Prison Time for Conspiracy to Acquire Controlled Substances by Fraud." FBI Pittsburgh Division, news release, November 15, 2012. https://archives.fbi.gov/archives/pittsburgh/press-releases/2012/mingo-county-pharmacist-sentenced-to-prison-time-for-conspiracy-to-acquire-controlled-substances-by-fraud.

Starnes, Todd. "Hey, Black Lives Matter, Stop Terrorizing Our Cities." Fox News, July 28, 2016. www.foxnews.com/opinion/hey-black-lives-matter-stop-terrorizing-our-cities.

State of West Virginia. "Meet the Attorney General: Patrick Morrisey." Office of the WV Attorney General, n.d. https://ago.wv.gov/about/Meet%20the%20AG/Pages/default.aspx.

Statista Research Department. "Percentage Added to the Gross Domestic Product (GDP) of the United States of America in 2020, by Industry." Statista, June 3, 2021. www.statista.com/statistics/248004/percentage-added-to-the-us-gdp-by-industry/.

———. "Religious Affiliation of Rural Americans in 2019, by Religion." Statista, June 21, 2022. www.statista.com/statistics/1009381/religious-affiliation-rural-americans/.

Stevens, Hannah R., Yoo Jung Oh, and Laramie D. Taylor. "Desensitization to Fear-Inducing COVID-19 Health News on Twitter: Observational Study." *JMIR Infodemiology* 1, no. 1 (2021).

Steverman, Ben. "Harvard's Chetty Finds Economic Carnage in Wealthiest ZIP Codes." *Bloomberg*, September 24, 2020. www.bloomberg.com/news/features/2020-09-24/harvard-economist-raj-chetty-creates-god-s-eye-view-of-pandemic-damage.

Stewart, Emily. "The Problem with America's Semi-Rich." *Vox*, October 12, 2021. www.vox.com/the-goods/22673605/upper-middle-class-meritocracy-matthew-stewart.

Stolz, Jörg. "'All Things Are Possible': Towards a Sociological Explanation of Pentecostal Miracles and Healings." *Sociology of Religion* 72, no. 4 (winter 2011): 456–482.

Storper, Michael. "Separate Worlds? Explaining the Current Wave of Regional Economic Polarization." *Journal of Economic Geography* 18, no. 2 (2018): 247–270.

Strathern, Alan. *Unearthly Powers: Religious and Political Change in World History*. Cambridge: Cambridge University Press, 2019.

Stuart, Paul H. "Conceptual and Historical Foundations of Rural Social Welfare." In *Rural Social Work: Building and Sustaining Community Capacity*, edited by T. Laine Scales, Calvin L. Streeter, and H. Stephen Cooper. Hoboken, NJ: John Wiley & Sons, 2014.

Suzman, James. *Work: A History of How We Spend Our Time*. London: Bloomsbury, 2020.

Taves, Ann. *Fits, Trances, and Visions: Experiencing Religion and Explaining Experience from Wesley to James*. Princeton, NJ: Princeton University Press, 1999.

Thompson, Derek. "The Myth of American Universities as Inequality-Fighters." *Atlantic*, August 31, 2017. www.theatlantic.com/business /archive/2017/08/universities-inequality-fighters/538566/.

Throsby, David. "Cultural Capital." *Journal of Cultural Economics* 23 (1999): 3–12.

Tickamyer, Ann R., and Cynthia M. Duncan. "Poverty and Opportunity Structure in Rural America." *Annual Review of Sociology* 16 (August 1990): 67–86.

Tokarczuk, Olga. "Olga Tokarczuk's Nobel Lecture: 'Tenderness Is the Most Modest Form of Love.'" *Irish Times*, December 13, 2019. www .irishtimes.com/culture/books/olga-tokarczuk-s-nobel-lecture -tenderness-is-the-most-modest-form-of-love-1.4113106.

Toner, Bill. "The Impact of Agreement Bias on the Ranking of Questionnaire Response." *Journal of Social Psychology* 127, no. 2 (1987): 221–222.

Topazio, Virgil W. "Voltaire, Philosopher of Human Progress." *Publications of the Modern Language Association of America* 74, no. 4 (1959): 356–364.

Trimble, Megan. "WHO: Anti-Vaccine Movement a Top Threat in 2019." *US News & World Report*, January 16, 2019. www.usnews.com/news /national-news/articles/2019-01-16/who-names-vaccine-hesitancy -as-top-world-threat-in-2019.

US Attorney's Office, District of Columbia. "GOLD, Simone Melissa." Case no. 1:21-cr-85. Last modified June 16, 2022. www.justice.gov /usao-dc/defendants/gold-simone-melissa.

US Bureau of Labor Statistics. "QCEW Field Layouts for NAICS-Based, Annual CSV Files." Quarterly Census of Employment and Wages. Last modified September 24, 2020. www.bls.gov/cew/about-data /downloadable-file-layouts/annual/naics-based-annual-layout.htm.

US Census Bureau. "American Community Survey 5-Year Data (2009–2020)." March 17, 2022. www.census.gov/data/developers/data-sets/acs-5year.html.

———. "Economic Census: NAICS Codes & Understanding Industry Classification Systems." Last modified August 19, 2022. www.census.gov/programs-surveys/economic-census/guidance/understanding-naics.html.

———. *2010 Census Regions and Divisions of the United States.* 2010. www.census.gov/geographies/reference-maps/2010/geo/2010-census-regions-and-divisions-of-the-united-states.html.

US Census Bureau and Opportunity Insights. "The Opportunity Atlas." Accessed 2022. www.opportunityatlas.org/.

US Department of Justice. "Justice Department Announces Global Resolution of Criminal and Civil Investigations with Opioid Manufacturer Purdue Pharma and Civil Settlement with Members of the Sackler Family." News release, October 21, 2020. www.justice.gov/opa/pr/justice-department-announces-global-resolution-criminal-and-civil-investigations-opioid.

US House Select Subcommittee on the Coronavirus Crisis. "Select Subcommittee Launches Investigation into Online Entities Pushing Coronavirus Misinformation and Selling Unproven Treatments." News release, October 29, 2021. https://coronavirus.house.gov/news/press-releases/select-subcommittee-launches-investigation-online-entities-pushing-coronavirus.

Vance, J. D. *Hillbilly Elegy: A Memoir of a Family and Culture in Crisis.* New York: Harper, 2016.

Van Dam, Andrew. "Trump Wasn't Just a Rural Phenomenon. Most of His Supporters Come from Cities and Suburbs." *Washington Post*, November 18, 2020. www.washingtonpost.com/business/2020/11/18/rural-city-trump-voters/.

Veblen, Thorstein. *The Theory of the Leisure Class: An Economic Study of Institutions.* New York, 1899.

Vedantam, Shankar. "Strangers in Their Own Land: The 'Deep Story' of Trump Supporters." In *Hidden Brain*, January 24, 2017. Podcast. www.npr.org/2017/01/24/510567860/strangers-in-their-own-land-the-deep-story-of-trump-supporters.

Verter, Bradford. "Spiritual Capital: Theorizing Religion with Bourdieu Against Bourdieu." *Sociological Theory* 21, no. 2 (2003): 150–174.

Vinopal, Courtney. "2 Out of 3 Americans Believe U.S. Democracy Is Under Threat." PBS, July 2, 2021. www.pbs.org/newshour/politics/2-out-of -3-americans-believe-u-s-democracy-is-under-threat.

Wacquant, Loïc. "Negative Social Capital: State Breakdown and Social Destitution in America's Urban Core." *Netherlands Journal of Housing and the Built Environment* 13, no. 25 (1998).

Wagner, Michael W., and Mike Gruszczynski. "Who Gets Covered? Ideological Extremity and News Coverage of Members of the U.S. Congress, 1993 to 2013." *Journalism & Mass Communication Quarterly* 95, no. 3 (2013): 670–690. https://doi.org/10.1177/1077699017702836.

Wallace, Jacob, Paul Goldsmith-Pinkham, and Jason L. Schwartz. "Excess Death Rates for Republicans and Democrats During the COVID-19 Pandemic." NBER working paper no. 30512, National Bureau of Economic Research, Cambridge, MA, September 2022. www.nber .org/papers/w30512.

Warde, Alan, David Wright, and Modesto Gayo-Cal. "Understanding Cultural Omnivorousness: Or, the Myth of the Cultural Omnivore." *Cultural Sociology* 1, no. 2 (2007): 143–164.

Warnock, Deborah. "Capitalizing Class: An Examination of Socioeconomic Diversity on the Contemporary Campus." In *Working in Class: Recognizing How Social Class Shapes Our Academic Work*, edited by Allison Hurst and Sandi Kawecka Nenga. Lantham, MD: Rowman & Littlefield, 2016.

Wayne, Teddy. "Tucker Carlson on the Alien Invasion." *New Yorker*, May 9, 2022. www.newyorker.com/magazine/2022/05/16/tucker-carlson -defends-the-aliens-extraterrestrial-ones.

Wehner, Peter. "David Brooks's Journey Toward Faith." *Atlantic*, May 7, 2019. www.theatlantic.com/ideas/archive/2019/05/second-mountain-brooks -discusses-his-faith/588766/.

Whitenton, Michael R. "Review: American Covenant." *Reading Religion*, December 5, 2017. https://readingreligion.org/9780691147673 /american-covenant/.

Wikipedia, s.v. "America's Frontline Doctors." Last modified July 13, 2022, 00:27. https://en.wikipedia.org/wiki/America's_Frontline_Doctors.

Wilkerson, Isabel. *Caste: The Origins of Our Discontents*. New York: Random House, 2020.

Williams, Raymond. *Marxism and Literature*. Oxford: Oxford University Press, 1977.

Willick, Jason. "The Man Who Discovered 'Culture Wars.'" *Wall Street Journal*, May 25, 2018. www.wsj.com/articles/the-man-who-discovered -culture-wars-1527286035.

Wines, Michael, and Nick Corasaniti. "Arizona Vote Review 'Made Up the Numbers,' Election Experts Say." *New York Times*, October 1, 2021. www.nytimes.com/2021/10/01/us/arizona-election-review.html.

Winfrey, Oprah, and David Brooks. "David Brooks: The Quest for a Moral Life." In *Oprah's Super Soul*, May 20, 2019. Podcast. https://podcasts .apple.com/us/podcast/david-brooks-the-quest-for-a-moral-life /id1264843400?i=1000438838518.

Wolff, Susanna. "We're Being So Safe." *New Yorker*, November 25, 2020. www.newyorker.com/humor/daily-shouts/were-being-so-safe.

World Population Review. "Muslim Population by State 2022." N.d. https:// worldpopulationreview.com/state-rankings/muslim-population-by -state.

Wuthnow, Robert. *In the Blood: Understanding America's Farm Families*. Princeton, NJ: Princeton University Press, 2015.

———. *The Left Behind: Decline and Rage in Small Town America*. Princeton, NJ: Princeton University Press, 2018.

———. "Religious Involvement and Status-Bridging Social Capital." *Journal for the Scientific Study of Religion* 41, no. 4 (2002): 669–684.

———. *Small-Town America: Finding Community, Shaping the Future*. Princeton, NJ: Princeton University Press, 2013.

Young, Michael. *The Rise of the Meritocracy*. London: Thames & Hudson, 1958.

Younge, Gary. "The View from Middletown: A Typical US City That Never Did Exist." *Guardian*, October 18, 2016. www.theguardian.com /membership/2016/oct/18/view-from-middletown-us-muncie-america.

Yuhas, Alan. "Der Spiegel Fires Award-Winning Writer, Citing Fabrication on 'Grand Scale.'" *New York Times*, December 19, 2018. www .nytimes.com/2018/12/19/world/europe/der-spiegel-claas-relotius .html?module=inline.

Notes

INTRODUCTION: GETTING INTO THE ROOM

1. "Census Reporter Profile Page for Danville, PA," American Community Survey 5-Year Estimates, US Census Bureau, https://censusreporter.org/profiles/16000US4218136-danville-pa/.

2. "Economy in Danville, Pennsylvania," Best Places, www.bestplaces.net/economy/city/pennsylvania/danville#:~:text=Danville%20has%20an%20unemployment%20rate%20of%204.8%25.

3. Analysis of *2016 ACS 5 Year Data of Census-Designated Places with 4k-15k Population*.

4. Philip Roth, *Sabbath's Theatre* (New York: Houghton Mifflin, 1995).

5. Robert Wuthnow, *The Left Behind* (Princeton, NJ: Princeton University Press, 2018).

6. Josh Kron, "Red State, Blue City: How the Urban-Rural Divide Is Splitting America," *Atlantic*, November 30, 2012, www.theatlantic.com/politics/archive/2012/11/red-state-blue-city-how-the-urban-rural-divide-is-splitting-america/265686/.

7. Ann R. Tickamyer and Cynthia M. Duncan, "Poverty and Opportunity Structure in Rural America," *Annual Review of Sociology* 16 (August 1990): 67–86; Kenneth Pigg, ed., *The Future of Rural America: Anticipating Policies for Constructive Change* (New York: Routledge, 2019).

8. Rich Morin, "Behind Trump's Win in Rural White America: Women Joined Men in Backing Him," Pew Research Center, November 16, 2017, www.pewresearch.org/fact-tank/2016/11/17/behind-trumps-win-in-rural-white-america-women-joined-men-in-backing-him/.

9. Nicholas Carnes and Noam Lupu, "The White Working Class and

the 2016 Election," *Perspectives on Politics* 19, no. 1 (2021): 55–72, https://doi.org/10.1017/s1537592720001267.

10. Andrew Van Dam, "Trump Wasn't Just a Rural Phenomenon. Most of His Supporters Come from Cities and Suburbs," *Washington Post*, November 18, 2020, www.washingtonpost.com/business/2020/11/18/rural-city-trump-voters/.

11. D. T. Lichter and D. L. Brown, "Rural America in an Urban Society: Changing Spatial and Social Boundaries," *Annual Review of Sociology* 37, no. 1 (2011): 565–592.

12. Tim Marema, "Rural Population Declines Slightly over Last Decade, Census Shows," *Daily Yonder*, September 7, 2021, https://dailyyonder.com/rural-population-declines-slightly-over-last-decade-census-shows/2021/09/07/; J. Crabtree, "A Different Path for Rural America," *American Journal of Economics and Sociology* 75, no. 3 (2016): 605–622.

13. Sarah Chaney Cambon and Andrew Mollica, "Rural Counties Are Booming, but Can It Last?," *Wall Street Journal*, June 28, 2022, www.wsj.com/articles/rural-counties-are-booming-pandemic-back-to-office-work-from-home-11656423785.

14. America Counts, "One in Five Americans Live in Rural Areas," US Census Bureau, August 9, 2017, www.census.gov/library/stories/2017/08/rural-america.html.

15. Shankar Vedantam, "Strangers in Their Own Land: The 'Deep Story' of Trump Supporters," January 24, 2017, in *Hidden Brain*, podcast, www.npr.org/2017/01/24/510567860/strangers-in-their-own-land-the-deep-story-of-trump-supporters.

16. Yanna Krupnikov and John Barry Ryan, *The Other Divide: Polarization and Disengagement in American Politics* (Cambridge: Cambridge University Press, 2022).

17. Ezra Klein and Barack Obama, "Obama Explains How America Went from 'Yes We Can' to 'MAGA'," June 1, 2021, in *The Ezra Klein Show*, podcast transcript, *New York Times*, www.nytimes.com/2021/06/01/opinion/ezra-klein-podcast-barack-obama.html.

18. Ezra Klein and George Saunders, "Ezra Klein Interviews George Saunders," February 19, 2021, in *The Ezra Klein Show*, podcast, www.nytimes.com/2021/02/19/podcasts/ezra-klein-show-george-saunders-transcript.html.

CHAPTER 1: WE ARE NOT SO DIFFERENT, YOU AND ME

1. Carmine Gallo, "Brené Brown's Presentation Caught Oprah's Attention. The Same Skills Can Work for You," *Forbes*, October 11, 2013, www.forbes

.com/sites/carminegallo/2013/10/11/brene-browns-presentation-caught
-oprahs-attention-the-same-skills-can-work-for-you/?sh=57a3f10653c1.

2. Edward-Isaac Dovere, "Democratic Governors Worry About Threat
to Democracy but Don't See It as a Winning Message for 2022," CNN, December 13, 2021, www.cnn.com/2021/12/12/politics/democratic-governors
-2022-messaging/index.html.

3. Bill Toner, "The Impact of Agreement Bias on the Ranking of Questionnaire Response," *Journal of Social Psychology* 127, no. 2 (1987): 221–222;
John J. Ray, "Acquiescence and Problems with Forced-Choice Scales." *Journal of Social Psychology* 130, no. 3 (1990): 379–399.

4. "Binary Choice Questions: Compelling Findings About the Coronavirus," Great Book, https://greatbrook.com/binary-choice-questions
-compelling-findings-about-the-coronavirus/#after_section_1.

5. Manuel Castells, "The Impact of the Internet on Society: A Global
Perspective," in *Change: 19 Key Essays on How the Internet Is Changing Our
Lives* (Bilbao, Spain: BBVA, 2014).

6. Richard Harwood, "The Alienated American Voter: Are the News
Media to Blame?," Brookings, September 1, 1996, www.brookings.edu/articles
/the-alienated-american-voter-are-the-news-media-to-blame/.

7. Gallup and Knight Foundation, *American Views: Trust, Media and
Democracy* (Washington, DC: Gallup, 2018).

8. Steven Pinker, "The Media Exaggerates Negative News. This
Distortion Has Consequences," *Guardian*, February 17, 2018, www
.theguardian.com/commentisfree/2018/feb/17/steven-pinker-media
-negative-news.

9. Katie Rogers, "What Is a Constant Cycle of Violent News Doing to
Us?," *New York Times*, July 15, 2016, www.nytimes.com/2016/07/16/health
/what-is-a-constant-cycle-of-violent-news-doing-to-us.html; Hannah R. Stevens, Yoo Jung Oh, and Laramie D. Taylor, "Desensitization to Fear-Inducing
COVID-19 Health News on Twitter: Observational Study," *JMIR Infodemiology* 1, no. 1 (2021).

10. Please see the previous chapter and the appendix for a more detailed description of the General Social Survey.

11. Some data sets include both 2014 and 2018 data because particular
questions are not asked in each year.

12. "Manchester, Kentucky," City-Data, www.city-data.com/city/Man
chester-Kentucky.html.

13. Danzy Senna, "Robin DiAngelo and the Problem with Anti-racist
Self-Help," *Atlantic*, August 3, 2021, www.theatlantic.com/magazine/archive
/2021/09/martin-learning-in-public-diangelo-nice-racism/619497/.

14. Justin Curtis, "The Effect of the 2020 Racial Justice Protests on Attitudes and Preferences in Rural and Urban America," *Social Science Quarterly* 103, no. 1 (January 2022): 90–107, https://doi.org/10.1111/ssqu.13105.

15. April Simpson, "Why Rural America Is Joining the Movement for Black Lives," *Stateline* (blog), Pew Charitable Trusts, June 12, 2020, www.pewtrusts.org/en/research-and-analysis/blogs/stateline/2020/06/12/why-rural-america-is-joining-the-movement-for-black-lives.

16. Curtis, "The Effect of the 2020 Racial Justice Protests."

17. Lawrence Bobo and Frederick Licari, "Education and Political Tolerance: Testing the Effects of Cognitive Sophistication and Target Group Affect," *Public Opinion Quarterly* 53, no. 3 (1998): 285–308; Herbert McClosky, "Consensus and Ideology in American Politics," *American Political Science Review* 58, no. 2 (1964): 361–382; Louk Hagendoorn and Shervin Nekuee, *Education and Racism: A Cross National Inventory of Positive Effects of Education on Ethnic Tolerance* (London: Routledge, 1999).

18. Mary R. Jackman, "General and Applied Tolerance: Does Education Increase Commitment to Racial Integration?," *American Journal of Political Science* 22, no. 2 (1978): 302–324.

19. Frank Newport, "Affirmative Action and Public Opinion," Gallup, August 7, 2020, https://news.gallup.com/opinion/polling-matters/317006/affirmative-action-public-opinion.aspx.

20. Pew Research Center, *Conflicted Views of Affirmative Action*, May 14, 2003, www.pewresearch.org/politics/2003/05/14/conflicted-views-of-affirmative-action/.

21. Isaac Chotiner, "A Political Scientist Defends White Identity Politics," *New Yorker*, April 30, 2019, www.newyorker.com/news/q-and-a/a-political-scientist-defends-white-identity-politics-eric-kaufmann-whiteshift-book.

22. Eric Kaufmann, "Americans Are Divided by Their Views on Race, Not Race Itself," *New York Times*, March 18, 2019, www.nytimes.com/2019/03/18/opinion/race-america-trump.html; also Eric Kaufmann, *Whiteshift: Populism, Immigration, and the Future of White Majorities* (New York: Abrams, 2018).

23. Danya E. Keene and Mark B. Padilla, "Race, Class and the Stigma of Place: Moving to 'Opportunity' in Eastern Iowa," *Health & Place* 16, no. 6 (November 2010): 1216–1223, https://doi.org/10.1016/j.healthplace.2010.08.006; Samuel P. Oliner and Jerrald D. Krause, "Racial and Ethnic Attitudes in Rural America: Focus on Humboldt County, California," *Humboldt Journal of Social Relations* 26, no. 1/2 (2001): 11–55.

24. B. Keith Payne, Heidi A. Vuletich, and Jazmin L. Brown-Iannuzzi, "Historical Roots of Implicit Bias in Slavery," *PNAS* 116, no. 24 (May 28, 2019): 11693–11698, https://doi.org/10.1073/pnas.1818816116.

25. Michèle Lamont et al., "Bridging Cultural Sociology and Cognitive Psychology in Three Contemporary Research Programmes," *Nature Human Behaviour* 1, no. 12 (December 2017): 866–872.

26. "Islamophobia: Understanding Anti-Muslim Sentiment in the West," Gallup, n.d., https://news.gallup.com/poll/157082/islamophobia-understanding-anti-muslim-sentiment-west.aspx.

27. Eugene K. Ofosu et al., "Same-Sex Marriage Legalization Associated with Reduced Implicit and Explicit Antigay Bias," *PNAS* 116, no. 18 (April 15, 2019), https://doi.org/10.1073/pnas.1806000116.

28. Sarah Boxer, "Truth or Lies? In Sex Surveys, You Never Know," *New York Times*, July 22, 2000, https://archive.nytimes.com/www.nytimes.com/library/arts/072200sex-surveys.html.

29. Please see appendix for more comprehensive GSS results on this topic.

30. Richard Rothstein, *The Color of Law: A Forgotten History of How Our Government Segregated America* (New York: Liveright, 2017); Kenneth T. Jackson, *Crabgrass Frontier: The Suburbanization of the United States* (New York: Oxford University Press, 1985); Isabel Wilkerson, *Caste: The Origins of Our Discontents* (New York: Random House, 2020).

31. Elizabeth Seale, "Coping Strategies of Urban and Rural Welfare Organisations and the Regulation of the Poor," *New Political Economy* 18, no. 2 (April 25, 2012): 141–170, https://doi.org/10.1080/13563467.2012.664124.

32. Paul H. Stuart, "Conceptual and Historical Foundations of Rural Social Welfare," in *Rural Social Work: Building and Sustaining Community Capacity*, eds. T. Laine Scales, Calvin L. Streeter, and H. Stephen Cooper (Hoboken, NJ: John Wiley & Sons, 2014).

33. Rachel Sherman, *Uneasy Street: The Anxieties of Affluence* (Princeton, NJ: Princeton University Press, 2017).

34. Rachel Sherman, "Conflicted Cultivation: Parenting, Privilege, and Moral Worth in Wealthy New York Families," *American Journal of Cultural Sociology* 5 (2017a): 1–33.

35. Rachel Sherman, "'A Very Expensive Ordinary Life': Consumption, Symbolic Boundaries and Moral Legitimacy Among New York Elites," *Socio-Economic Review* 16, no. 2 (2018): 411–433.

36. While, for the most part, this was my sense of how rural Americans viewed mobility, I would be remiss to not address some of the stereotyping around social policy in America. Notions of the "welfare queen," for example, permeate public media and shape Americans' views of who is on welfare (i.e., Black women who are not working hard to rise above obstacles

or have "uncontrolled fecundity"). See also Franklin D. Gilliam Jr., "The 'Welfare Queen' Experiment," *Nieman Reports* 53, no. 2 (1999): 49–52.

37. For more of Professor David Runciman's brilliance on Tocqueville and other great thinkers, please see his *Talking Politics* podcast. Here is the link to his discussion of Tocqueville, of which I have borrowed much: https://play.acast.com/s/history-of-ideas/tocquevilleondemocracy.

38. Patrick Healey, "What Surprised Us in Focus Groups with Voters About Jan. 6," *New York Times*, January 7, 2022, www.nytimes.com/2022/01 /07/opinion/voter-focus-groups-jan-6.html.

CHAPTER 2: YOU'D BE SURPRISED HOW WELL WE ARE DOING

1. William Cronon, *Nature's Metropolis* (New York: Norton, 1991), xiv.

2. Carnes and Lupu, "The White Working Class."

3. Arlie R. Hochschild, "How the White Working Class Is Being Destroyed," *New York Times*, March 17, 2020, www.nytimes.com/2020/03/17 /books/review/deaths-of-despair-and-the-future-of-capitalism-anne-case -angus-deaton.html.

4. Edward L. Glaeser and Albert Saiz, "The Rise of the Skilled City," *Brookings-Wharton Papers on Urban Affairs* (2004): 47–105.

5. Glaeser and Saiz, "The Rise of the Skilled City"; Paul M. Romer, "The Origins of Endogenous Growth," *Journal of Economic Perspectives* 8, no. 1 (1994): 3–22, https://doi.org/10.1257/jep.8.1.3; Paul M. Romer, "Increasing Returns and Long-Run Growth," *Journal of Political Economy* 94, no. 5 (1986): 1002–1037, https://doi.org/10.1086/261420.

6. Saskia Sassen, *The Global City: New York, London, Tokyo* (Princeton, NJ: Princeton University Press, 1991).

7. The data represents median numbers.

8. Comparisons to small towns is based on 2016 five-year ACS data. Statewide comparisons are derived from 2019 five-year data. Five-year data tends to be stable, and thus comparisons between the data are reasonable.

9. Eduardo Porter, "The Hard Truths of Trying to 'Save' the Rural Economy," *New York Times*, December 14, 2018, www.nytimes.com/interactive /2018/12/14/opinion/rural-america-trump-decline.html.

10. Dylan Shane Connor and Michael Storper, "The Changing Geography of Social Mobility in the United States," *PNAS* 117, no. 48 (November 16, 2020), https://doi.org/10.1073/pnas.2010222117.

11. J. D. Vance, *Hillbilly Elegy: A Memoir of a Family and Culture in Crisis* (New York: Harper, 2016); Anne Case and Angus Deaton, *Deaths of Despair and the Future of Capitalism* (Princeton, NJ: Princeton University Press, 2020).

12. Arthur Getis and Judith Getis, "Christaller's Central Place Theory," *Journal of Geography* 65, no. 5 (1966), https://doi.org/10.1080/00221346608982415.

13. L. M. Hartman and David Seckler, "Towards the Application of Dynamic Growth Theory to Regions," in *Regional Economics*, ed. Harry W. Richardson (London: Palgrave Macmillan, 1970), https://doi.org/10.1007/978-1-349-15404-3_8.

14. Richard S. Conway Jr., "Economic Base Theory of Regional Growth," in *Empirical Regional Economics*, 3–21 (Cham, Switzerland: Springer, 2022).

15. Richard Hernandez, "The Fall of Employment in the Manufacturing Sector," *Monthly Labor Review* (August 2018).

16. Jane Jacobs, *The Economy of Cities* (New York: Vintage, 1970); Edward L. Glaeser, *Triumph of the City: How Our Greatest Invention Makes Us Richer, Smarter, Greener, Healthier, and Happier* (New York: Penguin, 2011); Glaeser and Saiz, "The Rise of the Skilled City."

17. Sassen, *The Global City*; Manuel Castells, *The Information Age: Economy, Society and Culture*, 3 vols. (Cambridge, MA, and Oxford: Blackwell, 1996–1998).

18. Edward L. Glaeser and Jesse M. Shapiro, *City Growth and the 2000 Census: Which Places Grew, and Why* (Washington, DC: Brookings, 2001), www.brookings.edu/wp-content/uploads/2016/06/whygrowth.pdf; Edward L. Glaeser, "Urban Colossus: Why Is New York America's Largest City?" (NBER working paper no. 11389, National Bureau of Economic Research, Cambridge, MA, June 2005), www.nber.org/papers/w11398.

19. Romer, "The Origins of Endogenous Growth."

20. Romer, "Increasing Returns."

21. Statista Research Department, "Percentage Added to the Gross Domestic Product (GDP) of the United States of America in 2020, by Industry," Statista, June 3, 2021, www.statista.com/statistics/248004/percentage-added-to-the-us-gdp-by-industry/.

22. Paul Krugman, *Geography and Trade* (Cambridge, MA: MIT Press, 1992); Paul Krugman, "Increasing Returns and Economic Geography," *Journal of Political Economy* 99, no. 3 (June 1991).

23. Michael J. Handel, "Skills Mismatch in the Labor Market," *Annual Review of Sociology* 29, no. 1 (August 2003): 135–165.

24. Isabella Simonetti, "Over 360 Newspapers Have Closed Since Just Before the Start of the Pandemic," *New York Times*, June 29, 2022, www.nytimes.com/2022/06/29/business/media/local-newspapers-pandemic.html.

25. Technically called the "east south central division" by the Census.

26. Gregory F. Randolph and Elizabeth Currid-Halkett, "Planning in the Era of Regional Divergence: Place, Scale, and Development in Confronting Spatial Inequalities." *Journal of the American Planning Association* (2021): 1–8.

27. Mark Muro and Andre M. Perry, "Regional Divergence Is More than an Economic Dilemma—It's a Civil Rights Issue," Brookings, January 28, 2020, www.brookings.edu/blog/the-avenue/2020/01/28/regional-divergence-is-more-than-an-economic-dilemma-its-a-civil-rights-issue/.

28. "The Opportunity Atlas," US Census Bureau and Opportunity Insights, www.opportunityatlas.org/.

29. Enrico Moretti, *The New Geography of Jobs* (New York: HarperCollins, 2012).

30. Joseph Gyourko, Christopher Mayer, and Todd Sinai, "Superstar Cities," *American Economic Journal: Economic Policy* 5, no. 4 (2013): 167–199; Richard Florida, *The Rise of the Creative Class* (New York: Basic Books, 2002); Michael Storper, "Separate Worlds? Explaining the Current Wave of Regional Economic Polarization." *Journal of Economic Geography* 18, no. 2 (2018): 247–270.

CHAPTER 3: LIFE CHANCES

1. Horatio Alger, *Ragged Dick* (Boston: A.K. Loring, 1868).

2. Barbara Kingsolver, *Demon Copperhead* (New York: Harper, 2022).

3. Katherine M. Keyes et al., "Understanding the Rural–Urban Differences in Nonmedical Prescription Opioid Use and Abuse in the United States," *American Journal of Public Health* 104, no. 2 (February 1, 2014): e52-e59; Christine Hancock et al., *Treating the Rural Opioid Epidemic* (Washington, DC: National Rural Health Association, 2017), www.ruralhealth.us/NRHA/media/Emerge_NRHA/Advocacy/Policy%20documents/Treating-the-Rural-Opioid-Epidemic_Feb-2017_NRHA-Policy-Paper.pdf.

4. "Small Towns and Rural Areas Hit Hard by Opioid Crisis," CBHA, August 2020, www.cbha.org/about-us/cbha-blog/2020/august/small-towns-and-rural-areas-hit-hard-by-opioid-c/; National Center for Health Statistics, "Drug Overdose Mortality by State," CDC, last modified March 1, 2022, www.cdc.gov/nchs/pressroom/sosmap/drug_poisoning_mortality/drug_poisoning.htm.

5. National Center for Health Statistics, "Drug Overdose Mortality."

6. Eric Eyre, *Death in Mudlick: A Coal Country Fight Against the Drug Companies that Delivered the Opioid Epidemic* (New York: Scribner, 2020).

7. Chris McGreal, "Why Were Millions of Opioid Pills Sent to a West Virginia Town of 3,000?," *Guardian*, October 2, 2019, www.theguardian.com/us-news/2019/oct/02/opioids-west-virginia-pill-mills-pharmacies.

8. McGreal, "Why Were Millions."

9. Southern District of West Virginia US Attorney's Office, "Mingo County Pharmacist Sentenced to Prison Time for Conspiracy to Acquire Controlled Substances by Fraud," FBI Pittsburgh Division, news release, November 15, 2012, https://archives.fbi.gov/archives/pittsburgh/press-releases/2012/mingo-county-pharmacist-sentenced-to-prison-time-for-conspiracy-to-acquire-controlled-substances-by-fraud.

10. Eric Eyre, "Morrisey's Wife Lobbied on Opioids for Drug Firm, Disclosures Say," *Charleston Gazette-Mail*, April 28, 2018, www.wvgazettemail.com/news/politics/morriseys-wife-lobbied-on-opioids-for-drug-firm-disclosures-say/article_be3d9ee8-00e1-570c-b161-c7b59c7c31d0.html; Louis Jacobson, "A Closer Look at Patrick Morrisey's Family Ties to 'Big Pharma,'" *Politifact*, March 28, 2018, www.politifact.com/article/2018/mar/27/closer-look-patrick-morriseys-family-ties-big-phar/.

11. Jim Axelrod and Ashley Velie, "West Virginia AG's Past Work with Drug Companies Questioned," *CBS Evening News*, June 2, 2016, www.cbsnews.com/news/questions-raised-about-west-virginia-attorney-generals-past-with-drug-companies/; Jacobson, "A Closer Look."

12. Axelrod and Velie, "West Virginia AG's Past Work."

13. Brian Saady, "A Real Killing: How Greedy Corporate Pushers Caused the Opioid Crisis," *American Conservative*, January 23, 2019, www.theamericanconservative.com/how-the-corporate-pill-pushers-started-the-opioid-crisis/; Axelrod and Velie, "West Virginia AG's Past Work"; Julia Lurie, "He's Running as a Hero of the Opioid Epidemic. Here's the Catch," *Mother Jones*, July 13, 2018, www.motherjones.com/politics/2018/07/hes-running-as-a-hero-of-the-opioid-epidemic-heres-the-catch/; Story Hinckley, "One West Virginia City's Pioneering Approach to Opioid Crisis," *Christian Science Monitor*, May 22, 2017, www.csmonitor.com/USA/Society/2017/0522/One-West-Virginia-city-s-pioneering-approach-to-opioid-crisis.

14. Hinckley, "One West Virginia City's Pioneering Approach."

15. Courtney Hessler, "West Virginia Files Lawsuit Against Kroger for Opioid Distribution Practices," *Herald-Dispatch*, August 25, 2022, www.herald-dispatch.com/news/west-virginia-files-lawsuit-against-kroger-for-opioid-distribution-practices/article_3979d24c-5ee7-5ce9-983a-738ffdda8fef.html; Lurie, "He's Running as a Hero"; Chris Dickerson, "Jenkins Says Morrisey Has Conflict of Interest About Opioids," *West Virginia Record*,

February 6, 2018, https://wvrecord.com/stories/511331505-jenkins-says
-morrisey-has-conflict-of-interest-about-opioids.

16. See also Hinckley, "One West Virginia City's Pioneering Approach."

17. Axelrod and Velie, "West Virginia AG's Past Work"; Dickerson,
"Jenkins Says."

18. "Meet the Attorney General: Patrick Morrisey," Office of the WV
Attorney General, State of West Virginia, n.d., https://ago.wv.gov/about
/Meet%20the%20AG/Pages/default.aspx.

19. Caroline MacGregor, "West Virginia Reaches Landmark Settlement
with 'Big Three' Opioid Distributors," West Virginia Public Broadcasting,
August 1, 2022, www.wvpublic.org/government/2022-08-01/west-virginia
-reaches-landmark-settlement-with-big-three-opioid-distributors; Kris Maher, "West Virginia Reaches $400 Million Opioid Deal with Distributors,"
Wall Street Journal, August 2, 2022, www.wsj.com/articles/west-virginia
-reaches-400-million-opioid-deal-with-distributors-11659460919.

20. Dietrich Knauth, "West Virginia Cities Reach $400 Mln Opioid
Distributor Settlement," Reuters, August 1, 2022, www.reuters.com/business
/healthcare-pharmaceuticals/west-virginia-cities-reach-400-mln-opioid
-distributor-deal-2022-08-01/.

21. Corinne Ramey and Sara Randazzo, "McKesson, Amerisource-
Bergen and Cardinal Health Not Liable for Opioid Crisis in West Virginia, Court Rules," *Wall Street Journal*, July 5, 2022, www.wsj.com/articles
/distributors-not-liable-for-opioid-crisis-in-west-virginia-court-rules
-11657036182; Nate Raymond, "U.S. Drug Distributors Prevail in $2.5 Billion
West Virginia Opioid Case," Reuters, July 3, 2022, www.reuters.com/world
/us/us-drug-distributors-prevail-25-billion-west-virginia-opioid-case-2022
-07-04/.

22. Charles D. Kolstad, "What Is Killing the US Coal Industry?," Stanford Institute for Economic Policy Research, March 2017, https://siepr
.stanford.edu/publications/policy-brief/what-killing-us-coal-industry.

23. Hochschild, "How the White Working Class Is Being Destroyed."

24. Céilí Doyle and Sheridan Hendrix, "Trump Promised to Bring
Back Coal in Appalachia. Here's Why That Didn't Happen," *Columbus Dispatch*,
October 20, 2020, www.dispatch.com/story/news/environment/2020/10/20
/trump-promised-bring-back-coal-appalachia-has-he/5866420002/.

25. Atul Gawande, "Why Americans Are Dying from Despair," *New
Yorker*, March 23, 2020, www.newyorker.com/magazine/2020/03/23/why
-americans-are-dying-from-despair.

26. Angus Deaton, *The Great Escape: Health, Wealth, and the Origins of
Inequality* (Princeton, NJ: Princeton University Press, 2013).

27. Gawande, "Why Americans."

28. Case and Deaton, *Deaths of Despair*.

29. US Department of Justice, "Justice Department Announces Global Resolution of Criminal and Civil Investigations with Opioid Manufacturer Purdue Pharma and Civil Settlement with Members of the Sackler Family," news release, October 21, 2020, www.justice.gov/opa/pr/justice-department -announces-global-resolution-criminal-and-civil-investigations-opioid; Brian Mann and Martha Bebinger, "Purdue Pharma, Sacklers Reach $6 Billion Deal with State Attorneys General," NPR, March 3, 2022, www.npr .org/2022/03/03/1084163626/purdue-sacklers-oxycontin-settlement#:~: text=Purdue%20Pharma%20has%20admitted%20criminal,a%20separate %20settlement%20in%202020.

30. Dietrich Knauth, Jonathan Stempel, and Tom Hals, "Sacklers to Pay $6 Billion to Settle Purdue Opioid Lawsuits," Reuters, March 4, 2022, www.reuters.com/business/healthcare-pharmaceuticals/sacklers-will-pay-up-6-bln-resolve-purdue-opioid-lawsuits-mediator-2022-03-03/; Mann and Bebinger, "Purdue Pharma."

31. "A Time of Crisis for the Opioid Epidemic in the USA," *Lancet*, July 24, 2021, www.thelancet.com/journals/lancet/article/PIIS0140 -6736(21)01653-6/fulltext.

32. Ailsa Chang, Noah Caldwell, and Christopher Intagliata, "'Empire of Pain: The Secret History of the Sackler Dynasty' Profiles Pharma Family," NPR, April 13, 2021, www.npr.org/2021/04/13/986929541/empire-of-pain -the-secret-history-of-the-sackler-dynasty-profiles-pharma-family.

33. The HRS is a nationally representative, longitudinal panel study of Americans aged fifty-one and older. Through in-depth interviews, the HRS collects information on a rich set of health and socioeconomic characteristics for approximately twenty thousand respondents every two years. The data collected includes family structure and demographics; health behaviors and diagnosed conditions; employment, income, and wealth; and other information pertinent to studies of aging. This study used the RAND HRS Longitudinal File (2018, V1), a cleaned and stream-lined version of the HRS data created by the RAND Center for the Study of Aging.

34. Monica Potts, "Why Being Anti-Science Is Now Part of Many Rural Americans' Identity," *FiveThirtyEight*, April 25, 2022, https://fivethirty eight.com/features/why-being-anti-science-is-now-part-of-many-rural -americans-identity/.

35. See also Adriana Lleras-Muney, "The Relationship Between Education and Adult Mortality in the United States." *Review of Economic Studies*

72, no. 1 (2005): 189–221; and Adriana Lleras-Muney, "Education and Income Gradients in Longevity: The Role of Policy" (NBER working paper no. 29694, National Bureau of Economic Research, Cambridge, MA, January 2022), www.nber.org/papers/w29694.

36. David G. Blanchflower and Andrew J. Oswald, "Trends in Extreme Distress in the United States, 1993–2019," *American Journal of Public Health* 110, no. 10 (October 1, 2020): 1538–1544.

37. Anne Case and Angus Deaton, "The Great Divide: Education, Despair and Death" (NBER working paper no. 29241, National Bureau of Economic Research, Cambridge, MA, September 2021), www.nber.org/papers/w29241.

38. Jason Fletcher and Hamid Noghanibehambari, "The Effects of Education on Mortality: Evidence Using College Expansions" (NBER working paper no. 29423, National Bureau of Economic Research, Cambridge, MA, October 2021), www.nber.org/papers/w29423.

39. Fletcher and Noghanibehambari, "The Effects of Education on Mortality."

40. Anne Case and Angus Deaton, "Life Expectancy in Adulthood Is Falling for Those Without a BA Degree, but as Educational Gaps Have Widened, Racial Gaps Have Narrowed," *PNAS* 118, no. 11 (2021), www.pnas.org/doi/10.1073/pnas.2024777118.

CHAPTER 4: COGNITIVE DISSONANCE

1. F. Scott Fitzgerald, *The Crack-Up* (New York: New Directions, 1945).

2. Michael Wines and Nick Corasaniti, "Arizona Vote Review 'Made Up the Numbers,' Election Experts Say," *New York Times*, October 1, 2021, www.nytimes.com/2021/10/01/us/arizona-election-review.html; Ben Giles, "Arizona Recount of 2020 Election Ballots Found No Proof of Corruption," NPR, September 25, 2021, www.npr.org/2021/09/25/1040672550/az-audit.

3. Teddy Wayne, "Tucker Carlson on the Alien Invasion," *New Yorker*, May 9, 2022, www.newyorker.com/magazine/2022/05/16/tucker-carlson-defends-the-aliens-extraterrestrial-ones.

4. Emma Colton, "Arrests in Chicago Plummet to Historic Lows as Crime Rises and Police Admittedly Pull Back: 'No Way,'" Fox News, July 19, 2022, www.foxnews.com/us/arrests-chicago-plummet-historic-lows-crime-rises-police-admittedly-pull-back-no-way; Todd Starnes, "Hey, Black Lives Matter, Stop Terrorizing Our Cities," Fox News, July 28, 2016, www.foxnews.com/opinion/hey-black-lives-matter-stop-terrorizing-our-cities; Marco

Rubio, "Abortion Decision Exposes How Woke Corporations Are Hostile to American Families," Fox News, July 19, 2022, www.foxnews.com/opinion /abortion-decision-exposes-woke-corporations-hostile-american-families.

5. Edward W. Said, *Orientalism* (New York: Pantheon Books, 1978), 108.

6. Ernest Gellner, "The Mightier Pen? Edward Said and the Double Standards of Inside-Out Colonialism (Review of Culture and Imperialism by Edward Said)," *Times Literary Supplement*, February 19, 1993.

7. Bernard Lewis, "The Question of Orientalism," *New York Review of Books*, June 24, 1982.

8. Sean Illing, "A Princeton Sociologist Spent 8 Years Asking Rural Americans Why They're So Pissed Off," *Vox*, June 30, 2018, www.vox .com/2018/3/13/17053886/trump-rural-america-populism-racial-resentment.

9. Illing, "A Princeton Sociologist."

10. Said, *Orientalism*, 269.

11. Benedict Anderson, *Imagined Communities: Reflections on the Origins and Spread of Nationalism* (New York: Verso, 1991).

12. Akhil Gupta, "The Reincarnation of Souls and the Rebirth of Commodities: Representations of Time in 'East' and 'West,'" *Cultural Critique* 22 (1992): 187–211.

13. Sigmund Freud, *Civilization and Its Discontents* (1930).

14. Ezra Klein, *Why We're Polarized* (New York: Simon & Schuster, 2020). See also Stephen Metcalf, "Ezra Klein's 'Why We're Polarized' and the Drawbacks of Explainer Journalism," *New Yorker*, March 11, 2020, www .newyorker.com/books/under-review/ezra-kleins-why-were-polarized-and -the-drawbacks-of-explainer-journalism.

15. Akhil Gupta and James Ferguson, "Beyond 'Culture': Space, Identity, and the Politics of Difference," *Cultural Anthropology* 7, no. 1 (1992): 6–23.

16. Johannes Fabian, *Time and the Other: How Anthropology Makes Its Object* (New York: Columbia University Press, 1983).

17. Anderson, *Imagined Communities*.

18. Adeline Koh, "Imagined Communities, Social Media, and the Faculty," *Academe*, May–June 2016, www.aaup.org/article/imagined-communities-social -media-and-faculty#.YtbWcnbMJnI.

19. Gordon Allport and Bernard Kramer, "Some Roots of Prejudice," *Journal of Psychology* 22 (1946): 9–39.

20. Allport and Kramer, "Some Roots of Prejudice."

21. Irwin Katz, "Gordon Allport's *The Nature of Prejudice*," *Political Psychology* 12, no. 1 (1991): 125–157.

22. Thomas Pettigrew, "Intergroup Contact Theory," *Annual Review of Psychology* 49, no. 1 (1998): 65–85.

23. Marianne Bertrand and Esther Duflo, "Field Experiments on Discrimination," in *Handbook of Economic Field Experiments*, eds. Esther Duflo and Abhijit Banerjee, 309–393 (Amsterdam: North Holland, 2017).

24. See Katz, "Gordon Allport's *The Nature of Prejudice*."

25. Monica Potts, "In the Land of Self-Defeat," *New York Times*, October 4, 2019, www.nytimes.com/2019/10/04/opinion/sunday/trump-arkansas .html; Sarah Smarsh, "Dangerous Idiots: How the Liberal Media Elite Failed Working-Class Americans," *Guardian*, October 13, 2016, www.theguardian .com/media/2016/oct/13/liberal-media-bias-working-class-americans.

26. James Druckman et al., "(Mis-)Estimating Affective Polarization," *Journal of Politics* 84, no. 2 (April 2022).

27. James Druckman et al., "Affective Polarization, Local Contexts and Public Opinion in America," *Nature Human Behaviour* 5, no. 1 (2021): 28–38.

28. Druckman et al., "Affective Polarization."

29. Timothy Bella, "Tucker Carlson Falsely Claims Anthony S. Fauci 'Created' Covid," *Washington Post*, July 29, 2021, www.washingtonpost.com /health/2021/07/29/tucker-carlson-fauci-created-covid/.

30. Tiffany Hsu, "Despite Outbreaks Among Unvaccinated, Fox News Hosts Smear Shots," *New York Times*, July 11, 2021, www.nytimes.com/2021 /07/11/business/media/vaccines-fox-news-hosts.html.

31. Jacob Wallace, Paul Goldsmith-Pinkham, and Jason L. Schwartz, "Excess Death Rates for Republicans and Democrats During the COVID-19 Pandemic" (NBER working paper no. 30512, National Bureau of Economic Research, Cambridge, MA, September 2022), www.nber.org/papers/w30512.

32. Marlene Lenthang, "These Cities Have Reached Biden's 70% Vaccination Goal—and Beyond," ABC News, June 11, 2021, https://abcnews.go .com/Health/cities-reached-bidens-70-vaccination-goal/story?id=78195531.

33. Guy Lombardo and Linda Shahinian, "Letters to the Editor: We Need to Talk About Racism and 'Blue Lives Matter,'" *Los Angeles Times*, April 18, 2021, www.latimes.com/opinion/story/2021-04-18/racism-blue-lives-matter.

34. Jonathan Russell, "Here's What's Wrong with #BlueLivesMatter," *HuffPost*, July 9, 2016, www.huffpost.com/entry/heres-whats-wrong-with-bl _b_10906348.

35. Douglas Ahler and Gaurav Sood, "The Parties in Our Heads: Misperceptions About Party Composition and Their Consequences," *Journal of Politics* 80, no. 3 (2018): 964–981.

36. Eric Groenendyk, Michael Sances, and Kirill Zhirkov, "Intraparty Polarization in American Politics," *Journal of Politics* 82, no. 4 (2020).

37. Courtney Vinopal, "Two Out of Three Americans Believe US Democracy Is Under Threat," PBS Newshour, July 2, 2021.

38. Martin Pengelly, "Republican Party Calls January 6 Attack 'Legitimate Political Discourse,'" *Guardian*, February 4, 2022, www.theguardian.com/us-news/2022/feb/04/republicans-capitol-attack-legitimate-political-discourse-cheney-kinzinger-pence.

39. Emily Kubin and Christian von Sikorski, "The Role of (Social) Media in Political Polarization: A Systematic Review," *Annals of the International Communication Association* 45, no. 3 (September 21, 2021): 188–206, https://doi.org/10.1080/23808985.2021.1976070.

40. Kubin and von Sikorski, "The Role of (Social) Media."

41. Matthew Mendelsohn and Richard Nadeau, "The Magnification and Minimization of Social Cleavages by the Broadcast and Narrowcast News Media," *International Journal of Public Opinion Research* 8, no. 4 (Winter 1996): 374–389.

42. Bryan McLaughlin, "Commitment to the Team: Perceived Conflict and Political Polarization," *Journal of Media Psychology* 30, no. 1 (January 2018): 41–51, https://doi.org/10.1027/1864-1105/a000176.

43. John Fiske, *Media Matters: Race and Gender in U.S. Politics* (London: Routledge, 2016); Raymond Williams, *Marxism and Literature* (Oxford: Oxford University Press, 1977).

44. Sarah Sobieraj and Jeffrey M. Berry, "From Incivility to Outrage: Political Discourse in Blogs, Talk Radio, and Cable News," *Political Communication* 28, no. 1 (2011): 19–41, https://doi.org/10.1080/10584609.2010.542360.

45. Sobieraj and Berry, "From Incivility to Outrage."

46. Sobieraj and Berry, "From Incivility to Outrage"; D. A. Jones, "The Polarizing Effect of New Media Messages," *International Journal of Public Opinion Research* 14, no. 2 (2002): 158–174; Matthew Gentzkow and Jesse M. Shapiro, "What Drives Media Slant? Evidence From U.S. Daily Newspapers," *Econometrica* 78, no. 1 (January 2010): 35–71.

47. Nick Bowlin, "Joke's on Them: How Democrats Gave Up on Rural America," *Guardian*, February 22, 2022, www.theguardian.com/us-news/2022/feb/22/us-politics-rural-america.

48. Porter, "The Hard Truths of Trying to 'Save' the Rural Economy."

49. Gentzkow and Shapiro, "What Drives Media Slant?"; Matthew Gentzkow and Jesse M. Shapiro, "Media Bias and Reputation," *Journal of Political Economy* 114, no. 2 (April 2006): 280–316.

50. Michael W. Wagner and Mike Gruszczynski, "Who Gets Covered? Ideological Extremity and News Coverage of Members of the U.S. Congress, 1993 to 2013," *Journalism & Mass Communication Quarterly* 95, no. 3 (2013): 670–690, https://doi.org/10.1177/1077699017702836.

51. Toby Bolsen and Matthew A. Shapiro, "The US News Media, Polarization on Climate Change, and Pathways to Effective Communication," *Environmental Communication* 12, no. 2 (2018): 149–163.

52. Catherine "Dru" Glaze et al., "Visual Communications: An Analysis of University Students' Perceptions of Rural America Based on Select Photographs," *Journal of Applied Communications* 97, no. 1 (2013).

53. "You Asked, We Answered: Do the COVID-19 Vaccines Contain Aborted Fetal Cells?," Nebraska Medicine, August 18, 2021, www.nebraskamed .com/COVID/you-asked-we-answered-do-the-covid-19-vaccines-contain -aborted-fetal-cells; North Dakota Health, *COVID-19 Vaccines & Fetal Cell Lines*, August 17, 2022, www.health.nd.gov/sites/www/files/documents /COVID%20Vaccine%20Page/COVID-19_Vaccine_Fetal_Cell_Handout .pdf; Los Angeles County Department of Public Health, *COVID-19 Vaccine and Fetal Cell Lines*, April 20, 2021, http://publichealth.lacounty.gov /media/coronavirus/docs/vaccine/VaccineDevelopment_FetalCellLines.pdf.

54. Associated Press, "On COVID Vaccinations, Pope Says Health Care Is a 'Moral Obligation,'" NPR, January 10, 2022, www.npr.org /2022/01/10/1071785531/on-covid-vaccinations-pope-says-health-care-is-a -moral-obligation.

55. Owen Dyer, "Founder of America's Frontline Doctors Is Sentenced to Prison for Role in Capitol Riot," *BMJ*, June 22, 2022, www.bmj .com/content/377/bmj.o1533; Vera Bergengruen, "How 'America's Frontline Doctors' Sold Access to Bogus COVID-19 Treatments—and Left Patients in the Lurch," *Time*, August 26, 2021, https://time.com/6092368 /americas-frontline-doctors-covid-19-misinformation/; US House Select Subcommittee on the Coronavirus Crisis, "Select Subcommittee Launches Investigation into Online Entities Pushing Coronavirus Misinformation and Selling Unproven Treatments," news release, October 29, 2021, https:// coronavirus.house.gov/news/press-releases/select-subcommittee-launches -investigation-online-entities-pushing-coronavirus; Wikipedia, s.v. "America's Frontline Doctors," last modified July 13, 2022, 00:27, https://en.wikipedia .org/wiki/America's_Frontline_Doctors.

56. Spencer S. Hsu, "Anti-vaccine Doctor Sentenced to Prison for Jan. 6 Trespassing," *Washington Post*, June 16, 2022, www.washington post.com/national-security/2022/06/16/simone-gold-sentenced/; "GOLD, Simone Melissa," case no. 1:21-cr-85, US Attorney's Office, District of Columbia, last modified June 16, 2022, www.justice.gov/usao-dc/defendants /gold-simone-melissa; Stephanie Mencimer, "Doctor, Lawyer, Insurrectionist: The Radicalization of Simone Gold," *Mother Jones*, May 6, 2021, www.mother

jones.com/politics/2021/05/doctor-lawyer-insurrectionist-the-radicalization
-of-simone-gold/.

57. Michael Coren, "When True Believers Become a Danger to Themselves
and Others," *Globe and Mail*, August 13, 2021, www.theglobeandmail.com
/opinion/article-when-true-believers-become-a-danger-to-themselves-and
-others/; Mother Miriam, "COVID Vaccines Have Been 'Designed to Kill Off
the Population,'" October 7, 2021, in *Mother Miriam Live*, podcast, https://
play.acast.com/s/mother-miriam-live/covid-vaccines-have-been-designed-to
-kill-off-the-population.

58. Associated Press, "Wisconsin Priest Flouts 'Godless' COVID Protocols," *Catholic Reporter*, April 26, 2021, www.ncronline.org/news/coronavirus
/wisconsin-priest-flouts-godless-covid-protocols; Darragh Roche, "Priest Says
COVID Rules Enforcers Will Burn in 'Hottest Levels' of Hell," *Newsweek*,
April 27, 2021, www.newsweek.com/priest-says-covid-rules-enforcers-will
-burn-hottest-levels-hell-1586634.

59. Todd Richmond, "Father James Altman, Who Said Democrats Would
Burn in Hell and Called Covid Restrictions 'Nazi-Esque,' Removed by His
Bishop," *America*, July 9, 2021, www.americamagazine.org/faith/2021/07/09
/father-james-altman-removed-wisconsin-bishop-241015; CNA Staff, "La
Crosse Bishop Removes Father Altman from Ministry," Catholic News Agency,
July 9, 2021, www.catholicnewsagency.com/news/248326/la-crosse-bishop
-removes-father-altman-from-ministry.

60. Dan Merica, "Trump Met with Boos After Revealing He Received
Covid-19 Booster," CNN, December 21, 2021, www.cnn.com/2021/12/20
/politics/donald-trump-booster-shot-boos/index.html.

61. Sheera Frenkel, "The Most Influential Spreader of Coronavirus Misinformation Online," *New York Times*, July 24, 2021, www.nytimes.com/2021
/07/24/technology/joseph-mercola-coronavirus-misinformation-online.html.

62. In a 2008 article looking at rural views on immigration, the authors
found that many of the youth interviewed expressed "norms of tolerance
and civility." James G. Gimpel and J. Celeste Lay, "Political Socialization and Reactions to Immigration-Related Diversity in Rural America,"
Rural Sociology 73, no. 2 (June 2008): 180–204, https://doi.org/10.1526
/003601108784514561.

CHAPTER 5: THE MERITOCRACY BIAS

1. Interview with me, October 18, 2021.

2. Caroline M. Hoxby, "The Changing Selectivity of American Colleges," *Journal of Economic Perspectives* 23, no. 4 (Fall 2009): 95–118; Jeffrey

Selingo, "The College-Admissions Process Is Completely Broken," *Atlantic*, March 23, 2022, www.theatlantic.com/ideas/archive/2022/03/change -college-acceptance-application-process/627581/; Emily Brehe-Gunter, "1995 vs. 2020: How College Admissions Has Changed over the Past 25 Years," KD College Prep, June 26, 2020, https://kdcollegeprep.com/how -college-admissions-changed-last-25-years/.

3. Sonja Ardoin, *College Aspirations and Access in Working-Class Rural Communities: The Mixed Signals, Challenges, and New Language First-Generation Students Encounter* (London: Lexington Books, 2017).

4. Casey Parks, "The Tragedy of America's Rural Schools," *New York Times*, September 7, 2021, www.nytimes.com/2021/09/07/magazine/rural -public-education.html.

5. Pamela Druckerman, *Bringing Up Bébé: One American Mother Discovers the Wisdom of French Parenting* (New York: Penguin, 2012).

6. Emily Stewart, "The Problem with America's Semi-Rich," *Vox*, October 12, 2021, www.vox.com/the-goods/22673605/upper-middle-class -meritocracy-matthew-stewart.

7. Michael Young, *The Rise of the Meritocracy* (London: Thames & Hudson, 1958).

8. Phil Bell, "Book Review: The Meritocracy Trap by Daniel Markovits," *LSE Review of Books*, March 30, 2020, https://blogs.lse.ac.uk/lsereviewof books/2020/03/30/book-review-the-meritocracy-trap-by-daniel-markovits/.

9. Richard V. Reeves, *Dream Hoarders: How the American Upper Middle Class Is Leaving Everyone Else in the Dust, Why That Is a Problem, and What to Do About It* (Washington DC: Brookings Institution Press, 2017).

10. The study included data on students from public and private high schools who applied to nine highly selective colleges.

11. Thomas J. Espenshade and Alexandria Walton Radford, *No Longer Separate, Not Yet Equal: Race and Class in Elite College Admission and Campus Life* (Princeton, NJ: Princeton University Press, 2009), 92–94.

12. Espenshade and Radford, *No Longer Separate*, 98.

13. Douglas Belkin, "For Colleges, a Rural Reckoning," *Wall Street Journal*, December 1, 2017, www.wsj.com/articles/for-colleges-a-rural -reckoning-1512159888.

14. Patricia McDonough, *Choosing Colleges: How Social Class and Schools Structure Opportunity* (Albany, NY: SUNY Press, 1997).

15. Espenshade and Radford, *No Longer Separate*, 126.

16. Deborah Warnock, "Capitalizing Class: An Examination of Socio-economic Diversity on the Contemporary Campus," in *Working in Class:*

Recognizing How Social Class Shapes Our Academic Work, eds. Allison Hurst and Sandi Kawecka Nenga (Lantham, MD: Rowman & Littlefield, 2016).

17. Belkin, "For Colleges, a Rural Reckoning."

18. Belkin, "For Colleges, a Rural Reckoning."

19. Peter Sacks, *Tearing Down the Gates: Confronting the Class Divide in American Education* (Berkeley: University of California Press, 2007).

20. Peter Lemon, "Fox Host Tucker Carlson Says College Education 'Diminishes You' and 'Everyone Should Opt Out,'" *Newsweek*, April 24, 2021, www.newsweek.com/fox-host-tucker-carlson-says-college-education -diminishes-you-everyone-should-opt-out-1586212.

21. Caroline Hoxby and Christopher Avery, "The Missing 'One-Offs': The Hidden Supply of High-Achieving, Low Income Students" (NBER working paper no. 18586, National Bureau of Economic Research, Cambridge, MA, December 2012), www.nber.org/papers/w18586.

22. Hoxby and Avery, "The Missing 'One-Offs.'"

23. Jonathan Smith, Matea Pender, and Jessica Howell, "The Full Extent of Student-College Academic Undermatch," *Economics of Education Review* 32 (2013): 247–261.

24. Ardoin, *College Aspirations*.

25. Belkin, "For Colleges, a Rural Reckoning."

26. Julian Coman and Michael Sandel, "Michael Sandel: 'The Populist Backlash Has Been a Revolt Against the Tyranny of Merit,'" *Guardian*, September 6, 2020, www.theguardian.com/books/2020/sep/06/michael -sandel-the-populist-backlash-has-been-a-revolt-against-the-tyranny-of -merit.

27. Ardoin, *College Aspirations*.

28. Michael Corbett, *Learning to Leave: The Irony of Schooling in a Coastal Community* (Nova Scotia, Canada: Fernwood Publishing, 2007), 18.

29. Ardoin, *College Aspirations*.

30. Ardoin, *College Aspirations*.

31. Ardoin, *College Aspirations*.

32. Lynn O'Shaughnessy, "20 Surprising Higher Education Facts," *US News & World Report*, September 6, 2011, https://www.usnews.com/edu cation/blogs/the-college-solution/2011/09/06/20-surprising-higher -education-facts.

33. Raj Chetty et al., "Mobility Report Cards: The Role of Colleges in Intergenerational Mobility" (NBER working paper no. 23618, National Bureau of Economic Research, Cambridge, MA, July 2017), www.nber.org /papers/w23618.

34. Chetty et al., "Mobility Report Cards," 2017.

35. Suqin Ge, Elliott Isaac, and Amalia Miller, "Elite Schools and Opting In: Effects of College Selectivity on Career and Family Outcomes," *Journal of Labor Economics* 40, no. S1 (April 2022).

36. Derek Thompson, "The Myth of American Universities as Inequality-Fighters," *Atlantic*, August 31, 2017, www.theatlantic.com/business/archive/2017/08/universities-inequality-fighters/538566/.

37. Raj Chetty et al., "Mobility Report Cards: The Role of Colleges in Intergenerational Mobility," Equal Opportunity Project, 2018, https://opportunityinsights.org/wp-content/uploads/2018/03/coll_mrc_summary.pdf.

38. "Opportunity Atlas," accessed October 13, 2022.

39. To be clear, there are rural towns in deep poverty (just like some of our blighted inner-city neighborhoods). That is a significant problem that no amount of college prep programs will fix if we do not focus on the bigger structural issues and complete erosion of the local tax base. Underfunded urban schools get a lot of attention, and rightly so, but there are many more rural kids in greater poverty than even those attending urban public schools. As an article in the *New York Times* chronicled, rural schools often are missing books, Wi-Fi, and basic ventilation (an issue even before Covid). In a particularly poignant scene, the superintendent of a Mississippi school district asked the teachers if they had any final concerns. "The women told Henderson they had few complaints. Really, one woman whispered, there was only one. The school's drainage had stopped working, and sewage was spilling onto the kitchen floors." (Parks, "The Tragedy of America's Rural Schools.")

40. Stewart, "The Problem with America's Semi-Rich."

41. Gareth Cook, "The Economist Who Would Fix the American Dream," *Atlantic*, July 17, 2019, www.theatlantic.com/magazine/archive/2019/08/raj-chettys-american-dream/592804/.

42. Ben Steverman, "Harvard's Chetty Finds Economic Carnage in Wealthiest ZIP Codes," *Bloomberg*, September 24, 2020, www.bloomberg.com/news/features/2020-09-24/harvard-economist-raj-chetty-creates-god-s-eye-view-of-pandemic-damage.

43. Alex Bell et al., "Lost Einsteins: How Exposure to Innovation Influences Who Becomes an Inventor," *Vox EU*, December 24, 2017, https://voxeu.org/article/how-exposure-innovation-influences-who-becomes-inventor. See also Alex Bell et al., "Who Becomes an Inventor in America? The Importance of Exposure to Innovation," *Quarterly Journal of Economics* 134, no. 2 (2018).

44. Cook, "The Economist."

45. Raj Chetty et al., "How Does Your Kindergarten Classroom Affect Your Earnings? Evidence from Project Star," *Quarterly Journal of Economics* 126, no. 4 (2011): 1593–1660.

46. Valerie Michelman, Joseph Price, and Seth D. Zimmerman, "Old Boys' Clubs and Upward Mobility Among the Educational Elite," *Quarterly Journal of Economics* (2021).

47. David Brooks, "How the Bobos Broke America," *Atlantic*, August 2, 2021, www.theatlantic.com/magazine/archive/2021/09/blame-the-bobos -creative-class/619492/.

CHAPTER 6: MYTHOS AND LOGOS AND THE SEARCH FOR TRUTH

1. Erica Chidi and Gabby Bernstein, "The Power of Surrendering," February 15, 2022, in *The Goop Podcast*, podcast, https://goop.com/the -goop-podcast/the-power-of-surrendering/.

2. Alan Strathern, *Unearthly Powers: Religious and Political Change in World History* (Cambridge: Cambridge University Press, 2019).

3. Philip Gorski, "The Return of the King: The Politics of Immanence and the Disenchantments of Liberalism." *Hedgehog Review* (Spring 2022).

4. Richard Hofstadter, *Anti-intellectualism in American Life* (New York: Knopf, 1963).

5. Ann Taves, *Fits, Trances, and Visions: Experiencing Religion and Explaining Experience from Wesley to James* (Princeton: Princeton University Press, 1999); Jörg Stolz, "'All Things Are Possible': Towards a Sociological Explanation of Pentecostal Miracles and Healings," *Sociology of Religion* 72, no. 4 (winter 2011): 456–482.

6. Strathern, *Unearthly Powers*.

7. Strathern, *Unearthly Powers*.

8. Philip Gorski, *American Covenant: A History of Civil Religion from the Puritans to the Present* (Princeton, NJ: Princeton University Press, 2017).

9. Hofstadter, *Anti-intellectualism*.

10. Jessica Parr, "Guest Post: Cotton Mather and the Enlightenment in New England: Redefining the Holy Spirit," *Junto* (blog), June 26, 2017, https://earlyamericanists.com/2017/06/26/guest-post-cotton-mather -and-the-enlightenment-in-new-england-redefining-the-holy-spirit/; Cotton Mather, *Reasonable Religion. Or, the Truth of the Christian Religion, Demonstrated* (Boston, 1700); Cotton Mather, *A Man of Reason* (Boston, 1718); History.com Editors, "Great Awakening," History, March 7, 2018, www .history.com/topics/british-history/great-awakening.

11. David Sorkin, *The Religious Enlightenment: Protestants, Jews, and Catholics from London to Vienna* (Princeton, NJ: Princeton University Press, 2011).

12. Jon Butler, "Religion and Eighteenth-Century Revivalism," in *AP US History Study Guide* (New York: Gilder Lehrman Institute of American History, 2009), http://ap.gilderlehrman.org/history-by-era/religion-and -eighteenth-century-revivalism/essays/religion-and-eighteenth-century-rev; Christian Smith, *The Secular Revolution: Power, Interests, and Conflict in the Secularization of American Public Life* (Berkeley: University of California Press, 2003), 65–66.

13. Gorski, *American Covenant*.

14. Hofstadter, *Anti-intellectualism*, 68–69.

15. Gorski, *American Covenant*.

16. Hofstadter, *Anti-intellectualism*, 55; Smith, *The Secular Revolution*, 66.

17. Hofstadter, *Anti-intellectualism*.

18. Smith, *The Secular Revolution*, 12.

19. Philip Gorski, "The Long, Withdrawing Roar: From Culture Wars to Culture Clashes," *Hedgehog Review* 23, no. 2 (2021).

20. Gorski, *American Covenant*. Please also see this excellent review of Gorski's book: Michael R. Whitenton, "Review: American Covenant," *Reading Religion*, December 5, 2017, https://readingreligion.org/97806911 47673/american-covenant/.

21. Gorski, "The Long, Withdrawing Roar," 28.

22. Ross Douthat, "Can the Meritocracy Find God?," *New York Times*, April 10, 2021, www.nytimes.com/2021/04/10/opinion/sunday/religion -meritocracy-god.html.

23. Hofstadter, *Anti-intellectualism*.

24. Robert P. Jones et al., *The 2020 Census of American Religion* (Washington, DC: PRRI, 2021).

25. David Ley, "The Immigrant Church as an Urban Service Hub," *Urban Studies* 45, no. 10 (2008): 2057–2074, doi:10.1177/0042098008094873; C. Hirschman, "The Role of Religion in the Origins and Adaptation of Immigrant Groups in the United States," *International Migration Review* 38, no. 3 (2004): 1206–1233, doi:10.1111/j.1747-7379.2004 .tb00233.x.

26. Henry Louis Gates Jr., *The Black Church: This Is Our Story, This Is Our Song* (New York: Penguin Press, 2021).

27. Alexander Bloom, *Prodigal Sons: The New York Intellectuals and Their World* (Oxford: Oxford University Press, 1986). See also Marc Raphael, ed., *The Columbia History of Jews in America* (New York: Columbia University Press, 2008).

28. "U.S. Muslims Concerned About Their Place in Society, but Continue to Believe in the American Dream," Pew Research Center, July 26, 2017, www.pewresearch.org/religion/2017/07/26/findings-from-pew-research -centers-2017-survey-of-us-muslims/. See also "Muslim Population by State 2022," World Population Review, n.d., https://worldpopulationreview.com /state-rankings/muslim-population-by-state.

29. The General Social Survey (GSS) is a nationally representative survey of adults across the United States. Established in 1972, its surveys use a core set of questions annually and add various different special topic questions. Subjects include morality, psychological well-being, race, the environment, and social mobility, among many other topics.

30. See also Robert Putnam and David Campbell, *American Grace: How Religion Divides and Unites Us* (New York: Simon & Schuster, 2010).

31. Laura R. Olson, "Religion and American Public Life: A Discussion of Robert Putnam and David Campbell's *Saving Grace: How Religion Divides and Unites Us*," *Perspectives on Politics* 10, no. 1 (2012): 103–106.

32. Robert Wuthnow, "Religious Involvement and Status-Bridging Social Capital," *Journal for the Scientific Study of Religion* 41, no. 4 (2002): 669–684.

33. Bradford Verter, "Spiritual Capital: Theorizing Religion with Bourdieu Against Bourdieu," *Sociological Theory* 21, no. 2 (2003): 150–174.

34. Andrew Greeley, "Coleman Revisited: Religious Structures as a Source of Social Capital," *American Behavioral Scientist* 40, no. 5 (1997): 587–594.

35. Valerie A. Lewis, Carol Ann MacGregor, and Robert D. Putnam, "Religion, Networks, and Neighborliness: The Impact of Religious Social Networks on Civic Engagement," *Social Science Research* 42, no. 2 (2013): 331–346.

36. Lydia Bean, *The Politics of Evangelical Identity: Local Churches and Partisan Divides in the United States and Canada* (Princeton, NJ: Princeton University Press, 2014).

37. Gorski, "The Long, Withdrawing Roar," 28.

38. Smith, *The Secular Revolution*.

39. Tom Gjelten, "2020 Faith Vote Reflects 2016 Patterns," NPR, November 8, 2020, www.npr.org/2020/11/08/932263516/2020-faith-vote -reflects-2016-patterns; Michelle Boorstein, "A Horn-Wearing 'Shaman.' A Cowboy Evangelist. For Some, the Capitol Attack Was a Kind of Christian Revolt," *Washington Post*, July 6, 2021, www.washingtonpost.com/religion /2021/07/06/capitol-insurrection-trump-christian-nationalism-shaman/; Sarah Posner, "How the Christian Right Helped Foment Insurrection," *Rolling Stone*, January 31, 2021, www.rollingstone.com/culture/culture-features /capitol-christian-right-trump-1121236/.

40. David Brooks, "The Dissenters Trying to Save Evangelicalism from Itself," *New York Times*, February 4, 2022, www.nytimes.com/2022/02/04 /opinion/evangelicalism-division-renewal.html.

41. Philip Gorski and Samuel Perry, *The Flag and the Cross: White Christian Nationalism and the Threat to American Democracy* (Oxford: Oxford University Press, 2022).

42. Statista Research Department, "Religious Affiliation of Rural Americans in 2019, by Religion," Statista, June 21, 2022, www.statista.com /statistics/1009381/religious-affiliation-rural-americans/.

43. Jones et al., *The 2020 Census of American Religion*.

44. Ruth Braunstein, "A Theory of Political Backlash: Assessing the Religious Right's Effects on the Religious Field," *Sociology of Religion* (2021).

45. Susan Jacoby, *The Age of American Unreason in a Culture of Lies* (New York: Vintage, 2008), 67–69.

46. Jacoby, *The Age of American Unreason*.

47. For a more detailed explanation of the events around evolution teachings and social Darwinism documented in these pages, please see Jacoby, *The Age of American Unreason*, 69–71.

48. For a historical challenge to the notion of social Darwinism, please also see Thorstein Veblen, *The Theory of the Leisure Class: An Economic Study of Institutions* (New York, 1899).

49. Jacoby, *The Age of American Unreason*, 70–71.

50. Jacoby, *The Age of American Unreason*, 82.

51. Blakely, Jason. "Scientific Authority and the Democratic Narrative: How Did We Arrive at This Crisis of Scientific Authority?" *Hedgehog Review* 22, no. 3 (2020).

52. "What Is Scientism, and Why Is It a Mistake?," *Big Think*, December 9, 2021, https://bigthink.com/13-8/science-vs-scientism/.

53. Richard Dawkins, *The Selfish Gene* (Oxford: Oxford University Press, 1976).

54. Freddie Sayers and Richard Dawkins, "Richard Dawkins: 'Scientism' Is a Dirty Word," June 18, 2021, in *UnHerd with Freddie Sayers*, podcast, https://unherd.com/thepost/richard-dawkins-scientism-is-a-dirty-word/.

55. Marcelo Gleiser, "Can Scientists Overreach?," NPR, April 6, 2011, www.npr.org/sections/13.7/2011/04/06/135160725/can-scientists-overreach; Marilynne Robinson, "Hysterical Scientism," *Harper's*, November 2006, https: //harpers.org/archive/2006/11/hysterical-scientism/.

56. Hanna Rosin, "The Case Against Breastfeeding," *Atlantic*, April 1, 2009, www.theatlantic.com/magazine/archive/2009/04/the-case-against-breast-feeding/307311/.

57. Mark Rubinstein, "Rational Markets: Yes or No? The Affirmative Case," *Financial Analysts Journal* 57, no. 3 (May–June 2001): 15–29, www.jstor.org/stable/4480313.

58. Michael Lewis, *The Big Short: Inside the Doomsday Machine* (New York: W. W. Norton, 2010).

59. Jane E. Brody, "Farewell, Readers, It's Been a Remarkable Ride," *New York Times*, February 21, 2022, www.nytimes.com/2022/02/21/well/health-advice-diet-smoking.html.

60. Eric Merkley and Peter John Loewen, "Anti-intellectualism and the Mass Public's Response to the COVID-19 Pandemic," *Nature Human Behaviour* (2021): 706–715.

61. Mallory Simon, "Over 1,000 Health Professionals Sign a Letter Saying, Don't Shut Down Protests Using Coronavirus Concerns as an Excuse," CNN, June 5, 2020, www.cnn.com/2020/06/05/health/health-care-open-letter-protests-coronavirus-trnd/index.html.

62. Julia Marcus and Gregg Gonsalves, "Public-Health Experts Are Not Hypocrites," *Atlantic*, June 11, 2020, www.theatlantic.com/ideas/archive/2020/06/public-health-experts-are-not-hypocrites/612853/.

63. Patrick McGee, "How Connected Fitness Became the New Obsession," *Financial Times*, January 21, 2022, www.ft.com/content/8fe94eef-1077-4eaa-8192-26013f7931ea.

64. Chidi and Bernstein, "The Power of Surrendering."

65. Sophie De Rosée, "The Case for Manifesting," *Financial Times*, January 3, 2022, www.ft.com/content/6fed8d95-1917-4e78-91c6-b0bacf04f03c.

66. Courtney Bender, *The New Metaphysicals: Spirituality and the American Religious Imagination* (Chicago: University of Chicago Press, 2010).

67. Karen Armstrong, *The Case for God* (New York: Knopf, 2009), x–xii.

68. Armstrong, *The Case for God*, x–xii.

69. William Bristow, "Enlightenment," in *Stanford Encyclopedia of Philosophy*, 2017, https://plato.stanford.edu/entries/enlightenment/.

70. Sorkin, *The Religious Enlightenment*; Theo Hobson, "For Rousseau, It's Humanity That's Divine, Not Reason," *Guardian*, January 27, 2014, www.theguardian.com/commentisfree/2014/jan/27/rousseau-humanity-divine-not-reason#:~:text=Voltaire%2C%20the%20most%20famous,religion%20is%20known%20as%20deism.

71. Arthur M. Melzer, "The Origin of the Counter-Enlightenment: Rousseau and the New Religion of Sincerity," *American Political Science Review* 90, no. 2 (1996): 344–360.

72. Terence E. Marshall, "Rousseau and Enlightenment," *Political Theory* 6, no. 4 (1978): 421–455.

73. N. E. Cronk, "About Voltaire," Voltaire Foundation for Enlightenment Studies, University of Oxford, www.voltaire.ox.ac.uk/about-voltaire/; Virgil W. Topazio, "Voltaire, Philosopher of Human Progress," *Publications of the Modern Language Association of America* 74, no. 4 (1959): 356–364; René Henry Pomeau, "Voltaire: French Philosopher and Author," in *Encyclopedia Britannica Online*, accessed February 23, 2022, www.britannica.com/biography/Voltaire.

74. Melzer, "The Origin of the Counter-Enlightenment."

75. David Runciman, "Rousseau on Inequality," February 2, 2021, in *History of Ideas*, season 2, podcast, https://play.acast.com/s/history-of-ideas/s2-rousseauoninequality.

76. Jean-Jacques Rousseau, *Discourse on the Origin of Inequality* (Cambridge, MA: Hackett, 1992); Leo Damrosch, *Jean-Jacques Rousseau: Restless Genius* (Boston: Houghton Mifflin Harcourt, 2007).

77. Melzer, "The Origin of the Counter-Enlightenment."

78. Marshall, "Rousseau and Enlightenment."

79. *Encyclopedia Britannica Online*, s.v. "Lisbon Earthquake of 1755," accessed February 23, 2022, www.britannica.com/event/Lisbon-earthquake-of-1755.

80. Russell R. Dynes, *The Dialogue Between Voltaire and Rousseau on the Lisbon Earthquake: The Emergence of a Social Science View* (Newark, DE: Disaster Research Center, 1999).

81. Jean-Jacques Rousseau, *The Collected Writings of Rousseau*, vol. 3, eds. Roger D. Masters and Christopher Kelly (Hanover, NH: University Press of New England, 1990); Dynes, *The Dialogue*.

82. Dynes, *The Dialogue*.

83. Kathryn Lofton, *Consuming Religion* (Chicago: University of Chicago Press, 2017).

84. Richard J. Shinder, "The Very Real Threat in the Rise of Anti-Rationalism," *Hill*, June 27, 2021, https://thehill.com/opinion/campaign/559764-the-very-real-threat-in-the-rise-of-anti-rationalism.

CHAPTER 7: CULTURAL CAPITAL

1. Taken from Oprah's interview with Tara Westover: Michelle Darrisaw, "On SuperSoul Sunday, *Educated* Author Tara Westover Talks to Oprah Defining Love," *Oprah Daily*, May 4, 2019, www.oprahdaily.com/life

/relationships-love/a27359653/tara-westover-oprah-super-soul-sunday-interview/.

2. James Davison Hunter, *Culture Wars: The Struggle to Control the Family, Art, Education, Law, and Politics in America* (New York: Basic Books, 1991).

3. Shamus Khan, "Capital Inequalities," *Hedgehog Review* (Summer 2021), https://hedgehogreview.com/issues/distinctions-that-define-and-divide/articles/capital-inequalities.

4. Hunter, *Culture Wars*.

5. This research project resulted in the following two articles: Raj Chetty et al., "Social Capital I: Measurement and Associations with Economic Mobility," *Nature* 608 (2022): 108–121, https://doi.org/10.1038/s41586-022-04996-4; Raj Chetty et al., "Social Capital II: Determinants of Economic Connectedness," *Nature* 608 (2022): 122–134, https://doi.org/10.1038/s41586-022-04997-3.

6. Loïc Wacquant, "Negative Social Capital: State Breakdown and Social Destitution in America's Urban Core," *Netherlands Journal of Housing and the Built Environment* 13, no. 25 (1998).

7. Chetty et al., "Social Capital I."

8. Janet Bercovitz and Maryann Feldman, "The Mechanisms of Collaboration in Inventive Teams: Composition, Social Networks, and Geography," *Research Policy* 40, no. 1 (2011): 81–93; Maryann P. Feldman, "The New Economics of Innovation, Spillovers and Agglomeration: A Review of Empirical Studies," *Economics of Innovation and New Technology* 8, no. 1–2 (1999): 5–25; Howard S. Becker, *Art Worlds* (Berkeley: University of California Press, 1982); Elizabeth Currid, *The Warhol Economy: How Fashion, Art, and Music Drive New York City* (Princeton, NJ: Princeton University Press, 2007).

9. Pierre Bourdieu, "The Forms of Capital," in *Handbook of Theory and Research for the Sociology of Education*, ed. J. Richardson (Westport, CT: Greenwood, 1986), 241–258.

10. Khan, "Capital Inequalities."

11. David Throsby, "Cultural Capital," *Journal of Cultural Economics* 23 (1999): 3–12.

12. Peter Wehner, "David Brooks's Journey Toward Faith," *Atlantic*, May 7, 2019, www.theatlantic.com/ideas/archive/2019/05/second-mountain-brooks-discusses-his-faith/588766/; Oprah Winfrey and David Brooks, "David Brooks: The Quest for a Moral Life," May 20, 2019, in *Oprah's Super Soul*, podcast, https://podcasts.apple.com/us/podcast/david-brooks-the-quest-for-a-moral-life/id1264843400?i=1000438838518.

13. Putnam and Campbell, *American Grace*.

14. Interview with Robert Wuthnow. Please also see Robert Wuth-now, *Small-Town America: Finding Community, Shaping the Future* (Princeton, NJ: Princeton: Princeton University Press, 2013).

15. Erin Logan, "White People Have Gentrified Black Lives Matter. It's a Problem," *Los Angeles Times*, September 8, 2020, www.latimes.com/opinion /story/2020-09-04/black-lives-matter-white-people-portland-protests-nfl.

16. Lizzie Bowes, "Performative Wokeness Needs to Stop," *Varsity*, December 21, 2017, www.varsity.co.uk/violet/14313.

17. Wilfred McClay, "Performative: How the Meaning of a Word Be-came Corrupted," *Hedgehog Review* 23, no. 2 (Summer 2021).

18. Brian Mann and Elizabeth Baker, "Black Protest Leaders to White Allies: 'It's Our Turn to Lead Our Own Fight,'" NPR, September 22, 2020, www.npr.org/2020/09/22/913094440/black-protest-leaders-to-white -allies-it-s-our-turn-to-lead-our-own-fight.

19. Musa al-Gharbi, *We Have Never Been Woke: Social Justice Discourse, Inequality and the Rise of a New Elite* (Princeton, NJ: Princeton University Press, forthcoming).

20. George Packer, "How America Fractured into Four Parts," *Atlantic*, March 26, 2022, www.theatlantic.com/magazine/archive/2021/07 /george-packer-four-americas/619012/; Doug Chaya, "The Threat from the Illiberal Left," *Economist*, September 4, 2021, www.economist.com/leaders /2021/09/04/the-threat-from-the-illiberal-left.

21. Throsby, "Cultural Capital."

22. Douglas Holt, "Does Cultural Capital Structure American Con-sumption?," *Journal of Consumer Research* 25, no. 1 (1998).

23. See Veblen's *Theory of the Leisure Class* for a full analysis of the role of consumption and social status.

24. Alan Warde, David Wright, and Modesto Gayo-Cal, "Understand-ing Cultural Omnivorousness: Or, the Myth of the Cultural Omnivore," *Cultural Sociology* 1, no. 2 (2007): 143–164; Holt, "Does Cultural Capital."

25. We adopted a fractional probit regression framework to predict each of the consumption measures discussed, where consumption by household and year was pooled in a cross-sectional data set. Our precise specification for that framework is the following (vector variables are presented in bold text):

$Y_{it} = \beta_1 \, age_{it} + \beta_2 \, education_{it} + \textbf{race}_i\beta_3 + \textbf{income}_{it} \, \beta_4 + \beta_5 \, rural_{it} + \textbf{region}_{it} \, \beta_6 + \textbf{rural*region}_{it} \, \beta_7 + year_t \, \beta_8 + \textbf{year*region}_{it} \, \beta_9 + \varepsilon_{it}$

26. The only difference is that higher-income households devote a significantly smaller share of their milk expenditures on plant milk.

27. James Suzman, *Work: A History of How We Spend Our Time* (Lon-don: Bloomsbury, 2020). See also Ezra Klein and James Suzman, "Ezra

Klein Interviews James Suzman," June 29, 2021, in *The Ezra Klein Show*, www.nytimes.com/2021/06/29/podcasts/transcript-ezra-klein-interviews -james-suzman.html.

28. Philip Gorski, "The Long, Withdrawing Roar."

29. R. Putnam and D. Campbell, *American Grace: How Religion Divides and Unites Us* (New York: Simon & Schuster, 2010).

30. Charles Mathewes, "By Whose Waters We Wept. . ." *Hedgehog Review* 23, no. 1 (Spring 2021).

CHAPTER 8: THE THROUGH LINE

1. Olga Tokarczuk, "Olga Tokarczuk's Nobel Lecture: 'Tenderness Is the Most Modest Form of Love,'" *Irish Times*, December 13, 2019, www .irishtimes.com/culture/books/olga-tokarczuk-s-nobel-lecture-tenderness -is-the-most-modest-form-of-love-1.4113106.

2. Meghan Keneally, "Trump Tells Supporters: 'You're Not Forgotten Anymore,'" ABC News, January 20, 2017, https://abcnews.go.com /Politics/inauguration-festivities-officially-kick-off-dc/story?id=44875711.

3. Sassen, *The Global City*.

4. Megan Trimble, "WHO: Anti-Vaccine Movement a Top Threat in 2019," *US News & World Report*, January 16, 2019, www.usnews.com/news /national-news/articles/2019-01-16/who-names-vaccine-hesitancy-as -top-world-threat-in-2019; Maggie Fox, "Anti-vaccine Hot Spots on Rise Across U.S., Study Finds," NBC News, June 12, 2018, www.nbcnews.com /health/health-news/anti-vaccine-hotspots-rise-across-u-s-study-finds- n882461.

5. Olga Khazan, "Wealthy L.A. Schools' Vaccination Rates Are as Low as South Sudan's," *Atlantic*, September 16, 2014, www.theatlantic .com/health/archive/2014/09/wealthy-la-schools-vaccination-rates-are -as-low-as-south-sudans/380252/.

6. Sharon Otterman, "New York Confronts Its Worst Measles Outbreak in Decades," *New York Times*, January 17, 2019, www.nytimes.com /2019/01/17/nyregion/measles-outbreak-jews-nyc.html.

7. Manish Sadarangani, "Herd Immunity: How Does It Work?," Oxford Vaccine Group, April 26, 2016, www.ovg.ox.ac.uk/news/herd-immunity-how -does-it-work.

8. Elizabeth Currid-Halkett, *The Sum of Small Things: A Theory of the Aspirational Class* (Princeton, NJ: Princeton University Press, 2017).

9. "Breastfeeding Report Card: United States, 2022," CDC, last modified August 31, 2022, www.cdc.gov/breastfeeding/data/reportcard.htm.

10. Corinne Purtill, "If You Want to Get into an Elite College, You Might Consider Moving to One of These States," *Quartz*, April 4, 2016, https://qz.com/653167/if-you-want-to-get-into-an-elite-college-you-might-consider-moving-to-one-of-these-states/.

11. Cambon and Mollica, "Rural Counties Are Booming."

12. It was Michael Young who first coined the term "meritocracy" and saw the darkness in a society that established hierarchy through ostensible merit. For a dystopian critique of the meritocracy please see Young, *The Rise of the Meritocracy*.

13. Alejandro Portes, "Downsides of Social Capital," *PNAS* 111, no. 52 (December 22, 2014), www.pnas.org/doi/full/10.1073/pnas.1421888112.

14. Gawande, "Why Americans Are Dying from Despair."

15. For a more elaborated discussion of these ideas considered here please see Judith N. Shklar, *Ordinary Vices* (Cambridge, MA: Harvard University Press, 1985); Runciman's discussion of Shklar's philosophy: David Runciman, "Shklar on Hypocrisy," April 20, 2021, in *History of Ideas*, season 2, podcast, https://play.acast.com/s/history-of-ideas/shklaronhypocrisy.

16. Runciman, "Shklar on Hypocrisy."

17. Blake Smith, "Moral Cruelty and the Left," *Tablet*, June 17, 2020, www.tabletmag.com/sections/arts-letters/articles/judith-shklar-politics-of-fear.

18. Smith, "Moral Cruelty."

19. Runciman, "Shklar on Hypocrisy."

20. Krupnikov and Ryan, *The Other Divide*.

21. Krupnikov and Ryan, *The Other Divide*.

22. Galen Druke, "Americans Aren't as Polarized as the News Makes It Seem," February 10, 2022, in *FiveThirtyEight Politics*, podcast, https://fivethirtyeight.com/features/politics-podcast-americans-might-be-less-divided-than-you-think/.

23. David Runciman, "Nietzsche on Morality," March 2, 2021, in *History of Ideas*, season 2, podcast, https://play.acast.com/s/history-of-ideas/neitzscheonmorality.

24. Hunter, *Culture Wars*; Jason Willick, "The Man Who Discovered 'Culture Wars,'" *Wall Street Journal*, May 25, 2018.

25. Ezra Klein, "California Is Making Liberals Squirm," *New York Times*, February 11, 2021, www.nytimes.com/2021/02/11/opinion/california-san-francisco-schools.html.

26. Ronald F. Inglehart and Pippa Norris, "Trump, Brexit, and the Rise of Populism: Economic Have-Nots and Cultural Backlash" (HKS working paper no. RWP16-026, Harvard Kennedy School, Cambridge, MA, August 2016).

27. Ronald Inglehart, "Globalization and Postmodern Values," *Washington Quarterly* 23, no. 1 (2000): 215–228.

28. Winfrey and Brooks, "David Brooks."

29. Francis Fukuyama, "One Single Day. That's All It Took for the World to Look Away from Us," *New York Times*, January 5, 2022, www.nytimes.com/2022/01/05/opinion/jan-6-global-democracy.html?searchResultPosition=1.

30. Gary Younge, "The View from Middletown: A Typical US City That Never Did Exist," *Guardian*, October 18, 2016, www.theguardian.com/membership/2016/oct/18/view-from-middletown-us-muncie-america.

31. For a full transcript of the speech, please see: Tokarczuk, "Olga Tokarczuk's Nobel Lecture."

Index

Elizabeth Currid-Halkett is the James Irvine Chair in Urban and Regional Planning and professor of public policy at the University of Southern California. The recipient of a Guggenheim Fellowship, she currently holds the Kluge Chair in Modern Culture at the Library of Congress, and her research has been featured in the *New York Times*, *Wall Street Journal*, *Economist*, and *New Yorker*. The author of three previous books, she lives in Los Angeles, California.

https://elizabethcurridhalkett.com/